Reform the People

*Changing attitudes towards popular education
in early twentieth-century China*

Reform the People

Changing Attitudes Towards Popular Education
in Early Twentieth-Century China

PAUL J. BAILEY

EDINBURGH UNIVERSITY PRESS

© Paul J. Bailey 1990

Edinburgh University Press
22 George Square, Edinburgh

Set in Linotron Goudy
by Koinonia Ltd, Bury, and
printed in Great Britain by
The Alden Press, Oxford

British Library Cataloguing
　in Publication Data
Bailey, Paul
　Reform the people: changing attitudes towards
popular education in early 20th Century China.
1. China, Education, history
I. Title
370.951

ISBN 0 7486 0218 6

Contents

List of Figures	vii
List of Tables	vii
List of abbreviations	viii
Acknowledgements	ix

Introduction   1

1. The Reorientation of Official Thinking   17
Official Attitudes from the 1890s to 1904   18
The 1904 School System   31
The Board of Education and Educational Aims of 1906   36
Contrast with the West   41
Constitutionalism and Education   45

2. The Public Debate 1900-11   64
The Participants   66
The Concept of Social Education   69
The Reform of Customs and the Training of a New Citizenry   72
An Ambivalent Voluntarism   79

3. Popular Education Developments 1904-11   98
'Planning One's Livelihood and Managing the Family'   98
Half-Day Schools and Literacy Schools   102
Vocational Education   110
Changes in the Primary School Curriculum   116

4. The 1912 School System   134
The Widening Public Debate   135
The Republican Ministry of Education   139
The Role of Education in the New Republic   145
The School System of 1912   151
The Function of the New Schools: Hopes and Misgivings   163

5. Popular Educational Developments in the Early Republic   185
The Reform of Popular Culture   186
Public Lectures   194
Spare-time Schools and Libraries   200
Vocational Education and the Promotion of 'Hard and Diligent Work'   207

6. The Work-Study Movement 227
Li Shizeng and the French Connection 227
Chinese Labour in France and Work-Study 233
The Student Work-Study Movement 1917-21 236
Epilogue 246
Conclusion 263
Bibliography 273
Index 292

List of Figures

1. The 1904 School System 33
2. The 1912 School System 156

List of Tables

1. Number of Middle Schools and Lower Primary Schools in 1907 and 1909 — 44
2. Provincial Education Expenditures in 1909 — 45
3. Number of Vocational Schools in 1907 and 1909 — 46
4. Background of Primary School Teachers in 1909 — 47
5. Number of *Quanxuesuo*, Lecture Halls and Education Associations in 1907 — 101
6. Number of Half-Day Schools in 1907 and 1909 — 104
7. Provincial Expenditures on *Quanxuesuo*, Lecture Halls, Education Associations and Half-Day Schools in 1907 and 1909 — 105
8. Primary School Curricula for 1904, 1910 and 1912 — 140
9. Expenditures of the Nanjing Government, March 1912 — 143
10. Provincial Origin of Delegates to the 1912 Education Conference — 153
11. Sources of School Funds 1915-16 — 156
12. Number of Schools and Students in 1912-16, 1922 — 159
13. Number of Schools and Students in Zhejiang 1912-16 — 160
14. School Expenditures in Zhejiang 1912-16 — 161
15. Number of Schools and Students in Guangdong Province 1912-18 — 162
16. Number of Popular Education Associations in 1915 — 187
17. Items Considered Beneficial for Popular Education by the Education Ministry, 1913 — 188
18. Number of Lecture Institutes in 1916-17 — 195
19. Beijing Lecture Institutes in 1916 — 196
20. Number of Newspaper Reading Rooms in 1916 — 197
21. Number of Half-Day Schools and Literacy Schools in 1916 — 201
22. School Attendance in 1919 — 203
23. School Drop-out Rate in 1915 — 205
24. Popular Libraries in 1916, 1922 and 1930 — 206
25. Number of Readers in the Shaanxi Public Library (June 1918-May 1919) — 207
26. Number and Provincial Origin of Work-Study Students — 237

Abbreviations

The following abbreviations are used in the notes.

DFZZ *Dongfang zazhi*
DYJN *Diyici Zhongguo jiaoyu nianjian*
FFSL *Fufa qingong jianxue yundong shiliao*
JYZZ *Jiaoyu zazhi*
JZRB *Jingzhong ribao*
QGYD *Liufa qingong jianxue yundong*
XMCB *Xinmin congbao*
ZHJYJ *Zhonghua jiaoyujie*

Acknowledgements

It is a pleasure to express finally my thanks and appreciation to all those who have helped and encouraged me in the writing of this book. Firstly, I would like to thank Professor Edgar Wickberg of the University of British Columbia. He supervised my Ph.D. thesis on which the book is based and provided valuable guidance on the scope and content of the work. I also thank Professor Alexander Woodside of the University of British Columbia for reading some of the draft chapters of the thesis and giving me some useful pointers. I remember with gratitude the indispensable help always given by the staff of the University of British Columbia's East Asian Library.

I thank the Trustees of the Killam Estate for awarding me a pre-doctoral fellowship in 1978-1979 while at the University of British Columbia, and again in 1979-1980, which allowed me to carry out research in Paris. While I was in Paris I had the good fortune to attend a research seminar given by Professor Marianne Bastid-Bruguière, whose own work on late Qing educational reform first stimulated my interest in this aspect of China's modernization process. I benefited enormously from her erudition, advice and encouragement. A British Council Scholarship in 1980-81 gave me the opportunity to do research at Beijing University, where I was able to consult educational journals of the early Republican period not available elsewhere. A University of British Columbia Graduate Fellowship allowed me to complete the writing of the Ph.D. thesis.

The demands of teaching meant that a revision of the thesis took longer than I had anticipated. Some more research was necessary, however, and two grants from the University of Edinburgh's Travel and Research Fund gave me the chance to consult materials at the University of Columbia's East Asian Library in New York during the spring of 1986 and to do some further archival research in Paris in the summer of 1988. A grant from the Japan Foundation in the summer of 1987 allowed me to do research in Tokyo and Kyoto. While in Kyoto I had the pleasure of meeting Dr Kitamura Minoru, who kindly helped me to find my way at the Jimbun Kagaku Kenkyūsho at Kyoto University.

For the typing of the manuscript in its various stages here at the University of Edinburgh I am grateful for the kind and indispensable help given by the History Department secretaries, Gloria Ketchin, Alison Munro and Jill Marshall. I thank also the University of Edinburgh's Faculty of Arts Postgraduate Studies Committee for providing financial assistance.

Over the years I have enjoyed the company and benefited from the encouragement of good friends and colleagues, in particular Lloyd Kramer, David and Christine Mungello, Donald Burton, Ku Wei-ying, Don Starr, and Rhodri Jeffreys-Jones. Lastly, I would like to thank my wife Dawn whom I had the good fortune to meet as I was struggling to complete the book. She has brought much joy to my life and gave me the inspiration to overcome the final hurdle. To her I gratefully dedicate this book.

EDINBURGH
May, 1990

Introduction

In 1900 Chinese officials and intellectuals felt a deep sense of crisis. For many of them, China's defeat at the hands of Japan in 1895 and the 'scramble for concessions' in 1897-8 seemed to portend the partition of China among the western powers. China's potential fate was compared with that of luckless Poland.[1] In 1898 Yan Fu's translation of T.Huxley's *Evolution and Ethics* appeared, introducing into the Chinese vocabulary terms such as 'survival of the fittest' (*yousheng liebai*), 'natural selection' (*tian ze*), and 'struggle for existence' (*jing cun*).[2] Anguished cries of alarm could be heard warning of the eventual dispersal and even extinction of the Chinese race unless fundamental reforms were implemented. For a brief period in 1898 the reformers were able to gain the support of the Guangxu Emperor and a number of reform edicts were issued calling for institutional change, the promotion of industry and commerce, and the establishment of modern schools. A conservative backlash, led by the Emperor's aunt, the Empress-Dowager Cixi, quickly followed. The Guangxu Emperor was made a virtual prisoner, reformers such as Kang Youwei and Liang Qichao were forced to flee the country with prices on their heads, and the reform edicts were cancelled.[3] The worst fears of the reformers were confirmed in 1900 when the court actively encouraged and supported the anti-foreign Boxer uprising, which led to the occupation of Beijing by the powers and yet more humiliating demands made of the Chinese government.

By 1901 even Cixi recognised the need for change and the court embarked on a series of reforms designed to strengthen the country and secure the position of the Qing monarchy.[4] Constitutional reform included plans for the convening of a national assembly and the establishment of provincial and district assemblies.[5] Military modernisation was promoted in order to create a well-equipped national army.[6] Educational reform comprised plans to create a national hierarchical system of schools and the abolition of the traditional civil service examinations.

This latter reform, like all the others, failed to prevent the downfall of the dynasty and its replacement by a republic in 1911-12, but it did nevertheless represent a wider change in attitudes towards education that spanned the last years of the Qing dynasty and early years of the Republic, and, as such, constitutes an important element in China's modernisation process, a process defined recently as one 'by which societies have been and are being transformed under the impact of the scientific and technological revolution'.[7] During the latter half of the nineteenth century, Chinese officials and scholars had focused on the military and technological efficiency of the West as the key factor explaining her strength. By the end of the century the focus had shifted to government institutions. In the early years of the twentieth century yet another factor was perceived. Chinese officials, scholars and educators, inspired by the examples of Britain, Germany, Japan, France and the United States now emphasised the importance of an extensive educational system producing a patriotic, hard-working and united citizenry as a cause of national strength.[8]

Hitherto formal education in China had been closely associated with the recruitment of officials through examinations requiring extensive knowledge of the Confucian classics.[9] Government schools (*guanxue*) at the prefectural and district levels were established merely as places where civil service examination candidates on government stipends were meant to register. Confucian academies (*shuyuan*), originally founded during the Song dynasty (960-1279 AD) in the wake of the neo-Confucian movement and funded by officials or local wealthy patrons, had generally become by the nineteenth century institutions that promoted the state orthodoxy and in which scholars practised examination techniques.[10] Despite occasional interest in promoting a wider network of schools at local levels to inculcate Confucian morality amongst the populace (or, in the case of ethnic minorities, 'Confucian uniformity'),[11] the state had traditionally left whatever formal elementary education that did exist to local communities, gentry and lineages.[12] Although greater economic prosperity after the sixteenth century stimulated an increase in the number of such schools,[13] many of them often led a precarious existence.[14]

A more systematic attempt was begun in the early years of the twentieth century to provide all the people with an education, one that would not only 'reform' people's customs and behaviour by inculcating the virtues of patriotism, concern for the public good, and hard work, but also one that would accord with the relevant economic needs of the people. In addition to the government's attempt to create a formal system of modern schools, officials and gentry promoted and sponsored a wide variety of supporting measures such as literacy, half-day and vocational schools, public lectures, and newspaper reading rooms. Although they often referred to the example of the West, Chinese educators were also able to draw on a tradition, dating back to Confucius (551-479 BC), that placed great faith in the efficacy of education to mould a person's character.[15] The confidence in the positive benefits to be gained from a more widespread education contrasted sharply with the suspicion and hostility displayed in eighteenth- and nineteenth-century England, for example, in the wake of proposals for an expansion in popular education.[16]

This book sets out to analyse changing attitudes towards education, in particular popular education, during this crucial transition period that covered the last years of the Qing dynasty and early years of the Republic. Since many of the educational issues raised during this period anticipated the debates of post-1949 Communist China, an analysis of educational thought in this transition period will help place modern China's educational

Introduction

development in a wider context.

I have used a broad definition of 'popular education' for the purposes of this study. The two Chinese terms used for popular education in the early twentieth century were *shehui jiaoyu* (social education) and *tongsu jiaoyu* (common education). The former term was borrowed from the Japanese (*shakai kyōiku*) and was introduced into the Chinese vocabulary in 1902. In its Japanese context 'social education' referred to all informal educational activity outside the school that helped alleviate what was called, at the turn of the century, 'the social problem' (*shakai mondai*). This was a catchword for all the evils that Japanese bureaucrats and educators, casting a wary eye at the situation in the West, prophesied might befall Japan in the wake of her industrialisation programme: the growing gap between city and countryside, urban unrest and workers' strikes, conflicts between labour and capital, ruthless individualism on the one hand and the emergence of radical socialist parties on the other.[17] Social education was therefore meant to cement social unity.[18] The Chinese took over the meaning of this term.

The other Chinese term used for 'popular education' at this time, *tongsu jiaoyu*, also referred to educational activity outside the formal school, as well as to the 'reform' of popular literature, entertainment, and customs. *Tongsu* had the connotation of 'vulgar' or 'unrefined', in contrast to the highly refined culture or speech of the literary elite. As it was used in the early twentieth century, the term referred to both the *means* of educating the people (e.g. vernacular publications as opposed to the classical literary texts which catered for elite education) and to the *ends* of such an endeavour (i.e. the 'reform' of people's customs and behaviour).[19] Attempts by the Confucian elite to replace the 'corrupt' or 'superstitious' aspects of popular culture with values more acceptable to ruling class interests were, of course, a marked feature of Chinese tradition,[20] as witnessed, for example, by the official appropriation of popular cults and festivals or the distribution of popular morality books (*shanshu*).[21] Rather like Europe from the seventeenth century onwards,[22] however, early-twentieth-century China witnessed a more systematic and widespread attempt to reform the people's customs. For Chinese educators such an endeavour was closely linked to the very survival of the nation and of the race.

In the 1920s and 1930s, as more emphasis was placed on the existence of classes in Chinese society and the widening gap between them, new terms were introduced for 'popular education' such as *pingmin jiaoyu* (common people's education) and *minzhong jiaoyu* (mass education), which specifically referred to the education of less privileged adults and children.[23] Such terms, however, still designated educational activity outside the formal school. A 1919 article in the education journal *Pingmin jaoyu* (Education for the Common People) declared that 'everything in society has an educational function'.[24] The term *pingmin jiaoyu* came into widespread use especially with the movement initiated by James Yen (Yan Yangchu) in 1922 to provide literacy training for adults and children who had not attended school.[25] The term *minzhong jiaoyu* (mass education) was defined in 1930 as an education that would enlighten the people on hygiene, culture, and politics, as well as one that would provide instruction on earning a livelihood.[26] Some Chinese sources list 'mass education' as an element of 'social education', along with public lectures, entertainment and spare-time schools.[27]

In addition to describing developments in popular education, as the Chinese defined it, the book will also analyse developments in primary and vocational education, which the Chinese referred to as *putong jiaoyu* (general education).[28] This term came into general use after 1904 when a national school system was introduced, and was meant to contrast with the term *rencai jiaoyu* (education for talent), used by Chinese educators in the early twentieth century to describe traditional formal education with its emphasis on cultivating an elite for government service, as well as to refer to all kinds of 'elitist education'. Since primary education had never traditionally been considered as a function of the state, changing perceptions of primary education after 1905, when *putong jiaoyu* was emphasised by many as the most important feature of an educational system, are an important indicator of attitudes towards popular education in general. Changes in the primary school curriculum such as the elimination of the Confucian classics, for example, made education more accessible and therefore can be considered as contributions to popular education.

Changes in attitude towards vocational education are also significant since they reflected a growing view after 1900 that formal education was not necessarily synonymous with knowledge of the classical literary tradition. Two new terms (again borrowed from the Japanese) began to be used to describe vocational education: *shiye jiaoyu*, defined as an education that would 'train people to work in productive activities', and *zhiye jiaoyu*, defined as an instruction that would provide 'occupational knowledge and skills'.[29] By providing more facilities for vocational training and/or introducing practical subjects into the formal school system, Chinese officials and educators admitted the need for education to serve the people in more concrete ways than simply viewing it as an instrument of social control.

Finally, a chapter will be devoted to the work-study movement, which took place amongst Chinese students and workers who went to France between 1908 and 1920. Fired by the idealism that had gripped the Russian populists in the 1860s and 1870s,[30] Chinese intellectuals championed the sanctity of labour and the unity of mental and manual work. They hoped that work-study would not only raise the workers' cultural level but also help eliminate traditional elite attitudes towards physical labour. As such the movement contributed to the debate over the role and content of education .

Accompanying the changes in attitude towards education was the emergence during the last years of the Qing of a group of professional educators, a kind of educational 'lobby', who remained active throughout the early years of the Republic. Many of them were of gentry background who had studied abroad in Japan. They participated in educational conferences, worked in educational administration both at central and local levels, established schools, contributed to educational journals, and helped produce and edit school textbooks. Their activities, in fact, were part of a wider process in late-nineteenth and early-twentieth-century China in which gentry sought to increase their role in public affairs.[31] This 'educational lobby' has been neglected in western accounts of modern China, yet their contribution to the evolution of educational ideas and practice in early-twentieth-century China should not be underestimated. They not only advised officials and helped devise the new regulations and procedures concerning education but also, in introducing new ideas and approaches and analysing problems and their solutions, they contributed to a lively educational debate which was to have relevance well beyond the early years of the Republic.

This group of educators included Lu Feigui (1886-1941), at various times a teacher, book publisher and school textbook compiler, who was the first editor of *Jiaoyu zazhi* (The Educational Review);[32] Huang Yanpei (1878-1965), holder of the provincial degree (*juren*) under the traditional civil service examination system, who established schools, worked in provincial and district educational administration, and promoted vocational education;[33] Fan Yuanlian (1875-1927), a minister of education in the early years of the Republic who had studied in Japan and worked in educational administration during the last years of the Qing;[34] Luo Zhenyu (1866-1940), the editor of the first modern Chinese journal devoted to education and a school inspector during the last years of the dynasty;[35] Jiang Weiqiao (1874-?), head of the school textbook department of the Shanghai Commercial Press, who was a counsellor in the newly-established Ministry of Education in 1912 and head of the Jiangsu provincial education bureau in the 1920s;[36] Li Shizeng (1881-1973), who was the founder of the work-study movement;[37] Wu Da (1880-1913), holder of a lower degree (*shengyuan*) under the traditional civil service examination system, who worked in local education administration during the last years of the dynasty and promoted social education;[38] and, finally, Chen Zibao (1862-1922), a founder of primary schools who was a vigorous proponent of women's education and the use of vernacular (*baihua*) readers in school.[39]

The late nineteenth and early twentieth centuries also saw a proliferation of newspapers and journals in China. A recent study estimates that in the last decade of the Qing approximately one hundred journals were being published at any one time with a possible audience of between two and four million (roughly 1 per cent of the total population).[40] The first specialist journals devoted entirely to education, *Jiaoyu shijie* (Educational World) and *Jiaoyu zazhi* (The Educational Review), began publication in 1902 and 1909 respectively, reflecting both the increasing 'professionalisation' of education and an expanding public interest in educational issues. During the early years of the Republic, another long-running educational journal appeared. Beginning publication in 1913 *Zhonghua jiaoyujie* (The Chinese Educational World) continued until 1937.[41] At the same time a spate of shorter-lived educational journals were published, many of them produced by provincial education associations or societies. They included *Jiaoyu zhoubao* (Education Weekly, 1915-19), *Jingshi jiaoyubao* (Beijing Educational Review, 1914-19), *Jiaoyu yanjiu* (Educational Research, 1913-14), *Jiaoyu chao* (Educational Tide, 1919), and *Jiaoyu yu shiye* (Education and Industry, 1917-20).[42]

These journals discussed educational developments in China and abroad, as well as translating articles or book excerpts on education from foreign sources (mainly via the Japanese). Through an analysis of these journals one can see how Chinese educators perceived developments in the West and which aspects of western educational thought and practice they chose to emphasise. Many of the issues confronted by Chinese educators, in fact, were also being vigorously debated in the West at the same time. For example, the concerns of Chinese educators to see education more systematically organised and more economically relevant were voiced at precisely the time when western governments, in their attempt to pursue 'national efficiency', were planning to bring education under more coordinated control as well as to make it more practical and technically-oriented.[43] The discussion of these aims, and the benefits and disadvantages accruing from them, constituted an important element in the Chinese educational debate.

Little has been written in English on educational thought and practice in early-twentieth-century China. Some contemporary observers did comment in rather exaggerated terms on the educational reforms undertaken by the Qing. Thus Margaret Burton, writing in 1911 on girls' education in China, exclaimed: 'The past decade has witnessed in China what is probably the greatest educational renaissance the world has ever seen.'[44] Another observer, H. King, also writing in 1911, described the years 1905-11 as a 'revolution in Chinese education', and claimed that 'never has a country accomplished more in so short a time after the establishment of a new system of education'.[45]

More analytical English-language works were written by Chinese scholars (some of whom held doctorates from American universities) in the early years of the Republic and during the 1920s and 1930s.[46] Most of them sought to demonstrate the superiority of China's educational tradition over that of the West and confidently claimed that such a tradition had facilitated educational reform after 1905. Kuo Ping-wen, for example, a Ph.D. from Columbia University and the future president of Nanjing Higher Normal School, wrote in his 1915 work, *The Chinese System of Public Education*, that China had always had a 'democratic educational spirit', which was reflected in the new republican school system of 1912. In contrast to China, Kuo claimed, where the new schools were 'being utilized by all classes of society', other countries such as England, France, and the United States were undemocratic.⁴⁷ Such a view was also shared by H. Galt, an American educator who taught at Beijing University in the 1920s. He praised China's traditional system of education and its beneficial effect on the republican system after 1912. Galt's admiration for traditional Chinese education even prompted him to suggest a revival of the Confucian civil service examinations, which 'maintained a series of academic degrees that conserved educational standards and promoted respect' as well as possessing social forms and ceremonies 'valuable for social control and for maintaining kindliness and courtesy in social life'.⁴⁸

In the 1930s two western writers condemned recent educational development in China. In his book *Nationalism and Education in Modern China* C. Peake expressed horror at the growth of what he perceived as intolerant nationalism in Chinese education, which had been developing since the last years of the dynasty.⁴⁹ The one ray of hope, according to Peake, had been the brief interlude of 1919-22 when the influence of the American educator and philosopher John Dewey in China had led to more emphasis on democratic values and the importance of individual development.⁵⁰ V. Purcell, in his book, *Problems of Chinese Education*, took issue with Kuo Ping-wen, claiming that he did not give due credit to Christian influence on Chinese education which, Purcell implied, was more or less responsible for any improvements that did occur.⁵¹ Like Peake, Purcell noted that after 1925 Chinese educators jettisoned the democratic American model, in vogue since the May Fourth movement of 1919, and leant once more towards the less democratic German and Japanese models.⁵² Whether praising or damning recent Chinese educational development, therefore, the works published between 1912 and the 1930s were either too polemical or narrow in their focus to provide a substantial analysis of educational change in early-twentieth-century China.

Since the 1930s the few studies that have been done on Chinese education concentrate either on the attempts of provincial officials such as Li Hongzhang (1823-1901) and Zhang Zhidong (1837-1909) at the end of the nineteenth century to establish technical and military schools and reform the traditional civil service examinations,⁵³ or on the burst of enthusiasm for democratic and popular education supposedly aroused as a result of the May Fourth movement and the influence of John Dewey's educational philosophy in 1919.⁵⁴ In all of these studies the period between the abolition of the civil service examinations in 1905 and the May Fourth movement in 1919 is considered of little significance as far as China's educational development is concerned. Yet it was precisely during this period that attitudes towards the role of education changed dramatically.

Recently a number of excellent regional studies of China during the last years of the Qing dynasty have been published. Although useful information is given on the establishment of new schools, educational reform is primarily described in terms of the growing rivalry between gentry and government as each sought to control the reform process; of the growing divisions within the gentry class itself with the more conservative rural gentry opposing all modernising change promoted by urban gentry; or, finally, in terms of the widening gap between local elites and the populace as the burden of increased taxes needed to finance new schools increasingly fell on those less likely to receive the privilege of a modern education.[55]

The first study to analyse in depth changes in educational ideas and practice was M. Bastid, *Aspects de la réforme de l'enseignement en Chine au début du vingtième siècle* (Paris, 1971). It covers the period 1902-12 as seen through the activities and writings of Zhang Jian, an entrepreneur and educational reformer. The study is useful not only in analysing the political consequences of educational reform but also in revealing how and in what ways Japanese influence played a role in Chinese educational reform, as well as showing that it was during this period that importance began to be placed on such aspects as vocational education and specialised teacher training. A more recent study by S. Borthwick, covering the same period, focuses on the establishment of modern schools and the problems encountered during the process.[56]

This study sets out to complement these two works by providing a more in-depth analysis of educational thought during the last years of the Qing dynasty and early years of the Republic, since there is a very real continuity in attitudes towards education that spans the 1911 revolution. In the process I hope, firstly, to chart the debate over the role and content of education in a changing China; secondly, to reveal which aspects of western and Japanese educational thought and practice appealed to Chinese educators (and hence contribute to a more accurate understanding of the real nature of western educational influence on China); and thirdly, to point out how and in what ways the educational debates during this transitional period anticipated those of post-1949 China.

Three caveats need to be mentioned with regard to this study. Firstly, although details are given of educational developments when possible, it must be noted that apart from the fact that there are no systematic and detailed figures on such things as the funding of popular education (e.g. half-day and literacy schools), the educational statistics that are available are not always complete. The increasing political turmoil and the breakdown of central government control after 1912 meant that despite requests by the Ministry of Education for the provinces to send information many of them did not do so (or if they did such information was incomplete). Furthermore, figures from the same or differing sources often do not match. Thus in the first Chinese Education Yearbook (published in 1934) the number of lecture institutes in 1928 and 1929 are given as 551 and 2 071 respectively in volume 4 while in volume 3 of the same publication the totals are given as 535 and 2 894.[57] Statistics are given, therefore, only to indicate general developments.

Secondly, educational development during this period took place primarily in urban areas, although the promotion and establishment of half-day schools, literacy schools, and popular lecture institutes was evidence of an increasing concern to make education more widely available. Articles specifically on the problems of rural education began to appear only in 1919[58] and it was not until the 1920s and 1930s that *nongmin jiaoyu* and *xiangcun jiaoyu* (both meaning rural education) became commonly-used terms, particularly in connection with the rural reconstruction movements of the 1930s.[59]

Thirdly, schools (whether full-time or part-time) were attended mostly by boys during this period, although the number of girls in school slowly increased. I have not dwelt in detail on the debate over women's education, since this deserves a more extensive study in its own right.[60]

NOTES

1. See, for example, Liang Qichao, 'Puolan miewang ji' (An Account of Poland's Extinction), *Shiwu bao*, no. 3 (1896), pp. 138-41; Kang Youwei, 'Sanyue ershiqiri Baoguohui shang yanjiang huici' (Speech at a Meeting of the Protect the Nation Association on 27 March 1898), in Jian Bocan et al. (comp.), *Wuxu bianfa* (Shanghai, 1957), 4: 409-10. Kang warned that China might experience the same fate as Poland, India, Vietnam and Burma.
2. J. Grieder, *Intellectuals and the State in Modern China* (New York, 1981), p. 151. Yan Fu's translation of Huxley ushered in a period when Social Darwinism became a topic of lively interest amongst Chinese intellectuals, principally because it seemed to answer many of the questions Chinese were asking about China's situation in the world, as well as to offer prescriptions for the course China should follow. For a stimulating, although long-winded and tortuous, study of Darwinian influence on Chinese intellectuals, see J. Pusey, *China and Charles Darwin* (Cambridge, Mass., 1983).
3. For details of the Hundred Days Reform, M. Cameron, *The Reform Movement in China 1898-1912* (Stanford, 1931) is still useful. For a recent analysis of the political in-fighting during 1898, see L. Kwong, *A Mosaic of the Hundred Days* (Cambridge, Mass., 1984).
4. The best introduction to the 1901-11 Manchu reform period is M. Wright, 'Introduction: The Rising Tide of Change' in M. Wright (ed.), *China in Revolution: The First Phase 1900-1913* (New Haven, 1968) pp. 1-63.
5. The first full-length study of this aspect of Qing reform, unfortunately marred by a turgid writing style, is J. Fincher, *Chinese Democracy* (New York, 1981). See also his chapter 'Political Provincialism and National Revolution' in M. Wright (ed.), *ibid*, pp. 185-226.
6. An excellent study of late Qing military reform is E. Fung, *The Military Dimension of the Chinese Revolution* (Vancouver, 1980).
7. G. Rozman (ed.), *The Modernization of China* (New York, 1981).
8. This is not to say, of course, that Chinese educators were unaware of the differences in educational systems among western countries.

The centralised French system, for example, was often contrasted with the more decentralised structure of the American system. There was a tendency, however, among Chinese officials and educators to view all western countries alike in their ability to train loyal and disciplined citizens.
9. G.Rozman (ed.), *The Modernization of China*, Ch. 6.
10. For a study of academies in an earlier time when they were more innovative, see J.Meskill, *Academies in Ming China: A Historical Essay* (Arizona, 1982). See also T. Grimm, 'Academies and Urban Systems in Kwangtung' in G.Skinner (ed.), *The City in Imperial China* (Stanford, 1977), pp. 475-98. Even in the nineteenth century some academies provided a wider curriculum. The Gujing Qingshe Academy in Hangzhou (established in 1801), for example, examined students in astronomy, mathematics, and geography. See B. Elman, 'The Hsueh-hai T'ang and the Rise of New Text Scholarship', *Ch'ing-shih wen-t'i*, 4: 2 (December 1979), pp. 51-71. The Gezhi Shixue Academy in Shaanxi province, established in 1896, taught science, English and mathematics. Huang Yanpei, 'Qingji gesheng xingxue shi' (A History of the Promotion of Education in Each Province at the End of the Qing), *Renwen yuekan* 1: 7 (September, 1930), pp. 1-2.
11. During the Ming dynasty, for example, the Hongwu Emperor ordered in 1375 the wide-scale establishment of community schools (*shexue*). Little came of this initiative and those that were set up quickly became integrated with the civil service examination system. See Igarashi Shōichi, *Chūgoku Kinsei Kyōiikushi no Kenkyū* (Tokyo, 1979), pp. 7-8, 397. The phrase 'Confucian uniformity' comes from A. Woodside, 'Some mid-Qing Theorists of Popular Schools', *Modern China*, 9: 1 (January 1983), p. 9. For Qing policy towards ethnic minorities, see Pei Huang, *Autocracy at Work* (Bloomington, 1974), pp. 273-301.
12. For community schools during the Qing dynasty, see Hsiao Kung-ch'üan, *Rural China: Imperial Control in the Nineteenth Century* (Seattle, 1960), pp. 235-44; E. Rawski, *Education and Popular Literacy in Ch'ing China* (Michigan, 1979), pp. 33-53. Rawski argues that these schools played a useful role in promoting a more widespread literacy among the populace than has hitherto been thought possible by western sinologists. She defines the lowest level of literacy as the ability to recognise several hundred characters (p. 4), and concludes that mid- and late-nineteenth-century China may have experienced literacy rates of 30-45 per cent for men and 2-10 per cent for women (p. 140). Although Rawski notes that Japanese levels of male literacy during the late Tokugawa period were about the same, she does not pose the question whether studies of Japanese education use a different criterion for 'literacy' than her own.
13. E. Rawski, 'Economic and Social Foundations of Late Imperial Culture' in D. Johnson, A. Nathan, E. Rawski (eds.), *Popular Culture in Late Imperial China* (Berkeley, 1985), pp. 3-12; Ho Ping-ti, *The Ladder of Success in Imperial China* (New York, 1962), pp. 194-6.

14. Hsiao Kung-ch'üan, *Rural China*, refers to the short-lived existence of community schools and gentry-sponsored charitable schools (*yixue*). In one town alone, in Zhili province, none of the twelve *yixue* founded between 1685 and 1871 existed in 1911 (p. 250). Lack of funds or appropriation by the elite of educational funds for other purposes were often the reasons for this state of affairs. A. Woodside (*op. cit.*, pp. 5-6) also stresses the precarious existence of charitable schools.
15. For a discussion of early Confucian theories on the nature of man, see D. Munro, *The Concept of Man in Early China* (Stanford, 1969), esp. pp. 13-15, 22, 48-51, 82-3,163-5.
16. M. Jansen and L. Stone, 'Education and Modernization in Japan and England', *Comparative Studies in Society and History*, no. 9 (1967), pp. 208-32. Stone notes that from the seventeenth century onwards the English upper classes had tended to 'associate lower class education with political and social radicalism'. See also C. Kaestle, 'Between the Scylla of Brutal Ignorance and the Charybdis of a Literary Education: Elite Attitudes Towards Mass Schooling in Early Industrial England and America', in L. Stone (ed.), *Schooling and Society* (Baltimore, 1976), pp. 177-91; H. Chisick, *The Limits of Reform in the Enlightenment* (Princeton, 1981), pp. 279-90.
17. B. Marshall, 'The Late Meiji Debate Over Social Policy' in H. Wray, H. Conroy (eds.), *Japan Examined: Perspectives on Modern Japanese History* (Honolulu, 1983), pp. 158-62. The Association for the Study of Social Policy (*Shakai seisaku gakkai*), comprising intellectuals and bureaucrats, was founded at the turn of the century with the specific aim of devising policies to avoid the 'social problem'.
18. It is interesting to note that social education continues to be a subject of interest among educators. See, for example, J. Sandven (ed.), *The Role of Educational Research in Social Education* (Oslo, 1963), a collection of papers from the Third International Congress for the University Study of Education.
19. The first definition of *tongsu jiaoyu* I have come across is in a 1906 article in DFZZ, 3: 5, *jiaoyu*, p. 65 in which the term refers to the 'reform' of society through the agency of public lectures, newspapers and popular publications.
20. D. Johnson, 'Communication, Class, and Consciousness in Late Imperial China' in D. Johnson, A. Nathan, E. Rawski (eds.), *Popular Culture in Late Imperial China*, pp. 46-8.
21. For an example of the promotion of an approved state cult in imperial China, in this case Tian Hou, the patron goddess of fishermen, sailors and maritime merchants, see J. Watson, 'Standardizing the Gods: The Promotion of T'ien Hou Along the South China Coast 960-1960', in D. Johnson, A. Nathan, E. Rawski (eds.), *Popular Culture in Late Imperial China*, pp. 292-324. On the compilation of popular morality books, see Tadao Sakai, 'Confucianism and Popular Educational Works', in Wm. de Bary (ed.), *Self and Society in Ming Thought* (New York, 1970), pp. 331-

62. One of the most prolific compilers of such works was Lü Kun (1536-1618), the Ming dynasty scholar who wrote didactic works for women, children and the poor. See J. Handlin, *Action in Late Ming Thought* (Berkeley, 1983).
22. P. Burke, *Popular Culture in Early Modern Europe* (London, 1978). Burke argues (pp. 27-9) that during the course of the seventeenth and eighteenth centuries the educated classes gradually withdrew from participation in popular culture and embarked on a systematic attempt 'to change the attitudes and values of the rest of the population' (p. 207). See also the review article by W. Beik, 'Popular Culture and Elite Suppression in Early Modern Europe', *Journal of Interdisciplinary History*, 11: 1 (1980),pp.97-103.
23. *Pingmin* was originally used as the Chinese expression to translate 'proletariat 'during the early years of the twentieth century when Chinese revolutionaries and reformers were debating the 'social problem'. Neither group at that time believed that China exhibited glaring class differences (described in terms of the gap between rich and poor) characteristic of the West. See Song Jiaoren's article in *Min bao* 1: 5 (1906), p. 79, where 'bourgeois' and 'proletariat' are rendered as *fushen* (lit. 'rich gentry') and *pingmin* (lit. 'the ordinary people'). Another revolutionary, Zhu Zhixin, in the same issue of *Min bao*, p. 52, used the expression *ximin* (the populace) for 'proletariat' and *haoyu* (lit. 'an esteemer of unrestrained extravagance') for 'bourgeois'. The expression *minzhong jiaoyu* was first used at the Guomindang-sponsored Education Conference of 1928, which called for the widespread creation of mass schools to provide a training in literacy and arithmetic for 15-50 year-olds. For a report on the conference proceedings, see *Quanguo jiaoyu huiyi baogao* (Shanghai, 1928), 2 vols. The resolution on mass schools is in vol. 2. pp. 398-9.
24. *Wusi shiqi qikan jieshao* (Beijing, 1979) 1.1: 338.
25. For a discussion of this literacy campaign, see *Pingmin jiaoyu chubu chengji baogao* (Shanghai, 1925); Yang Maoru, 'Pingmin jiaoyu yundong de jingguo', JYZZ, 19: 1 (1927), pp. 1-5; Wu Xiangxiang, 'Pingmin jiaoyu yundong de chuqi shishi', *Shi bao* (17 February 1980) pp.18-9, (24 February 1980), p 25-7, (2 March 1980), pp.20-1.
26. *Jiaoyu yu minzhong*, 2: 1 (1930), *lunzhu*, pp. 1-2.
27. *Shehui jiaoyu jiangyan dagang* (Kaifeng 1929), p. 58.
28. Kuo Pingwen, *The Chinese System of Public Education* (New York, 1914), p. 100, regards popular education as comprising not only literacy, half-day and primary schools, but also middle schools. English language works on popular education also show diversity in their definitions of the concept. H. Silver, *The Concept of Popular Education* (London, 1965) notes (p. 15) that 'popular education is used in this study...as an after-the-event shorthand to cover a range of thinking about the education of the poor and deprived, from the most limited and condescending charitable approach to the labouring classes, to the most ambitious plans for national education'. H. Pollard, *Pioneers of Popular Education 1760-1850* (London, 1956),

although never defining specifically what he means by popular education, seems to equate the concept with the instruction of the poor, new innovative methods in teaching children, and the creation of state-funded and controlled primary school systems.

29. Jingshi yixue guan (comp.), *Jiaoyu cihui* (Beijing, 1904), pp. 148, 164. This was a compilation of educational terms published by the government translation bureau. In most cases the bureau used Japanese translations from the German.
30. M. Canovan, *Populism* (London, 1981), pp. 71-83.
31. Wang Ermin, 'Qingji xuehui huibiao' (A Record of Study Societies during the Late Qing), *Dalu zazhi* 26: 2 (January 1962), pp. 14-20, 26: 3 (February 1962), pp. 16-23; M. Bastid, *L'Evolution de la Société Chinoise à la fin de la Dynastie des Qing 1873-1911* (Paris, 1979), pp. 37-49.
32. *Minguo renwu zhuan* (Beijing, 1981), 3: 230-6; *Zhuanji wenxue*, 30: 3 (March 1977), p. 126.
33. H. Boorman, R. Howard (eds.), *Biographical Dictionary of Republican China* (New York, 1967), 2: 210-13. Huang lived on to participate in political life after the establishment of the People's Republic. In 1954 and 1958 he attended the National People's Congress as the representative of Jiangsu province. His funeral was attended by such CCP dignitaries as Zhou Enlai and Deng Xiaoping. *Guangming ribao* (25 December 1965).
34. H. Boorman, R. Howard (eds.), *Republican China*, 2: 14-5.
35. Hashikawa Tokio, *Chūgoku Bunka Kai Jimbatsu Sōkan* (Beijing, 1940), pp. 785-6.
36. Hashikawa Tokio, *ibid.*, pp. 797-8; J-P Drège, *La Commercial Press de Shanghai 1897-1949* (Paris, 1978), p. 238.
37. H. Boorman, R. Howard (eds.), *Republican China*, 2: 319-21.
38. Liu Shaotang (ed.), *Minguo renwu xiaozhuan* (Taibei, 1975),1: 38-9.
39. Chen Rong'gun *Chen Zibao xiansheng jiaoyu yiyi* (Guangzhou, 1952), pp. 293-7.
40. Leo Ou-fan Lee, A. Nathan, 'The Beginnings of Mass Culture: Journalism and Fiction in the Late Ch'ing and Beyond' in D. Johnson, A. Nathan, E. Rawski (eds.), *Popular Culture in Late Imperial China*, pp. 370-2.
41. *Jiaoyu zazhi* continued publication until 1948. *Zhonghua jiaoyujie* briefly resumed publication in 1947 until December 1950. *Cihai: jiaoyu xinli fen'ce* (Shanghai, 1980), p. 60
42. I was fortunate to have access to these journals, many of them not available in the West, while doing research at Beijing University in 1980-1.
43. N. Stone, *Europe Transformed 1878-1919* (London, 1983), pp. 96, 389-90.
44. M. Burton *The Education of Women in China* (New York, 1911), p. 149.
45. H. King, *The Educational System of China as Recently Reconstructed* (Washington, 1911), p. 103.

46. See, for example, Chai-Hsuan Chuang, *Tendencies Toward a Democratic System of Education in China* (Shanghai, 1922); Kuo Pingwen, *The Chinese System of Public Education* (New York, 1914); Chiling Yin, *Reconstruction of Modern Educational Organizations in China* (Shanghai, 1926); Yen Sun Ho, *Chinese Education from the Western Viewpoint* (New York, 1913); T. Y. Teng, T. T. Lew, *Education in China* (Beijing, 1925); You-Kuang Chu, *Some Problems of a National System of Education in China* (Shanghai, 1933); Tsang Chiu-sam, *Nationalism in School Education in China since the Opening of the Twentieth Century* (Shanghai, 1933); T. Hsiao, *The History of Modern Education in China* (Shanghai, 1935). A number of accounts were also written in Chinese at this time, but they were mostly concerned with a description of government regulations and laws. See, for example, Jiang Shuge, *Zhongguo jindaii jiaoyu zhidu* (Shanghai, 1934) and Chen Qitian, *Zuijin sanshinian Zhongguo jiaoyushi* (Shanghai, 1936). Recent Chinese accounts continue this practice and contain little in-depth analysis of changes in educational attitudes. See Chen Jingpan, *Zhongguo jindai jiaoyushi* (Beijing, 1979) and Chen Yuanhui, *Zhongguo xiandai jiaoyushi* (Beijing, 1979).
47. Kuo Pingwen, *The Chinese System of Public Education*, p. 4. Like many Chinese officials during the last years of the Qing, Kuo insisted that in the Zhou dynasty (1122-256 BC) China had possessed a well organised school system providing education for all. T. Hsiao, *The History of Modern Education in China*, p. 4, takes seriously the claim presented in the Classic of Rites (*Li ji*) that there was a school for every twenty-five families in pre-Zhou times.
48. H. Galt, *Oriental and Occidental Elements in China's Modern Educational System* (Beijing, 1929), pp. 14-15. Bertrand Russell, who visited China during the May Fourth movement, stressed in 1922 that Chinese educational development was not necessarily behind that of the West. As an example he pointed to the acceptance of women at Beijing University and contrasted this with the situation at Cambridge. *The Problem Of China* (London, 1922), p. 236.
49. C. Peake, *Nationalism and Education in Modern China* (New York, 1932). Peake's unsympathetic and, at times, rather ludicrous approach is shown when he gives an example of what he calls 'selfish nationalism' - the decision taken by the Tenth Annual Conference of the National Federation of Education Associations in 1924 to remove English from the primary school curriculum and make it 'elective only' in junior middle schools. The idea of teaching a foreign language at primary level has hardly been adopted today, least of all in the United States. Peake, as an American, could also have done well to study the results of a survey carried out among American educators in the late 1920s (cited in You-Kuang Chu, *Some Problems of a National System of Education in China*, p. 30). 81 per cent of those questioned agreed with the statement that 'every boy and girl in American schools should be taught to give unquestioned and unlimited respect and support to the American flag for whatever cause it may be unfurled'.

50. On Dewey in China, see W. Brickman (ed.), *John Dewey's Impressions of Soviet Russia and the Revolutionary World: Mexico, China, Turkey* (New York, 1964); R. Clopham, Tsuin-chen Ou, *John Dewey: Lectures in China 1919-1920* (Honolulu, 1973).
51. V. Purcell, *Problems of Chinese Education* (London,1936), p. 51.
52. Ibid., p. 71.
53. W. Ayers, *Chang Chih-tung and Educational Reform in China* (Cambridge, Mass., 1971); K. Biggerstaff, *The Earliest Modern Government Schools in China* (Ithaca, 1961); W. Franke, *The Reform and Abolition of the Chinese Examination System* (Cambridge, Mass., 1960).
54. Chow Tse-tsung, *The May Fourth Movement* (Cambridge, Mass., 1960); B. Keenan, *The Dewey Experiment in China* (Cambridge, Mass., 1977).
55. J. Esherick, *Reform and Revolution: The 1911 Revolution in Hunan and Hubei* (Berkeley, 1976); C. Lewis, *Prologue to Revolution: The Transformation of Ideas and Institutions in Hunan Province 1891-1907* (Cambridge, Mass., 1976); E. Rhoads, *China's Republican Revolution: The Case of Kwangtung 1895-1913* (Cambridge, Mass., 1975). Japanese scholars have also devoted attention to the establishment of modern schools during the late Qing. See, for example, Abe Hiroshi, 'Shinmatsu no kindai gakkō, kōsei-shō o chūshin ni' (Modern Schools at the End of the Qing, concentrating on Jiangxi Province), *Rekishi Hyōron*, no.1 (January 1965), pp. 47-60, no. 3 (March 1965), pp. 56-66; Saito Akio, 'Chūgoku gakusei kaikaku no shisō to genjitsu' (Theory and Practice in the Reform of China's Educational System), *Senshū Jimbun Ronshū* (December 1969), pp. 1-25.
56. S. Borthwick, *Education and Social Change in China* (Stanford 1983).
57. *Diyici Zhongguo jiaoyu nianjian* (Shanghai, 1932; reprint Taibei, 1971) 3: 694-5.
58. See, for example, Wu Yuandi, 'Wuguo nongye jiaoyu zhi quexian ji gaige fangfa zhi shangque' (A Discussion of the Defects in our Country's Agricultural Education and the Methods to Reform It), ZHJYJ, 8: 1(1919), pp. 31-8.
59. For rural education in Ding *xian*, Hebei, see the two-volume collection edited by Wu Xiangxiang, *Dingxian nongmin jiaoyu* (Taibei, 1971). For rural reconstruction in Shandong province, see G. Alitto, *The Last Confucian: Liang Shu-ming and the Chinese Dilemma of Modernity* (Berkeley, 1979), pp. 192-278. One result of the increasing interest in rural education was the publication of a number of manuals for potential rural teachers. Two examples are Cheng Benhai, *Xiangcun shifan jingyantan* (Shanghai, 1939) and Gan Cao, *Xiangcun jiaoyu* (Shanghai, 1938).
60. Western missionaries in China during the nineteenth century pioneered the establishment of girls' schools and it is no coincidence that two of the earliest studies of women's education in China were written by missionaries. See M. Burton. *The Education of Women in China* (NewYork, 1911); I. Lewis, *The Education of Girls in China*

(New York, 1919). For a recent study of the women's movement in China during the last years of the Qing dynasty, which includes a discussion of education, see C. Beahan, 'The Women's Movement and Nationalism in Late Ch'ing China' (Ph.D. Thesis, Columbia University, New York, 1976).

1. The Reorientation of Official Thinking

The large-scale rebellions of the mid-nineteenth century and the occupation of Beijing in 1860 by Anglo-French forces to ensure Chinese ratification of newly revised treaties symbolised the classic danger of *neiluan waihuan* (internal disorder and foreign aggression). Primarily in response to the rebellions, and, in particular, the Taiping rebellion (1850-64), Zeng Guofan (1811-72), Li Hongzhang (1823-1901) and other provincial leaders promoted the idea of self-strengthening (*ziqiang*), designed to reinvigorate the Confucian political and social order through both a renewed emphasis on traditional moral values and the importation of western technology, particularly in the military sphere.[1] Two of the earliest 'self-strengthening' projects, for example, were the construction of the Jiangnan arsenal, near Shanghai, in 1865 and the Fuzhou shipyard in 1866.

It was in the wake of this self-strengthening movement, from the 1860s to the early 1890s, that China's first government-sponsored modern schools emerged. The earliest proponent of such schools was Feng Guifen (1809-94), an important scholar and administrative assistant to Li Hongzhang when he was Governor of Jiangsu in 1864-5.[2] In 1861 Feng argued that China needed to produce competent experts on western learning and hence avoid dependence on either foreigners or unreliable Chinese compradores in the treaty ports. In addition to military technology, Feng urged the adoption of western technology in agriculture and textile manufacture. China must learn about, and adopt, all technology, Feng insisted, that was of benefit to the country and to the people, although he warned that 'freakish skills and artful devices' (*qiji yinqiao*) were to be avoided.[3]

The modern schools established during this period included not only the training schools attached to the Jiangnan arsenal and Fuzhou shipyard, but also foreign language schools at Beijing, Shanghai and Guangzhou, military and naval academies, a telegraph school, and a school of mining and engineering.[4] As a study of these schools has made clear, they were essentially specialist training schools designed to produce graduates who would serve the government mainly in the military or diplomatic spheres.[5] As such the education given accorded with the traditional Chinese ideal of producing *rencai* (human talent for government service). Feng, in his 1861 proposal, had poured scorn on village and charitable schools in his home district precisely because they had failed, in his view, to produce 'exceptional talent'.[6] It should also be noted that these schools did not in any way infringe upon the dominance of the traditional civil service examinations as the principal route to civil office.[7]

Yet by the last years of the dynasty (1904-11) the terms of the discourse had fundamentally changed. The traditional civil service examinations were abolished and replaced by a national system of schools. Greater emphasis was placed on educating all the people and allowing more scope for individual needs. Finally, national wealth and strength was now located in the qualities of the populace rather than in the specialised training of experts.[8] What was the course of this transition and what were the terms of debate over popular education during the last years of the dynasty?

OFFICIAL ATTITUDES FROM THE 1890S TO 1904

The limited results of the self-strengthening movement were clearly illustrated with China's defeat at the hands of France in 1885. The growing French presence in Vietnam, long regarded as a tributary vassal of the Middle Kingdom, prompted the court to declare war on France in 1884. A humiliating defeat ensued (during which the Fuzhou shipyard was destroyed) and in 1885 China was compelled to recognise French dominance in Vietnam. Ten years later China was defeated by Japan in an attempt to halt increasing Japanese influence in Korea, another tributary vassal. Voices were raised criticising the narrow focus of the self-strengthening movement. In the 1890s schools sponsored by government officials offered a wider course of training. Yet the rationale behind these schools remained the same: to recruit 'talent' for government service. Two important officials involved in the promotion of such schools were Sheng Xuanhuai (1844-1916) and Zhang Zhidong (1837-1909).

Sheng, the first director of the officially-sponsored China Merchants Steam Navigation Company in 1873, and the Director-General of the Imperial Railway Administration in 1896, sponsored two modern schools: the Sino-Western School (*Zhongxi xuetang*) in Tianjin (1896) and the Nanyang Public School (*Nanyang gongxue*) in Shanghai (1897).[9] The Sino-Western School was to comprise two sections, each having 120 students; English, geography, astronomy, mathematics, mining, engineering and law were some of the courses offered.[10] In his memorial of 1895 proposing the creation of the school, Sheng noted: 'I investigated the road to self-strengthening and saw that cultivating talent (*rencai*) was the basis [of it]. For the way to seek talent, it is especially fitting that schools be established first.'[11] Sheng thus regarded new schools as a means to cultivate and select talent for government service. He pointed to the example of Japan, where the government chose 'talent' not only from military and naval schools but also from law, mining, and engineering institutes. Furthermore, Sheng was particularly concerned that the students chosen to be trained in new specialist schools should come from the intellectual elite:

> There are many capable people to be found in China, but it is first necessary to select and use the talented from among the many who are conversant with literature and calligraphy. If we select artisans and apprentices, who are ignorant of literary and mathematical skills, to be trained in industry we would definitely be unable to fulfil our desire

to catch up, and compete, with the other countries.¹²

The Nanyang Public School was meant to complement the Sino-Western School by providing a better grounding in Chinese history and literature.¹³ Although it had a section for teacher training, and hence constituted China's first normal school, Sheng saw the school's most important function as the training of able administrators. It is significant, for example, that he compared the potential role of Nanyang to that of the École d'Administration, a school created in France in 1848 to train civil servants.¹⁴

Zhang Zhidong, one of the most important provincial officials during the last years of the dynasty, was also a vigorous promoter of new higher level schools, but he emphasised that candidates for such schools were to be confined to a restricted few in order that 'talent' be produced as soon as possible for government service.¹⁵ The modern schools that Zhang founded in the 1890s bore this out. In 1893 he established the Self-Strengthening School (*ziqiang xuetang*) in Wuchang, Hubei. It was to be restricted to 120 students from Hubei and Hunan aged between fifteen and twenty-four years who came from families of officials or gentry above the rank of *shengyuan* (lower-degree holder).¹⁶ Pointing to the example of western countries where higher schools charged fees, Zhang later changed the regulations for the school and announced that as of 1897 fees would be charged.¹⁷ (The traditional Confucian academies, or *shuyuan*, had generally provided subsidies for the students.) In his memorial proposing the creation of the school, Zhang stressed that the 'art of government' had as its basis 'the cultivation of talent'. The school would offer instruction in current affairs, foreign languages, science, mathematics and commercial affairs in order 'to provide the country with able officials'.¹⁸

In 1896 Zhang established the Hubei Military Preparatory School (*wubei xuetang*) and the School for Gathering Talent (*chucai xuetang*) The former was designed to train military officials (*wuguan*). The quota of students was restricted to 120 and they had to be 'expectant civil or military officials, men with civil or military degrees, students of the Classics, and the sons of reputable gentry'. ¹⁹ Zhang later noted that more than 4 000 had applied and he made it clear that an extremely selective choice would be made in order to make training quick and easy. This was inevitable, he maintained, since training was to be the basis of an official career.²⁰ The School for Gathering Talent was to provide knowledge of international affairs, agriculture, industry, and commerce. A wide training of talent, Zhang claimed, was 'the fundamental basis for the planning of wealth and strength'.²¹

The schools founded by Zhang Zhidong in the 1890s were therefore specialist training schools designed to produce well-qualified officials or experts working for the state. He was not advocating at this point a more widespread system of education available to larger groups of people. A recent study of Zhang Zhidong and his educational policies by W. Ayers has concluded that Zhang contributed to the broadening of the scope of education and the spreading of its benefits.[22] One should bear in mind, however, that Zhang only began to propose a genuinely national system of education after 1903 and even then, as will be shown later, he continued to oppose vigorously the education of girls.

Ayers also maintains that Zhang anticipated the Chinese Communist Party in urging that a higher status be given to soldiers and artisans and in criticising students' reluctance to engage in manual labour.[23] This is simply not borne out in the reasons Zhang gave for the establishment of his modern schools, which were in no way to threaten the dominance and prestige of Confucian learning. The one official who *did* strike a new note was Zuo Zongtang (1812-85), a prominent official who had participated in the suppression of the Taiping rebellion and became Governor-General of Minzhe (Fujian and Zhejiang) and, later, of Shen'gan (Shaanxi and Gansu). It was Zuo who initiated the Fuzhou shipyard project in 1866 and in a memorial discussing the aims of the shipyard and its technical school to train ship engineers and navigators, Zuo drew attention to the traditional contempt held for manual and technical work and called on students to embark on technical, rather than academic or official careers.[24] After 1903–4 criticism of the traditional ideal of 'studying to become an official' (*dushu zuoguan*), which Zuo had anticipated, was to become more widespread.[25]

In contrast to the priorities laid down by such officials as Zhang Zhidong and Sheng Xuanhuai, others suggested a different emphasis. In 1896 Li Duanfen (1833-1907), vice-president of the Board of Punishments and a former education commissioner for Yunnan, presented a memorial proposing the creation of a national school system.[26] In contrast to the brief references to this memorial in western accounts of Chinese education, Chinese writers attribute great importance to Li's memorial, hailing it as a pioneering proposal for popular education.[27] One writer sees in Li's suggestion to increase the number of schools the beginnings of 'mass education' (*minzhong jiaoyu*).[28] Others view Li's memorial as the beginning of the advocacy of 'social education' in that it referred to education outside the school, reaching a wider range of people.[29]

Li drew on ideas already raised by scholars and reformers. The first written accounts of national school systems and the implied recommendation that such a school system would be appropriate in China appeared in a missionary journal, the *Jiaohui xinbao* ,(Church News), which was founded by the American Southern Methodist, Young J. Allen, in 1868.[30] The *Jiaohui xinbao*, although begun as a news magazine specifically for Chinese Christians, soon began to aim at a wider audience and published a wide variety of articles on scientific and general subjects as well as on religious knowledge.[31] Beginning in 1871 a German missionary, Ernst Faber, published articles on western educational systems as well as contributing a detailed analysis of German schools in 1874.[32] By way of an introduction to Faber's account, a Chinese commentator noted in the magazine that schools were the source of Germany's strength and urged the Manchu court to establish schools since the 'reform of the people [*huamin*] and customs [*chengsu*] must inevitably arise from study'.[33] Confucianism had always underlined the importance of education as a means of cultivating the moral self, but this was the first time national wealth and strength were specifically linked with the reform of the people's character and customs. Such a theme was to be increasingly heard after 1900.

The first Chinese to suggest a plan for a school system in China was the compradore and scholar Zheng Guanying (1842-1923). Zheng also managed a wide variety of modern enterprises and, in the words of one writer, was the first to enunciate a self-styled ethos for the merchant and commercial class.[34] Being a treaty-port Chinese, Zheng was exposed early on to western political, social and economic ideas and it is almost certain that he had read issues of *Jiaohui xinbao*. Zheng advocated educational reform and in 1884 proposed the establishment of state-financed academies in each province to teach western studies, which were to form a separate category in the civil service examinations.[35] Superior students were to be sent to a university in the capital. This university, Zheng stressed, should be a *real* one like those that existed in the West, and not like the Beijing School for Foreign Languages (*tongwenguan*) which had been opened in 1861 to train linguists for the newly-created Office for Foreign Affairs (*zongli yamen*).[36] As far as Zheng was concerned, the *Tongwenguan* was no better than a primary school and he implied that westerners did not take the school seriously. This revealed for the first time (although certainly not the last) the sensitivity certain Chinese reformers felt towards the potential or actual criticisms foreigners might make of Chinese institutions and customs.

Zheng then went on to propose that all traditional private schools and academies be converted into a two-stream system of primary schools (in the district capitals) and secondary schools (in the prefectural or provincial capitals) for civil and military studies respectively. His rationale for this system was that it would provide a greater pool of specialised students from which 'talent' could be selected. Referring to the emphasis in Japan and western countries on specialisation, particularly in shipping, engineering, and military technology, Zheng made it clear that his proposed primary and secondary schools would be feeder institutions for the university in Beijing. His only concession to popular education was to make the vague statement that each rural district should establish 'family and public schools' for everyone alike.[37] In 1892 Zheng again stressed that 'schools are the places for creating human talent and the fundamental basis for governing the empire'.[38] Zheng's approach, therefore, did not diverge radically from that of officials like Zhang Zhidong, except that he advocated a larger network of specialised schools. He praised the efficiency of the German school system in 'training talent' and only as an afterthought did he note that there also existed in Germany a large number of schools for the poor.[39]

Two other reformers who must have influenced Li Duanfen were Kang

Youwei and Liang Qichao, who were both to play key roles in the 1898 reform movement. In 1895, after China had signed the Treaty of Shimonoseki ending its war with Japan, which conceded to Japan the island of Formosa (Taiwan), recognised Japanese dominance in Korea, and allowed Japanese manufacturing enterprises to be established in the treaty ports (this privilege automatically being extended to the other foreign powers because of the most-favoured-nation clause), Kang Youwei led a vigorous protest movement. Kang, who was to gain notoriety through his new interpretations of Confucius and the Confucian classics as a way of justifying his reform programme, presented a memorial in Beijing, signed by hundreds of other students who were in Beijing to take the metropolitan examination, which called on the court to implement reforms in order that China could 'keep up with the times'. Kang also urged that education be made more widespread otherwise, he warned, 'talent' would not emerge amongst peasants, artisans, and merchants.[40] Furthermore, if such action was not taken, 'the reform of the people's customs [*huamin chengsu*], the mending of their ways, and their changing towards the good will be difficult to carry out'.[41] Kang, in contrast to Zheng Guanying, was now talking of both a knowledgeable and morally reformed citizenry (*caizhi zhi min*) as the basis of a strong country. This theme was to be taken up by Chinese officials after 1904.

Concrete proposals, however, were thin and sketchy. Kang himself, in his 1895 memorial, simply proposed the creation of technical academies (*yixue shuyuan*) at district, prefectural and provincial levels at which fifteen-year-olds would be selected to attend. Liang Qichao, in his reform journal *Shiwu bao* (The Chinese Progress), also discussed the desirability of establishing schools. 'Enlarging the people's intelligence' (*kai minzhe*) was the first priority, Liang exclaimed, and he referred to the broad and general education extended to peasants, artisans, merchants and soldiers in the West.[42] Yet even in his reform essays of 1896 dealing with schools, Liang saw the overall aim of a wide network of schools as the production of useful talent for the country.[43] There was little attention to specific details or consideration of the special needs of people as individuals. Calculating enrolment figures from comparisons with those in western countries, and allowing for certain limitations in China's current situation, Liang estimated with glee that a national school system in China could produce eight thousand university graduates after ten years, who could then be used by the state in a variety of ways.[44] One important aspect of Liang's reform proposals was his suggestion that the civil service examinations be integrated with a network of modern schools.[45]

Li Duanfen's memorial of 1896 is important not only because it was the first *official* proposal for a national school system, but also because it was the first to present a coherent and reasonably detailed plan. It therefore deserves closer analysis. Li began his memorial by stressing the urgent need for talent, the usual theme in reform proposals hitherto: 'Times are difficult and the need for talent is extremely urgent. I humbly propose to increase the number of schools in order to encourage human talent and to provide the means necessary to withstand national shame.'[46] The amount of talent a country had, Li continued, determined whether a country was strong or weak. He was astounded that so few talented men existed in China, given the large size of her population: 'Now the Chinese people number hundreds of millions but scholars amongst them only number 100 000 or so. For human talent to be so deficient as this signifies is not a question of no natural talent being born but rather that the direction in which teaching is going is not perfected.'[47]

Li listed five reasons for this state of affairs, of which the fifth one was the most significant:

> As for a large building, it is not one [beam] of wood that supports it, nor is it just one pillar that resists stress. We have to seek for more scholars and make a beginning in solving our problems. Today the eighteen provinces only have a few official schools. Each school has only several tens of students. Those who want to study cannot, either because they live in remote rural areas and cannot get to school, or because the quotas for students are full up and they are not permitted to attend. Even if every student in the schools were useful afterwards, it would still not be sufficient to provide enough talent for serving the kingdom.[48]

Li advocated the creation of schools at provincial, prefectural, and district levels, and while Zhang Zhidong's regulations for his various schools had called for recruitment from among families of 'upright gentry', Li proposed selecting students from among the people so that youths between the ages of twelve and twenty could enter school. Li evidently had in mind continuing the traditional practice carried out in the academies (*shuyuan*) whereby no tuition fees were levied and grants given to students. In fact, when modern schools began to be established during the early years of the century many of them did not at first levy tuition fees, the result being that many had to close down through lack of funds.[49] This is what happened in Hunan, for example, so that in 1910 the Governor was compelled to order that henceforth all students were to pay fees and be responsible for their own lodgings.[50]

Li proposed that schools below the provincial level should have a 'mixed' curriculum, which would include the Confucian classics, foreign languages, mathematics, geography and foreign history. Schools at provincial level would select students under twenty-five years of age (again no specific requirement concerning status) and the curriculum would comprise the Classics and Chinese history, as well as courses on industry, agriculture, commerce, mining, current affairs and communications. To counter protests that his scheme would cost too much, Li advised converting provincial and district academies into modern schools. He also brushed aside potential objections that there would not be sufficient qualified teachers by noting that at the preliminary stage sophisticated and complicated knowledge need not be taught. With this system, Li explained, China would not only successfully imitate western practice, but would also resurrect the ideals of the early Zhou dynasty (1122BC–771BC), during which a wide network of schools was believed to have existed.[51]

Li went on to note that 'those who go to schools can advance daily, but those who cannot go to school do not have the help of classroom lectures. This is not the way to improve customs.'[52] Li suggested two ways to overcome this problem, prompting some Chinese writers to regard Li as a pioneer in the development of social education.[53] Firstly, he proposed the creation of public libraries in all the provinces for those who could not afford a formal education. Such libraries would accumulate useful books and would: 'allow all people to enter and read them. From each area those who are good at studying and who are competent would be selected to manage the library. Being like this, those who formerly had no books with which to study will all be able to exert themselves and there will be no wastage of talent.'[54]

Li therefore anticipated the creation of libraries in a modern context (i.e. places freely open to a wider public); this was aptly shown in his use of the recently coined term for 'library', *tushuguan* (literally an institution for books), rather than the traditional term, *zangshulou* (literally a place for storing and conserving books), which referred to the private book collections of scholars and bibliophiles.[55]

Secondly, Li urged the publication of more newspapers to allow for a more informed public, criticising the ineffectiveness of the contemporary Chinese press, which was limited to treaty-port cities such as Shanghai and Guangzhou.[56] Once again, Li pointed to the practice in western countries where a wide variety of newspapers enabled everyone to be acquainted with current affairs. As a result, Li noted: 'Those at the top cannot cover up anything while carrying out their duties and those below can use their thorough acquaintance with the political situation in their dealings with officials. The source of wealth and strength is certainly to be found in this approach.'[57]

In Li's estimation, therefore, those 'below' were not to be merely passive observers of the political process. An active acquisition of knowledge on their part would, in Li's view, automatically induce those in authority to act more circumspectly.

Li's proposal for a school system, like those of Zheng Guanying and Kang Youwei before him, did not make clear the connection it was to have with the traditional examination system. The question was not to be resolved until the examination system was finally abolished in 1905. In 1896, however, the throne was not prepared to institute a national system of schools. In its acknowledgement of Li's memorial, the throne concurred with the idea of a national university, but ignored the rest of Li's plan.[58]

The idea of a national school system was revived in 1898 during the

Hundred Days Reform. Kang Youwei, gaining access to the Guangxu Emperor, was able to convince him of the need for a bold programme of reform. China's defeat at the hands of Japan in 1895 and the increasing demands of the powers in 1897-8 for concession areas and economic privileges prompted Kang to warn of the danger of imminent partition. He urged the Emperor to emulate Peter the Great of Russia and the Meiji Emperor of Japan by implementing political, economic and military reforms to make the country 'wealthy and strong' (*fuqiang*). At the same time Kang also pointed to the negative example of Louis XVI of France, whose failure to 'act with the times' and implement reform had led to revolution and the loss of his throne.[59] In a burst of enthusiasm the Guangxu Emperor issued edicts calling for the abolition of sinecure posts, the promotion of industry and commerce, and the wide-scale establishment of schools.[60]

Kang's proposal on education involved the conversion of Confucian academies, ancestral and clan temples (and hence appropriating their wealth and property) into a structured hierarchy of primary, middle and higher level schools, to be under the administration and supervision of a national university in the capital. Once again, the system was to co-exist with the examination system. Kang cited the example of Frederick the Great of Prussia, who established a wide network of schools and higher institutions of specialised learning providing the country with a wider pool of talent on which the state could draw. This was the main thrust and purpose of Kang's scheme, although he did mention that in addition to providing the candidates for the higher level specialised schools, primary and secondary schools were also places that trained public-minded citizens (*guomin*).[61] Kang also recommended that China learn from Japan whose education system had been described by Huang Zunxian (1848-1905), a diplomat and reformer who had spent time in Japan and whose book *Riben guozhi* (An Account of Japan) was published in 1895.[62]

Zhang Zhidong, in his treatise *Quanxue pian* (Exhortation to Learning), which was distributed among officials on the eve of the Hundred Days Reform, also called for the establishment of schools and the promotion of overseas study.[63] Zhang made it clear, however, that primary and secondary schools, were to be 'feeders' for the proposed new national university in the capital and, unlike Kang, stressed the importance of traditional learning to be carried out in the schools. The Confucian classics were to have pride of place in the curricula for both primary and secondary schools, summed up in Zhang Zhidong's phrase 'traditional learning as the foundation, new learning [i.e. western studies] for application' (*jiuxue wei ti xinxue wei yong*). Although Zhang suggested that both administrative techniques (*zheng*) and vocational skills (*yi*) be taught in the schools, he assigned priority to the former.

Like Kang Youwei, Zhang advocated the appropriation of Confucian academies and clan temples to provide the funds and locations of the new schools. He also included charity halls, theatres, Buddhist and Daoist monasteries as potential sites for the new schools, although Zhang had a secondary motive for the conversion of Buddhist and Daoist monasteries. Such action, he noted, would contribute to the revival and expansion of Confucian scholarship.[64]

Kang Youwei preferred to emphasise much more the connection between the appropriation and transformation of popular religious institutions and the reform of the people's customs. His contempt for such institutions was aptly illustrated by his description of them as 'decadent and licentious' (*yin*).[65] Revealing a sensitivity to foreign opinion noted earlier in the case of Zheng Guanying, Kang claimed in a memorial that western visitors to China held the Chinese people up to scorn and ridicule because of their 'extravagant and decadent superstitions and beliefs' (*yinji*). Unlike other countries, Kang remarked, where only one god was worshipped, the Chinese worshipped a plethora of spirits and gods. Because of their 'barbaric customs', Kang lamented, westerners regarded the Chinese as no different from the 'uncivilised' peoples of Java, India and Africa. He suggested that Confucian churches be opened in every locality in which all the people would regularly assemble and worship Confucius. In this way, Kang concluded, the Chinese would be able to keep on the right moral path as their counterparts in the West were able to do.[66] The idea that the Chinese people had to be transformed, like those in the West, into hard-working, disciplined and morally upright citizens was to be an important theme in discussions of popular education after 1900.

The brief period of reform incurred the hostility of conservatives and was ended when the Emperor's aunt, the Empress-Dowager Cixi, retook the reins of power and rescinded all of the reform edicts. Only the new imperial university remained unscathed.[67] The conservative reaction led to the fatal support given by the throne to the anti-foreign Boxer movement. Beginning with attacks on Chinese Christians and western missionaries in Shandong province, the Boxers extended their activities to the Beijing metropolitan area where, with official encouragement. they attacked the foreign legations. The ensuing occupation of Beijing by a nine-power expeditionary force in 1900 forced the court to flee to Xian in Shaanxi province. The court was obliged to accept a humiliating settlement, which included the imposition of a large indemnity, punishment of responsible officials, the stationing of foreign troops between Beijing and Tianjin, and the suspension of the civil service examinations in areas that had witnessed Boxer activity.

This marked a turning-point in the court's attitude towards reform. On 29 January 1901 Cixi issued an edict underlining the need to 'adapt to the times and establish new institutions' (*yinshi lizhi*).[68] The edict discussed the necessity for China to learn from the foreigners and implement reforms in order 'to strengthen the country and benefit the people' (*qiang'guo limin*). Although the edict stressed the need to reform old laws and customs, it is significant that priority was still given to obtaining 'men of talent'. It noted that 'we have too many run-of-the-mill officials and not enough outstanding officials'. If such people could be found, the edict continued, 'then there will be no difficulty in rectifying bad laws; if we cannot find such people, then laws alone are useless'. As will be discussed later, gentry reformers drew a different lesson from the Boxer uprising and insisted that the people as a whole needed to be reformed.

On 14 September 1901, echoing the ideas of the 1898 reformers, the throne ordered the conversion of provincial academies into higher-level schools and the creation of middle and primary schools at the prefectural and district levels. The Confucian classics were to form the basis of the curriculum, supplemented by history, Chinese and foreign government, and sciences (*yixue*). Once again, the edict stressed the importance of human talent as the basis of government.[69] The court evidently thought the provinces were not taking prompt enough action since it issued another edict in November 1901 urging them to establish schools in order to 'accumulate talent' (*chucai*). This was, the court noted, 'truly the most urgent task facing us today'.[70]

The edicts issued by the throne on educational reform drew on the proposals put forward by such provincial officials as Zhang Zhidong and Yuan Shikai, the Governor of Shandong. In July 1901 Zhang, together with Liu Kunyi (1830-1902), the Governor-General of Liangjiang, had suggested the adoption of a school system modelled on that of Japan.[71] Zhang praised the Japanese and western systems of education because they were similar to the school system that had existed in Chinese antiquity. Such similarities, in Zhang's view, included the simultaneous study of civil (*wen*) and military (*wu*) affairs, and the teaching of both morality (*dao*) and vocational skills (*yi*).[72] More significantly, Zhang stressed, as he had done in his 1898 treatise, the efficient organisation and centralised control which he perceived as characteristic of education systems in the West and, in particular, the issue of government-approved standardised textbooks and appointment of school supervisory officials. Huang Zunxian, in his written account of Japan published in 1895, had also drawn attention to western practices in education that the Japanese government had adopted. These included the use of nationally standardised curricula, adherence to uniform school hours and schedules, the wearing of school uniforms, and the teaching of students in common.[73]

Zhang's 1901 plan suggested that each district establish a primary school (*xiao xuetang*) and higher primary school (*gaodeng xiao xuetang*). The primary schools would cater for the 12-15-year-old age group (Zhang thus left the question of elementary education in abeyance) and the curriculum would comprise the Confucian classics, elementary geography, arithmetic, Chinese history and government. The higher primary schools, for the 15-18-year-old age group, would provide a more in-depth instruction of these subjects in addition to teaching a foreign language and military drill.[74] At eighteen students would enter a middle school in the prefectural capital where, after three years, graduates would be awarded the traditional civil service degree of *linsheng*.⁷⁵ All this Zhang defined as 'general education' (*putong jiaoyu*). After three years at a higher school in the provincial capital graduates would be sent as apprentices (*lianxisheng*) to a government office. At twenty-five students would again be examined and awarded the provincial-level degree (*juren*). Such students could thereupon either be given an official appointment or be allowed to enter the Imperial University. Graduates of the university would be awarded the highest civil service degree (*jinshi*). The court accepted the idea of integrating modern schools with the traditional examination system and issued an edict to this effect in December 1901.⁷⁶

As W. Franke has observed, the whole thrust of Zhang's plan was to train future officials rather than to give an education to the general public.⁷⁷ Zhang had nothing to say about the education of children under twelve and even the primary schools were mainly regarded as preparatory training for the higher schools. Furthermore, although Zhang bewailed the fact that 'knowledge was not widespread', and despite the correlation he perceived between Japan's growing strength and the number of schools in the country, he saw a more immediate task, to take precedence over establishing a wide network of lower-level schools: 'Today, in order to save the situation... it is first necessary to establish middle schools... Then select energetic and bright lower-degree holders of character and quickly educate them, first instructing them in general subjects and then in specialised subjects'.⁷⁸ Zhang concluded his memorial in terms typical of official suggestions hitherto proposed:

> These four items (i.e. the creation of schools, the reform of the civil service examinations, abolition of the military examinations and the sending of students abroad) are the first task in seeking talent for administration... If one does not obtain talent one cannot count on the survival of the country. If one does not encourage the establishment of schools, talent cannot be cultivated.⁷⁹

The other important provincial official on whose ideas the court drew was Yuan Shikai (1859-1916), the governor of Shandong from 1899 to 1901 and creator of the Beiyang army, China's first modernised military force. In 1901 he presented a plan to the throne outlining a three-tiered system of schools for Shandong province, which he equated with primary (*xiaoxue*), secondary (*zhongxue*) and university (*daxue*) levels. The apex of the system was to be a college in the provincial capital, Jinan.⁸⁰ Yuan explained: 'A country's weakness or strength depends on human talent. The flourishing of human talent has its origin in the schools... Today, at a time of rapid change and great difficulty, if we want to use people to assist in government, we must encourage education to nurture talent.'⁸¹

As one historian has noted, Yuan's scheme was designed for no other reason than for 'the traditional purpose of training better officials to serve the dynasty'.⁸² It is significant, for example, that the provincial college was to be built first and the court instructed the other provinces to use its regulations as a model.[83] Also, as with Zhang Zhidong, Yuan ignored the question of primary education before the age of thirteen, preferring to leave it to the initiative of local communities.

Zhang Zhidong and Yuan Shikai were two of a number of high provincial officials who had managed to keep the areas of their jurisdiction free from foreign invasion during the Boxer uprising. They had done this by giving guarantees to foreign consuls concerning the protection of property and the safety of foreign nationals. Yet despite the disasters brought upon the throne and prestige of the country in the wake of the Boxer uprising, Zhang and Yuan still thought in terms of the traditional ideal of *rencai* (human talent) as a solution to China's problems, testimony to the powerful Confucian tradition that assigned priority to men over laws and institutions. Of course, traditional Confucianism stressed the importance of the morally-cultivated scholar, a 'generalist' rather than a specialist, whereas the term *rencai*' as used by Zhang and Yuan referred specifically to the technically-trained specialist working in administration or in other capacities on behalf of the state although Zhang, more than Yuan, also underlined the necessity for a solid background in Confucian learning. Zhang Zhidong, after all, was a member of the Confucian elite, being a holder of the highest civil service degree, whereas Yuan Shikai was only the holder of a purchased lower degree.

There was, however, another strand in the Confucian tradition which, as we shall see, exerted increasing influence after 1904. This involved a faith in the efficacy of education to bring about the moral perfectibility of man.[84] It was to be this faith that lay behind the confidence of the throne, officials and educators that widespread education would automatically produce a patriotic, public-minded and hard-working citizenry.

In January 1902 the court appointed Zhang Baixi as Chancellor of the Imperial University (*guanxue dachen*) and instructed him to present regulations on a new school system.[85] Zhang Baixi was a keen supporter of educational reform, especially with regard to the university. Foreigners had ridiculed the university, he noted, as a 'small boys' school and he warned that if educational reform was not implemented 'the contempt of outsiders will be evoked and the prestige of the country injured'.[86] Zhang's plan was sanctioned by the court, which instructed the provinces to carry out its provisions, 'with the general expectation that real talent will emerge to be made use of by the state'.[87] Zhang proposed the creation of elementary, primary and secondary schools under the control and supervision of the national university. With the potential criticism of conservatives in mind, Zhang maintained that his plan would simply revive a school system that had existed during the Zhou dynasty but which had since fallen into disuse. Unlike Zhang Zhidong's 1901 plan, Zhang Baixi's scheme now envisaged a state system of education that began with elementary schools, as well as for the first time suggesting the implementation of compulsory schooling: 'At the age of nine they will enter primary school for three years. After each area has established a school, then everyone, of whatever rank, should receive these seven years of education. After this they can follow whatever occupation they like'.[88] Zhang also suggested that charitable and private schools (*yishu, jiashu*) be converted into primary schools. However, the plan made no provision for girls' education and little provision for any kind of supplementary education.

Nevertheless, Zhang Baixi's proposal still aroused much opposition at court. Conservatives feared that such a system would undermine Confucian learning. In 1903 the throne first appointed Rong Qing, and then Zhang Zhidong as Zhang Baixi's assistants and ordered them to devise a new set of regulations that would assign a larger part of the curriculum to traditional learning.

Meanwhile, provincial officials were showing an interest in extending education to a wider populace. One such official was Duan Fang (1861-1911), the Governor of Hubei.[89] In 1902 he noted the large number of vagrants (*yumin*) in the provincial capital, many of whom resorted to criminal activities. This was due, Duan claimed, to the fact that the benefits of education had not been extended to all. To correct this oversight Duan proposed the creation of 'universal schools' (*puji xueshu*) for 15–20 year-olds.[90] There were to be thirty such schools in the provincial capital and its suburbs and they were to be officially subsidised. Although Duan noted that these schools were to benefit the illiterate and the unemployed, it is evident that he had more groups in mind. Thus the regulations stipulated that before attending a 'universal school' a student had to register his name and occupation. Elsewhere the regulations stated that employers were not to discourage their employees from attending these schools and noted that such schools would especially benefit petty shop clerks, traders, peddlers and labourers (e.g. rickshaw-pullers).

With the opening of these schools, Duan confidently predicted, the streets would henceforth be cleared of crime. Furthermore, once everyone had received an education, Duan continued, it would be impossible for anyone to be cheated or deceived by others: 'The more the people are literate, the more they understand the principles of human intercourse, and this is beneficial to the business (*puhu*) and to the family.'[91]

It is significant that Duan did not insist on the wearing of a uniform, in marked contrast to the regulations on charity schools in eighteenth-century England which deliberately insisted on the wearing of a 'sober' uniform to impress upon the children their lowly status and the fact that they were the recipients of charity. It was not until 1906, following his participation in an official mission to Europe and North America to investigate government and education, that Duan Fang advocated the wearing of uniforms at school as a way of imposing discipline upon children.[93] As will be shown later, however, some Chinese educators continued to oppose the wearing of school uniforms at primary level because the costs involved would be disadvantageous for poorer families.

The interest shown by some provincial officials in extending education to a wider populace is also shown in the regulations on official lectures (*xiangyue*) issued by the Governor of Hunan in 1903. Traditionally, *xiangyue* referred to the public duty of local gentry to expound on Confucian virtues and official proscriptions (laid down, for example, by the Sacred Edicts of the Kangxi and Yongzheng emperors in the seventeenth and eighteenth centuries).[94] The 1903 regulations issued by the Governor of Hunan enjoined the gentry to lecture on current affairs and encourage the opening of kindergartens and girls' schools. The Governor also insisted that gentry were to use colloquial language (*baihua*) and avoid obscure literary allusions.[95] During the last years of the Qing, in fact, reformers and revolutionaries promoted the use of a more accessible written language free of the rigidities and obfuscation of the classical literary style. Also, the encouragement to open girls' schools is an example of how provincial or local initiative (official or gentry) often pre-empted central government action, since the court was not to issue regulations on girls' schools until 1907.

THE 1904 SCHOOL SYSTEM

The impasse brought about by the court's decision to have the 1902 school regulations revised highlighted the need to draw up a uniform administrative system in order to impose control over the schools. Furthermore, the few modern schools that had been founded had to compete with the traditional civil service examinations. Shu Xincheng, a prominent educator and writer of the 1920s and 1930s, recounts in his autobiography the disdain with which the new primary school was met in the capital of his native district of Xupu, Hunan.[96] In 1903 the district magistrate had been ordered to convert a traditional academy into a higher primary school but the inhabitants, including Shu's mother, dismissed it as a 'foreign-type school' and preferred to see their children continuing their preparation for the civil service examinations in private or family schools (*sishu*). Such schools, run by one teacher and instructing pupils on an individual basis, concentrated on the rote memorisation of the Confucian classics.[97]

In 1903 Zhang Zhidong and Yuan Shikai proposed the abolition of the examinations because, since they were considered the only route to 'profit and emolument' (*lilu* i.e. an official career), they were obstructing the development of modern schools and hence 'the state will never have the talent to suit the times'.[98] Yuan Shikai, in another memorial in 1903, urged the speedy adoption of a national school system and referred to the common practice in the West to extend education to everyone between the ages of seven and twelve.[99]

In January 1904 the new school regulations were promulgated and were to remain in force until 1911.[100] Administrative control over the school system was wrested from the Imperial University and placed in the hands of a Director of Education (*zongli xuewu dachen*) and a Bureau of Educational Affairs (*xuewuqu*). The period of compulsory education was reduced to five years and greater emphasis was placed on the Confucian classics in the primary school curriculum. In a teaching schedule comprising six hours a day for a twelve-day week, Zhang Baixi's 1902 plan had assigned twelve hours (out of a total of seventy-two) to the teaching of the Classics in elementary and primary schools,[101] whereas the 1904 regulations assigned twelve hours (out of a total of thirty in a six-day teaching week) to the Classics in lower primary schools and twelve hours (out of a total of thirty-six) in higher primary schools.[102]

A feature of both the 1902 and 1904 plans was the addition of 'moral training' (*xiushen*) to the curriculum. The concept had been borrowed from Japan (*shūshin* in Japanese) where, in 1880, Nishimura Shigeki, in charge of the newly-formed compilation bureau (*hensankyōku*) at the Ministry of Education, issued the *Shōgaku Shūshin Kun* (Moral Primer for Elementary Schools). This was to be the first of many moral primers produced in reaction to the extreme westernisation that some Japanese officials and educators feared had pervaded the school curriculum. In contrast to the cosmopolitan bias in school textbooks and the praise of such western values as individualism during the 1870s, Japanese moral primers after 1880 were concerned exclusively with Japan and stressed traditional virtues such as loyalty and public service.[103] In 1902 Zhang Baixi, as rector of the Imperial University, was presented with an entire set of textbooks used in government schools in Japan by the Japanese minister at Beijing.[104]

In Zhang's 1902 regulations moral training occupied an important part of the curriculum and sought to instil traditional virtues such as 'filial piety and fraternal duty [*xiaodi*], faithfulness and sincerity [*zhongxin*], correct etiquette and a sense of shame [*liyi lianchi*], and respect for elders and teachers [*jingzhang zunshi*]' as well as encouraging 'loyalty to the monarch and love of country' (*zhongjun aiguo*).[105] The 1904 school system also incorporated moral training into the curriculum:

> The main aim is to impose reasonable discipline without overbearing coercion, and moreover to illustrate the words and deeds of past historical figures in order to stimulate in the pupils feelings of admiration and the desire to emulate them. In this way moral training will cultivate the pupils' inherent good nature and they will then not be tempted into banditry or indulge in unrestrained or undisciplined behaviour.[106]

Moreover, the regulations noted moral training would acquaint pupils with the public good and hence 'lay the foundation for feelings of patriotism when they become adults'.

Despite the conservative bias of the 1904 school system as illustrated in the greater weight attributed to the Classics in the primary school curriculum, it did represent a significant change in official attitudes. The new system was more elaborate, allowing a greater scope for vocational and elementary education (see Figure 1). For the first time also physical education was recognised as an important aspect of primary education,

The Reorientation of Official Thinking 33

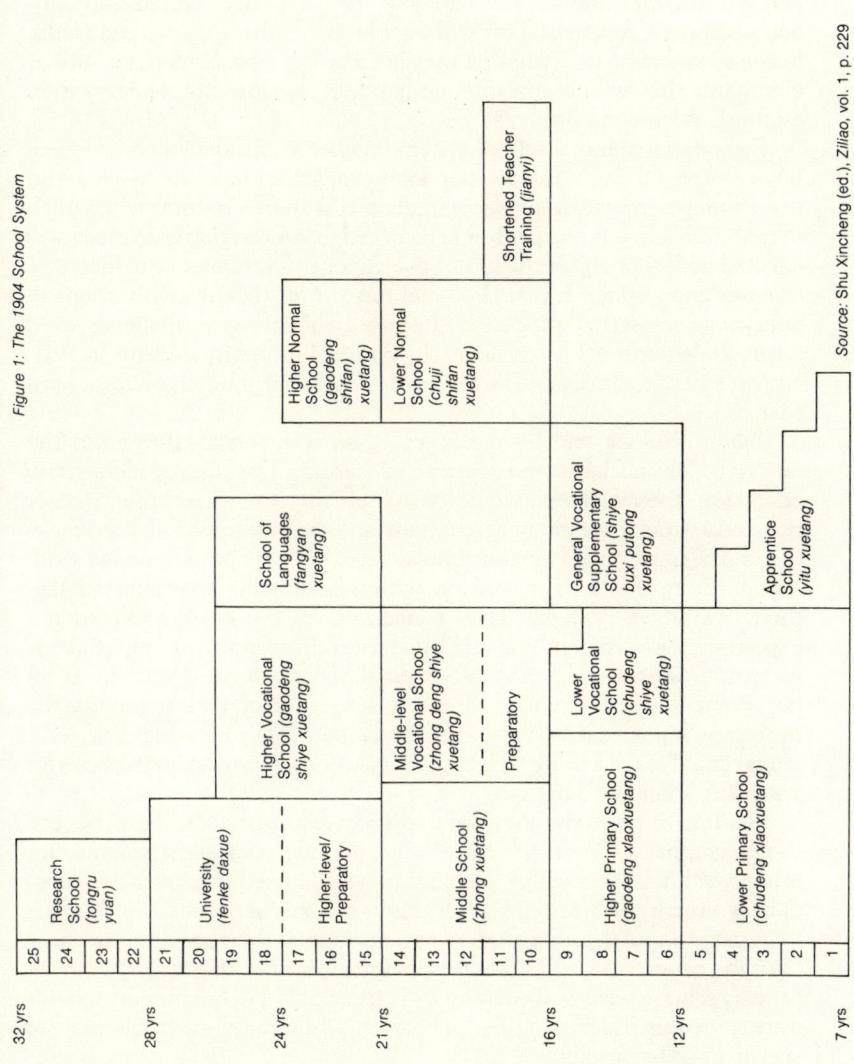

Figure 1: The 1904 School System

Source: Shu Xincheng (ed.), Ziliao, vol. 1, p. 229

while the increasing interest in vocational education was shown in allowing for handicrafts to be taught as an optional subject in lower and higher primary schools. The preamble to the 1904 regulations stated: 'All perverse theories and slander will have to be strictly resisted and condemned by the teachers. This will enable the students to succeed in the future so that no matter whether they become scholars, farmers, artisans or merchants they will all, on the one hand, be patriots and, on the other, establish themselves firmly.'[107]

The official aim of a school system had been considerably broadened: schools were now not only to train talent for government service but also to encourage patriotism and allow students to acquire a training with which to maintain a livelihood. It should be noted, however, that patriotism was equated with support for the Qing government. The reference to 'perverse theories and slander' revealed official distrust of student involvement in politics, a distrust that was clearly illustrated when the government cracked down on demonstrations organised by Beijing University students in 1903 against recent treaties signed with Russia which had granted concessions in Manchuria.[108]

Zhang Zhidong and his colleagues then went on to distinguish the rationale for specialist and general education. The aim of elementary education, they declared, would enable all the people, whether 'rich or poor, aristocrat or commoner', to understand the 'rules of social intercourse (*li*)' and be transformed into 'virtuous citizens'. Higher primary and secondary education would equip students with the necessary knowledge to plan their livelihood.[109] Higher-level education, on the other hand, sought expertise in government and administration through instructing students in various specialised fields. Vocational schools were described as an important element of general education since their aim was to provide the necessary 'knowledge and techniques' (*caizhi zhiyi*) with which the individual could make a living. This, the regulations insisted, was the basis for a wealthy people and nation.

The importance now attached to primary education could also be seen in the emphasis on teacher training to provide competent teachers for primary schools[110] as well as recognition of the need to implement compulsory primary education, both in terms of the state's duty to provide it (*yiwu jiaoya*) and the obligation of parents to send their children to school (*qiangbo jiaoyu*).[111] Unlike Zhang Zhidong's earlier plan in 1901, lower primary schools were now to be for 6–11-year-olds. Higher primary schools were aimed at the 11–15-year-old range, while middle schools were to accept 15–20-year-olds.

Zhang, however, continued to oppose education for girls:
> Since the Three Dynasties girls have also had education so as to be equipped to read the Classics. What was taught was that which prepared girls to be wives and mothers. In China the distinction between the sexes is prudently adhered to. It is not appropriate to allow young

girls to enter school in large groups and to wander about the streets. Moreover, it is even more inappropriate to let them read western books and study foreign customs which will gradually cause them to act independently and have contempt for their parents-in-law.[112]

Zhang concluded that 'if at this time, with China's situation as it is, we establish girls' education the damage done will be extensive'.[113] What *was* appropriate, as far as Zhang was concerned, was very clearly expressed: 'Therefore, girls can only be educated within the family and receive instruction from the mother or from the nurse to enable them to have a basic grasp of literacy and be conversant with necessary family affairs and with the appropriate tasks befitting a woman.'[114] Although regulations for girls' primary and normal schools were later promulgated in 1907,[115] the official aim was still to train 'virtuous mothers and good wives' (*xian'mu liangqi*). In the final analysis whatever educational benefits girls were to receive were seen more in terms of the advantages for future generations than for the girl herself.

Unlike earlier plans, the 1904 regulations provided for a system of vocational and supplementary education. In addition to lower and higher vocational schools for primary school graduates, general supplementary vocational schools were to be established for those who had either worked before or who wanted to learn a trade.[116] Such schools were to be attached to primary, middle or vocational schools and use was to be made of their teachers, equipment and dormitories. Although fees were to be charged, children from less-well-off families were exempted from paying. General subjects to be taught included moral training, Chinese culture, arithmetic and physical education. Vocational subjects were subsumed under agriculture, industry and commerce. These schools could also teach skills appropriate for local conditions such as machine-manufacturing, printing, or brewing. Even the general subjects had to bear some relation to the skills taught: 'The general supplementary vocational schools, although they teach general subjects, must pay attention to co-ordinating them with reality and make them relevant. For example, if a school stresses agriculture, then the study of Chinese language must relate to agriculture.'[117]

To provide a basic vocational education for those between seven and twelve years of age who could not go to lower primary schools, the 1904 system called for the creation of apprentice schools (*yitu xuetang*), also to be attached to lower or higher primary schools.[118] Although the regulations insisted on the need for apprentice schools to teach moral training and Chinese culture it was clear that the principal aim of the schools was to train students for an occupation. Courses were to last from six months to four years and, like the supplementary vocational schools, teaching could take place in the evenings or during the slack season.

The new school system also provided for the creation of teacher training institutes to supply instructors for the vocational schools.[119] Significantly, the regulations stipulated that after completing the course, graduates had to undergo a compulsory teaching period of not less than six years. In 1902 the entrepreneur and educational reformer, Zhang Jian, had advocated the establishment of normal schools specifically to train teachers (in this case for the new primary and middle schools).[120] The regulations on vocational teacher training institutes thus continued the trend of emphasising the importance of training *professional* teachers.

In an attempt to integrate the civil service examinations with the modern schools, the 1904 system allowed for the awarding of traditional degrees to school graduates at various levels,[121] and this has led one scholar to describe the modern schools as the path 'to social prestige and privileged position, as well as a civil service career'.[122] Yet the provision for supplementary vocational schools and the increasing importance attached to primary education revealed a change in official attitudes towards the role and scope of education. In addition to representing a shift from the traditional emphasis on 'education for talent' to a concern with implementing a genuinely national system of education, such features of the 1904 system as the use of government-approved and standardised textbooks, the drawing up of curricula with uniform hours and schedules, the stress on discipline, and the training of government-licensed professional teachers aimed to achieve a greater uniformity and official control over the educational process than had hitherto existed. As such, the changes set in motion by the 1904 school system closely parallel those that occurred in nineteenth-century Europe during the course of educational reform.[123]

THE BOARD OF EDUCATION AND EDUCATIONAL AIMS OF 1906

Japan's victory over Russia in the summer of 1905 in a war fought over who would have dominant influence in Manchuria and Korea stimulated further demands for reform in China. Citing the Meiji government's promulgation of a constitution and creation of a national diet in 1890, Chinese reforming officials hailed Japan's victory as the triumph of constitutionalism over autocracy. In 1901, in the wake of the Boxer uprising and allied occupation of Beijing, the Manchu court had already created a Bureau for the Management of Administrative Affairs *(duban zhengwu chu)* to consider reform proposals. Now, in November 1905, a Commission to Examine Government *(kaocha zhengzhi guan)* was set up to discuss the possibilities of constitutional government and plans made to send official missions abroad to Europe and North America.

Japan's victory also lent urgency to official suggestions that the traditional civil service examinations be abolished and priority given to modern schools. In August 1905 a joint memorial by five Governors-General – Zhang Zhidong, Yuan Shikai, Duan Fang, Zhou Fu and Cen Chunxuan – underlined the importance of universal education and thus confirmed the shift of emphasis that had taken place in 1904:[124] 'The establishment of schools is not only for accumulating talent but is mainly for expanding the people's knowledge and to enable everyone to receive an education.'[125] The

The Reorientation of Official Thinking

memorialists attributed Prussia's defeat of France in 1871 and Japan's defeat of Russia in 1905 to universal education. Widespread education in China, they continued, would foster patriotism and unity, as well as equipping the people with the knowledge and skill to 'plan their livelihood' (*zimou qi sheng*). With the abolition of the civil service examinations in 1905 a serious obstacle to the further development of modern schools was removed.[126] Whereas the higher primary school in Shu Xincheng's native district in Hunan had been shunned by the local residents in 1903, the Chinese writer Guo Moruo notes in his autobiography that the higher primary school in his home district of Jiading, Sichuan, received 1200 applications to take the entrance examinations (including one from a forty-year-old lower degree holder).[127]

In December 1905 a separate Board of Education (*xuebu*) was created to administer the schools.[128] The court was once again able to draw upon the pioneering initiatives of provincial officials. Yuan Shikai, Governor-General of Zhili since 1901, had already established a provincial Bureau of Education (*xuewuchu*) in 1903 comprising departments dealing with supervision, accounts, overseas students, ordinance survey, specialist schools, vocational schools, and general education.[129] The new Board of Education was headed by a secretary (*shangshu*) and two assistants, and comprised five departments: general affairs (*zongwusi*), general education (*putongsi*), specialist education (*zhuanmensi*), vocational education (*shiyesi*) and accounts (*kuaijisi*). The department of general education was to supervise teacher training, middle schools, primary schools and popular education (*tongsu jiaoyu*), which dealt with such matters as public lectures. Libraries evidently were not considered an item of popular education at this time since they were under the supervision of the department of specialist education. Reflecting the concern to impose control and uniformity, the Board of Education quickly issued a spate of regulations on such matters as teachers' duties, the wearing of school uniforms, examination and course schedules, classroom and playground rules, rewards and punishments, and ceremonial.[130]

Under the Board of Education were provincial education commissioners (*tixue*), who presided over a provincial Education Office (*xuewu gongsuo*) organised along the same lines as the Board of Education.[131] A glance at the personnel of the Henan Education Office in 1907 reveals the seriousness with which officials now tackled the question of education. The Henan office clearly attracted young and ambitious members of the upper gentry elite. Thus out of a total personnel of forty-three, the average age was thirty-five. The head of the Education Office was a metropolitan degree-holder and his two assistants were holders of the provincial civil service degree, while the head of the department of general education was a former member of the Hanlin Academy and the head of the vocational education department was a former district magistrate.[132]

Duan Fang and Dai Hongci (President of the Board of Rites), on their return from an official trip to Europe and North America in 1906 to investigate constitutional government, reinforced the idea that general education was the most important priority for the state.[133] They criticised the education systems in Russia and Italy because they felt too much attention was paid to higher-level schools at the expense of general education, with the result that in those countries 'the path to acquiring a livelihood is restricted and beggars daily increase'. They singled out Germany for special praise because of its equal attention to both specialist and general education. Unlike China, Duan and Dai lamented, where people only have regard for their personal interests, Germany has produced a patriotic citizenry trained in the virtue of 'performing their duties and keeping order'. The modern schools being established in China, they urged, must instil patriotism, loyalty and concern for the public good and not develop along the same path as the traditional civil service examinations, which scholars had merely exploited for individual prestige and profit. It was for this reason that 'education for the people' had to take priority over higher education. The two officials therefore proposed higher tuition fees for higher-level schools to provide the funds necessary for an increase in the number of primary schools.[134] Furthermore, they claimed, if students at middle- and higher-level schools had to contribute more to their education as opposed to relying on government grants, they would be less arrogant and extravagant.

In their memorial Duan Fang and Dai Hongci also stressed the importance of a centralised education system capable of imposing common and uniform standards. Again they praised the example of Germany (and, conversely, simply noted without comment that the United States had a decentralised education system).[135] It is no coincidence that the Chinese officials focused on Germany. In Europe the beginnings of state involvement in education and attempts to restrict church activity in this area took place in the German states during the late eighteenth century.[136] In 1774 the expulsion of the Jesuits from Austria was quickly followed by the promulgation of the *Allgemeine Schul-Ordnung*, which called for the complete co-ordination of school facilities into a national centralised system. A Commission on Education and Censorship (*Studien und Zensur Hofkommission*) was also created to ensure that schools used standardised and prescribed textbooks. In Prussia Frederick William I had signalled the beginning of his state's involvement in education with the issue of the *Landschul-Reglement* in 1763 making elementary schooling compulsory. In the wake of Prussia's defeat at the hands of Napoleon in 1806 officials preached the necessity of implementing wide-scale primary education to create a disciplined and patriotic citizenry. The creation of a Prussian Ministry of Public Instruction in 1817 set the pattern for bureaucratic control of education which was to be followed by other German states.[137]

In order to emphasise the importance of a uniform education system Duan Fang and Dai Hongci even compared schools with machine factories (*jichang*).[138] Just as the individual components of a machine had to be produced to common specifications to ensure co-ordination and efficiency, so the schools, by adhering to uniform curricula and regulations, would produce a united citizenry. As part of this standardisation, Duan and Dai highlighted the need to employ fully-trained professionals in teaching and administration. It was no longer feasible, they argued, to rely simply, as had been done in the past, on local gentry whose classical literary attainments did not necessarily equip them to master the new skills of school management or the teaching of modern subjects. Reflecting the influence of social Darwinist concepts in vogue since the late 1890s, Duan Fang and Dai Hongci referred to 'competition in the educational field' (*xuejie jingzheng*) and argued that a centralised and uniform school system staffed by trained experts would equip China to compete with the powers, whose own education systems had contributed so much to their wealth and strength.

When the Board of Education issued its educational aims in March 1906 it reiterated the opinion advanced by Duan and Dai that general education had to be given priority: 'Looking at the educational systems of foreign countries there are two main divisions: one is called specialist and the other is called general. But general education is given more attention. It does not lie in creating a talented few, but in creating a majority of citizens'.[139]

This general education was to inculcate the five principles of honouring the monarch, Confucius, the public good, a martial spirit, and practical study. Referring to Japan, the Board of Education remarked that due to widespread education the people associated their own interests with those of the monarch and state: 'Therefore, everyone has the public-minded desire to wash away national shame, and regards the ruler's joy or sorrow as the nation's glory or insult. Thus the glory or shame of the country is their own happiness or sadness. This is what is meant by ruler and people being one (*junmin yiti*)'.[140]

Another justification for extending education to all was that a country's strength was not just dependent on a few heroes, but on the collective will and strength of the people. This collective will would be fostered in the schools, where a sense of camaraderie and co-operation extending beyond the traditional group loyalties of region, clan and family would be developed. The patriotism that the Board of Education hoped to encourage in the primary schools would hopefully contribute to the people's martial spirit. Pointing to the example of the West and Japan where everyone 'greeted compulsory military service with joy', the Board of Education noted:

> The Chinese people's concern with daily living is large, while their loyalty and devotion are meagre. Their own lives count for much, while they have little concern for the state. If we want to solve these deficiencies, then we must use education as the tool to improve customs. All textbooks in middle and primary schools must contain elements of militant citizenry-ism (*junguomin zhuyi*)... History and geography textbooks should describe battles on land and sea and contain illustrations of cannon, battleships and flags...'[141]

In England, also, during the second half of the nineteenth century educators were stressing both the utility of history in arousing patriotism and drill in imposing a sense of order and discipline upon the children of the working classes.[142] Yet whereas the Board of Education underlined the importance of military drill in so far as it trained a public-minded and martial people prepared to fight for their country, in England drill (which had become a regular part of the curriculum in voluntary and board schools by the 1880s) was seen more in terms of reinforcing social relationships. One English educator in 1880, for example, described the advantages of teaching drill thus:

> The habit of obedience to authority, of immediate obedience to demands, may tend to teach the working classes a lesson ... that immediate obedience and submission to authority, deference to others, courtesy to equals, respect to superiors ... are the real marks of manly self respect and independence, and not the vulgar and pernicious doctrine that one man is as good as another, and that courtesy or deference is the property of a servile nature.[143]

By associating the welfare of the state with the survival of the dynasty, of course, the Qing hoped that the patriotism and martial spirit to be encouraged in the schools would guarantee the people's loyalty to the throne. Yet the Board of Education's emphasis on the more practical role education should play represented a significant departure from the traditional official view that had associated education with knowledge of the classical literary canon. Education, it was claimed, was only valuable in so far as it could be put to practical use:

> If one talks in an elevated way about human nature and reveres the abstract, then this has absolutely no benefit for the country's or people's livelihood ... In the past we have had abundant scholarship, but no literature of everyday books or letters; we have had subtle studies of mathematical principles but have found no way for doing everyday accounts.[144]

In addition to Chinese and moral training, practical subjects such as arithmetic and handicrafts were emphasised. The Board of Education continued:

> In each country of the world practical benefits are stressed. Industry is especially considered important. Everyone must obtain the skill of being a farmer, industrial worker or merchant. On the one hand, this benefits people's livelihood, on the other it benefits the state. This is the key element in making the state wealthy and strong, and the *most beneficial* part of education.[145]

By admitting that education had functions to perform other than producing the cultivated scholar versed in the Confucian classics and by associating the learning of individual economic skills with the increase of national wealth, the Board of Education enhanced the potential prestige of vocational education. It is during the last years of the dynasty, therefore, that an interest in such education occurred, rather than during the May

The Reorientation of Official Thinking

Fourth period as some scholars have maintained.[146]

CONTRAST WITH THE WEST

Official discussions on education in China during this period did not betray a fear that education for the lower classes would result in their being transformed into idlers or potential rebels. Such a fear characterised the debate over popular education in England, where obscurantist attitudes (i.e. opposition to any kind of mass schooling) persisted into the first half of the nineteenth century.[147] In England it was argued that ignorance for the poor was their opiate, 'a cordial administered by the gracious hand of providence'. An 'ill-judged and improper education' would only frustrate this benevolent purpose. The comments made by a Member of Parliament during a House of Commons debate in 1807 summed up the fear that popular education might disrupt the social order: 'Giving education to the labouring classes of the poor ... would be prejudicial to their morals and happiness; it would teach them to despise their lot in life, instead of making them good servants in agriculture and other laborious employments. Instead of teaching them subordination it would render them fractious and refractory'.[148]

Charity schools for the poor generally limited themselves to religious instruction. The purpose of such education was made clear by a Reverend Wilson in London, who observed in 1817:

> In every country, but especially in this free state, the mass of your poor, like the base of a cone, if it be unsteady and insecure, will quickly endanger every superincumbent part. Religious education, then, is the spring of public tranquillity ... by infusing the higher sentiments of penitence and faith and gratitude and the love of God, communicates the elements of a cheerful and uniform subjection to all lawful authority.[149]

When other subjects were allowed they were mainly limited to arithmetic and drawing for boys and needlework for girls. The readers used by the two religious societies providing educational facilities for the poor (the Society for Promoting the Education of the Poor in the Principles of the Established Church and the British and Foreign School Society) during most of the nineteenth century contained little vocationally instructive material 'given that children were trained to know their place in life, and that only limited occupations would be available to them'.[150]

Although the obscurantist position gradually lost ground in early-nineteenth-century England, concessions to popular education were very much prompted by defensive and negative attitudes. Elite control of popular education was felt to be safer than allowing the working classes to devise educational institutions of their own, while in the wake of the Industrial Revolution prominent thinkers such as Thomas Malthus, Jeremy Bentham and Adam Smith justified mass education as a means to rescue the working classes from vice, overpopulation and antagonism towards the upper classes.¹⁵¹ Diehard attitudes still persisted however. When Mechanics Institutes were opened in 1823 for the diffusion of science among the working classes they were met with bitter opposition, despite the fact that they were under middle-class leadership and that moral and political science were barred from the curriculum.¹⁵² A prominent conservative publication noted in 1825:

> We cannot be ignorant that the education of the working adults of a great nation is without precedent and on which experience throws no light, save what is abundantly discouraging. We cannot be ignorant that hitherto wherever the lower orders of any great state have obtained a smattering of knowledge, they have generally used it to produce national ruin.¹⁵³

In France, too, the implementation of popular education was seen as a guarantee of social stability. Despite the grandiose faith late eighteenth-century *philosophes* proclaimed in the power of education to improve human potential, they ultimately viewed early socialisation in terms of maintaining social stability and the social hierarchy.¹⁵⁴ When Guizot introduced his law in 1833 obliging every commune to open a school he placated potential critics by insisting that 'universal primary education is one of the greatest guarantees of order and social stability'. As evidence of the essentially conservative nature of the measure, moral and religious instruction constituted the most important part of the primary school curriculum.¹⁵⁶

Even in the United States, where, as one writer has noted, there was less hostility to mass schooling than in England during the early nineteenth century because of the absence of a Tory opposition,¹⁵⁷ popular education was regarded very much as a defensive measure. Daniel Webster, the noted Whig politician and orator, argued in 1820 that in an age of popular suffrage public instruction was not so much of a luxury as a 'wise and liberal system of police by which property, and life, and the peace of society are secured'.¹⁵⁸ Caleb Mills, future superintendent of public instruction for Indiana, advised the Indiana legislature in 1846 that common schooling would 'discipline people so that they would not threaten private property or disobey their employers'.¹⁵⁹

For Chinese officials also, extending education to more people would result in greater social harmony, but there was more confidence in the people's potential and less fear that education might make them lazy and rebellious. They would never have agreed, for example, with Bernard Mandeville's observation in 1714 (still cited by nineteenth-century opponents of mass schooling) that idleness and criminality amongst the English working classes were due to a surfeit of education.¹⁶⁰ In contrast to the pessimism shown by some nineteenth-century English educators in their criticism of the natural depravity of the lower classes,¹⁶¹ Chinese officials confidently expected that widespread education would automatically level the distinctions in Chinese society. In 1906 Cen Chunxuan, the Governor-General of Yunnan and Guizhou, argued that education would unite the people in their understanding of li (social and moral propriety) and gradually level off the divisions between the 'knowledgeable and foolish, cultured and barbaric'.[162]

Duan Fang was even more explicit in his stress on the egalitarian function of popular education. In 1905 he advocated the creation of elementary schools (*mengyangyuan*) for three-to-six-year-olds. Not only would such schools lay the foundations of patriotism through the teaching of music, and technological skills through the teaching of handicrafts but, more importantly for Duan, they would train the children of the lower classes so that they could attend primary schools along with children of the rich:

> The basic purpose of elementary schools is to take the children of the poor and cultivate them so that wealthy and aristocratic parents will not fear their children picking up bad habits by being in the same class with them. With these good intentions, in the future primary schools will not discriminate between rich and poor, aristocrat and commoner, and will be able to carry out education in common. This is the method through which equal education (*tongdeng jiaoyu*) will be carried out.[163]

Cen and Duan evinced a confidence and optimism in the role of education that was an important element of the Confucian tradition. Confucius himself believed that everyone could achieve individual self-improvement through education (i.e. knowledge of the rites and rules of social etiquette), while Mencius (372 BC–289 BC) emphasised man's inherent good nature, which only the lack of education distorted. As Jiang Menglin, educational reformer and Chancellor of Beijing University in 1919, remembers, one of the first texts read by pupils in the private and family schools that prepared their charges for the civil service examinations was the Trimetrical Classic (*Sanzi jing*). It began with the words of Mencius: 'Man's nature (*xing*) is originally good. By nature men are alike and it is only through practice that they diverge. If education is not provided, man's nature changes [from its original goodness]'.[164] The egalitarian implications of Confucian educational thought were often seized upon by individual scholars and reformers, particularly in the late Ming when followers of the philosopher Wang Yangming such as Wang Ken (1483–1540) proclaimed their faith in the potential of the common man to achieve wisdom.[165] It was this tradition that lay behind the consensus amongst official circles in early-twentieth-century China concerning the positive results that would accrue from widespread education.

The existence of such a consensus distinguishes educational reform in China from that of Russia. In Russia, too, in the 1890s, a vigorous campaign to promote universal primary education was launched by members of the professional class (doctors, statisticians, and agronomists) who worked for the state or city councils (*dumas*).[166] As with China, educational reform had originally concentrated on the development of higher education. Peter the Great, for example, in the eighteenth century had opened specialist schools

Table 1 Number of Middle Schools and Lower Primary Schools in 1907 and 1909

Province	1907[a] Middle Schools	1907[a] Lower Primary	1909[b] Middle Schools	1909[b] Lower Primary
Zhili	31 (2 039)	7 596 (133 884)	31 (2 419)	10 259 (209 668)
Fengtian	4 (342)	1 208 (37 566)	5 (505)	2 460 (84 284)
Jilin	4 (331)	6 (234)	5 (526)	215 (7 468)
Heilongjiang	2 (169)	44 (1 280)	1 (156)	116 (3882)
Shandong	19 (1 050)	3 201 (39 872)	22 (1 206)	31 536 (461 174)
Shanxi	25 (1 639)	510 (12 173)	15 (1 360)	1 650 (46 804)
Shaanxi	13 (771)	1 879 (36 839)	14 (943)	2 324 (50 856)
Henan	22 (1 331)	1 270 (23 309)	22 (2 551)	2 948 (63 770)
Jiangsu	12 (1 473)	626 (18 335)	11 (1 639)	829 (26 309)
Anhui	21 (988)	121 (2 262)	25 (1 844)	421 (10 419)
Zhejiang	32 (2 025)	301 (12 571)	23 (2 430)	1 288 (42 850)
Jiangxi	23 (1 473)	181 (3 588)	33 (2 286)	555 (11 675)
Hubei	17 (1 391)	1 306 (40 645)	21 (2 560)	2 437 (721 937)
Hunan	39 (3 220)	419 (11 492)	47 (3 992)	833 (25 061)
Sichuan	52 (5 356)	6 924 (202 923)	51 (5 828)	9 132 (294 650)
Guangdong	25 (2 600)	776 (29 338)	29 (3 122)	862 (33 347)
Guangxi	8 (458)	916 (26 279)	15 (1 700)	819 (27 394)
Guizhou	1 (146)	325 (12 181)	4 (445)	456 (16 968)
Fujian	14 (1 095)	141 (4 909)	15 (1 044)	275 (9 406)
Gansu	11 (477)	385 (8 233)	11 (372)	977 (19 637)
Xinjiang	–	99 (1 080)	1 (21)	88 (2 126)

Note: Number of students are in brackets.
a. Source: Diyici jiaoyu tongji tubiao (1909), pp. 35–6.
b. Chen Qitian, Zuijin sanshinian Zhongguo jiaoyushi, pp. 97–100.

to train technically proficient servants of the state, and throughout the nineteenth century the greater part of the state's educational budget went towards financing universities and secondary schools.[167] The educational reformers of the 1890s bemoaned the state's lack of interest in primary education. Like their Chinese counterparts they viewed it as a universal panacea that would create a rational citizenry shorn of its superstitious beliefs and backward customs and thus ensure stability, economic development and military strength.

From the start, however, the campaign was hindered by a suspicious bureaucracy who feared the disruptive effects on the social order such education might bring. In contrast to the situation in China, the state more often than not placed itself in opposition to the campaign for universal and secular primary schooling by continuing to underwrite (from the mid-1880s) an alternative network of parish schools under the control of the church. For the conservative bureaucracy such schools, offering a shorter course of study and concentrating on moral and religious instruction, were

Table 2 Provincial Education Expenditures in 1909 (in *taels*)

Province	Specialist Schools	Vocational Schools	Normal Schools	Middle Schools	Primary Schools
Zhili	394 180	107 926	233 730	226 946	1 173 056
Fengtian	113 186	123 118	155 684	50 367	1 095 456
Jilin	46 261	35 892	75 897	67 691	248 S79
Heilongjiang	–	27 849	37 549	11 283	167 423
Shandong	157 779	75 037	135 069	63 491	384 177
Shanxi	146 610	31 972	76 656	91 638	310 200
Shaanxi	100 189	30 513	49 392	70 219	273 357
Henan	84 074	48 650	102 282	116 783	428 831
Jiangsu	88 576	42 490	67 757	181 585	561 026
Anhui	69 592	16 484	99 393	148 537	350 177
Zhejiang	69 572	36 252	108 150	133 062	786 024
Jiangxi	56 926	29 848	62 912	143 447	372 728
Hubei	183 825	118 080	124 515	151 593	614 384
Hunan	99 179	138 461	202 087	247 047	594 979
Sichuan	142 292	78 266	65 722	321,823	1 078 213
Guangdong	161 303	102 281	90 467	224 708	1 269 958
Guangxi	82 602	55 269	79 842	80 142	339 881
Yunnan	62 002	60 731	118 698	20 241	266 620
Guizhou	19 496	15 926	43 906	39 555	161 982
Fujian	69 982	51 245	53 780	45 153	278 109
Gansu	32 870	17 512	17 156	15 484	62 465
Xinjiang	17 609	27 305	–	44 858	95 310

Source: *Disanci jiaoyu tongji tubiao* (1911), pp. 19-20.

a safer guarantee of social stability. By 1900, for example, the funds allotted by the state treasury for church parish schools amounted to twice the amount spent on secular primary schools. Such a situation was not to be significantly reversed until after 1905.

CONSTITUTIONALISM AND EDUCATION

In September 1906, five months after the publication of the government's educational aims, the throne issued an edict proclaiming the necessity to establish a constitution. Claiming that constitutional practice in the West and Japan had led to national wealth and strength by identifying the people's interest with that of the government, the Qing hoped to rally gentry support behind the throne by allowing their participation in the political process. In 1907 the Commission to Examine Government (*kaocha zhengzhi guan*) became the Commission for Constitutional Arrangements (*xianzheng biancha guan*). Regulations were issued on the creation of provincial assemblies (*ziyiju*), which were to convene in 1909. In 1908 a nine-year constitutional programme was announced which envisaged the estab-

Table 3 Number of Vocational Schools in 1907 and 1909

Province	1907[a] Higher	1907[a] Lower	1909[b] Higher	1909[b] Lower
Zhili	2 (279)	6 (391)	2 (243)	14 (384)
Fengtian	0	5 (204)	1 (118)	1 (32)
Jilin	0	0	0	3 (78)
Heilongjiang	0	0	0	3 (365)
Shandong	1 (118)	5 (131)	1 (138)	12 (454)
Shanxi	0	0	1 (105)	1 (120)
Shaanxi	0	0	0	1 (45)
Henan	0	5 (89)	0	16 (846)
Jiangsu	1 (85)	5 (208)	1 (48)	6 (280)
Anhui	0	0	0	6 (158)
Zhejiang	0	2 (68)	1 (189)	12 (190)
Jiangxi	1 (120)	0	1 (34)	0
Hubei	1 (86)	5 (464)	1 (104)	9 (727)
Hunan	0	2 (80)	1 (227)	2 (52)
Sichuan	0	0	1 (239)	6 (252)
Guangdong	1 (210)	9 (850)	1 (221)	8 (493)
Yunnan	0	8 (231)	0	12 (438)
Xinjiang	0	0	0	3 (90)

Note: Number of students are in brackets.
a. Source: *Diyici jiaoyu tongji tubiao* (1909), pp. 31-2.
b. Chen Qitian, *Zuijin sanshinian Zhongguo jiaoyushi*, p. 134.

lishment of a national assembly (half the members being appointed by the throne and half elected by the provincial assemblies) and the holding of national elections for a parliament in 1917.[168]

Officials stressed the key role general education was to play in the constitutional process by training a loyal, disciplined and socially responsible citizenry. After 1906 the attention given to general education bore fruit in the rapid expansion of primary schools (see Table 1). In Zhili province the number of lower primary schools increased from 7596 (with 133 884 students) in 1907 to 10 259 (with 209 688 students) in 1909. Most other provinces registered a considerable increase in primary schools, while the number of middle schools remained the same or even, in some cases, decreased. In Hubei, where Zhang Zhidong had pioneered the creation of higher-level specialist schools in the 1890s, just over 32 per cent of the educational budget in 1907 was spent on primary education, whereas only 4 per cent was spent on higher-level education.[169] Figures for 1909 issued by the Board of Education on provincial educational expenditures also reveal a significant proportion of provincial budgets going towards primary education (see Table 2). While Zhili, for example, allotted 394 180 *taels* to

Table 4. Background of Primary School Teachers in 1909

	Higher Primary				Lower Primary	
Province	Normal School Grads.	Other Grads.	Non-Grads.	Foreigners	Normal School Grads.	Others
Zhili	534	95	168	5	8 092	2 543
Fengtian	159	144	267	2	907	2 342
Jilin	95	32	25	–	254	113
Heilongjiang	89	8	31	–	137	45
Shandong	270	162	242	2	1 487	2 218
Shanxi	174	85	162	–	906	1 356
Shaanxi	69	42	235	–	736	1 677
Henan	265	99	112	11	21 091	2 054
Jiangsu	316	254	265	2	1 180	1 957
Anhui	281	242	455	–	450	1 135
Zhejiang	380	443	1413	2	538	2 750
Jiangxi	292	171	786	1	181	841
Hubei	589	125	219	3	2 419	1 291
Hunan	666	173	581	–	1 266	1 169
Sichuan	769	353	603	1	7 320	3 290
Guangdong	279	112	251	–	1 755	2 177
Guangxi	299	50	202	–	815	965
Yunnan	160	23	58	–	879	763
Guizhou	257	24	139	–	623	256
Fujian	529	235	470	–	246	427
Gansu	87	43	55	–	71	593
Xinjiang	–	–	–	–	75	201
Total.	6 559	2 915	6 739	29	32 428	30 163

Source: Chen Qitian, *Zuijin sanshinian Zhongguo jiaoyushi*, pp. 94-5.

specialist schools, 1 173 056 *taels* were spent on primary schools.[170] Although official statistics do not reveal a large expansion in vocational education before 1911 (see Table 3), what increase took place occurred amongst lower vocational schools.

In addition to the expansion of primary education, an attempt was made to put into practice official calls for the professionalisation of teaching. In 1909 over one third of the 16242 higher primary school teachers were normal school graduates, while the number of lower primary school teachers with a normal school training exceeded those who did not have such a training (see Table 4).[171]

Finally, a symbolic confirmation of the importance the court now attributed to general education occurred in 1906 when it was ordered that the Board of Education should take precedence over the Board of Rites (*Li bu*) in the administrative hierarchy.[172] Traditionally, the Board of Rites had ranked third among the Six Boards (Civil Appointments, Revenue, Rites, War, Punishments, Public Works), overseeing court ritual, the examination system, state sacrifices, editing the Imperial Calendar and managing tributary relations with foreign rulers. With the creation of a Ministry of Foreign Affairs in 1901 and the abolition of the civil service examinations in 1905 the Board of Rites' functions were already greatly reduced. Now, however, even the management of ceremonies and ritual, so long a crucial aspect of Chinese political practice, was not considered as important as the building of a national school system.

NOTES

1. On the self-strengthening movement, see M. Wright, *The Last Stand of Chinese Conservatism* (New York, 1967); Ting-yee Kuo, 'Self-Strengthening: The Pursuit of Western Technology' in J. Fairbank (ed.), *The Cambridge History of China*, Vol. 10 (Cambridge,1978), pp. 491-542.
2. A. Hummel, *Eminent Chinese of the Ch'ing Period* (Washington,1943), 1: 241-3.
3. Feng Guifen, 'Cai xixue yi' (Proposal to adopt Western learning) in Shu Xincheng (ed.), *Zhongguo jindai jiaoyushi ziliao* (Beijing,1979), 3: 894-7. It was Feng's 1861 proposal that first enunciated the formula for the self-strengthening movement: 'If we have Chinese ethics and teachings *(lunchang mingjiao)* as the foundation, and supplement this with the techniques of other countries for wealth and strength, surely this would be the ideal.' *Ibid.*, p. 896.
4. On these schools, see K. Biggerstaff, *The Earliest Modern Government Schools in China* (Ithaca, 1961). See also Zhu Youxian (ed.), *Zhongguo jindai xuezhi shiliao* (Shanghai, 1983), 1.1: 214-78, 329-467.
5. Biggerstaff, *ibid.*, pp .74-5.
6. Shu Xincheng (ed.), *Ziliao*, 3: 895. There was a hint, however, in Feng's proposal that he was also thinking in terms of extending education to everyone when he remarked, almost as an aside, 'In discussing learning today, a really important task is for China to allow her people to excel more *(xiumin)*, so that they surpass the foreigners and thus gain victory over them.' *Ibid.*, p. 896.
7. Feng did suggest that successful graduates from his proposed new schools of western learning be awarded the traditional provincial-level degree *(juren)*, but nothing came of this idea. Li Hongzhang also attempted, without success, to have 'foreign learning' as an examination category. K. Biggerstaff, *op. cit.* pp. 26-7. In 1884 another official, Pan Yantong, advocated a special examination category devoted to technical subjects *(yixueke)* again without meeting official approval. Shu Xincheng (ed.), *Ziliao*, 1: 29-34. Pan's idea was to entice those with official aspirations to study scientific and technical subjects. Answering critics that this was a dangerous proposal since it might lead to everyone becoming acquainted with modern military technology, Pan declared that less wealthy people would not present problems since they would be unable to purchase

modern weapons and, anyway, all candidates for the proposed exam would have to meet with gentry approval. *Ibid.*, pp .30–1.
8. The civil service examination system had been criticised by prominent Song reformers such as Fan Zhongyan (989–1052) and Wang Anshi (1021–86). Wang even proposed a wide network of national and local schools to replace the examination system. Such a network, however, was to have a similar function – the selection of officials. Wang merely thought that schools would be a more effective tool to indoctrinate potential officials. See L. Walton-Vargo, 'Education, Social Change and Neo-Confucianism in Sung-Yuan China' (Ph.D. thesis, University of Pennsylvania, 1978), pp. 5-7. See also T. Hong-chi Lee, 'Education in Northern Sung China' (Ph.D. thesis, Yale University, l974).
9. Sheng's memorials on these schools are in Shu Xincheng (ed.), *Ziliao* 1: 138–43, 153–7. Sheng Xuanhuai was one of a growing number of 'foreign affairs' *(yangwu)* experts employed by high provincial officials such as Li Hongzhang. Although only a lower-degree holder, Sheng was appointed to a variety of posts ranging from customs intendant to director of officially-sponsored textile mills. Later he was able to profit from his official contacts and public funds to launch business ventures of his own. M. Bastid, *L'Evolution de la Société Chinoise à la fin de la Dynastie des Qing 1873–1911*, pp. 31, 39. On the involvement of officials in modern economic enterprises during the late Qing, see W. Chan, *Merchants, Mandarins, and Modern Enterprise in Late Ch'ing China* (Cambridge, Mass., 1977).
10. It was in Sheng's memorial that the idea of an organised hierarchy of educational levels was broached. Each of the two sections (higher and lower) was to have four classes and students were to proceed higher up the ladder as they specialised more. Candidates had to be conversant with the Classics and tuition fees were charged. Sheng may well have been influenced by the example of the Anglo-Chinese School opened in 1882 by the American missionary, Young J. Allen, in Shanghai. It had a three-tiered structure – primary schools, two secondary schools and one college. See A. Bennett, *Missionary Journalist in China* (Athens, Georgia, 1983), pp. 89-95. Sheng called the lower level of his school (for 13–15-year-olds) a 'primary school' *(xiao xuetang)* and the upper level a 'university' *(da xuetang)* Graduates were to be sent abroad for further training or be appointed in administration dealing with 'foreign matters' *(yangwu)* .
11. Shu Xincheng (ed.), *Ziliao* 1: 138.
12 *Ibid.*, p. 138 .
13. In 1905 the Nanyang Public School became a school of technology under the newly created Ministry of Commerce. A. Feuerwerker, *China's Early Industrialization: Sheng Hsuan-huai (1844–1966) and Mandarin Enterprise* (Cambridge, Mass., 1958), pp. 69–70.
14. Shu Xincheng (ed.), *Ziliao* 1: 155. The Ecole d'Administration was the forerunner of the Ecole Nationale d'Administration (ENA)

established in 1946.
15. For a good account of Zhang's self-strengthening projects, see Wang Lanyin, 'Zhang Zhidong zhi fuqiang zhengce' (Zhang Zhidong's policies for wealth and strength), *Shida yuekan* (17 December 1934), pp. 1–73
16. Wang Lanyin, ibid., pp. 15-16. See also Shu Xincheng (ed.), *Jindai Zhongguo jiaoyu shiliao* (Shanghai, 1928),1: 15. Information on the Self-Strengthening School can also be found in Zhu Youxian (ed.), *Zhongguo jindai xuezhi shiliao* 1.1: 306–22. A recent study notes that before 1895 Zhang favoured a 'double-track system', with academies (teaching the Confucian Classics) co-existing with the new schools teaching 'western learning'. Thus in Guangdong Zhang established both the Guangya Academy and the Self-Strengthening School. After 1895, the study concludes, Zhang tended to merge the two. See Su Yunfeng, *Zhang Zhidong yu Hubei jiaoyu gaige* (Taibei, 1976), p. 26.
17. *Zhang Wenxiang gong quanji* (Taibei, 1963), 4: 2226. Room and board, in addition to school supplies like ink and paper, continued to be supplied free of charge.
18. Cited in Wang Lanyin, 'Zhang Zhidong zhi fuqiang zhengce', p. 15.
19. Zhu Youxian (ed.), *Zhongguo jindai xuezhi shiliao* 1.1.541–6. See also W. Ayers, *Chang Chih-tung and Educational Reform in China* (Cambridge Mass.,1971),p. 117; Wang Lanym, 'Zhang Zhidong zhi fuqiang zhe'ngce', pp. 7–10. The Military Preparatory School was converted in 1906 to a military primary school. Su Yunfeng,*Zhang Zhidong yu Hubei jiaoyu gaige*, p. 114.
20. *Zhang Wenxiang gong quanji*, 4: 2222. Zhang's Industrial School (*gongyi xuetang*), created in 1898, did, however, relax its entrance requirements because not enough gentry were interested. The school called for 'intelligent and healthy 12–16-year-olds who could read 2 000 characters and the Four Books'. Su Yunfeng, *Zhang Zhidong yu Hubei jiaoyu gaige* p. 145; Wang Lanyin, 'Zhang Zhidong zhi fuqiang zhengce', p. 20.
21. Wang Lanyin, 'Zhang Zhidong zhi fuqiang zhengce', p. 17. Zhang referred to the benefits accruing to both the state and the people's livelihood (*guoji minsheng*), but did not elaborate on this latter aspect. In 1898, however, Zhang founded the Agricultural School (*nongwu xuetang*) to train 'upright gentry' to teach the populace, in an official capacity, new agricultural techniques. Shu Xincheng (ed.). *Ziliao*, 1: 158-9.
22. W. Ayers, *Chang Chih-tung and Educational Reform*,p. 253.
23. *Ibid.*
24. Zuo's memorial is printed in Zhongguo shi xuehui (comp.), *Yangwu yundong* (Shanghai, 1961), 5: 5–9. Another recent study of Zhang Zhidong attempts to portray him as a reforming bureaucrat who advocated nationwide change at the expense of conservative, locally-based gentry. See D. Bays, *China Enters the Twentieth Century: Chang Chih-tung and the Issues of a New Age* (Michigan, 1978), p. 220. This attempt to show, like Ayers, that Zhang led the way in

'modernising' China is again misleading, especially as far as education is concerned. As will be shown later, whatever ideas Zhang had on education were very much the result of the influence exerted by local notables such as Zhang Jian and Luo Zhenyu. Also, in contrast to the thought and activities of local gentry, Zhang's position on education was quite conservative. To give but two examples – schools for girls were being established in the early years of the century *despite* Zhang's well-known opposition to the principle of women's education, and while educators discussed the irrelevance of the Confucian Classics in modern primary schools, Zhang desperately tried to safeguard tradition by promoting the creation of Schools for the Preservation of Antiquity (*cungu xuetang*) after 1907. Chen Qingzhi, *Zhongguo jiaoyushi* (Shanghai, 1936), pp. 618-19.

25. It is interesting to note that in 1975 both Liu Shaoqi and Lin Biao were accused of using the slogan *dushu zuoguan* to influence educated youth and hence obstruct one of the key elements of Maoist educational philosophy (i.e. sending intellectuals to the countryside). See *Hongqi*, no. 12 (1975), p. 29. T. Bernstein, *Up to the Mountains and Down to the Villages: The Transfer of Youth from Urban to Rural China* (New Haven, 1977), p. 5, notes that the campaign to send city youths to the countryside during the late 1950s and early 1960s was designed, amongst other things, to combat the idea of *dushu zuoguan*.

26. Li's memorial is in *Donghua lu*, Guangxu reign (Taibei, 1963), 27: 3773–6. It is also reprinted in Mai Zhonghua (comp.), *Huangchao jingshi wen xinbian* (Taibei, 1973), 1: 368–72; Shu Xincheng (ed.), *Shiliao*, 1: 1-5; Jian Bocan (comp.), *Wuxu bianfa* (Shanghai, 1953), 2: 292–7. Li was a metropolitan degree-holder (*jinshi*) and Hanlin compiler from Guizhou province. In 1898 he was appointed Secretary of the Board of Rites, but was later dismissed and exiled to Kashgaria for his association with the One Hundred Days reform movement. Pardoned in 1902, he returned to Guizhou as education commissioner. It would be tempting to link Li's stress on the expansion of education (in contrast to Zhang Zhidong's emphasis on the creation of higher-level specialist schools) with the fact that he came from the comparatively poor province of Yunnan. For information on Li, se *Diyici Zhongguo jiaoyu nianjian* (Taibei, 1971), 5: 437. See also the chapter on him by Liang Qichao (his brother-in-law) in Meng Erchang (comp.), *Beizhuan jibu* (Beijing, 1932), *zhuan* 5: 5b–8b. According to one source, Liang helped Li with the draft memorial, although Liang makes no mention of this in his chapter on Li. See Luo Dunhe, 'Jingshi daxuetang chengli ji' (An Account of the Establishment of Beijing University), *Yongyan* (June 1913), pp. 1–5.

27. For references in English to Li's memorial, see W. Franke, *The Reform and Abolition of the Traditional Chinese Examination System*, pp. 37–9; C. Peake, *Nationalism and Education in Modern China*, pp. 25–8; R. Lund, 'The Imperial University of Peking' (Ph.D. Thesis, University of Washington, 1956), pp. 50–8.

28. Gao Xiansi, 'Sanshiwu nian lai zhi minzhong jiaoyu' (Mass Education in the Last Thirty-five Years), in Zhuang Yu (ed.), *Zuijin sanshinian zhi Zhongguo jiaoyu* (Shanghai, 1931), p. 153.
29. Jiang Jianbai, *Zhongguo shehui jiaoyu xingzheng* (Shanghai, 1937), pp. 7-8; Zhong Lingxiu, *Shehui jiaoyu xingzheng* (Taibei, 1968), p.177; Zhongguo jiaoyu xuehui (ed.), *Shehui jiaoyu yanjiu* (Taibei, 1968), pp. 1–2.
30. On Young J. Allen, see A. Bennett, *Missionary Journalist in China* (Athens, Georgia, 1983).
31. A. Bennet, *ibid.*, p. 62. Bennett notes (p. 97) that *Jiaohui xinbao* and its successor, *Wanguo gongbao* (The Globe Magazine), were the most important journals of ideas in China before 1894–5 because of their consistency of publication (1868-83; 1889-1907) and their relatively widespread distribution. By 1874 circulation of *Jiaohui xinbao* amounted to 2 000 copies a week. Bennett thinks (pp. 159-60) that the journal was not only read by educated treaty-port Chinese but also by all important officials in the capital and provinces.
32. A. Bennett, *ibid.*, pp. 123–4.
33. A. Bennett, *ibid.*, p. 124.
34. Yen-p'ing Hao, *The Comprador in Nineteeth Century China* (Cambridge, Mass., 1970), p. 205.
35. Zheng Guanying, 'Kaoshi' (On Examinations) in Shu Xincheng (ed.), *Ziliao*, 3: 897-902. These proposed academies would be for 15–20-year-olds conversant with Chinese and western culture. See also S. Borthwick, *Education and Social Change in China* (Stanford, 1983), pp 40–1.
36. On the Zongli Yamen and the Tongwenguan, see M. Banno, *China and the West 1858–1861: The Origins of the Tsungli Yamen* (Cambridge, Mass., 1964).
37. Zheng Guanying, 'Kaoshi', p. 901.
38. *Zheng Guanying ji* (Shanghai, 1982), p. 245.
39. *Ibid.*, p. 246. Zheng also referred to Germany's enactment of compulsory education for all boys and girls over five years of age, as well as to the wide range of German educational institutions such as schools of agronomy and art, night schools, publishing societies, and delinquent homes. Zheng Guanying, 'Xixue' (On Western Learning) in Shu Xincheng (ed.), *Ziliao*, 3: 904, 907.
40. Shu Xincheng (ed.), *Ziliao*, 3: 917. S. Borthwick, *Education and Social Change in China*, pp. 44–5, notes that 'talent had by this time lost its exclusive connection with scholarship and government service'. While it is true that Kang Youwei and Liang Qichao now talked of extending education to peasants and artisans, the main rationale for all major official educational reform proposals up to 1904 continued to be the training and recruitment of talent for government service.
41. Shu Xincheng (ed.), *Ziliao*, 3: 917.
42. Liang Qichao, 'Lun xuexiao: youxue' (A Discussion of Elementary Education), *Shiwu bao*, no. 16 (1897), p. 1034.
43. Liang Qichao, 'Lun xuexiao: zonglun' (A General Discussion of

Schools), *Shiwu bao*, no. 5 (1896), pp. 271–6, no. 6 (1896), pp. 936–44. Liang's essays are also reprinted in Shu Xincheng (ed.), *Ziliao*, 3: 936–44.
44. Shu Xincheng (ed.), *Ziliao*, 3: 944. See also S. Borthwick, *Education and Social Change in China*, pp. 46–7.
45. Liang Qichao, 'Lun xuexiao: keju' (A Discussion of Examinations), *Shiwu bao*, no. 7 (1896), pp. 413–20, no. 8 (1896), pp. 483–8. See Also Abe Yō, 'Ryō kei-chō no kyōiku shisō to sono katsudo' (Liang Qichao's Educational Thought and Activities), *Kyushū Daigaku Kyō iku Kiyō*, no. 6 (1959), p. 314. Tan Sitong, one of the 1898 reformers, was the first to propose such an integration, in 1894. Shu Xincheng (ed.), *Ziliao*, 3: 919–22.
46. *Donghua lu*, Guangxu reign, 27: 3773.
47. The phrase that I have translated as 'not yet perfected' is *wei jin*. In the version printed in Jian Bocan (comp.), *Wuxu bianfa*, 2: 292-7, the phrase appears as *wei shan*. *Jin* seems to imply quantity rather than quality, whereas *shan* perhaps implies the reverse. If this is the case, when Li referred to the 'imperfect state' of teaching he meant that not enough people were receiving an education, rather than that the methods of teaching or the schools themselves were of an inferior quality.
48. *Donghua lu*, Guangxu reign, 27: 3773. The other four reasons were: (1) The modern schools simply taught western languages and civilisation and ignored basic questions such as how to govern the state and make it strong; (2) Those studying science and industry were not committed to these subjects; (3) Students were not encouraged to specialise in a particular skill or vocation; (4) There were no practical demonstrations or investigations abroad to consolidate what had been learnt academically.
49. See the report on modern schools in Hunan by M. Rocher, son of the French consul, in *Asie Française*, no. 113 (August 1910), pp. 340–4.
50. JYZZ, 3: 3 (1910), *jishi*, pp. 25-6.
51. *Donghua lu*, Guangxu reign, 27: 3774. All reforming scholars and officials harked back to a golden age in the early Zhou dynasty as described in the *Zhouli* (Rituals of Zhou), a text that was traditionally believed to have been written by the Duke of Zhou in the twelfth or eleventh century bc and which purported to describe government organisation. Although modern-day scholars generally believe that the text was written much later (probably in the third or fourth century bc) and that it presented a rather idealised version of how government operated in the early Zhou dynasty, Chinese reformers in the late nineteenth and early twentieth centuries often justified educational reform by referring to the extensive network of schools as described in the *Zhouli*. See also Kuo Ping-wen, *The Chinese System of Public Education*, pp. 15–32, for an account of education in the early Zhou dynasty.
52. *Donghua lu*, Guangxu reign, 27: 3775.
53. Gao Jiansi, 'Sanshiwu nian lai zhi minzhong jiaoyu', p. 153. On

social education during the late Qing, see Zheng Shiyu, *Xiandai jiaoyu shi* (Taibei, 1981), pp. 81–4.
54. *Donghua lu*, Guangxu reign, 27: 3775.
55. R. Pelissier, *Les Bibliothèques en Chine pendant la première moitié du XXème siècle* (Paris, 1969), pp.8–13. Li himself, however, still used the traditional term, *zangshulou*.
56. Li did not specify if newspapers should be privately or government owned. In 1859 Hong Renkan, an important Taiping leader, had proposed the use of newspapers to 'gather public opinion' and allow for a more informed populace. By 1894-5 there were approximately twelve newspapers being published in the major treaty-port cities. Zhang Zhidong, while Governor at Guangzhou in 1884, and Yuan Shikai, while Governor of Shandong in 1899–1901, both revived the practice of circulating official newspapers *(guanbao)*. A recent study has shown that newspapers in the treaty-port cities began to expand their circulation after 1895, as well as publishing more political, rather than commercial, news. Leo Ou-fan Lee, A. Nathan, 'The Beginnings of Mass Culture: Journalism and Fiction in the Late Ch'ing and Beyond', pp. 360–8. See also R. Britton, *The Chinese Periodical Press* (Taibei, 1968), pp. 37,108, 110. For the increasing importance of newspapers and journals in the forming of a 'public opinion' in China at this time, see A. Iriye, 'Public Opinion and Foreign Policy' in A. Feuerwerker *et al.* (eds.), *Approaches to Modern Chinese History* (Berkeley, 1967), pp. 216–38.
57. *Donghua lu*, Guangxu reign, 27: 3775-6. Li also proposed the creation of machinery workshops, to be attached to schools, the sending of students abroad, and the opening of a translation bureau that would supply more up-to-date translations of western works. Ma Jianzhong, a returned student from France and the first Chinese to receive the *baccalauréat* (in 1879), had also suggested in 1894 the establishment of a government translation bureau. See *Shike zhai jiyan* (Beijing 1970), pp. 89–94.
58. Shu Xincheng (ed.), *Shiliao*, 1: 6-7; R. Lund, 'The Imperial University of Peking', p. 58. Other official proposals in 1897 merely continued the theme of 'creating' or accumulating talent' *(zaojiu rencai, yuchu rencai)*. Thus the Anhui Governor suggested an increase in the number of schools by having each provincial capital open a school for 13–15-year-olds from good families. Such schools were to be feeders for the proposed University of Beijing. *Xiangxue xinbao*, no. 1 (1897), pp. 39–41.
59. Kang Youwei, 'Jincheng faguo geming jixu' (Memorial on the French Revolution), in Jian Bocan (comp.), *Wuxu bianfa* 3: 7–9.
60. M. Cameron, *The Reform Movement in China 1898–1912*, pp. 23–55.
61. Kang Youwei, 'Qing kaixue zhe' (Petition to Open Schools) in Shu Xincheng (ed.),*Ziliao*, 1: 151–3.
62. Huang Zunxian was a counsellor in the Chinese legation in Tokyo in 1877. Later he became Consul-General in San Francisco and Singapore. A. Hummel, *Eminent Chinese of the Ch'ing Period*, 1: 350–1. See also N. Kamachi, *Reform in China: Huang Tsun-hsien and the*

Japanese Model (Cambridge, Mass., 1981). A recent Chinese biography praises Huang's contribution to China's modernization. Zheng Hailin, *Huang Zunxian yu jindai Zhongguo* (Beijing, 1988).
63. Zhang Zhidong, 'Quanxue pian' (Exhortation to Study), in Shu Xincheng (ed.), *Ziliao*, 3: 971–84.
64. *Ibid.*, p. 976. See also Wang Ermin, *Wanqing zhengzhi sixiang shilun* (Taibei, 1969), p. 95; S. Borthwick, *Education and Social Change in China*, pp. 47–8.
65. Kang Youwei, 'Qing shi gesheng gai shuyuan yinsi wei xuetang zhe' (Petition requesting that all provinces convert academies and decadent temples into schools), in Shu Xincheng (ed.), *Ziliao*, 1: 80-2. Hsiao Kung-ch'üan, *A Modern China and a New World* (Seattle, 1975), p. 380, in referring to Kang's suggestion, translates *yin* as 'unauthorised', which hardly conveys the scorn Kang had for popular culture
66. Kang Youwei, 'Qing zun Kong sheng wei guojiao li jiaobu jiaohui yi Kongzi jinian er fei yin ji zhe' (Proposal to elevate Confucianism as a state religion and establish a Board of Religion and religious associations to commemorate Confucius and eliminate decadent forms of worship), in Jian Bocan (comp.), *Wuxu bianfa*, 2: 231–6. Writing in the journal *Xiangbao* in 1898 Kang reiterated his fear of western contempt for the Chinese: 'Ever since the Japanese disgraced us, the Westerners have belittled us and treated us as barbarians… Before, they called us a half civilized country. Now they class us with the servile blacks. Before, they hated us for pride and self-esteem. Now they call us stupid, deaf, and blind.' Cited in J. Pusey, *China and Charles Darwin*, p. 142.
67. R. Lund, 'The Imperial University of Peking', p. 128.
68. *Da Qing Dezong (Guangxu) Jinghuangdi shilu* (Taibei edition, 1964), 476: 4378–9. The edict also called on officials to 'seek truth from facts' *(shishi qiu shi)*, a slogan made much of recently by Deng Xiaoping in his programme of economic reform.
69. *Ibid,.* 486: 4475 .
70. *Ibid,.* 488: 4500 .
71. *Zhang Wenxiang Gong quanji*, 2: 939–49. See also W. Franke, *The Reform and Abolition of the Chinese Examination System*, pp. 49–50; W. Ayers, *Chang Chih-tung and Educational Reform in China*, pp. 157, 205–15. In 1872 the new Meiji government issued its Fundamental Code of Education *(gakusei)*, which planned for a nationwide system of primary, secondary and higher-level schools. It was largely based on the centralised French model (although most of the funding for the schools was to come from local communities) and envisaged eight years of compulsory schooling. After a brief experiment with a more decentralised *laissez-faire* approach in 1879–80 education was once again recentralised (with the period of compulsory schooling reduced) and greater emphasis was placed on moral training. School attendance figures, however, did not exceed 90.per cent until after 1902. Michio Nagai, 'Westernization and Japanisation: The Early Meiji Transformation of Education' in D.

Shively (ed.), *Tradition and Modernization in Japanese Culture* (Princeton, 1971), pp. 35–76; H. Passin, *Society and Education in Japan* (New York, 1965), pp. 69–85.
72. Zhang's distinction between morality and vocational skills bears an interesting similarity to Mao Zedong's emphasis on the equal importance of being both 'red' (adhering to correct ideology) and 'expert' (possessing technological expertise).
73. Noriko Kamachi, *Reform in China: Huang Tsun-hsien and the Japanese Model*, pp. 78-9. Zhang Zhidong had referred to these practices in his 1898 treatise. Interestingly, Zhang had also pointed to the western practice of arranging classes by ability so that the less bright students could be hived off.
74. For Zhang's stress on the importance of military drill at school, see *Donghua lu*, Guangxu reign, 27: 3735.
75. *Linsheng* were lower-degree holders (*shengyuan*) who were entitled to take the provincial examinations and who received government stipends. Chung-li Chang, *The Chinese Gentry* (Seattle, 1970), pp. 17–18.
76. R. Lund, 'The Imperial University of Peking', p. 152.
77. W. Franke, *The Reform and Abolition of the Chinese Examination System*, p. 50.
78. *Zhang Wenxiang Gong quanji*, 2: 945.
79. *Ibid.*, 2: 948.
80. D. Buck, *Urban Change in China: Politics and Development in Tsinan, Shantung 1890–1949* (Madison, 1978), p. 55.
81. *Yang Shouyuan zouyi jiyao* (Beijing, 1937), 10: 4b. Yuan emphasised a similar point in a 1902 memorial: 'Times are difficult and we should realise that reform and the seeking of talent are today's urgent tasks' *Yuan Shikai zouzhe zhuanji* (Taibei, 1971), 2: 559–60.
82. D. Buck, 'Educational Modernization in Tsinan 1899–1937' in M. Elvin, W. Skinner (eds.), *The Chinese City Between Two Worlds* (Stanford, 1974) p. 175.
83. R. Lund, 'The Imperial University of Peking', p. 152.
84. For an excellent discussion of early Confucian theories on the nature of man, see D. Munro, *The Concept of Man in Early China* (Stanford, 1969). Munro notes that Confucians believed all men were equally endowed at birth with an 'evaluating mind' and that the growth and development of this capability was very much dependent on education. Education, therefore, was the key in the solution of political and social problems.
85. The regulations are printed in Taga Akigorō (ed.), *Kindai Chūgoku Kyōiku Shi Shiryō* (Tokyo, 1972),1:128-84. Zhang's memorial proposing the new system is in Shu Xincheng (ed.), *Ziliao*, 1: 195-6. See also Chen Qitian, *Zuijin sanshinian Zhongguo jiaoyushi*,(Shanghai, 1930), p. 80; DYJN, 1: 23; M. Bastid, *Aspects de la Réforme*, pp. 40–1.
86. R. Lund, 'The Imperial University of Peking', pp. 165–6.
87. Taga Akigorō (ed.), *Shiryō*, 1:119.
88. *Ibid.*, 1: 167. A memorial written by Zhang Zhidong in 1902 on

educational progress in Hubei revealed a change in his approach. In the memorial he noted the importance of primary education in other countries and the fact that it was the state's duty to provide it. Such an education, Zhang remarked, taught morality and practical skills, as well as laying the foundations for patriotism. He called such a training 'citizen education' (*guomin jiaoyu*). *Zhang Wenxiang Gong quanji*, 2: 1016.

89. Duan was later Governor of Hunan (1904–5), Governor-General of Zhili (1909) and Governor-General of Jiangsu and Jiangxi (1910). In 1905 he was one of the five commissioners sent to Europe and North America to study constitutional government. In 1910 he helped organise an Industrial Exhibition in Nanjing. At the time of the 1911 Revolution he was acting Governor-General of Sichuan, where he was killed by his own troops. A. Hummel, *Eminent Chinese of the Ch'ing Period*, 1: 780–2.
90. The regulations for these schools are in Shu Xincheng (ed.), *Ziliao* 1: 100–2.
91. Shu Xincheng (ed.), *Ziliao*, l: 102.
92. H. Silver, *The Concept of Popular Education*, p. 32
93 *Qingmo choubei lixian dang'an shiliao* (Beijing, 1979), 2: 970.
94. In 1652 the Shunzhi Emperor promulgated six maxims (*liuyu*), which urged his subjects to practice virtue and lead a peaceful life. Lower-degree holders over sixty years of age were nominated to expound on the maxims in each locality. In 1670 the Six Maxims were superseded by a new set issued by the Kangxi Emperor, known as the Sacred Edict. These were supplemented by the *Shengyu guangxun* (Amplified Instructions of the Sacred Edict), promulgated by the Yongzheng Emperor in 1724. The main concern was to impress upon the people the need to obey the laws, pay taxes, and avoid 'heretic creeds'. One study has noted that the *xiangyue* system was gradually transformed from 'a lecturing device' to an institution of police surveillance. Hsiao Kung-ch'üan, *Rural China*, pp. 185–205.
95. Jiang Jianbai, *Zhongguo shehui jiaoyu xinzheng*, pp. 8–10. In the past, innovative scholars had proposed using the colloquial language in public lectures. This was particularly the case during the late fifteenth and early sixteenth centuries, which witnessed vigorous activity in the realm of popular education as a result of the influence of the famous Ming philosopher Wang Yangming. See J. Handlin, *Action in Late Ming Thought* (Berkeley, 1983).
96. Shu Xincheng, *Wo he jiaoyu* (Shanghai, 1945), pp 49–50. See also Saitō Akio, 'Chūgoku gakusei kaikaku no shisō to genjitsu', pp. 1–8. Interestingly, it was only after Shu had convinced his parents that he would receive a traditional degree after graduating from the new school and that it would not involve any increased costs for the family that he was allowed to attend. This suggests again that not all modern education (when making use of traditional schools), in its initial stages at least, was necessarily more espensive than traditional schooling, as M. Bastid (*Aspects de la Réforme*, p. 84) maintains.

97. For an account of these traditional schools, see Tanaka Kenji, 'Kyū Shina ni okeru jidō no gakujuku sei katsu' (Student Life in the Private Schools of Traditional China), *Tōhō Gakuhō* 15: 2 (January 1945), pp. 217–32. See also S. Borthwick, *Education and Social Change*, pp. 17–30; M. Bastid, *Aspects de la Réforme*, pp. 34–5. Guo Moruo, in his autobiography, also gives a vivid description of the harsh regimen he experienced at a traditional school. *Moruo zizhuan* (Hong Kong, 1978), 1: 30–5
98. Cited in Chen Qitian, *Zuijin sanshinian Zhongguo jiaoyushi*, p. 23.
99. *Donghua lu*, Guangxu reign, 29: 4979-82.
100. The aims outlined by these officials (*xuewu gangyao*), as well as the description and regulations of the new schools, are in *Zouding xuetang zhangcheng* (reprint, Taibei, 1972).The *xuewu gangyao* is reprinted in Shu Xincheng (ed.), *Ziliao*, 1: 199–220, and in Taga Akigorō (ed.), *Shiryō*, 1: 208–25. The regulations for the new schools are also in Taga Akigorō (ed.), *Shiryō*, 1: 226–408. See also M. Bastid, *Aspects de la Réforme*, pp. 42–6.
101. Shu Xincheng (ed.), *Ziliao*, 2: 400, 406–7.
102. *Ibid.*, 2: 421–4, 437–9.
103. I. Hall, *Mori Arinori* Cambridge. Mass., 1973), pp. 351–3. Ironically, the Japanese Education Ministry had borrowed the idea of moral training from French educational practice during the Third Republic, which prescribed moral instruction (drawn from Roman Catholicism) as part of the curriculum. After 1890 the government also began to exert an increasing monopoly over the publication of textbooks and in 1897 the Japanese Diet agreed that at least ethics textbooks should be compiled and published by the government. By 1903 a government committee had compiled all ethics texts used in elementary grades. W. Fridell, 'Government Ethics Textbooks in Late Meiji Japan', *Journal of Asian Studies*, 29: 4 (August 1970), pp. 823–33. It has been pointed out, however, that 1880 did not represent such a clear turning point. Thus even in the 1870s traditional moral values were still taught, while after 1880 language readers tended to contain much less traditionalist or statist morality than the ethics textbooks. E. Patricia Tsurumi, 'Meiji Primary School Language and Ethics Textbooks: Old Values for a New Society?', *Modern Asian Studies*, 8: 2 (1974), pp, 247–61.
104. Wang Feng-gang, *Japanese Influence on Educational Reform in China from 1895 to 1911* (Beijing, 1931), pp. 63–4.
105. Shu Xincheng (ed.), *Ziliao*, 2: 399.
106. *Ibid.*, 2: 419.
107. *Zouding xuetang zhangcheng*, p. 45.
108. Yang Tianshi et al. (comp.), *Ju'E yundong* (Beijing, 1979), pp. 145–55; Beijing daxue lishixi, *Beijing daxue xuesheng yundong shi* (Beijing, 1979), p. 2.
109. *Zouding xuetang zhangcheng*, p. 46. Zhang Baixi's 1902 plan had viewed middle schools primarily as the foundation for higher-level education, whereas in the 1904 regulations they were also 'to enable those who do not want to proceed on the educational ladder

to practice various trades'. Taga Akigorō (ed.), *Shiryō*, 1: 157, 166, 279; *Zouding xuetang zhangcheng*, p. 431. In 1909, however, it was decided to adopt the German pattern and divide middle schools into specialist branches of arts and sciences(*wenshi*). They were thus seen more as a preparation for advanced and specialised learning. This division was abolished in 1911 and the more general middle school re-adopted.
110. It was also proposed that all western books be translated quickly so as to reduce dependence on foreign teachers.
111. The frequent use of *yiwu jiaoyu* rather than *qiangbo jiaoyu* suggests a concern with persuasion as opposed to arbitrary force, although both terms are translated as 'compulsory education'. D. Munro, *The Concept of Man in Contemporary China* (Michigan, 1977), p. 180 has pointed to the tension in contemporary China between 'persuasion' (*shuofu*) and 'coercion' (*zhenya*). Perhaps this explains the use of the two terms for compulsory education. When plans were put forward in the early twentieth century to implement compulsory education they were generally phrased in terms of building more schools rather than in terms of passing laws that would penalise uncooperative parents. It seemed to be assumed that once the schools were built and the people aware of the government's call for universal education, parents would automatically send their children to school.
112. Taga Akigorō (ed.), *Shiryō*, 1: 311.
113. *Zouding xuetang zhangcheng*, p. 485.
114. *Ibid.*, pp. 492–3.
115. Shu Xincheng (ed), *Ziliao*, 3: 800–13.
116. *Ibid.*, 2: 775–8
117. *Ibid .*, 2: 777.
118. *Ibid.*, 2: 783-5. An interesting feature of the regulations for these apprentice schools, as well as for the general vocational schools, was the provision for a 'consultative group' (*shangyiyuan*) comprising those experienced in industry or commerce to 'discuss matters concerning the school'.
119. Taga Akigorō (ed.), *Shiryō*, 1: 339–42.
120. Zhang Jian's memorial proposing the creation of a normal school for Nantong and Haimen (Jiangsu) is translated in M. Bastid, *Aspects de la Réforme*, pp. 116-24. Zhang's attempt to secure school teachers paralleled that of the Japanese Minister of Education, Mori Arinori. On becoming Minister in 1885 he issued an ordinance on normal schools which stipulated that graduates had to serve as primary-school teachers for at least ten years in order to stop the practice (prevalent since 1872) of students enrolling simply to get a secondary education. I. Hall, *Mori Arinori*, p. 149.
121. Graduates of higher primary schools admitted to middle school were to be awarded the degrees of *linsheng*, *zengsheng*, or *fusheng*. Graduates of middle schools admitted to higher schools were to be awarded the degrees of *gongsheng*, *yu gongsheng*, or *suigongsheng* Graduates of higher-level schools were to be awarded the degree of

juren while graduates of the Imperial University were to receive the *jinshi*.
122. W. Franke, *The Reform and Abolition of the Chinese Examination System*, p. 67. The noted Japanese historian of Chinese education, Taga Akigorō, believes, however, that the 1904 school system demonstrates Zhang Zhidong's 'conversion' to citizen education. Taga Akigorō (ed.), *Shiryō*, 1 :42.
123. For an excellent discussion of the social effects of school reform in nineteenth century Europe, see Mary Jo Maynes, *Schooling in Western Europe* (New York, 1985).
124. W. Franke, *The Reform and Abolition of the Chinese Examination System*, p. 70 sees this memorial as representing a 'new note' in official attitudes towards education.
125. *Donghua lu*, Guangxu reign, 29: 5372.
126. In some provinces, however, the creation of modern schools was well under way by 1905. For some examples, see M. Bastid, *Aspects de la Réforme*, p. 46.
127. Guo Moruo, *Moruo Zizhuan*, 1: 57–8 .
128. The regulations for the new Board of Education are in Taga Akigorō (ed.), *Shiryō*, 1: 418–21. See also DYJN, 1: 28; Shu Xincheng (ed.), *Ziliao*, 1: 274–6; Chen Baoquan, *Zhongguo jindai xuezhi bianqian shi* (Taibei, 1972), pp. 64–7; S. Borthwick, *Education and Social Change*, p. 73. For a general account of administrative changes in education during the last years of the Qing, see Lei Guodian, *Zhongguo jiaoyu xingzheng zhidu shi* (Taibei, 1983), pp. 1–157. The first Secretary of the Board of Education was a Mongol bannerman, Rong Qing.
129. S. Mackinnon, *Power and Politics in Late Imperial China* (Berkeley, 1980), p. 145. The year before, in 1902, Yuan had set up a schools office (*xuexiaosi*) to supervise colleges, middle and primary schools.
130. Chen Qitian, *Zuijin sanshinian Zhongguo jiaoyushi*, pp. 92–3.
131. Regulations for provincial education are in Taga Akigorō (ed.), *Shiryō*, 1: 421–3.
132. *Xuebu guanbao*, no. 28 (1907), *jingwai xuewu baogao*, pp. 202–3.
133. *Qingmo choubei lixian dang'an shiliao*, 2: 961–74.
134. An article in *Jiangning xuewu zazhi*, vol. 2 (1907), *zalu*, pp. 5–12 reiterated Duan's proposal that higher-level education should be made more expensive to enable primary- and middle-level education to be provided free.
135. It should be noted, however, that at the municipal level the early years of the twentieth century saw a concerted campaign by professionals and big business to wrest control of schools from local ward trustees and boards. By the second decade of the twentieth century most major city educational systems in the United States had been centralised. D. Nasaw, *Schooled to Order* (New York, 1979), p. 111.
136. Mary Jo Maynes, *Schooling in Western Europe*, p. 49.
137. J. Black, *Citizens for the Fatherland* (New York, 1979), pp. 7, 12; R. Samuel, R. Thomas, *Education and Society in Modern Germany*

(London, 1949), pp. 2–3. Throughout most of the nineteenth century, however, education was not entirely controlled by the state, since the Church continued to have a supervisory role in elementary education and teacher training. Furthermore, after the unification of Germany in 1871 the individual states (*Länder*) retained jurisdiction over education. Strictly speaking the first countries to adopt a state system of education were Switzerland, in 1798, and Holland, in 1806, in both cases as a result of French occupation. H. Pollard, *Pioneers of Popular Education 1760–1850* (London, 1956), pp. 71–8.
138 *Qingmo choubei lixian dang'an shiliao*, 2: 965.
139. This important document is in *Donghua lu*, Guangxu reign, 30: 5474–9. It is reprinted in Shu Xincheng (ed.), *Ziliao*, 1: 220–6; Taga Akigorō (ed.), *Shiryō*, 1: 634–5; DYJN, 1: 29–31. One Chinese scholar maintains that the Board of Education's educational aims of 1906 mark the beginnings of 'utilitarian educational thought' (*shili jiaoyu sixiang*). Ren Shixian, *Zhongguo jiaoyu sixiang shi* (Taibei, 1964), p. 341.
140. *Donghua lu*, Guangxu reign, 30: 5474.
141. *Ibid.*, 30: 5476.
142. J. Hurt, 'Drill, Discipline and the Elementary School Ethos' in P. McCann (ed.), *Popular Education and Socialization in the Nineteenth Century* (London, 1977), p. 182.
143. *Ibid.*, p. 180. By this reckoning, of course, the upper classes had no need for drill. Team sports such as football and cricket were considered quite sufficient.
144. *Donghua lu*, Guangxu reign, 30: 5477. The Board of Education cited the Ming philosopher Wang Yangming as a pioneer of 'practical study', despite the fact that Wang's philosophy was not part of the official canon.
145. *Ibid.*, 30: 5477.
146. See, for example, Chow Tse-tsung, *The May Fourth Movement* (Cambridge, Mass., 1969), pp. 259–60; and M. Gewurtz, 'Social Reality and Educational Reform: The Case of the Chinese Vocational Education Association 1917-1927', *Modern China* 4: 2 (April 1978). Gewurtz does refer to the isolated attempts of gentry-entrepreneurs like Zhan Jian before 1911 to encourage vocational education, but generally she ignores the basic change in attitudes towards vocational education that occurred during these years.
147. Mary Jo Maynes, *Schooling in Western Europe*, p. 54. L. Stone notes that since the seventeenth century the English upper classes had tended to 'associate lower class education with political and social radicalism'.
148. V. Neuberg, *Popular Education in Eighteenth Century England* (London, 1971), pp. 3–4.
149. P. McCann, 'Popular Education, Socialization and Social Control: Spitalfields 1812–1824, in P. McCann (ed.), *Popular Education and Socialization in the Nineteenth Century*, p. 1.
150. J. Goldstrom, 'The Content of Education and the Socialization of

the Working Class Child 1830–1860', in P. McCann (ed.), *Popular Education and Socialization in the Nineteenth Century*, p. 99.
151. Mary Jo Maynes, *Schooling in Western Europe*, p. 55; C. Kaestle, 'Between the Scylla of Brutal Ignorance and the Charybdis of a Literary Education: Elite Attitudes Toward Mass Schooling in Early Industrial England and America', in L. Stone (ed.), *Schooling and Society* (Baltimore, 1976), p. 179.
152. H. Silver, *English Education and the Radicals* (London, 1975), p. 41.
153. H. Silver, *The Concept of Popular Education* (London, 1965), p. 21.
154. For an excellent discussion of the educational views of the *philosophes*, see H. Chisick, *The Limits of Reform in the Enlightenment* (Princeton, 1981). See also R. Palmer, *The Improvement of Humanity* (Princeton, 1985), pp. 57–8; M. Jo Maynes, *Schooling in Western Europe*, pp. 43–4. Maynes makes the interesting point (*ibid.*, p. 39) that the obscurantist warnings of the potentially disruptive effects of popular education took on a special meaning precisely because of the late-eighteenth-century faith in the transformative power of education.
155. M. Jo Maynes, *Schooling in Western Europe*, p. 54.
156. A. Peterson, *A Hundred Years of Education* (London, 1971), p. 16. R. Anderson, *Education in France 1848–1870* (Oxford, 1975), p. 17.
157. C. Kaesle, 'Between the Scylla of Brutal Ignorance and the Charybdis of a Literary Education', p. 182.
158. D. Nasaw, *Schooled to Order*, p. 52.
159. *Ibid.*, p. 47.
160. Mandeville, referring to the increasing crime rate in London, remarked: 'I intend to examine into the real causes of these mischiefs so justly complained of, and doubt not but to make it appear that charity schools, and everything else that promotes idleness, and keeps the poor from working, are more accessory to the growth of villainy than the want of reading and writing, or even the grossest ignorance and stupidity'. He concluded that 'to make the society happy and people easy under the meanest circumstances, it is requisite that the greatest numbers of them should be ignorant as well as poor.' *Fable of the Bees or Private Vices and Public Benefits* (London, 1714; Oxford edition, 1957), pp. 271, 287–8.
161. J. Hurt, 'Drill, Discipline and the Elementary School Ethos' in P. McCann (ed.), *Popular Education and Socialization in the Nineteenth Century*, p. 171.
162. *Qingmo choubei lixian dang'an shiliao*, 2: 975.
163. Shu Xincheng (ed.), *Ziliao*, 2: 395.
164. Jiang Menglin, *Xichao* (Taibei, 1974), p. 22. For a discussion of the educational thought of Confucius, Mencius, and Xunzi, see Ren Shixian, *Zhongguo jiaoyu sixiang shi* (Taibei, 1964) pp. 40–72.
165. Wm. de Bary, 'Individualism and Humanitarianism in Late Ming Thought' in Wm. de Bary (ed.), *Self and Society in Ming Thought* (New York, 1970), pp. 145–225.
166. The following discussion is based on A. Sinel, 'The Campaign for

Universal Primary Education in Russia 1890–1904'. I am grateful to Professor Sinel for letting me have a copy of his paper.
167. J. Black, *Citizens for the Fatherland*, pp. 23–4; J. McClelland, *Autocrats and Academics* (Chicago, 1979), p. 9.
168. J. Fincher, *Chinese Democracy* (New York, 1981), pp. 71, 73, 80.
169. Su Yunfeng, *Zhang Zhidong yu Hubei jiaoyu gaige* (Taibei, 1976), p. 200.
170. The tael *(liang)*, approximately an ounce of silver in the form of an oval ingot, was the standard unit of exchange during the Qing period. In theory it was equivalent to 1 000 copper cash but could be worth up to 1 500 cash. There were also several kinds of tael – custom taels, treasury taels, and Shanghai taels. In August 1911 one custom tael was worth $1.5 Mexican. At the same time, to complicate matters even further, dollar coins (Mexican, Spanish, Hong Kong) were used for domestic and retail transactions along the coast while Chinese dollar coins were also issued by provincial mints in the last years of the Qing. In 1910 the silver dollar *(yuan)* was adopted as the unit of currency for the Empire. H. Montague, H. Woodhead (comp.), *The China Year Book, 1912* (London, 1912), pp. 66–7, 273–81. Statistics for the end of the Qing often use taels and *yuan* interchangeably.
171. Most of these normal school graduates were students who had taken the shortened 'crash courses' *(sucheng)* in teacher training, mostly in Japan. By way of contrast less than one-third of middle school teachers were normal school graduates. Chen Qitian,*Zuijin sanshinian Zhongguo jiaoyushi*, pp 109–12.
172. The edict is in *Xuebu guanbao*, no. 1 (1906).

2. The Public Debate 1900–11

While the immediate reaction of the Qing court after the Boxer uprising had been to call for the recruitment of 'honest and talented' officials, gentry reformers were convinced that the people as a whole needed to be reformed. The Boxers' violent xenophobia, their use of magical practices, which they claimed made them invulnerable to bullets, and their destruction of railroad and telegraph lines, which they perceived as violating the natural harmony of the land, seemed to confirm the observation made by Kang Youwei in 1898: the Chinese people were backward, ignorant and superstitious and as such damaged China's prestige in the world. In the journal *Qingyi bao* (Pure People's Discussion), founded by Liang Qichao on his arrival in Japan after he had fled Beijing in 1898, Mai Menghua wrote in 1900 that the Boxers had caused 'foreigners increasingly to curse us as uncivilised savages [*yeman*] and insult us as an uncouth and boorish people [*guangzhong*] so that our four hundred million countrymen have lost face vis-à-vis the foreigners'.[1] For Mai Menghua, the Chinese people themselves were responsible for China's weakness, and not the lack of honest officials or the unscrupulous actions of the foreign powers.

The urgent need to improve the people's character and customs led to increasing public discussion of, and interest in, popular education that predated the change in official policy towards education described in Chapter One. This debate was carried out in a number of journals that began to be published after 1900, both in China and Japan, where large numbers of Chinese overseas students and political exiles were congregated. In contrast to the early treaty-port Chinese-language newspapers, which had tended to concentrate on business and commercial news,[2] the periodical press after 1900 covered a wide range of topics from politics to literature. Approximately one hundred such journals may have been published at any one time during the last years of the dynasty, with an average of 3 000 copies per issue and reaching an audience of between two and four million.[3]

In 1901 the first Chinese journal devoted entirely to education, *Jiaoyu shijie* (Educational World), began publication, followed in 1909 by another specialist journal of education, *Jiaoyu zazhi* (Educational Review). The latter was one of many journals published by the Shanghai Commercial Press, which was to become by the 1920s China's most important publishing firm.[4] It had been founded in 1897 with an initial capital of 4 000 Chinese dollars (*yuan*) and by the last years of the dynasty was capitalized at 1·5 million *yuan*. In 1903 the Commercial Press opened its first branch in Hankou and in 1905 established a subsidiary printing works in Beijing.

In 1904 the Commercial Press began publishing *Dongfang zazhi* (Eastern Miscellany), a reformist journal of current affairs that was to run until 1948. Like the other two journals devoted to education, *Dongfang zazhi*, although adopting a moderate political stance, felt free to make critical comments on government policy and regulations concerning education, as well as to offer advice and suggestions of its own.

The proliferation of the periodical press after 1900 compelled the Qing court to issue a press law in 1908 prohibiting the publication of edicts and government proclamations before they had appeared in the official gazettes (*guanbao*) and obliging every journal to submit each issue to inspection by a government censorship bureau prior to publication.[5] It remained a dead letter, especially as many journals were published in the International Settlement in Shanghai and hence escaped Chinese official jurisdiction.

The discussion over education that took place in the periodical press must be seen within the larger context of political and social change during the last years of the dynasty. With its programme of political and educational reform after 1900 the Qing court had in fact opened up a Pandora's box, as growing numbers of people now assumed the right to debate official government policy so long restricted to the inner circles of officialdom. An increasingly vociferous public opinion began to make itself felt as gentry, merchants and students sought to influence national affairs. In the realm of foreign affairs, for example, these groups manifested their determination to make their opinions known. Boycott campaigns were organised in 1905 against the United States to protest American immigration policy that discriminated against Chinese, and in 1908 against Japan after the confiscation by Chinese officials of a Japanese gun-running cargo vessel along the Guangdong coast had prompted high-handed demands by the Tokyo government for an official apology and payment of an indemnity.[6] Growing opposition to foreign economic influence in China led to a 'rights recovery movement' during the last years of the dynasty in which gentry and merchants sought to repurchase railroad and mining concessions granted to the foreign powers by the Qing government.[7]

Likewise, the court's programme of constitutional reform widened the political debate. The announcement in 1906 of plans to prepare for a constitution was quickly followed by the creation of gentry and merchant associations to publicise the merits of self-government (*zizhi*).[8] These associations varied in name from the Public Association to Prepare for the Establishment of a Constitution in Shanghai to the Public Association of Constitutional Politics in Hunan and the Merchants Self Government Society in Guangdong.[9] They held public meetings and presented memorials to the throne outlining their ideas and suggestions on constitutional preparation. When the provincial assemblies were elected in 1909 they soon came into conflict with both provincial governors as they sought to debate matters not within their jurisdiction, and with the court as they demanded the convocation of a national parliament earlier than had originally been laid down.[10]

Education, therefore, like politics and foreign affairs, became very much a *public* issue after 1900. No longer the preserve of Confucian scholars, nor exclusively associated with the training of a governing elite, education became a legitimate field of debate in which specialists and non-specialists alike participated.

THE PARTICIPANTS

Three principal groups were involved in the educational debate. The first group comprised those who were associated with, and contributed to, *Educational World*, *The Educational Review* and *Eastern Miscellany*. Many were from official or gentry families who had either studied in, or visited, Japan and who often combined the roles of educators, publishers, and advisers to government officials. In a sense they can be seen as a new class of professional educators, involved in all aspects of education, whether it be teaching, publishing school textbooks, working in educational administration or contributing to pedagogic theory.

The founder of *Educational World* was Luo Zhenyu (1866-1940), whose father had been an assistant magistrate. In 1883 Luo passed the district-level civil service examinations but failed the provincial-level examinations in 1891. In 1896 he helped organise the Agronomy Society (*nongxuehui*) in Shanghai, which translated over one hundred books on agriculture, mainly from Japanese. Luo's interest in Japan led him to establish in 1898 the Eastern Culture Society (*dongwen xueshe*), which offered courses in Japanese. In 1900 Luo worked in the Bureau of Agriculture set up by Governor-General Zhang Zhidong in Hubei. Zhang sent Luo on an official mission to Japan in 1901 to investigate education there and on his return was consulted by important provincial officials such as Cen Chunxuan and Duan Fang. In the first two issues of *Educational World* Luo translated the regulations for the Japanese Ministry of Education (*Mombushō*) as well as for Japanese primary, middle and normal schools.[11] It was through Luo that officials such as Zhang Zhidong and educational reformers such as the entrepreneur Zhang Jian first became acquainted with, and influenced by, Japanese educational practice. Zhang Jian's normal school, founded in his native district of Nantong, Jiangsu, in 1902,[12] and the organisation of the Board of Education with its division into specialist departments dealing with higher and general education, for example, were inspired by Japanese practice.[13] In 1906 Luo was assigned to the newly-created Board of Education as a school inspector, touring Zhili and Shanxi in 1907 and Shandong, Henan, Jiangxi and Anhui in 1908. In 1909 he was appointed Dean of the agricultural college at the Imperial University.[14]

Lu Feigui (1886-1941), the chief editor of *The Educational Review*, also came from an official family, his father having worked in provincial government and his mother being a niece of the important nineteenth-century official, Li Hongzhang.[15] Lu studied English at an early age and soon became involved in publishing. In 1906 he worked for a Shanghai book firm and later studied in Japan. In 1908 he joined the staff of the Commercial Press, becoming head of the publications department. Lu created his own book company in 1912, the *Zhonghua Shuju* (China Bookstore), which competed with the Commercial Press in the publication of primary and middle-school readers.[16] After the 1911 Revolution Lu was to help in drawing up the official regulations for general education (see Chapter Four).

Other contributors to *The Educational Review*, such as Jiang Weiqiao, Gao Fengqian and Zhuang Yu, were also involved in translation and compilation work for the Commercial Press. In addition to being an editor of *The Educational Review*, Jiang Weiqiao was the director of a vocational school opened by the Commercial Press from 1909 to 1912. In 1912 Jiang was to become an official in the new Republican Education Ministry.[17] Gao Fengqian had been a supervisor of Chinese students in Japan and translated Japanese articles on education for *Educational World*. He later became head of the translation bureau for the Commercial Press.[18] Zhuang Yu compiled many of the primary school texts during the last years of the dynasty and, like Jiang Weiqiao, joined the staff of the newly-created Education Ministry in 1912.

The chief editor of arguably the most important journal of current affairs in twentieth-century China, *Eastern Miscellany*, was Zhang Yuanji (1866-1959), a metropolitan degree holder (*jinshi*) and member of the prestigious Hanlin Academy. Although Zhang had supported the 1898 reform movement, he was not adversely affected by the conservative reaction. Soon afterwards he joined the staff of the Commercial Press and became involved in the publication of school texts. In 1920 he became a supervising manager of the Commercial Press and was elected chairman of the Board of Directors in 1930.[19]

The second group that contributed to the educational debate comprised those reformers associated with Liang Qichao (1873-1929). Like Kang Youwei, Liang had been forced to flee China with a price on his head for his involvement in the 1898 reform movement. He settled in Japan where he continued his publishing activity promoting the cause of political and social reform. In his writings Liang introduced a wide range of western political and social thought and wrote the first articles in Chinese on western socialism.[20] In contrast to his former mentor Kang Youwei, who was busily organising the Protect the Emperor Society (*baohuang hui*) to work for the restoration of the Guangxu Emperor, Liang adopted a hostile stance with regard to the Manchu dynasty in the years immediately following 1898. At one point it seemed he might join forces with Sun Yatsen, the western-educated revolutionary who had created the Revive China Society (*xingzhong hui*) in 1895 with the purpose of promoting the establishment of a republic. Liang did not cross into the revolutionary camp, however. A

1903 visit to North America, where he was appalled at the corruption, parochialism and degradation of overseas Chinese communities there, convinced Liang that China was not yet ready for a republic and after 1903 he began to advocate the benefits of 'enlightened despotism', which would usher in the reforms necessary to train a responsible, public-spirited, and educated citizenry. His views, and those of his followers, were published in *New People's Miscellany* (*Xinmin congbao*) which appeared between 1902 and 1907. [21]

Liang's reformist stance and his argument that revolution in China would result in chaos, disunity, and foreign control were fiercely condemned by Chinese radical students in Japan, the third group involved in the educational debate. Chinese government students had begun to go to Japan in 1896, in the wake of official encouragement of overseas study. Zhang Zhidong recommended Japan both because of the short distance involved and the similarities of the two cultures. By 1902 there were 270 Chinese students in Japan. Japan's attraction as a place for overseas study was enhanced by her defeat of Russia in 1905. For many young Chinese of the time, Japan represented the concrete example of an Asian country that had imbibed the secrets of western wealth and strength to create a modern and dynamic state capable of inflicting defeat upon a western power. By 1906 there were between 8 000 and 10 000 Chinese students in Japan, many of whom were privately financed.[22] While in Japan, many students were attracted to western concepts of nationalism and democracy. Increasingly hostile to the Manchu dynasty, which they portrayed as corrupt and weak rulers responsible for China's weakness and her continued humiliation at the hands of foreign powers, Chinese radical students condemned the government's constitutional programme as a ploy to perpetuate autocratic rule, and referred to Liang as a stooge of the Manchus.[23] These student radicals published a number of short-lived journals, drawing attention to China's plight and outlining their ideas on political, social and educational change. Most of these journals were associated with students from a particular province, such as *Jiangsu*, *Tides of Zhejiang* (*Zhejiang chao*), and *Hubei Student World* (*Hubei xueshengjie*).[24]

Discussions of popular education in the periodical press before 1911 not only drew attention to the necessity of consolidating social unity and training a patriotic citizenry shorn of its superstitions and backward beliefs, but also underlined the key role education had to play in producing economically self-reliant and productive individuals, a new aim for education not present in traditional thought. In the process Chinese educators began to describe society in very untraditional terms. At the same time such discussions were marked by a profound ambivalence towards the lower classes. On the one hand reformers and radicals described them in contemptuous terms and implied they needed guidance from their intellectual betters. On the other, they evinced an almost mystical faith in the power of the people and confidently assumed that immediate benefits were to be gained from a morally invigorated and knowledgeable people. These contradictory outlooks stemmed from two strands of traditional Confucian political and educational thought: the elitism and paternalism that surrounded the role of the scholar ('those who worked with their minds') in his duty to provide a moral example for the uneducated ('those who worked with their hands') and the notion that the people not only constituted the basis of the state but also were capable of being transformed through education.

THE CONCEPT OF SOCIAL EDUCATION

In the aftermath of the Boxer Rebellion, some Chinese educators emphasised the function of popular education in promoting social stability. It is in this context that Luo Zhenyu in 1902 translated a Japanese article in *Jiaoyu shijie* on 'social education' (*shehui jiaoyu*).[25] The article is important because it introduced into Chinese the notion of 'society' (*shehui*), a term borrowed from the Japanese (*shakai*), as a distinct entity separate from, and independent of, both the state and the traditional ruler–subject relationship.[26] Defining society as a 'collectivity of people with an ordered hierarchy', the article referred to the existence of three potentially conflicting 'classes' (*jieji*) – the upper, middle and lower levels (*shangliu, zhongliu, xialiu*). The 'upper levels' were defined as the high officials and the wealthy, the 'middle levels' as those with moderate wealth and education (e.g. intellectuals and students) and the 'lower levels' as the poor, helpless and those 'lacking in morality' (e.g. convicts).

The article reflected the fear of Japanese educators that industrialisation was leading to both increasing class differentiation, as 'officials and capitalists' (*zibenzhu*) became clearly distinct from 'workers' (*laoyizhe*), and the emergence of social conflict (what was euphemistically to be called the 'labour problem'). This resulted in the decline of morality, increasing crime rates, factory strikes, and the breakdown of the family system.

No doubt the original author of the article exaggerated the extent and impact of industrialisation in Japan. Although a beginning had been made after 1868 with the state's sponsorship of modern heavy industry, figures from 1865 to 1905 reveal that industrial operations were still carried out on a relatively small scale.[27] The number of factories using any type of industrial power comprised less than half the total by 1905. The number of workers per factory also remained small, averaging 60 in 1905. In 1903 there were 483 839 factory workers[28] in a population of 46·1 million. Nevertheless, the effects of the Sino-Japanese War of 1895 did boost industrial growth, laying the foundations for a modern capitalist economy and an independent class of modern wage workers. By the end of the nineteenth century railway engineers, mechanics and printers had begun to organise their own trade unions, which prompted hostile government reaction in the form of a Public Police Law (*chian keisatsu hō*) in 1900 curbing their activities. The number of labour disputes fluctuated in the last years of the nineteenth century and early years of the twentieth from forty-three in 1898 (involving 6 293 workers) to nineteen in 1905 (involving 5 013 workers).

If the article exaggerated the impact of industrialisation in Japan it might seem even more paradoxical that Luo Zhenyu felt the article had relevance for China. A modern proletariat was beginning to emerge in the last years of the dynasty, but it was a minimal proportion of China's total population and was confined mainly to the treaty ports, in particular, Shanghai. Between 1900 and 1910 there were in Shanghai 76 000 workers in factories with over 500 employees out of total of 240 000 workers in factories and mines throughout China. The number of strikes, although small, increased during this period, however. In 1898-9 there were ten strikes, while after 1909 there were twenty-four strikes.[29] In a wider sense, however, society during the last years of the dynasty was becoming more diverse and complex, principally because industrial capitalism affected divisions within the ruling elite itself. A new officer class trained in modern military academies, foreign affairs specialists, compradore merchants and financiers, gentry-entrepreneurs and a westernised treaty-port intelligentsia were all the products of China's contact with the capitalistic West.[30] It was this growing complexity in society and the potential tensions to which it might give rise that evidently struck a chord with Luo Zhenyu.

In addition to this Luo was clearly impressed with the article's stress on society as an organic unit, with each group dependent on the other, and the importance it attributed to the 'middle levels' of society, who were to perform a crucial harmonising role. According to the article, 'social education' would make the upper and middle levels of society aware of their duties and responsibilities while at the same time integrating the lower levels and convincing them that they were a necessary component of a unified society.[31] Since school education was inevitably concerned with *individual* achievement, the article noted, social education would complement this by stressing the need for social unity and the importance of the collective interest. Such an education would be carried out, for example, in factories and prisons as well as in an extensive network of poor people's schools. Luo Zhenyu, in an earlier article in *Jiaoyu shijie*, had also advocated the building of public libraries and museums in each district capital.[32]

Liang Qichao, in his reformist journal *Xinmin congbao* (New People's Miscellany) also introduced the concept of social education as a means to cement social unity.[33] Like Luo Zhenyu, Liang was a fervent admirer of the Japanese education system[34] and in 1904 he translated a Japanese article on educational aims in which social education was assigned the important role of harmonising the upper and lower classes. The upper classes would be educated to assume their social responsibilities and commitment to the well-being of the people, while the lower classes would be trained to become hard-working members of society with a natural disposition to serve and obey the law (*fucong xingzhi*).[35] Once again emphasis was placed on the crucial role of the middle levels of society – intellectuals and students – in actively pursuing and promoting social unity.[36] Such an emphasis was to be repeated by Chinese educators in the early years of the Republic.

Chinese student radicals in Japan also described society in terms of upper, middle and lower levels, but unlike the moderate educators they defined social education as revolutionary propaganda aimed at the lower classes. A 1903 article in a journal edited by Hunanese students argued that the lower classes constituted the 'backbone' (*zhongjian*) of the revolution whereas the middle classes (defined as 'intellectuals') were to be the 'vanguard' (*qianli*). Social education, through the medium of public lectures, would forge a link between the two and would enable the middle classes to penetrate the world of 'labourers, soldiers, and secret societies'.[37]

Like the reformers associated with *Educational World* and *New People's Miscellany*, therefore, student radicals assigned the leading role in social education to the 'middle classes'. Yang Dusheng, in his 1903 tract 'New Hunan' (*Xin Hunan*), declared that the middle levels of society had to give 'guidance and help to the lower levels in the task of transforming the upper levels of society'[38] and Chen Tianhua, a student who was to commit suicide in 1905 in protest against China's humiliation during the Russo-Japanese War (China, a neutral, watched helplessly as the two combatants fought on Chinese soil), claimed that 'only the middle levels of society know the significance of revolution, and this awareness will gradually reach the lower levels of society'.[39] The importance both moderates and radicals attributed to the 'middle classes' reflected their assumption that the initiatives to be taken in promoting education would naturally be taken by the emerging group of professional educators on the one hand, and the new student class educated in modern schools on the other. In both cases the traditional gentry and official elite would be displaced.

Notwithstanding the definition of social education made by some student radicals before 1911 as a means of fostering a revolutionary alliance between the middle and lower classes,[40] 'social education' by the last years of the dynasty had generally become associated with the notion of using a wide range of facilities (such as theatres and museums) to emphasise the organic unity of society and the public interest, thereby complementing the 'individualistic' education offered in formal schools. This view was to be shared by all Chinese educators, whether progressive or conservative. Shu Xincheng, for example, the promoter of modern educational methods like the Dalton Plan in the 1920s, commented in 1927: 'To use these public institutions [reading-rooms, cinemas, museums] to educate the general public is social education. The aim is to promote the people's general knowledge and encourage public order.'[41] At the same time social, or popular, education would 'reform customs' and train an economically self-reliant citizenry.

THE REFORM OF CUSTOMS AND THE TRAINING OF A NEW CITIZENRY

In 1895 the manifesto of Sun Yatsen's first revolutionary organisation, the Revive China Society, had attributed China's ills to the backwardness and selfishness of the people and had called for the 'reform of the people's customs' (*huamin chenyu*).[42] After the Boxer uprising in 1900 'the reform of customs' became inextricably linked with popular education in the minds of both moderates and radicals.

Thus in 1902, the same year in which Liang Qichao began writing his series of articles advocating the transformation of the Chinese people into self-reliant, dynamic and public-minded citizens,[43] a group of educators that included Cai Yuanpei and Jiang Weiqiao founded the Chinese Educational Association in Shanghai to promote 'the education of the Chinese people and the improvement of their character and morals'.[44] They set up a department of social education to encourage 'the reform of customs' (*gailiang fengxi*) and to compile reading material for the edification of the people.[45] All 'backward' customs and beliefs such as *fengshui* (popular notions of geomancy), gambling, extravagant weddings and funerals, and 'outlandish' religious festivals and ceremonies were to be eliminated, especially as they were seen as both economically wasteful and detrimental to China's prestige in the world. This concern with backward popular customs was to become a recurring theme in both official and intellectual discourse and has persisted to the present day.

The periodical press after 1900 consistently railed against popular customs. Journals such as the *Ningbo baihua bao* (Ningbo Vernacular Journal) in 1903-4 condemned village festivals (*saihui*) and the people's proclivity for gambling.[46] The *Anhui suhua bao* (Anhui Vernacular Speech Journal), edited in 1904 by the future founder of the Chinese Communist Party, Chen Duxiu, criticised marriage customs and notions of geomancy. Chen was particularly critical of popular Buddhist beliefs which, in his view, not only led to people wasting their money on charms but also made the people appear ridiculous to the outside world.[47] In 1904, the radical Shanghai journal, *Jingzhong ribao* (Alarm Bell Daily), whose editorials nevertheless were often reprinted in *The Eastern Miscellany*, urged educators to 'infiltrate' popular amusements. As an example, the journal suggested that mah-jong tiles be inscribed with terms of current affairs and general knowledge such as 'constitutional monarchy' (*lixian*), 'republic' (*gonghe*), and 'autocracy' (*zhuanzhi*), as well as newly-coined words for modern phenomena such as *tielu* (railways), *dianxin* (electricity) and *qiquan* (steamship).[48] Liang Qichao argued in 1903 that China needed genuine national festivals, as in France or the United States, that commemorated important events in the nation's history and celebrated the virtues of public-minded heroes.[49]

Not everyone, however, joined in the general condemnation of popular customs. One notable example was the author of a 1905 article in Liang

Qichao's journal, *New People's Miscellany*, on the betrothal practices of the Miao people in Guizhou province. Known as the 'moon dance' (*tiaoyue*) it involved groups of young men and women singing to each other from opposite sides of a river. Those couples who were mutually attracted were free to become betrothed. Such freedom of marriage, the article noted, was something that even the most civilised western country would do well to emulate.[50]

The call to reform customs was also accompanied by criticism of traditional drama and literature. In 1897 Yan Fu (1853-1921), the translator of Adam Smith and Herbert Spencer, had stressed the social function of literature. In 1902 Liang Qichao pleaded for a new fiction that would 'renovate the people' (*xiumin*) by uplifting morality and improving customs.[51] Both Yan and Liang condemned traditional popular fiction as decadent and corrupt, inciting 'robbery and lust' (*huidao huiyin*).[52] In Liang's view, this popular form needed to be appropriated by the elite and suffused with new values. A fiction describing the heroic and selfless activities of a Washington or a Cavour, Liang noted, would assist China's political transformation and the training of a patriotic citizenry.

Traditional drama, also, came under attack for its failure to stimulate patriotism and for its propensity to portray superhuman figures and unlikely events that bore no connection with reality. In 1904 Chen Duxiu expressed disappointment with the failure to exploit drama's potential. He saw drama as a more useful educational tool than either schools or newspapers, describing the theatre as a 'giant school for the people'(*zhongren di da xuetang*).[53] Chen pointed to the harmful effect of traditional drama on the Boxers, whose mystical and unrealistic faith in their invulnerability to bullets had been influenced by the 'heavenly warriors and generals' portrayed in popular drama.[54] Chen also condemned 'pornographic drama' (*yinxi*) and plays that encouraged selfish ambition to seek wealth and prestige instead of promoting an interest in the well-being of the country.[55]

In their campaign to reform popular culture, Chinese educators and writers in the last years of the Qing promoted the use of the vernacular (*baihua*), thus anticipating one of the rallying cries of the New Culture Movement after 1915. A vernacular supplement had been added to the first modern-style Chinese newspaper, *Shen bao*, in 1876[56] and the reformist official Huang Zunxian had discussed the need to unify the written and spoken languages in 1887.[57]

The first educator to advocate the use of the vernacular in schools was Chen Zibao (1862-1922), a disciple of Kang Youwei, who began to use vernacular readers in the school he founded in Macao in 1899. In an 1897 article Chen stressed the relativity of language, arguing that the classical idiom (*wenyan*) had no absolute value, and that everyday language relevant to the people should be used in schools.[58] (One positive result of such a measure, Chen noted, was that parents' hostility to modern schools would be dispelled because they would still feel able to communicate with their children.) By 1899 Chen even dismissed the Confucian classics as relevant teaching material.[59] He also suggested that schools use the dialect of the region in which they were located, in contrast to the later view that one standard form should be uniformly imposed.[60]

Others took up the cause. Qiu Renliang, a supporter of Liang Qichao, created the Association to Promote the Vernacular (*baihua xuehui*) in 1898. The classical language, Qiu observed, had prevented the emergence of a knowledgeable citizenry. He predicted that a vernacular movement would destroy the cultural arrogance of the literati and would bring the classics to the common people in the same way as the vernacular had made the Bible more accessible in the West.[61] The manifesto of his projected vernacular book store in 1898 was as radical as anything written in the first years of the New Culture Movement:

> We desire to unite with like-minded colleagues to set up a vernacular book store to translate widely from useful Chinese and western books in order to satisfy the country's need for intellectual nourishment. We will strive to allow a literate people to expand their knowledge, to encourage their determination and become involved in scholarship, and to sweep away entirely in one go the obstacles of the last two thousand years erected by the literati.[62]

After 1900 vernacular journals proliferated, all of them castigating the backwardness and ignorance of the people that gentry educators believed had been so visibly demonstrated during the Boxer uprising.[63] As one journal put it in 1903, the aim of vernacular publications was to reach 'peasants, artisans, merchants, soldiers, and the young' so as to encourage the development of a knowledgeable and public-minded people.[64] Lu Feigui added his weight to the campaign when he announced in the opening issue of *The Educational Review* in 1909 that articles written in the vernacular would be accepted for the journal's literary section, as well as echoing Chen Zibao's view that the vernacular should be used in schools.[65]

For the contributors to these vernacular journals, it was not simply a question of educating a new citizenry. They also underlined the connection between widespread literacy and national survival itself. In the *Hangzhou Vernacular Journal* (*Hangzhou baihua bao*) a contributor argued in 1901 that if everyone were literate, foreigners would never be able to dominate China completely because its culture would continue to flourish among the people. As a warning he referred to the example of Poland where, because the people were illiterate, the proscription of the Polish language by the country's Russian masters had been easily carried out.[66] This idea was taken up by Luo Zhenyu in 1902 when he emphasised the necessity for a country to control its own education, again referring to the ease with which Russia had subjugated Poland by prohibiting the use of the Polish language.[67]

Radical students also pointed to the link between widespread education and the continued existence of China as a nation state.[68] Anticipating the official view after 1905 they argued that survival was now focused on the 'struggle to promote education' (*xuezhan*).⁶⁹ Poland, India and Vietnam had all been conquered, it was maintained, because they had failed to develop education.⁷⁰ On the other hand, both Russia (in Poland) and the United States (in the Philippines) had imposed their respective languages on the indigenous population in order to foster loyalty and obedience, thus precluding any possibility of national resistance.⁷¹

Chinese educators also hoped that women would be included amongst the potentially enlarged readership brought about by the publication of vernacular journals. A number of journals, in fact, written wholly or partially in the vernacular, and addressed specifically to women, began to be published after 1900.⁷² By 1911 seventeen such journals had appeared, the first of them – *Journal of Women's Education* (*Nüxue bao*) – appearing in Shanghai in 1902 edited by a woman, Chen Xiefan.⁷³ Another prominent woman activist, Qiu Jin, founded the *Chinese Women's Journal* (*Zhongguo nübao*) in Shanghai shortly before she was executed in 1907 after having been implicated in an abortive anti-Manchu uprising.⁷⁴ Some of the ideas expressed in these journals exuded boundless faith in women's potential. A 1903 article in the *Women's Journal* (*Nüzi bao*), for example, asserted that the liberation of women in China would be more extensive than that in the West. Chinese women had three qualities, the article asserted, that made them not only superior to their western counterparts but also to Chinese men as well. They had a greater capacity for devotion and loyalty (making them potentially the best patriots), for compassion (making them potentially the most benign rulers) and for uncompromising resolve (making them potentially the most dedicated of revolutionaries). All they needed was education, which would allow their natural talents to flourish.⁷⁵

Most of these women's journals, however, were published and edited by men – including Jiang Weiqiao, who edited *Women's World* (*Nüzi shijie*) from 1904-6⁷⁶ – and although they championed the cause of women's education as an essential precondition for China's revival, the reasoning behind the campaign as well as the proposed content of women's education were decidedly ambiguous as far as women themselves were concerned.

Such ambiguity characterised the first proposals for women's education by pioneering reformers like Zheng Guanying (1842-1923) and Liang Qichao. In 1894 Zheng argued that although women need not necessarily be as highly educated or learned as men, an education that made them morally upright, literate, numerate and competent in 'handling everyday matters' (e.g. embroidery, cooking, accountancy) would greatly assist their husbands and bring virtue to the household.⁷⁷ In Zheng's words, they would thus become 'worthy women, worthy wives, and worthy mothers' (*xian'nü, xianfu, xianmu*). In 1897 Liang Qichao maintained that education for women would not only enable them to be 'producers' (*shengli*) rather than 'consumers' (*fenli*), but would also make them fitter mothers (morally and physically) for the upbringing of their children. The quality of China's future generations would thus be enhanced.[78]

After 1900 women's education was seen as an important aspect of social education: it would contribute to the reform of customs (e.g. by promoting the abolition of footbinding)[79] and to the correct domestic training of the young. As one article noted in 1905, women were the 'mothers of the nation's citizens'.[80] Even when it was urged that women should be educated so as to earn a living, the argument was often phrased in terms of benefiting men: with the financial pressure of supporting their wives eased, life would be more bearable for them.[81] Furthermore, the limits of women's education were clearly specified. A 1904 article in Liang Qichao's *New People's Miscellany* warned that education for boys and girls should be differentiated. If girls were given too advanced an education they would begin to look down on boys and might rebel against becoming mothers.[82] Jiang Weiqiao in 1909 bewailed the fact that girls attending school were often unable or unwilling to perform household chores on their return home, and suggested that girls' schools pay particular attention to the teaching of domestic science.[83]

Chinese educators hoped that education would promote two other virtues among the people, virtues that in their view had either been neglected or scorned by traditional education. First, there was the virtue of martial vigour, which would transform the people into a 'militant citizenry' (*junguomin*). Liang Qichao often contrasted the *bushidō* (way of the warrior) spirit in Japan with the more pacifist outlook in China. He was particularly attracted to the 'lively military outlook' in Japan and how the military set an example for the public. Even in the United States, Liang noted, primary school children sang songs about military heroes.[84]

One contributor to *New People's Miscellany* even advocated the militarisation of society. In his view the army should embody patriotism and public morality and he proposed military training in schools as the first step in organising the nation on a military basis. The school was compared to an army battalion and would virtually become a military preparatory school. Role models would be military figures rather than upright Confucian scholars. With society emulating the military, the writer concluded, discipline, courage and martial skills would be instilled into every citizen.[85]

Not everyone was prepared to go as far as to suggest a militarisation of society, but most moderate and radical journals underlined the need to train a militant citizenry. This was accompanied by an increasing emphasis on the importance of physical education and competitive games, particularly after 1900. Luo Zhenyu at the turn of the century introduced Aristotle's distinction between moral, intellectual and physical education (*deyu, zhiyu, tiyu*) with the radical notion that all were equally important.[86] Such an outlook became widely accepted. Luo himself recommended the use of temples as physical education training centres with army cadets as teachers.[87] A radical student journal in 1906 asserted that physical education was even more important than intellectual or moral training, since it would equip China to 'struggle' in the international arena.[88] Anglo-Saxon education was particularly praised for training robust and physically fit citizens,[89] while Jiang Weiqiao in 1909 spoke highly of the western emphasis on sport and competitive games, and urged Chinese schools to follow suit.[90] When Mao Zedong wrote his first article in 1917 condemning the traditional disdain for physical exercise he was merely echoing a view held by many Chinese educators since the last years of the Qing dynasty.[91]

Some writers, of course, insisted that the Chinese people *did* have a martial spirit, which only awaited education for it to be profitably utilised. A 1904 article in *The Eastern Miscellany* claimed that a martial spirit had always existed in the rural areas because of the constant struggle for resources.[92] Such a spirit was especially prevalent amongst bandits and pirates. With a widespread education emphasising patriotism, the article predicted, the spontaneous energy and courage exhibited by rural folk and bandits in their private feuds could be channelled into a united, nationalist struggle against all foreign aggressors.[93]

The second virtue promoted by educators was economic self-sufficiency. It was in this context that after 1900 they began for the first time to link education with economic development. In particular they bemoaned the laziness of the people and called for an education that would train self-reliant and hard-working citizens who would, by benefiting themselves, benefit the country. One indication of this trend can be seen in the change of attitudes towards beggars, vagrants, and the unemployed. The relatively tolerant Qing attitude towards migrating paupers has been contrasted with that of mercantilist Europe, where each unemployed person was perceived as an economic traitor to be confined to hospitals, factories or houses of correction.[94] This was to change after 1900 when a concerted effort was made in China to provide vocational facilities for the poor and unemployed. It is significant, for example, that in his 1902 articles on self-government, Kang Youwei proposed the creation of technical and industrial arts institutes which beggars, vagrants and the unemployed would be compelled to attend.[95]

It is no coincidence either that Chinese educators during this period began to focus on the problems of juvenile delinquency. Articles in *The Educational Review* focused on the growing crime rate amongst 14-21-year-olds in Britain, France, Germany and the United States as a result of unemployment,[96] in addition to describing corrective institutions and borstals in England.[97] China, too, it was feared, would experience an increase in juvenile delinquency if unemployment and poverty were not combated.[98] Significantly, the fears of Chinese educators were echoed by their counterparts in the United States where juvenile crime was becoming a frequent topic of discussion.[99]

The concern for what was perceived to be prevalent idleness led to an emphasis on hard work and the inculcation of a sense of autonomy to free the people of their slavish habits of dependence. In journals such as *The*

Eastern Miscellany after 1904, and The Educational Review after 1909, constant references were made to the people's 'lazy and pleasure-seeking natures' (duoyi), which contrasted with the hard-working and energetic nature of western citizens.[100] A contributor to The Eastern Miscellany argued in 1905 that people were poor because they were lazy and squandered their resources on gambling and 'decadent, extravagant forms of worship'. The widespread creation of industrial training centres (gongyi zhuchang), he concluded, would counteract this by channelling people into productive work.[101]

Such a concern even extended to those already in employment. Meng Zhaochang, a prominent gentry member of the Jiangsu Education Association, proposed in 1908 the establishment of 'citizen schools' (gongmin xuetang) for farmers, artisans and traders, amongst whom, Meng claimed, idleness and irresponsibility prevailed. Farmers, Meng observed, lost their land because of gambling debts or general negligence. The time they spent whiling away the hours 'going to tea-houses' or 'watching decadent entertainment' could profitably be used for an education that would stress the virtues of hard work and self-reliance. In this way, Meng insisted, people would come to realise that 'working to profit one's person and family was the way to work for the public interest of the locality, and the way to build a healthy state'.[102] This was the first occasion in which individual and family prosperity were equated with the public good, and contrasted with Liang Qichao's earlier attempt in 1902 to distinguish private from public morality. It was a trend of thought that was to cause disquiet among some educators during the early years of the Republic.

Long before the May Fourth critique of Confucian tradition for its stifling of individual development, Chinese educators were calling for a new sense of autonomy amongst the people. Chen Zibao in 1899 criticised the custom of inheritance (yichan guan'nian) and argued that schools needed to foster a sense of competitiveness, since only competition led to progress. He singled out the young in particular for criticism, claiming that they were far too dependent on their families. Whereas in the West, he observed, people often donated their money to worthwhile public causes, in China people saved money for their sons and grandsons. This, according to Chen, prevented the young from becoming morally and economically independent.[103]

The emphasis on thrift, hard work, and individual autonomy was echoed in the choice of western writings that were translated or discussed in the early years of the century. Thus excerpts from Samuel Smiles' Self Help, translated from the Japanese, appeared in several issues of Educational World in 1902-3 [104] (Self Help was to become part of the public lecture material used in the early years of the Republic), while articles on Herbert Spencer's educational thought appeared in The Educational Review, which stressed Spencer's philosophy of self autonomy and 'not depending on others'.[105]

Hard work and productivity, in fact, were elevated as the most crucial

factor in determining the nation's survival. A 1904 article in *The Eastern Miscellany* proclaimed that only those who were 'hard-working and diligent' (*qin*) would succeed, whereas the lazy (*duo*) would bring harm to themselves as well as to the country:
> What I call rich is not a reference to the rich capitalist of American trust companies or European corporations. Rich merchants and traders in our country must exist everywhere and be evenly distributed, with each one capable of managing his own business. If the number of whose who depend on others and who detract from the benefit of the whole daily decreases, then our country will be fortunate indeed and will avoid the fate of extinction.[106]

This stress on economic self-sufficiency led some Chinese writers to analyse Chinese society in a very untraditional way. Reflecting the awareness of the 'labour problem' in the West and what was seen to be the growing differences between rich and poor there, a 1904 editorial in *The Eastern Miscellany* divided the population into two groups; but rather than the traditional view of society which postulated a distinction between the literati (those steeped in the Confucian literary tradition) and the rest of the population, the 1904 editorial divided the people between those who 'produced wealth' (*shengcai zhi ren*) and those who 'consumed wealth' (*fencai zhi ren*). China's weakness, the editorial claimed, was that the latter group – comprising superfluous and petty officials, yamen clerks, servants, priests and monks, bandits, women, teachers, degree-holders and 'profligate sons of the rich' – outnumbered the former.[107]

This theme was taken up in a 1910 article, which divided the Chinese population into six groups (*pinlei*). The first three, comprising peasants, artisans and workers, merchants and small traders, were 'productive' (*shenglizhe*), while the other three, comprising officials and gentry, soldiers, and priests and monks, were 'consumers' (*fenlizhe*) Taking into account the unproductive members of the first three groups (the old, young, handicapped, unemployed), the article continued, the number of 'consumers' far outweighed that of the productive population. As such, it concluded, China was unique in the world and it was therefore imperative that education train more productive citizens.[108] The stress on economic productivity led to more prestige being attached to manual labour, which was to become a significant feature of educational debates in the early Republic. Schools, for example, were now recommended to inculcate a 'love of labour' (*hao laodong zhi xiguan*) among their pupils.[109]

AN AMBIVALENT VOLUNTARISM

Underlying the public debate on popular education during the last years of the dynasty was a profound ambivalence towards the people. Both moderates and radicals wavered between contempt for the lower classes and a voluntaristic faith in their potential. The reformer, Zhang Yuanji, advocating a campaign to 'develop the people's knowledge' (*kaifa minzhi*) in 1902 noted

that:
> Many of our people are stupid. Apart from food, drink and sex, they practically know nothing of anything else. They do not take into account, or show concern about, the possible disappearance of the state or of the race... Faced with a people like this, although there might be good administration, the carrying out of it will be met with hostility.[110]

Despite this gloomy assessment of the Chinese people, reformers exuded confidence in the power of education to create a 'new people' aware of their rights and duties and contributing to the public good (gongde).[111] A 1905 editorial in *The Eastern Miscellany* declared that within thirty years, when all the people were educated, their virtue (daode) and intelligence (zhihun) would be restored.[112] It was also assumed that the people themselves possessed a similar confidence in education. Thus it was proposed that the authorities publicly display the amount of taxes needed for specific purposes. Once the people knew that a certain sum was destined for education, they would willingly pay taxes.[113]

Luo Zhenyu, in one of the few specific discussions of rural education at this time, argued in 1906 that although people in the countryside were as 'stupid as deers and pigs', rural society was not yet polluted by the evils of modern urban life and that it would therefore be easier to carry out extensive moral education by taking advantage of the 'unsophisticated, natural and uninhibited nature' of rural inhabitants. The results would be law-abiding and harmonious communities.[114]

Student revolutionaries also referred to the people in ambivalent terms. In 1904 Chen Tianhua warned his compatriots that the Chinese people, like the Africans, had become the targets of western scorn. As with Zhang Yuanji, he painted a sombre picture:
> The upper, middle and lower levels of society no longer have any conscience and they have no sense of shame or sincerity. They are not in any way enlightened and they do not have the slightest knowledge. They have a stubborn attachment to outmoded ideas and resolutely adhere to corrupt customs, believing in ghosts and demons. The men smoke opium and the women have bound feet. Vagrant bands gather everywhere and thieves and brigands spread across the land. Places of residence are like livestock pens and behaviour is like that of savages. Words have no sincerity and people love money as if it was their life.[115]

Yet at the same time Chen declared that China had nothing to fear from foreign aggressors. Anticipating Mao Zedong's 'paper tiger' thesis of 1946,[116] Chen argued that, with 400 million people ready to die, China did not need to stand in awe of any foreign power, no matter how advanced its military technology was.[117]

Such ambivalence is prevalent in all revolutionary student publications. A 1903 article in *Hubei Student World*, for example, contrasted the backwardness of China's lower classes (described as 'brutes and animals') with the more far-sighted and civilised' peoples of the West, and asserted that it was up to the students to perform the tasks necessary to build China into a prosperous and strong nation because they were the only group with patriotic commitment.[118] Yet later, in the same article, the writer observed that the lower levels of society were the 'masters' (*zhuren*) of a country and that *only* when students had inculcated in them a 'spirit of independent self sufficiency' would China become vigorous enough to compete in the international arena.

A pervading sense of optimism, nevertheless, characterised all writings on education, whether by moderates or radicals.[119] For student radicals a widespread system of schools would eliminate the differences between 'aristocrat and commoner, rich and poor'. With education, a student wrote, 'the people's strength will expand and will extend the country's authority abroad' by achieving three aims: forming 'complete individuals', who would be both patriotic and economically productive; consolidating national unity and creating a 'great collectivity' (*da tuanti*); and equipping people with the means to 'struggle with the outside world'.[120]

Another article in the *Hubei Student World* predicted grandiose results from widespread education. Everyone would become 'independent in spirit, naturally inclined to become part of the collectivity, self-autonomous, capable of striving for progress, and sufficiently spirited to resist foreign aggression'.[121] Individual autonomy and the desire to become part of a larger collectivity were often juxtaposed by educators and writers in this period. Abandoning egoistic interests and particularistic loyalties (such as to the family or clan) was considered an act of individual self-assertion, an important theme in the later May Fourth Movement.

Furthermore, although reformers and revolutionaries expressed disparaging views of the people, there were also many statements praising the innate capabilities of the people.[122] One radical journal described the Chinese people as 'naturally diligent and hard-working, patient and intelligent'. It had merely been the lack of education that had prevented the people from gaining the expertise with which to compete economically in the world.[123] Another journal even pointed out that the poor in China had much to teach those who were not. They were patient, had stamina and were naturally intelligent, a result of their constant struggle to survive. Unlike those with money, who never took any risks, the article continued, the poor had a 'spirit of adventure'(*maoxianxing*), as well as the hopes and aspirations necessary for an entrepreneurial outlook. All they lacked was the means, which education would provide them.[124]

This ambivalent voluntarism is perhaps nowhere better illustrated than in a series of articles on poor people's education by a Shanghai primary school teacher, Li Yanhan, which appeared in *The Educational Review* between 1909 and 1911.[125] The general tone of his articles was one of condescension and Li, as a member of the educated class, referred to poor people almost as if they were a different race. Nevertheless, in his advocacy of schools for poor people, Li evinced the extraordinary faith in education so typical of his time.

Beginning by criticising the emphasis on quality (*jingmei*), defined as 'elitist education', at the expense of widespread availability (*puji*) of education, Li argued that with a wide network of schools for the poor, they would rapidly be able to join the ranks of farmers, workers, merchants and soldiers. Education for the poor, however, was not simply to train them for menial and lowly jobs, neither was it to inculcate in them attitudes of subservience. Li underlined the fact that sages and heroes in the past had often come from the lower classes and therefore proved that poor people could benefit just as much from education as the more well-off. Although schools for the poor should have shorter courses and larger classes (with no age limits), Li saw no reason why graduates from these schools should not transfer to regular higher primary schools.

For Li, poor people's schools would instil in their students a sense of independence and autonomy. His vision of what graduates might do afterwards was rather novel. One suggestion was that after having studied arithmetic, commercial subjects, and foreign languages, they should form 'trading groups' (*fufantuan*) that could go abroad to investigate market conditions and consumer tastes. In this way, they would contribute to the improvement of China's trading position by recommending which were the most appropriate goods for China to export. (Li even suggested that such trading groups could 'spy' for the Chinese government and investigate the situation of foreign countries in general.) Li foresaw that ultimately these trading groups would form wholesale companies with original members becoming stockholders.

In discussing the organisation and administration of poor people's schools, Li demonstrated a rare sensitivity to the feelings and situation of poor students. He warned that a danger existed of their innate feelings of inferiority being confirmed by the arrogant attitudes of their teachers. In an intriguing anticipation of the Maoist approach, Li suggested that teachers conduct 'self criticism' at regular intervals in order to lessen the gulf between teacher and pupil. Li also stressed the importance of professional management of such schools. As complete professionals teachers should not be overly strict in discipline but rather should be flexible in their approach and not bombard the students with complex and detailed rules and regulations (including the wearing of uniforms). Self-esteem and self-pride had to be fostered and the choice of educational 'models' was to focus on those who had successfully emerged from obscurity and poverty. Li was keen to emphasise that agriculture, industry and commerce could all produce 'heroes' in their own right and did not necessarily have to emerge from the ranks of scholarship or officialdom.

Li was also one of a number of educators at this time who saw poverty as an advantage. Children from such a background, in Li's view, were accustomed to the habits of 'arduous struggle' (*qinku*) and would therefore form a hardy citizenry in the future. He advised teachers to inculcate in their students a pride in their background. It was the idle rich, he suggested, who should feel ashamed. To emphasise his point, Li proposed that teachers should participate in manual or menial tasks at school.

Li's attitude to girl students, however, was decidedly more ambiguous. Although he advocated schools for poor girls his proposed curriculum was generally conservative (moral training, household management, social etiquette, but also arithmetic and physical education), and he criticised 'modern' attitudes which resulted in girls thinking above their station. They did not need to know, he argued, about current international and national politics in the same way boys did. Yet he did suggest that girls be taught the skills necessary for them to become secretaries, bookkeepers and accountants as well as to train them in artistic or design work. Thus, Li concluded, in addition to being 'virtuous mothers and good wives' girls from poor people's schools would become independent and 'talented, useful members of society' (*shehui banshi zhi rencai*). The contrast with Governor-General Zhang Zhidong's more hostile attitude towards education for girls (see Chapter One) is revealing.

For the most part, therefore, moderates and radicals exhibited boundless confidence in the power of education to bring about positive change and transform the people into a patriotic and economically productive citizenry.[126] The debate over popular education during the last years of the Qing also brought in its wake two significant developments.

Firstly, whereas traditionally education had been perceived as an unchanging and fixed process to inculcate Confucian morality, both Liang Qichao and student radicals often referred to education as a 'tool' (*zhu*) or 'instrument' (*qixie*), by means of which a modern citizenry would be forged. Liang argued that each civilisation or society had its own particular educational aims in accordance with its own needs *at a particular time*.[127] It was this pragmatic view of education, in addition to the widespread view that China's survival in a hostile and competitive world depended on the quality of its people, that prompted increasing numbers of educators and writers to highlight the importance of popular education.

Not everyone, of course, subscribed to this solution. Wang Guowei (1877-1927), a colleague of Luo Zhenyu and joint editor of *Educational World*, vociferously opposed the immediate creation of an extensive network of primary schools.[128] In 1906 he condemned what he called 'levelling-ism' (*pinfang zhuyi*) and advocated 'elitism' (*guizu zhuyi*) instead:

> What I call elitism is not political elitism, but intellectual elitism... Today we should selectively examine all middle school students and assemble the brightest... afterwards they should be given specialist training on an intensive two-year preparatory course. I am confident that the results will certainly be superior when compared with those obtained by the foreign system of proceeding through a hierarchical

and structured system of primary and middle schools.¹²⁹ For Wang, priority had to be given to higher education. The only concession he made towards popular education was his suggestion that the lower classes be taught religion so as to offer them hope for a better life after death.¹³⁰

It was Lu Feigui, however, who clearly represented the majority opinion when he argued in 1909 that widespread availability of education took precedence over its quality. It was no coincidence that Lu regarded the newly established literacy schools (see Chapter Three) as the most important educational innovation currently being implemented.¹³¹

Secondly, discussions of popular education drew on new ways of analysing society, which was now seen as a complex entity comprising different 'classes' (*jieji*) or levels' (*liu*) that might potentially come into conflict. Such a view was influenced by the increasing awareness of what was called 'the labour problem' in the West. Relying principally on Japanese sources, Chinese intellectuals wrote of the growing tensions and conflicts between rich and poor, capitalist and labourer in western societies. Such conflicts had led to industrial unrest, class division, the formation of militant trade unions, and the emergence of socialism. References to socialism appeared in Liang Qichao's journals after 1899, while in 1906 Zhu Zhixin, a student radical in Japan, translated parts of the Communist Manifesto.¹³²

Chinese educators, when looking at their own society, now became more sensitive to its complexity. In general, when they talked of different classes or levels they defined them in terms of rich and poor, or educated and uneducated. For example, a 1904 article in *Zhongguo baihua bao* differentiated the 'upper levels' (*shangliu*) of society, which comprised officials, gentry, capitalists (*zuo cai zhu*), and those who studied, from the 'lower levels' (*xialiu*), which comprised peasants, artisans, merchants and soldiers.¹³³ Popular education was seen as a panacea that would help cement social unity by breaking down these differences. More significant than this, however, was that at a time when a more thorough Chinese knowledge of Marxism and the strictly Marxian definition of class had to await the aftermath of the May Fourth Movement,¹³⁴ some Chinese writers were beginning to focus on the difference between those who produced wealth and those who consumed it as the most important characteristic of society. With increasing prestige accorded to productive labour, education could no longer be viewed as the prerogative of the well-to-do literary elite, neither could it be identified solely as the inculcation of an unchanged Confucian morality. Priority had to be given to educating the whole people, as well as to reshaping the content of education so that the people would become both public minded and economically productive.

The parameters of the debate over popular education had therefore been set by the time the Qing dynasty was overthrown in 1911. The debate was not ended, however, and was to continue during the early years of the Republic and even beyond 1949.

NOTES
1. Shangxin ren (pseud.), 'Lun yimin yu luanmin zhi yi' (A discussion of the difference between a righteous people and a disorderly people), *Qingyi bao* (Pure Discussion Journal), no. 52 (26 July 1900), pp. 3361-6. For information on *Qingyi bao*, which was published in Yokohama between 1899 and 1901, see *Xinhai geming shiqi qikan jieshao* (Beijing, 1982), 1: 1-30.
2. Leo Ou-fan Lee, A. Nathan, 'The Beginnings of Mass Culture: Journalism and Fiction in the Late Ch'ing and Beyond', pp. 362-3.
3. *Ibid.*, pp. 371-2.
4. J.-P. Drège, *La Commercial Press de Shanghai 1879-1949* (Paris, 1978); Zhuang Yu, 'Sanshiwu nian lai zhi Shangwu Yinshuguan' (The Commercial Press during the last thirty-five years) in Zhuang Yu (ed.), *Zuijin sanshinian zhi Zhongguo jiaoyu* (Shanghai, 1931), pp. 1-62.
5. R. Britton, *The Chinese Periodical Press* (Taibei, 1968), p. 110; J.-P. Drège, *La Commercial Press de Shanghai 1879-1949*, p. 24.
6. On the emergence of public opinion and its interaction with foreign policy, see A. Iriye, 'Public Opinion and Foreign Policy', in A. Feuerwerker *et al.* (eds.), *Approaches to Modern Chinese History* (Berkeley, 1967), pp. 216-38. On the anti-American boycott, see M. Hunt, *The Making of a Special Relationship: The United States and China to 1914* (New York, 1983), pp. 234-9. On the anti-Japanese boycott, see E. Rhoads, *China's Republican Revolution: The Case of Kwangtung 1895-1913* (Cambridge, Mass., 1975), pp. 136-9.
7. W. Chan, *Merchants, Mandarins, and Modern Enterprise in Late Ch'ing China*, pp. 129-45; Li Zongyi, 'The Bourgeois Revolutionaries in the Movement to Regain Economic Rights towards the end of the Qing dynasty', in Etō Shinkichi, H. Schiffrin (eds.), *The 1911 Revolution in China* (Tokyo, 1984), pp. 154-7.
8. For a stimulating discussion of the theory and practice of local self-government from the last years of the dynasty to the 1920s, see P. Kuhn, 'Local Self-Government Under the Republic', in F. Wakeman, C. Grant, (eds.), *Conflict and Control in Late Imperial China* (Berkeley, 1975), pp. 257-98. The concept of *zizhi* had been introduced by Huang Zunxian (1848-1905) in the 1890s. Influenced by the example of Japan, where a local self-government code had been promulgated in 1888, Huang stressed the importance of local activism as the foundation of a strong and unified state. Kang Youwei, in 1902, advocated *zizhi* as the means whereby elites could be mobilised to contribute to national economic development.
9. M. Bastid, *Aspects de la Réforme de l'Enseignement*, p. 70; J. Fincher, *Chinese Democracy*, p. 103.
10. Voters for the provincial assemblies were limited to males over twenty-five years of age who possessed one of the following qualifications: (1) Three years teaching experience; (2) Chinese or

foreign middle school education; (3) Holder of a traditional civil service degree; (4) Owner of capital or property valued at 5 000 Chinese dollars. Although provincial assemblies were empowered only to discuss and fix provincial budgets, and supervise local self-government societies, they insisted on discussing such matters as foreign policy and were particularly critical of the use of foreign loans for railroad development. Their pressure on the court in 1910 to convene a national parliament before the prescribed date of 1917 resulted in the Qing government promising to establish a parliament in 1913. J. Fincher, *Chinese Democracy*, pp. 100, 109, 133, 149, 170.

11. For information on *Jiaoyu shijie*, see *Xinhai geming shiqi qikan jieshao*, 1: 114-40. The journal ran until 1908. For a list of translations from the Japanese on education that appeared in *Jiaoyu shijie*, see Sanetō Keishū, *Chūgokujin Nihon Ryūgaku Shi* (Tokyo, 1960), pp. 257-8. Between 1901 and 1904, out of 48 works on education that were translated into Chinese, 39 were from the Japanese. *Ibid.*, p. 238.
12. M. Bastid, *Aspects de la Réforme de l'Enseignement*, pp. 116-26.
13. *Jiaoyu shijie*, no. 1 (May 1901) noted the division of the Mombushō into bureaux responsible for specialist and general education. Popular education (*tongsu jiaoyu*) came under the jurisdiction of the bureau for general education.
14. For information on Luo Zhenyu, see H. Boorman, R. Howard (eds.), *A Biographical Dictionary of Republican China*, 2: 426-7; Hashikawa Tokio, *Chūgoku Bunka Kai Jimbutsu Sōkan*, pp. 785-6; M. Bastid, *Aspects de la Réforme de l'Enseignement*, pp. 52-4. After the 1911 Revolution, Luo settled in Japan devoting himself to archaeological research. He remained a supporter of the deposed last Emperor, Puyi, and in 1932, he became associated with the Japanese puppet state of Manchukuo which had Puyi as its figurehead ruler. For this reason Luo has remained a *persona non grata* for the CCP and the Guomindang. Ironically, however, Puyi seems to have had little regard for Luo and maintained that much of his scholarship was a sham. Aisin-Gioro Puyi, *From Emperor to Citizen* (Beijing, 1964), 1: 174.
15. *Minguo renwu zhuan*, 3: 230-6.
16. Most of the primary- and middle-school texts after 1906 were privately published, mainly by the Commercial Press. By 1910 the Commercial Press had produced 300 titles. J.-P. Drège, *La Commercial Press de Shanghai 1879-1949*, pp. 17-19; Li Zezhang, 'Sanshiwu nian lai Zhongguo zhi chubanye' (Chinese publishing in the last thirty-five years), in Zhuang Yu (ed.), *Zuijin sanshinian zhi Zhongguo jiaoyu*, pp. 259-78.
17. Hashikawa Tokio, *Chūgoku Bunka Jimbutsu Sōkan*, pp. 707-8. Like Lu Feigui, Jiang was to develop an interest in Buddhism towards the end of his life, writing a history of Chinese Buddhism in 1929.
18. Wang Yunwu, *Gexin shidai jiaoxue sixiang* (Taibei, 1971), pp. 42-5.
19. H. Boorman, R. Howard (eds.), *A Biographical Dictionary of Republican China*, 1: 138-140; J.-P. Drège, *La Commercial Press de Shanghai*

1879-1949, p. 241; J. Grieder, *Intellectuals and the State in Modern China*, p. 155. Zhang sponsored the large-scale reprinting of rare books in the 1920s and 1930s, in particular the dynastic histories. After Liberation in 1949 Zhang continued to be active, being appointed a member of the East China Administrative Commission in 1953. He was elected as deputy to the National People's Congress in 1954 and 1958.

20. Li Yu-ning, *The Introduction of Socialism into China* (New York, 1971), pp. 7-12. For a general discussion of the debate between reformers and revolutionaries over the merits of socialism, see M. Bernal, *Chinese Socialism to 1907* (Ithaca, 1976).

21. For Liang's intellectual thought, see Hao Chang, *Liang Ch'i-ch'ao and Intellectual Transition in China 1890-1907* (Cambridge, Mass., 1971); P. Huang, *Liang Ch'i-ch'ao and Modern Chinese Liberalism* (Seattle, 1972). For information on *Xinmin congbao*, see *Xinhai geming shiqi qikan jeshao*, 1: 141-88.

22. On Chinese students in Japan, see R. Scalapino, 'Prelude to Marxism: The Chinese Student Movement in Japan 1900-1910', in A. Feuerwerker *et al*. (eds.), *Approaches to Modern Chinese History*, pp. 190-215; M. Jansen, 'The Japanese and the Chinese Revolution of 1911', in J. Fairbank, Kwang-ching Liu (eds.), *The Cambridge History of China*, vol. 11 (Cambridge, Mass., 1980), pp. 348-53; Liu Wangling, '1896-1906 nianjian Zhongguo liuri xuesheng' (Chinese Students in Japan between 1896 and 1906) in *Xinhai geming lunwenji* (Guangzhou, 1980), pp. 333-44; Huang Fuqing, *Qingmo liuri xuesheng* (Taibei, 1975); Sanetō Keishū *Chūgokujin Nihon Ryū gaku Shi* (Tokyo, 1960).

23. For an analysis of the intellectual debate between Chinese reformers and revolutionaries in Japan, see M. Gasster, *Chinese Intellectuals and the 1911 Revolution* (Seattle, 1969).

24. *Xinhai gming shiqi qikan jieshao*, 1: 239-58, 269-89, 329-45. Zhang Nan, Wang Renjie (comp.), *Xinhai geming qian shinianjian shibian xuanji* (Hong Kong, 1962), 1.1: 966-8.

25. *Jiaoyu shijie*, no. 33 (1902), pp. 1-33.

26. Entrepreneurs and educational reformers like Zhang Jian were increasingly to refer to this concept in their reform proposals. M. Bastid, *Aspects de la Réforme de l'Enseignement*, pp. 85, 173. M. Bastid notes that before 1907 Zhang Jian thought of the population as mere 'subjects' linked to the ruler or authority. Thus he referred to the people as *xia* (inferiors) in relation to *shang* (superiors), or *min* (people) in relation to *guan* (officials). After 1907 Zhang specifically referred to 'society' as an independent entity, having its own demands and requirements with which the state had to comply.

27. The following information is taken from J. Crump, *The Origins of Socialist Thought in Japan* (London, 1983), pp. 7, 8-9, 18, 21, 22.

28. Of whom 301 435 were women.

29. M. Bastid, *L'Evolution de la société Chinoise à la fin de la dynastie des Qing 1873-1911* (Paris, 1979), pp. 59, 62. See also Zhao Qin, 'Xinhai geming qianhou de Zhongguo gongren yundong' (The

workers' movement in China before and after the 1911 Revolution), *Lishi yanjiu*, no. 2 (1959), pp. 1-16.
30. M. Bastid, *L'Evolution de la société Chinoise*, pp. 19-43.
31. The anarchy and disorder of the French Revolution were specifically mentioned as a warning of what might happen if one group was set against another, thus destroying the finely-balanced equilibrium that held any society together.
32. Luo Zhenyu, 'Jiaoyu siyi' (Personal proposals on education), *Jiaoyu shijie*, no. 1 (1901). See also Jiang Jianbai, *Zhongguo shehui jiaoyu xingzheng*, pp. 3-4.
33. Copies of *Xinmin congbao*, like those of the radical student journals, reached audiences in China. They were often smuggled in by returning students from Japan who took up teaching positions in modern schools. One contemporary recalls that *Xinmin congbao* reached his family village 400 li from Hangzhou and that it was also read in Chengdu and Chongqing. Leo Ou-fan Lee, A. Nathan, 'The Beginnings of Mass Culture: Journalism and Fiction in the Late Ch'ing and Beyond', p. 370. The authors estimate that the journal had a circulation of 14 000 by 1906 (p. 365).
34. See Liang's 1902 proposals on educational policy in Shu Xincheng (ed.), *Ziliao*, 3: 947-54.
35. 'Jiaoyu mudi lun' (A Discussion of the Purposes of Education), *Xinmin congbao*, 13: 67 (1904), pp. 1-19.
36 The article remarked that China was weak precisely because the 'middle classes' had not assumed their responsibilities in promoting unity.
37. 'Minzu zhiyi zhi jiaoyu' (Nationalist Education), *Youxue yibian*, no.10 (1903), pp. 1-9.
38. Yang Dusheng, 'Xin Hunan' (The New Hunan), in Zhang Nan, Wang Renzhi (comp.), *Xinhai geming qian shinianjian shibian xuanji*, 1.2: 615.
39. Cited in Chen Jingpan, *Zhongguo jindai jiaoyushi*, p. 214. Both Liang Qichao and Chen Tianhua argued that Chinese revolutions in the past had failed because they had not been under middle-class leadership.
40. Such a prospect alarmed moderate educators. A 1911 article in *Jiaoyu zazhi* argued that such a threat to social order could only be averted if the middle levels of society (in particular school graduates) were given the job opportunities so that they could play their appropriate harmonising role in society. JYZZ, 3: 6 (1911), *yanlun*, pp. 62-8. The contributor no doubt had in mind the participation of frustrated scholars (unable to pass the civil service examinations or to gain official posts) in previous rebellions. The fear was frequently expressed in the early twentieth century that a surplus of modern school graduates with no job opportunities was a fertile recruiting ground for rebellion.
41. Shu Xincheng, *Jiaoyu tonglun* (Shanghai, 1927), pp. 180-1.
42. *Geming wenxian* (Taibei, 1953), 3: 275-6.
43. Liang Qichao's articles, under the general heading of 'Xinmin shuo'

(The Theory of a New People) are in XMCB (1902-4), and *Yinbing shi quanji* (Tainan, 1986), pp. 1-100. Excerpts are reprinted in Zhang Nan, Wang Renzhi (comp.), *Xinhai geming qian shinianjian shibian xuanji*, 1.1: 118-51. For analyses in English, see P. Huang, *Liang Ch'i-ch'ao and Modern Chinese Liberalism*, pp. 58-65; Hao Chang, *Liang Ch'i-Ch'ao and Intellectual Transition in China 1890-1907*, pp. 151-7.
44. JZRB, no. 42 (1904). *Jingzhong ribao*, edited by Cai Yuanpei, was the successor to *Eshi jingwen* (Warnings About Russia), which had been founded by radicals in 1903 as a forum for criticism of Russian policy in Manchuria. W. Duiker, *Ts'ai Yuan-p'ei* (Penn., 1977), p. 12. Cai Yuanpei (1868-1940), a metropolitan degree holder, was later to support Sun Yatsen's anti-Manchu revolutionary movement. He studied in Germany during the last years of the dynasty and was to become the first education minister under the Republic. See Chapter Four.
45. For Jiang Weiqiao's recollections of the Chinese Education Association, see *Xinhai geming* (Shanghai, 1957), 1: 485-96. See also *Xinhai geming huiyi lu* (Beijing, 1961-3), 4: 63-77. For information in English, see M. Rankin, *Early Chinese Revolutionaries* (Cambridge, Mass., 1971), pp. 50-69. The Association also established the Patriotic School (*aiguo xueshe*) to cater for the more than one hundred students who had withdrawn from the Nanyang Public School in Shanghai in protest against the expulsion of two students. Both Cai and Jiang taught at the school, while one of the pupils was Huang Yanpei, later to become a prominent educator in the last years of the dynasty and early years of the Republic. The protest at Nanyang represented one of the first examples of unrest in the modern schools, later characterized as the "student tide" (*xuesheng chao*). See Chapter Four.
46. *Xinhai geming shiqi qikan jieshao* 1: 431-40.
47. Chen Duxiu, 'E'su~bian' (A Discussion of Evil Customs), *Anhui suhua bao*, nos. 3, 4, 6, 7 (1904). See also *Xinhai geming shiqi qikan jieshao*, 2: 163-90; Lee Feigon, *Chen Duxiu* (Princeton, 1983), pp. 66-8
48. 'Majiang pai gaige yi'an' (Proposal to Reform Mahjong), JZRB, no. 14 (1904).
49. Liang Qichao, 'Jing'gao wo guomin' (A Warning to Our Citizens), XMCB, 5: 25 (1903), pp. 1-9.
50. XMCB, 10: 53 (1905), *zhuangjian*, pp. 1-2. This article, therefore, provides a precedent for the folklorist movement after 1919 when writers promoted the virtues of folk literature with its description of the natural and spontaneous attitudes and behaviour of the common people. Chang Tai-hung, *Going to the People: Chinese Intellectuals and Folk Literature 1918-1937* (Cambridge, Mass., 1985).
51. See Liang's article 'Lun xiaoshuo yu qunzhi zhi guanxi' (A Discussion of the Relationship between Fiction and Popular Rule), in *Xin xiaoshuo*, 1: 1 (1902), *lunshuo*, pp. 1-8. See also Leo Ou-fan Lee, A. Nathan, 'The Beginnings of Mass Culture: Journalism and Fiction

in the Late Ch'ing and Beyond' pp. 379-80; Shu-ying Tsau, 'The Rise of New Fiction' in M. Dolozelova-Velingerova (ed.), *The Chinese Novel at the Turn of the Century* (Toronto, 1980), pp. 18-37; M. Dolezelova-Velingerova, 'The Origins of Modern Chinese Literature' in M. Goldman (ed.), *Modern Chinese Literature in the May Fourth Era* (Cambridge, Mass., 1977), pp. 31-3; C. T. Hsia, 'Yen Fu and Liang Ch'i-ch'ao as Advocates of New Fiction' in A. Rickett (ed.), *Chinese Approaches to Literature from Confucius to Liang Ch'i-ch'ao* (Princeton, 1978), pp. 221-57.

52. Liang particularly condemned traditional novels such as *Dream of the Red Chamber* and *Water Margin*. Not all agreed with Liang's negative appraisal however. A 1907 article in *Yueyue xiaoshuo* (Monthly Fiction) argued that traditional novels *did* have a serious purpose and referred to *Dream of the Red Chamber* as a social and ethical love story. Shu-ying Tsau, 'The Rise of New Fiction', p. 30. In 1908 *Water Margin* was described as one of China's foremost political novels; another critic in the same year labelled it as a socialist and nihilist novel. C. T. Hsia, 'Yen Fu and Liang Ch'i-ch'ao as Advocates of New Fiction', pp. 246-7.

53. Chen Duxiu, 'Lun xiqu' (A Discussion of Drama), *Anhui suhua bao*, no. 11 (1904), *lunshuo*, pp. 1-6.

54. Jian Zhiyou, an associate of Liang Qichao, also attributed the military failure of the Boxers to the fighting techniques learned from stage warriors. For the views of Chen Duxiu and Jian Zhiyou, see Qian Xingcun (A Ying), comp. *Wanqing congchao; xiaoshuo yanjiu juan* (Beijing, 1960), pp. 50, 54. For an excellent discussion of the interaction of popular drama and the Boxers, see B. Doar, 'The Boxers and Chinese Drama: Questions of Interaction', *Papers on Far Eastern History*, no. 29 (March 1984), pp. 91-118. Doar concludes that although Guanyu (God of War) and other heroes were part of the Boxer pantheon, there was no direct relationship between Boxerism and the popular theatre because of the rapid spread of the movement. Improvised folk art forms such as the folk song and wall placard were used, however, in the propaganda arsenal of the Boxers. Doar's view differs from that of J. Esherick, *The Origins of the Boxer Uprising* (Berkeley, 1987), pp. 62-5, who argues that Boxer practices and ideology drew extensively from popular literature and opera.

55. See also JZRB, nos. 95, 96, 97 (1904) for a three-part article on the reform of drama. The article claimed that the reform of drama was the first step in the reform of society. Like other writers of the time, the author condemned traditional drama for 'propagating sex and violence'.

56. Ge Gongzhen, *Zhongguo baoxue shi* (Hong Kong, 1964), p. 76; Zeng Chubai, *Zhongguo xinwenshi* (Taibei, 1966), 1: 149. See also M. Dolezelova-Velingerova, 'The Origins of Modern Chinese Literature', pp. 19-20; P. Link, *Mandarin Ducks and Butterflies* (Berkeley, 1981), pp. 101-2.

57. Huang Zunxian, 'Riben guozhi wenxue shi' (A Record of Japan and

its Literature) in *Jindaishi ziliao* no. 2 (1963), pp. 114-6. This was to form a chapter in Huang's larger work on Japan published in 1898. Huang, in fact, pointed to Japan as a negative example of a country in which the written and spoken languages were separate, due to the country's use of the Chinese script. See also Tan Bi'an, *Wanqing de baihuawen yundong* (Wuhan, 1956), p. 5.

58. Chen Zibao, 'Suhua shuo' (Theory of Everyday Language), in *Chen Zibao xiansheng jiaoyu yiyi* (Guangzhou, 1952), pp. 17-9. Chen's school in Macao was one of the first Chinese schools to accept both boys and girls, in 1903. In 1918 he moved the school to Hong Kong. In 1898 Chen had visited Japan, where he was much attracted to the educational thought of Fukuzawa Yukichi.

59. Chen Zibao, 'Lun xunmeng yi xian jiezi' (In Teaching the Young it is Necessary First to Understand the Words), in *Chen Xibao xiansheng jiaoyu yiyi*, pp. 21-5.

60. One suggestion, increasingly popular towards the end of the Qing, was to use the Beijing dialect as the standard. See, for example, *Jinghua xinbao* (Beijing Speech Journal), no. 259 (1906).

61. See Qiu's 1898 article, 'Lun baihua wei weixin zhi ben' (The Vernacular is the Basis of Reform)l in *Jindaishi ziliao*, no. 2 (1963), pp. 120-3.

62. *Jindaishi ziliao*, no. 2 (1963), p. 112.

63. These included *Hangzhou baihua bao* (1901-4), *Suzhou baihua bao* (1901-2), *Yangzi jiang baihua bao* (1904-5), *Zhili baihua bao* (1905) and *Jilin baihua bao* (1907-8). For information on these journals, see *Xinhai geming shiqi qikan jieshao*, 2: 63-80, 81-7, 210-7, 210-19, 286-9, 548-62. 64.

64. *Xinhai geming shiqi qikan jieshao*, 1: 442.

65. Lu Feigui, 'Putong jiaoyu dang caiyong suben zhi' (General Education Should Adopt Everyday Words), *JYZZ*, 1: 1 (1909).

66. 'Quan ren shizi shuo' (On Urging People to be Literate), *Hangzhou baihua bao*, no. 2 (1901).

67. Luo Zhenyu, 'Jiaoyu wuyao' (Five Prerequisites of Education), *Jiaoyu shijie*, no. 9 (1902). Interestingly, Luo later urged that China should also emulate the powers and use education to extend her influence. He urged the Chinese government to promote education amongst Chinese communities in Thailand. With a well educated Chinese population there, Luo surmised, China's influence in Thailand would automatically increase. 'Lun Zhenxiang Xianluo zhi zhimin jiaoyu' (The Promotion of Chinese Education in Thailand), *Jiaoyu shijie*, no. 141 (1906).

68. See, for example, 'Jiaoyu lun' (A Discussion of Education), *Youxie yibian*, no. 1 (1902)

69. Yun Wo, 'Jiaoyu tonglun' (A General Discussion of Education), *Jiangsu*, no. 3 (1904).

70. Lin Cang, 'Tiexue zhuyi zhi jiaoyu' (Blood and Iron Education), *Zhejiang chao*, no. 10 (1904).

71. *Hubei xueshengjie*, 1: 1 (1904). See also *JYZZ*, 1: 9 (1909), *pinglun*, pp. 13-16, for a discussion of the affects of cultural imperialism and

how foreign educational influence could stunt the development of nationalism.
72. C. Beahan, 'Feminism and Nationalism in the Chinese Women's Press 1902 –1911' *Modern China*, 1: 4 (October 1975) pp. 379-416; R. Scalapino, G. Yu, *Modern China and its Revolutionary Process* (Berkeley, 1985), pp. 214-7.
73. C. Beahan, 'Feminism and Nationalism in the Chinese Women's Press 1902-1911', p. 387.
74. On Qiu Jin, see J. Spence, *The Gate of Heavenly Peace* (New York, 1981), pp. 50-60; M. Rankin, 'The Emergence of Women at the End of the Ch'ing: The Case of Ch'iu Chin' in M. Wolf, R. Witke (eds.), *Women in Chinese Society* (Stanford, 1975), pp. 39-66; C. Gipoulon, *Qiu Jin: Pierres de l'Oiseau Jingwei* (Paris, 1976). Qiu Jin's manifesto for the *Zhongguo nübao* is printed in *Geming wenxian* (Taibei, 1974), 66: 266-8. For a discussion of the journal, see *Xinhai geming shiqi qikan jieshao*, 2: 446-53.
75. 'Zhongguo nüzi zhi quantu' (The Future of Chinese Women), *Nüzi bao*, no. 4 (1903), printed in Li Youning, Zhang Yufa (comp.), *Jindai Zhongguo nüquan yundong shiliao* (Taibei, 1975), 1: 393-6. In Jiaxing, Zhejiang, a women's martial society was organised because it was felt that men were too 'debauched' to lead the struggle in saving the nation. R. Keith Schoppa, 'Politics and Society in Zhejiang 1907-1927' (Ann Arbor University Microfilm, 1974), pp. 16-7.
76. *Xinhai geming shiqi qikan jieshao*, 1: 461-73.
77. Zheng Guanying, 'Nüjiao' (On Women's Education), in *Zheng Guanying ji*, 1: 287-90.
78. C. Beahan, 'The Women's Movement and Nationalism in Late Ch'ing China', pp. 102-11. In 1902 Liang suggested that early marriages be prohibited since they damaged the couple and produced physically inferior children. *Ibid.*, pp. 122-3.
79. Zheng Guanying's opposition to footbinding (echoed by the student revolutionary Chen Tianhua in 1904) in 1894 also entailed a new aspect: the custom was causing China to be ridiculed by foreigners. As already noted, this sensitivity to foreign opinion underpinned much of the debate over the reform of popular culture.
80. Cited in Li Youning, Zhang Yufa (comp.), *Jindai Zhongguo nüquan yundong shiliao*, 1: 606-7.
81. See for example, a 1904 article in the radical student journal *Yunnan*, printed in Li Youning, Zhang Youfa (comp.), *Jindai Zhongguo nüquan yundong shiliao*, 1: 657-60.
82. 'Jiaoyu mudi lun' (On the Aims of Education), XMCB, 13: 67 (1904), *jiaoyu*, pp. 1-19. The low regard in which some Japanese educators and writers held of women's education (and, indeed, of women in general), which is evident in this article and many others that were translated into Chinese at this time, may have reinforced Chinese traditional stereotypes of women. It was frequently observed in Japanese writings that girls were naturally less daring and more subservient than boys. If girls were given too advanced an

education, it was argued, they might lose their submissive natures and this would be a danger to society. See JYZZ, 2: 12 (1910), *jiaoshou guanli*, pp. 147-52 for an article, translated from the Japanese, on the physical and mental differences between boys and girls. It made the usual assertion that boys were physically and mentally equipped to work in society whereas girls were suited to working in the home.
83. Li Youning, Zhang Yufa (comp.), *Jindai Zhongguo nüquan yundong shiliao*, 1: 645.
84. Liang Qichao, 'Junguomin bian' (On a Militant Citizenry), XMCB, 1: 1 (1902), *bingshi*, pp. 1-10. Interestingly, Liang's notion of a pacifist Chinese culture parallels that of the Jesuits in the eighteenth century, who had pointed to the lack of a martial tradition amongst the Chinese. One noted that China without doubt 'was the most pacific nation in the world and the least likely to have those outstanding qualities that made good soldiers'. *Mémoires Concernant l'Histoire, Les Sciences, Les Arts, Les Moeurs, Les Usages des Chinois* (Paris, 1771), 7: 3.
85. Bai Li, 'Junguomin zhi jiaoyu' (Education for a Militant Citizenry), XMCB, 4: 22 (1903), *junshi*, pp. 1-20. The author also implied that girls needed to be given a military training since he constantly referred to the *inspiring* example of Sparta, where both boys and girls received a military education. For the promotion of military virtues among the people and the campaign to elevate the status of the army, see E. Fung, *The Military Dimension of the Chinese Revolution*, pp. 88-99.
86. *Jiaoyui shijie* no. 77 (1904). This journal also introduced a host of other important western educators, including Locke, Rousseau, Pestalozzi and Hebart.
87. Luo Zhenyu, 'Gesheng she tizao zhuanxiso yi' (A Proposal that Each Province Establishes a Physical Training Centre), *Jiaoyu shijie*, no. 32 (1903), 1a-b. Another suggestion was that the army should carry out literacy training amongst the people. *Jiangning xuewu zazhi*, no. 5 , (1907), *xuandai*, pp. 1-5.
88. Bo Lin, 'Tiyu' (Physical Education), *Yunnan zazhi*, no. 1 (1906), pp. 43-50.
89. 'Ying'gelu suxun renzhong shi jiaoyu bing Zhongguo jinri jiaoyu zhi fangzhen' (Anglo-Saxon Education and the Direction of China's Current Education), *Zhejiang chao*, no. 1 (1904), pp. 1-7.
90. Jiang Weiqiao, 'Lun xuetang qingshi tiyu zhi fei' (On the Error of Schools to Belittle Physical Education) JYZZ, 1: 6 (1909), pp. 76-8. On the introduction of games into the school curriculum during the last years of the Qing, see S. Borthwick, *Education and social Change in China*, pp. 138-9.
91. Mao's 1917 article, 'A Study of Physical Education', has been translated and introduced by S. Schram, *Une Etude de l'Education Physique* (Paris, 1962). An annotated translation also appears in M. Henri Day, *Mao Zedong 1917-1927: Documents* (Stockholm, 1975), pp. 21-38.

92. Chong You, 'Lun Zhongguo minqi zhi keyong' (China's Martial Spirit Can Be Utilized), DFZZ, 1: 1 (1904), *sheshuo*, pp. 1-7. The term that I have translated here as 'martial spirit' (*minqi*) can also be translated as 'people's spirit' or 'people's energy'. An article in Liang Qichao's *Qingyi bao* described the Boxers as the 'representatives of the Chinese people's *minqi* and the pioneers in expelling the foreigner' (Zhang Nan, Wang Renzhi, comp., *Xinhai geming qian shinianjian,shibian xuanji*, 1.1: 62), while the Board of Education, reporting on the increasing number of non-official schools in 1908, declared that this was proof 'the people's *minqi* was expanding' (JYZZ, 3: 3, *jishi*, pp. 21-2). Other articles referred to the *minqi* being suppressed by the old education and that it needed to be 'released' by a new system that would stress practical and creative studies. DFZZ, 2: 8 (1905), *sheshuo*, pp. 154-6. It is therefore misleading simply to define *minqi* as 'anti-foreign sentiments of the Chinese people'. See J. Ch'en, *Yuan Shih-k'ai* (Stanford, 1972), p. 204.
93. A contributor to Chen Duxiu's journal also noted in 1904 that the province of Anhui had a 'heroic military culture', demonstrated by the courage of its troops in helping Li Hongzhang suppress the Taipings. *Anhui suhua bao* no. 14 (1904), *lunshuo*, pp. 1-2. J. Esherick, in his recent study of the Boxers, has also drawn attention to the fact that popular culture in western Shandong had long stressed martial values and that martial arts teachers were a common sight in the region. *The Origins of the Boxer Uprising*, pp. 38-9, 45-6.
94. A. Woodside, 'Some mid-Qing Theorists of Popular Schools', pp. 27-8.
95. Kang Youwei, 'Gongmin zizhi bian' (On Citizen Self Government), XMCB, 2: 7 (1902), *zhengzhi*, pp. 1-12.
96. JYZZ, 1: 1 (1909).
97. JYZZ, 1: 4 (1909), *zazuan*, pp. 25-36.
98. JYZZ, 1: 4 (1909), *sheshuo*, pp. 41-8.
99. D. Nasaw, *Schooled to Order* (New York, 1979), pp. 87-95. See also S. Troen, 'The Discovery of the Adolescent by American Educational Reformers 1900-1920: An Economic Perspective' in L. Stone (ed.), *Schooling and Society* (Baltimore, 1976).
100. See, for example, DFZZ, 1: 9 (1904), *jiaoyu*, p. 198; JYZZ, 2: 6 (1910), *sheshuo*, pp. 69-72. Popular education, in fact, was often described in terms of changing the people's 'lazy nature' into a 'diligent' one.
101. DFZZ, 2: 5 (1905) *shiye*, pp. 45-7.
102. DFZZ, 4: 12 (1908), *jiaoyu*, p. 105.
103. See Chen's articles, 'Lun Zhongguo ren wu zili zhi xingzhi' (Chinese People Have no Sense of Independence) and 'Zhengsheng guren lun' (The Need to Strive to do Better Than One's Predecessors) in *Jiaoyu yiyi*, pp. 25-6, 34-6. Such an argument even extended to school fees. One writer noted that school subsidies and free tuition only encouraged people's sense of dependence. XMCB,

5: 30 (1903), *jiaoyu shiping*, pp. 1-2. See also 'Lun Zhongguo renmin yilaixing zhi qiyuan' (The Origins of the Chinese People's Sense of Dependence), JZRB, no. 109, (June 1904).
104. *Jiaoyui shijie*, nos. 46, 47, 48, 49, 50 (1902-3). *Self Help* had been translated into Japanese by Nakamura Keiu in 1871. With its stress on hard work, diligence, frugality and perseverance and its underlying theme that national progress was brought about by the individual industry and energy of the people, Smiles' work proved enormously popular in Meji Japan. See E. Kinmonth, *The Self-Made Man in Meiji Japanese Thought* (Berkeley, 1981).
105. JYZZ, 1: 2 (1909), *zazuan*, pp. 11-12.
106. DFZZ, 1:18 (1904), *sheshuo*, pp. 175-7.
107. DFZZ, 1: 6, (1904), *sheshuo*, pp. 115-120. Although the writer did not specify who the 'productive' group was, the implication was that it included peasants, workers, and traders.
108. This article is reprinted in *Laodong*, no. 1 (March 1918), pp. 25-8. Unfortunately, although the article is dated 1910, there is no reference to the original publication. Since it is similar in approach to the previous article cited in DFZZ, it is likely that the article was published in a reformist journal. It is significant that when a revolutionary like Zhang Binglin analysed classes in Chinese society he defined them in terms of their *moral* qualities rather than their economic capabilities. See 'Geming zhi daode' (Revolutionary Morality), in Zhang Nan, Wang Renzhi (comp.), *Xinhai geming qian shinianjian shibian xuanji*, 2.1: 509-20.
109. See, for example, XMCB, 11: 59 (1904), *jiaoyu*, p. 6.
110. Cited in *Xinhai geming shiqi qikan jieshao*, 1: 116.
111. Liang Qichao, perhaps more than anyone else at the time, stressed the relationship between democracy (*minquan*) and education. 'In the past,' he declared, 'when rulers wanted to suppress the people's rights, they were forced to block the people's knowledge as the first priority. Now, if they want to promote people's rights, they have to expand the people's knowledge.' Cited in Chen Jingpan, *Zhongguo jindai jiaoyushi*, p. 137.
112. DFZZ, 2: 17 (1905), *sheshuo*, pp. 138-141.
113. DFZZ, 1: 4 (1904) *jiaoyu*, p. 77.
114. Luo Zhenyu, 'Lun cuntian jiaoyu' (On Village Education), *Jiaoyu shijie*, no. 133 (1906), *lunshuo*, pp. 1-6. A contributor to *Jiaoyu zazhi* in 1909 took issue with the image of an uncorrupted rural environment congenial for education by arguing that students would be more liable to develop wasteful habits in the countryside. In the cities, on the other hand, they would be more disciplined. Besides, the writer concluded, the countryside was altogether a dirty, unsafe and uncivilised place. JYZZ, 1: 10 (1909), *sheshuo*, pp. 120-9. In 1922 the noted sociologist, Tao Menghe, was to agree with Luo's view of village life as one based on trust and co-operation. With the invasion of urban values, Tao noted sadly, the strong, healthy and virtuous peasant had become like the soft, lazy and weak city dweller. *Shehui yu jiaoyu* (Shanghai, 1922), pp. 170-1.

115. *Xinhai geming*, 2: 133, 155.
116. In 1946 Mao told the American journalist Anna Louise Strong that China had nothing to fear from the US nuclear threat since people were always in the end more important than weapons in determining the outcome of any war. *Selected Readings From The Works of Mao Tsetung* (Beijing, 1971), p. 349.
117. Sun Zhifen, 'Chen Tianhua di aiguo geming sixiang', in *Xinhai geming wushi zhounian jinian lunwenji* (Beijing, 1962), 2: 380. See also Saitō Akio, Najima Atsuyoshi, *Chūgoku Gendai Kyōikushi* (Tokyo, 1962), pp. 75-6.
118. Zhang Nan, Wang Renzhi (comp.), *Xinhai geming qian shinianjian shibian xuanji*, 1.1: 452. For information on the journal, see *Xinhai geming qikan jieshao*, 1: 239-58.
119. This optimism has led M. Rankin to refer to the radical students' 'voluntaristic' faith in education. See *Early Chinese Revolutionaries: Radical Intellectuals in Shanghai and Chekiang 1902-1911* (Cambridge, Mass., 1971), p. 37. Another historian sees the students' optimism as part of a common trend observable both in the West and Japan at this time which proclaimed faith in the 'possibilities and promise of the educated man'. R. Scalapino, 'Prelude to Marxism: The Chinese Student Movement in Japan 1900-1910' in A. Feuerwerker *et al.* (eds.) *Approaches to Modern Chinese History*, p. 204. Both Rankin and Scalapino tend to gloss over the profound ambivalence of student attitudes towards the lower classes, as well as to ignore the fact that this 'voluntarism' characterised *all* writings on education at this time, whether by political moderates or radicals. Scalapino's description of the faith in education as part of a contemporary world-wide trend also overlooks the indigenous, Confucian roots of such a faith.
120. *Hubei xueshengjie*, 1: 1 (1903), *jiaoyu*, pp. 1-3.
121. *Hubei xueshengjie*, 1: 2 (1903), p. 9. The article pointed to the heroic resistance of the Filipinos against the Americans to show what a 'spirited citizenry' could do.
122. It might be noted, however, that such confidence was often tinged with a virulent racism. In his journal *Qingyi bao* Liang Qichao, for example, wrote: 'Someday in the twentieth century we Chinese will be the most powerful race in the world... who will have the power in days to come to open up the world. The whites are arrogant and not up to hardship. The blacks and browns lazy and unintelligent. Therefore, except for us yellows, there is no race that could undertake such a task...' Cited in J. Pusey, *China and Charles Darwin*, p. 313.
123. *Hubei xueshengjie*, 1: 4 (1903), p. 5.
124. Zhang Nan, Wang Renzhi (comp.), *Xinhai geming qian shinianjian shibian xuanji*, 1.2: 918-21.
125. These series of articles, entitled 'Pinmin jiaoyu tan' (A Discussion of Poor People's Education) are in JYZZ, 1: 3, 4, 5, 6, 7, 8, 9 (1909); 2: 1, 3 (1910); 3: 1, 8, 9, 10 (1911); 3: 11, 12 (1912). They are reprinted in Li Yanhan, *Pinmin jiaoyu tan* (Shanghai, 1911), and

Jiaoyu conggao (Shanghai, 1921), pp. 1-136.
126. Some revolutionaries, like Zhang Binglin, saw no need for education and argued that only revolution could increase the people's knowledge. Chen Jingpan, Zhongguo jindai jiaoyushi, p. 207.
127. Liang Qichao, 'Lun jiaoyu dang ding zongzhi' (Education Should Set Itself a Guiding Aim), XMCB, 1: 1 (1902), pp. 1-8. Liang pointed to the different educational aims and processes of ancient Athens and Sparta as an example.
128. For a recent study of Wang Guowei, see J. Bonner, *Wang Kuo-wei: An Intellectual Biography* (Cambridge, Mass., 1986). Wang joined Luo Zhenyu's Agronomy Society in 1897 and studied in Japan in 1901-2. Like Luo Zhenyu he worked for the Board of Education in the department of general affairs until 1911. After 1911 he devoted his time to research on oracle bones and became a professor at Qinghua University in 1925. In 1927, on the eve of the Guomindang occupation of Beijing, he committed suicide.
129. *Jiaoyu shijie*, no. 117 (1906). Reprinted in Shu Xincheng (ed.), Ziliao, 3: 1011.
130. *Jiaoyu shijie*, no. 129 (1906), lunshuo, p. 105. For a discussion of Wang's educational thought, see J. Bonner, *Wang Kuo-wei*, pp. 31-44. Wang's elitism is underscored by the fact that he later condemned the vernacular movement and repudiated his earlier studies of the vernacular. As Bonner notes: 'Odious to him... no doubt, was Hu Shi's ambition to make the written world accessible to peasants as well as to intellectuals, at the heart of which lies the radical rejection of a fundamentally traditional value, namely the sharp distinction between ruler and ruled, between those who labour with their minds and those who labour with their hands.' (p. 218) Interestingly, Wang's elitism and sense of horror at the prospect of social egalitarianism was shared by Lu Xun in this period. W. Lyell, *Lu Xun's Vision of Reality* (Berkeley, 1976), pp. 91-4; Leo Ou-fan Lee, *Voices From The Iron House* (Bloomington, 1987), pp. 20-1.
131. Lu Feigui, 'Lun jianyi shizi yi xian dingwei yiwu jiaoyu' (Literacy must be the First Aim of Compulsory Education), JYZZ, 1: 5 (1909), sheshuo, pp. 63-7.
132. On this, see Li Yu-ning, *The Introduction of Socialism Into China* (New York 1971).
133. 'Lun hechun' (Unite the Collectivity), Zhongguo baihua bao, no. 16 (1904).
134. It was not until after 1919 that the major works of Marxism were translated into Chinese.

3. Popular Education Developments 1904–11

With the creation of the Board of Education in 1904 and the Qing court's appeal for an expansion in education, regulations flowed from Beijing on a wide range of measures that included lecture institutes, half-day schools, and literacy schools. These regulations in many cases sanctioned a process already begun, as reform-minded gentry and entrepreneurs enthusiastically devoted themselves to the task of educating the people.

Gentry initiative in promoting education and establishing schools can, in fact, be seen as part of a larger process described recently by historians of social change in late Qing China. As early as the late sixteenth century local elites were increasingly taking over previously state-supervised activities such as the establishment and administration of orphanages and hospitals. From the eighteenth century onwards this trend towards private philanthropy was accelerated, and throughout the Qing formal city government was often replaced by an expanding sphere of *ad hoc* public activities run by local elites. These included the organisation of emergency famine relief, the setting up of granaries and the establishment of traditional schools. By the early twentieth century, in a city like Shanghai, local elites were becoming increasingly involved in the running of municipal services.[1]

While it is clear that the court's primary motive in promoting education was the desire to cement loyalty to the dynasty, concern had also been expressed to benefit the people in more practical ways than had hitherto been the case. For the gentry, the expansion of education would guarantee an orderly and disciplined society, but accompanying this general aim was a vigorous attempt to provide facilities for literacy and vocational training. Previous studies of reform in the late Qing have tended to concentrate on the modern primary and secondary schools, most of which were concentrated in important urban areas and catered to a well-off minority amongst school-age children. The result has been an incomplete description of educational developments during the last years of the dynasty.

'PLANNING ONE'S LIVELIHOOD AND MANAGING THE FAMILY'

In addition to the Board of Education and the creation of a provincial directorship of education (*tixue*), a new educational administration was established at the local level in May 1906. Lest no-one forget the court's determination to ensure that the educational process remain under centralised control, the Board of Education later made it clear that educational administration at the provincial and district levels was to come under the direct jurisdiction of the Board rather than under the provincial governor.[2]

At the department (*zhou*) and district (*xian*) levels, education was to come under the jurisdiction of the Education Promotion Bureau (*quanxuesuo*).³ The director of the Bureau, appointed by the district inspector of education, was to select assistants (*quanxueyuan*) from among 'upright gentry' and assign them to supervise an educational district (*xuequan*) comprising 3–4 000 households.⁴ As noted earlier this was part of a wider attempt by the central government to co-opt the gentry in the running of public affairs, although ultimately the bureaucracy and the gentry were to diverge in their objectives concerning educational reform.⁵

The increasing emphasis on professionalism in education is evident in the duties that the gentry assistants were expected to perform. These included lecturing to the public, researching methods of educational administration, acquainting themselves with pedagogic theory, advertising the new schools, and encouraging school attendance.⁶ With regard to the last duty, the regulations insisted that only persuasion was to be used. Some gentry assistants may have been excessively enthusiastic, since a report from Zhili in 1907 reproached a number of assistants for imposing fines and ordering the arrest of recalcitrant parents who had not sent their children to school.⁷

The Education Promotion Bureau was also expected to establish lecture halls (*xuanjiangsuo*) and newspaper reading rooms. Lecture halls could be opened next to the Bureau, in Confucian temples, or even on the street and, ideally, lecturers were to be either normal school graduates or primary school teachers. Anyone could attend these lectures although, as the regulations for the Beijing Education Promotion Bureau noted, women for the time being were to be excluded in order to 'prevent abuses' (*biduan*). It was still considered contrary to the rules of propriety to have the sexes intermingling in a public place.⁸

The lecture halls were expected to encourage parents to send their children to school on the basis that there was no other way to advance in life now that the civil service examinations had been abolished. Interestingly, earlier appeals to self interest had at least been couched in patriotic terms, as the following 1903 verse designed to 'encourage study', illustrates:

> The black and red races are all subjugated,
> But we the yellow race have still not awoken to this.
> One must be quick in studying.
> The beautiful pear and peach blossoms
> Only have a limited time,
> And cannot put off for ever the ravages of time.
> When one is old, one can only have self-pity.
> Let us follow the model of Japan nearby,
> And that of Europe and America far away,,
> And join the ranks of the world's civilised countries.
> When we are young we should all energetically
> Be concerned with ourselves.
> Time will not come again.⁹

Now, school attendance was to be described bluntly as the best way to 'plan one's livelihood and manage the family' (*mousheng zhijia*).

In September 1906 the Board of Education issued a list of suitable lecture material deemed appropriate for popular education.[10] This included Zhang Zhidong's 1898 treatise 'Exhortation to Learning' (*quanxue bian*); a vernacular text on law and order; a work (translated from the Japanese) on European and American education; a translation of *Robinson Crusoe*, a biography of Nelson, and a work on the British colonisation of Australia, all of which stimulated an 'adventurous spirit' and encouraged the forsaking of a 'subservient and dependent outlook'; texts on agriculture and commerce; and, finally, a translation of *Uncle Tom's Cabin*, which, it was hoped, would arouse feelings of patriotism among the people by warning them that they might experience a similar fate as that which had befallen blacks in the United States.[11] Lectures, therefore, aimed at fostering a loyal, patriotic and law-abiding populace while also hoping to encourage individual initiative.[12] Furthermore, by underlining the benefits of education in terms of 'planning one's livelihood', lectures were also to appeal to people's self interest.[13] Such a trend was to persist in the early years of the Republic and led to a vigorous debate over the relative merits of individual profit on the one hand, and the collective interest on the other.

Statistics reveal that the establishment of local educational administration was very uneven. By 1907, for example, the metropolitan province of Zhili had opened the largest number of Education Promotion Bureaux (154), while Xinjiang had only opened one. They were located in a variety of places that included former academies and traditional schools, obsolete examination halls, Confucian temples and temples to the God of War (*Guandi*).[14] The number of gentry assistants employed in the Bureaux also varied considerably. Thus while the number of Bureaux in Shandong was less than that in Zhili, there were 1 299 gentry assistants employed in the former province compared to 713 in the latter.[15] Furthermore, the number of Education Promotion Bureaux did not necessarily correspond with the number of lecture halls, indicating that in some cases the promotion of public lectures was a private, rather than official, initiative. In Shanxi province, for example, there were over two hundred lecture halls in 1907 although the province only had forty Education Promotion Bureaux (see Table 5).

A notable feature of the 1907 statistics is that the traditionally poorer provinces of Guangxi, Yunnan and Guizhou could boast a considerable number of lecture halls in response to the government's advocacy of popular education. By 1910 Guizhou had established 1 167 lecture halls.[16] As with Education Promotion Bureaux, lecture halls were housed in former public buildings, although some localities constructed new edifices for the purpose. A new lecture hall in Tianjin, for example, cost 6 000 *jin* to build and could accommodate eight hundred people.[17]

The court also sanctioned the creation of another organisation in 1906 to promote education, calling on local gentry to form education associa-

Table 5. Number of *Quanxuesuo*, Lecture Halls and Education Associations in 1907

Province	Quanxuesuo	Lecture Halls[a]	Education Associations
Zhili	154	135	35
Fengtian	31	37	9
Jilin	4	4	0
Heilongjiang	11	4	1
Shandong	100	311	33
Shanxi	40	234	20
Shaanxi	45	229	27
Henan	79	114	41
Jiangsu	20	61	15
Anhui	36	0	12
Zhejiang	44	78	11
Jiangxi	18	18	19
Hubei		No figures available	
Hunan	49	56	3
Sichuan		No figures available	
Guangdong	61	0	0
Guangxi	48	30	6
Yunnan	78	123	14
Guizhou	49	167	0
Fujian	26	20	16
Gansu	29	0	0
Xinjiang	1	0	0
Total:	923	1621	262

[a] By 1909 the number of lecture halls had increased considerably in most provinces. For example, Jilin had 35, Shanxi had 265, Shaanxi had 327, Anhui had 60, Zhejiang had 117, Sichuan had 392 and Guizhou had 1176. *Di sanci jiaoyu tongji tubiao* (1911), pp. 40-1.
Source: *Di yici jiaoyu tongji tubiao* (1909), *passim*.

tions (*jiaoyuhui*).[18] In the process the court hoped to bring the numerous 'study societies' (*xuehui*) – independent and informal gentry associations which had mushroomed since the founding of the Self Strengthening Society (*qiangxuehui*) by Kang Youwei in 1895 – under official supervision.[19] These study societies had included agricultural research societies, anti-footbinding societies, and societies to reform traditional schools. A prominent educator of the time, Huang Yanpei, later remarked that the creation of education associations was a clever scheme by the Qing to halt the development of these informal associations.[20]

The new education associations, described as 'public institutions', were to aid the administration of education under the supervision of the provincial education office. They were allotted a wide range of specialist and general functions that included the setting up of pedagogical research centres, the collection of educational statistics, the building of libraries, and the organisation of educational exhibitions and public lectures 'in order to correct people's minds and improve customs, to destroy superstition, emphasise hygiene and reform immoral and corrupting plays and songs'.[21]

Provincial education associations had been set up in most provinces by 1911, although the number of branch associations varied greatly among provinces.[22] Thus in 1910 Zhili and Sichuan each had sixty-five branch associations, while Gansu and Xinjiang only had four and one respectively. Overall, however, there was a significant increase in the number of education associations, increasing from 262 in 1907 to 723 in 1909, with a reported membership of 48 432.[23]

Education associations were extremely active in the years preceding the 1911 Revolution. The Jiangsu education association opened a school of law and a teacher training institute, as well as organising worker education programmes.[24] The Fujian education association also created a training institute of law in 1907, in addition to opening twenty primary schools.[25] A local education association in Shanxi opened a girls' school and a kindergarten in 1909.[26] The education association in Hangzhou (Zhejiang), which had been organised in 1904 (i.e. before the government issued formal regulations on education associations), set up a physical education lecture bureau (*tiyu jiangxi suo*) to train physical education teachers. Interestingly, instruction was given on weapons training and calisthenics as well as on sports (*youxi ticao*). Each year the association also planned to hold an athletics meet (*yundonghui*), something that became increasingly popular in the last years of the dynasty as more educators stressed the importance of physical fitness.[27]

HALF-DAY SCHOOLS AND LITERACY SCHOOLS

In 1906 the Board of Education approved the creation of half-day schools (*banri xuetang*) with the specific aim of catering to children from poorer families. Echoing a concern earlier expressed by one of its councillors, the Board noted that only the rich were able to benefit from the modern schools since only they had the time and resources for such a luxury.[28] Jiang Weiqiao, writing in *The Educational Review*, partly attributed this to the fact that many schools insisted on the wearing of a uniform, hence placing poorer families at a disadvantage.[29]

All districts were called upon to establish a wide network of half-day schools that would not charge fees or insist on any age qualifications. Ideally, one half-day school would serve 2–300 households regardless of whether they were located in an urban or rural area. This way, the Board commented, 'people's education will become universal'.[30] In addition to reading and writing, half-day schools were also empowered to teach arithmetic, history and geography.[31] Officials and gentry had in fact already begun to open half-day schools before 1906. In Hunan there were twenty-four such schools in 1904, while in Shandong in the same year the first half-day school was opened in the provincial capital.³²

The insistence on the non-charging of fees was significant when one considers that formal primary schools were about to levy tuition fees. Although in 1902 and 1904 the government had waived fees for primary schools, by the beginning of 1907 additional regulations took into account the financial difficulties of the new schools by allowing lower primary schools to charge up to 30 cents a month in tuition fees, higher primary schools up to 60 cents a month, and middle schools up to 1-2 *yuan* a month.³³ Many schools which could not rely on inherited property from former academies in fact charged more than the stipulated maximum.³⁴

In 1907 there was a reported total of 614 half-day schools with an enrolment of 18 246.³⁵ By 1909 the number had increased to 941 with an enrolment of 24 699 (see Table 6). Although there was considerable variation among the provinces - Sichuan, for example, had 203 half-day schools whereas Shaanxi had none - the distribution of half-day schools that *were* established may go some way in modifying the common assertion that educational reform in early-twentieth-century China was confined to the important urban areas. Certainly, such an assertion is valid for most primary and middle schools.³⁶ In Henan, for example, most district primary schools were located in district capitals or large towns.³⁷ In 1907, twenty-one of Zhili's middle schools were situated in Beijing,³⁸ while in Shandong in 1911 there were seven government schools at the secondary level and above in the provincial capital, more than in any other place in the province.³⁹ Yet the province with the highest number of half-day schools in 1909 was Xinjiang, still very much a frontier region. Even in the metropolitan province of Zhili, half-day schools were not necessarily all opened in large towns or cities. Twenty-four such schools were located in six districts in the south-western part of the province, an area not noted for large urban centres.⁴⁰

Statistics on educational expenditures for 1907 indicate that the state's rhetorical commitment to popular education was not initially matched by financial commitment and that non-offical funds played an essential role in the enterprise. In 1907 the Board of Education spent 12 000 *taels* on the Education Promotion Bureaux, lecture halls and half-day schools. In contrast, 150 072 *taels* were spent on scholarships for those studying abroad and 192 000 *taels* on the Imperial University.⁴¹ (It should be noted, however, that expenditures on the Education Promotion Bureaux and lecture halls were to be shared by the provinces.)⁴²

In the case of provincial budgets, also, a small proportion seems to have gone towards the upkeep of half-day schools (see Table 7). In Shandong province, for example, while 256 *taels* were spent per student in higher level schools and 35 *taels* per student in middle and primary schools in 1907, only 4 *taels* were spent per student in half-day schools.⁴³ Yet official expenditures on half-day schools and lecture halls *did* increase over the next few years. In Shandong expenditures on half-day schools increased from 28 *taels* in

Table 6. Number of Half-Day Schools in 1907 and 1909

Province	1907[a]		1909[b]	
Zhili	149	(3 026)	166	(3 853)
Fengtian	3	(161)	3	(137)
Jilin	1	(20)	3	(161)
Heilongjiang	3	(92)	1	(47)
Shandong	39	(797)	50	(884)
Shanxi	5	(149)	23	(622)
Shaanxi	0		0	
Henan	15	(313)	52	(1 240)
Jiangning	32	(1 133)	–	
Jiangsu	91	(3 887)	12	(457)
Anhui	1	(19)	13	(481)
Zhejiang	47	(1 518)	65	(2 219)
Jiangxi	9	(206)	9	(246)
Hubei	9	(319)	27	(1 492)
Hunan	15	(576)	32	(1 215)
Sichuan	160	(4 725)	203	(6 352)
Guangdong	11	(601)	9	(715)
Guangxi	11	(312)	10	(295)
Yunnan	7	(211)	3	(76)
Guizhou	1	(51)	5	(130)
Fujian	5	(130)	7	(137)
Gansu	–		7	(152)
Xinjiang	–		241	(3 788)
Total:	614	(18 246)	941	(24 699)

Note: Number of students are in brackets.
[a] Source: Di yici jiaoyu tongji tubiao (1909), pp. 35-6.
[b] Source: Chen Qitian, Zuijin sanshinian Zhongguo jiaoyushi, pp. 97-100.

1907 to 2 024 taels in 1909, while in Hubei expenditures on lecture halls increased from 322 taels to 6 390 taels during the same period. As will be shown later, this official effort was more than matched by the achievements of gentry and merchant benefactors in the creation of half-day, literacy and vocational schools.

In 1909 the government issued regulations on basic literacy schools (jianyi shizi xuetang) to provide both adults and children from poor backgrounds with the rudiments of a basic education.[44] They could either be attached to the modern schools or located in temples and other public buildings. As with half-day schools, no tuition fees were to be charged and courses were to last from one to three years.[45] It was envisaged that in one year students could learn up to 1 600 characters and in three years up to 3 200 characters.[46] The Board of Education prescribed two texts for the literacy schools, An Essential Reader for the Citizen, which would enlighten the people with respect to 'being loyal to the monarch and grateful for the

Table 7. Provincial Expenditures on *Quanxueso* Lecture Halls Education Associations and Half-Day Schools in 1907 and 1909 (in *taels*)

Province	Total 1907[a]	Total 1909[b]	Quanxueso 1907	Quanxueso 1909	Lecture Halls 1907	Lecture Halls 1909	Education Associations 1907	Education Associations 1909	Half-Day Schools 1907	Half-Day Schools 1909
Zhili	1 059 502	2 404 443	—	104 344	—	7 650	—	2 893	—	4 683
Fengtian	404 488	1 879 742	34 138	107 875	7 478	6 217	5 737	9 834	1 765	1 477
Jilin	122 739	590 596	8 615	41 475	1 038	8 022	7 856	1 251	439	1 849
Heilongjiang	792 556	351 405	11 412	47 799	833	955	4 864	—	915	266
Shandong		911 369	1 742	20 014	7 576	5 395	100	1 746	28	2 024
Shanxi		738 835	475	14 815	855	1 891	—	14 640	—	—
Shaanxi		639 236	9 938	22 599	852	1 167	—	7 773	—	113
Henan	546 838		17 499	32 345	1 428	1 321	2 866	4 371	974	2 357
Jiangsu	1 688 223	1 237 947	3 462	105 799	665	788	1 462	27 013	6 938	6 227
Anhui	451 810	757 592	2 268	3 224	—	—	2 026	3 185	140	1 623
Zhejiang	829 178	1 275 313	13 566	52 270	306	28	1 064	1 678	4 876	1 463
Jiangxi	450 755	970 182	2 227	9 375	—	302	3 021	11 058	119	950
Hubei	974 092	1 868 940	107 644	121 832	322	6 390	3 830	3 941	511	4 875
Hunan	1 074 251	1 444 413	58 132	89 146	984	1 311	—	2 806	355	707
Sichuan		2 186 864	—	408 139	—	2 423	—	2 219	—	9 263
Guangdong	287 890	2 115 860	—	53 333	—	—	—	2 032	—	599
Yunnan	492 327	519 965	17 306	37 621	2 552	2 672	500	2 348	641	172
Guizhou	201 722	349 631	9 771	40 473	2 819	7 492	—	—	64	418
Fujian	382 819	539 741	1 988	3 423	536	1 138	—	5 826	193	367
Guangxi		—	8 040	37 182	485	1 849	4 641	2 032	—	—
Gansu		160 554	—	2 941	—	344	331	20	—	74
Xinjiang		233 391	—	11 474	—	1 677	—	—	—	5 888

a. Source: *Di yici jiaoyu tongji tubiao* (1909), pp. 42-4.
b. Source: *Di sanci jiaoyu tongji tubiao* (1911), pp. 17-20.

sincere benevolence of the state', and a simple character text designed to acquaint students with characters for everyday use and to teach them 'practical ethics'. With such a training, it was hoped, those unable to go on to a higher school could 'plan their livelihoods' without 'slipping into evil and heretical ways'.[47]

There were two significant aspects to the regulations on literacy schools. Firstly, it was stipulated that those who had completed three years at a literacy school could transfer to the fourth year of a lower primary school (and hence enter the regular track that led to middle and higher schools).[48] China, therefore, did not adopt a rigid dual track system comparable to the one that had emerged in Germany, where the *Volksschule* (common schools) were strictly separated from the preparatory schools leading to higher institutions of learning. Secondly, graduates of literacy schools were also to receive certificates testifying to the number of characters they could read,[49] a concrete symbol of the achievements of popular education that would break the monopoly on educational attainment traditionally held by the gentry elite. Moreover, in a culture that prized the written word, such certificates would bestow a sense of self-worth and even prestige to thousands of children and adults who had never seen the inside of a formal school or immersed themselves in the Confucian canon.

Just as in the case of half-day schools, provincial officials and gentry had already begun experimenting with literacy schools before 1909. In 1904, for example, the Hunan provincial education office had outlined a literacy programme for the province, while in early 1909 ten model literacy schools had been opened in the Jiangsu provincial capital, teaching arithmetic in addition to reading and writing. A special institute was also set up within the provincial education office to train teachers for the literacy schools.[50] After 1909 there was a rapid growth in the number of literacy schools. By 1911 Sichuan had the highest number, totalling 4596 with an enrolment of 47 611 students.[51] (Sichuan also had the second highest number of half-day schools in 1911. The province continued to have a very high number of such schools during the early years of the Republic although it reportedly had one of the lowest *formal* school attendance rates in 1919.) Zhili came next with 4 160 literacy schools and 69 405 students.[52] The figure of over 500 such schools in Fujian is particularly striking since only the previous year, in 1910, the Governor-General had reported a total of only seven literacy schools in his province.[53]

The statistics on literacy schools given by the Board of Education were complemented by the reports of provincial governors, who often included the number of literacy schools in their assessment of constitutional preparation in their provinces. In early 1911 the Governor of Shandong, Sun Baoqi, estimated a total of 901 literacy schools in his province, an increase of 199 over the previous year.[54] The Governor-General of Hunan and Hubei reported that every district in Hubei except one had established a literacy school, the provincial figure totalling 1 070.[55] The Governor-

General of Shanxi reported a total of 504 literacy schools, an increase of 188 over the previous year in 1910.[56] Even the less prosperous provinces were able to document an increase. The Governor-General of Yunnan and Guizhou noted that before 1911 there had only been 59 literacy schools; now there were 232, with 5 580 pupils.[57] The Governor of Xinjiang noted that many literacy schools in his province had been combined with Chinese-language schools (*hanyu xuetang*),[58] indicating that the promotion of popular education was often accompanied by increased efforts to 'sinicise' ethnic minorities.

For the most part, literacy and half-day schools were housed in existing public buildings rather than new ones. In Tianjin night classes were held in lower primary schools. One such night class had seventy pupils, mostly industrial and agricultural workers, studying reading, writing and arithmetic for two hours every evening.[59] Some literacy classes made use of school facilities and equipment, as in Changzhou, Jiangsu, where the school principal also participated in literary instruction.[60] Sometimes, even former academies, the very symbol of elite education under the old examination system, were appropriated. In Yusheng district, Henan, a former academy was converted into a half-day school with over eighty students.[61]

Perhaps the most commonly used buildings for literacy classes were Buddhist temples and monasteries, temples in honour of official protective deities such as the City God (*cheng huang*) and God of War (*Guandi*), and Confucian temples (*wen chang chao*). The official organisation of religion often mirrored the assumptions of bureaucratic behaviour (e.g. official gods were graded in a hierarchical structure) and official religious ceremonies were seen as instruments of ideological control.[62] The City God, for example, was the other-worldly equivalent of the district magistrate and the temple was organised along the lines of the magistrate's yamen with the image of the City God dressed in official robes and flanked by images of yamen runners.[63] While the magistrate solicited the assistance of the City God in governing his district, the temple also served as a symbolic meeting point between official and popular religion. Popular worship involved the seeking of favours and on the City God's birthday (the City God was usually designated as the spirit of a former deceased official) the temple grounds witnessed the holding of markets and theatrical performances. By appropriating temples, officials and gentry attempted to channel religious beliefs to serve the secular cause of popular education. Thus in Tianjin a literacy school was housed in the City God temple, where two hours of instruction were given each evening, and another such school in Xieshen, Zhejiang, was opened in the temple to the God of War.[64]

It was Buddhist temples and monasteries, however, that comprised the majority of religious buildings used to house literacy and other spare-time classes. This was not surprising given their large number; in 1668, at the beginning of the Qing dynasty, there may have been up to 80 000 Buddhist temples throughout China.[65] The Qing dynasty's attitude towards Buddhism had always been an ambivalent one, on the one hand keen to prove its Confucian credentials by taking a stern approach towards Buddhism (which involved bringing it under close state control and supervision) and on the other patronising the religion in its role as the ruler of a multi-ethnic and multi-religious empire.[66] It was this ambivalence that allowed the court to support the suggestion put forward by Zhang Zhidong at the end of the nineteenth century to appropriate Buddhist temples for modern primary schools (see Chapter One).

Reformers such as Kang Youwei had also proposed using Buddhist institutions to house modern schools although here again attitudes towards Buddhism were ambivalent. While reformers like Kang bewailed the deleterious effects of Buddhist 'superstition' on the mentality of the people, they also retained a lifelong interest in Buddhism, arguing that it could be a genuinely Chinese counterpart to Christianity and that it could foster the appropriate morality needed for national salvation.[67]

After 1904 the dynasty gave its full approval to the appropriation of Buddhist property and funds in its campaign to promote popular education. Such property was not inconsiderable. In Shandong, for example, Buddhist temples owned as much as 5 *qing* of land (1 *qing* = 6.67 hectares).[68] In some cases, Buddhist temples resisted official and gentry pressure; in Zhaoqing, Guangdong, armed troops had to be used in 1904 to compel a number of Buddhist temples to 'contribute' funds for education.[69] In both Guangdong and Fujian cases were reported of temples transferring ownership of their property to *Japanese* Buddhist temples in order to avoid confiscation.[70]

On the other hand Buddhist monks often took the initiative in promoting popular education themselves so as to enhance their patriotic credentials. A 1904 article entitled 'Buddhist monks also appreciate patriotism' eulogised a Buddhist temple in Guangdong for donating funds to education and hence contributing to the wealth and strength of the nation.[71] A temple in Nanzhang, Hubei, gave up some of its land for a school and actually paid an annual sum to finance it.[72] In 1905 a Buddhist monk, returning from Japan, donated the large sum of 20 000 *taels* to finance a school on temple lands.[73] In Yangzhou, Jiangsu, several Buddhist temples banded together to erect a school of their own in order to forestall any official appropriations.[74] The head monk of a temple in Chengdu, Sichuan, was able to resist gentry attempts to appropriate temple land by paying a lump sum for education.[75]

The use of existing buildings meant that no great extra outlay was required to finance popular education. Another reason was that teachers were either volunteers[76] or paid much less than those who taught in regular schools. One literacy school in Haijian district, Jiangsu, paid its teachers 4 *yuan* a month in 1910.[77] (In that same year, shoemakers could earn 21 *yuan* a month, machine workers 15 *yuan* and women textile workers 8 *yuan*.)[78] At the Nanchang Higher Primary School, Jiangxi, in 1907, teachers earned from 8 *taels* to 17 *taels* a month.[79] An even more stark contrast was with higher schools, where teachers could earn up to 80 *taels* a month.[80] Foreign teachers, of course, were paid even more. The eleven Japanese teachers at the Nanjing Normal School in 1903 were each paid 2–300 *yuan* a month, in addition to receiving free board and lodging.[81]

At the Jiangxi Higher Vocational School in 1907, where native teachers earned between 20 and 74 *taels* a month, the Japanese teacher there earned 200 *taels* a month.[82] This did not necessarily deter the continued establishment of literacy and half-day schools. After all, the salaries of primary school teachers in Japan, where compulsory education had almost been fully implemented by the turn of the century, were low in comparison with other occupations.[83]

In fact, the number of literacy schools evidently continued to grow because in 1910 the Jiangsu provincial education association complained that the increase in literacy schools was very much at the expense of primary schools, since the former were being used to substitute for the latter. To remedy the situation the association proposed that lower primary schools only accept children of school age, while literacy schools should only accept adults.[84] Later in the same year the Jiangsu provincial assembly reiterated the fear that the creation of literacy schools would be used as an excuse to delay the establishment of primary schools.[85] Zhuang Yu, a prominent contributor to *The Educational Review*, voiced a different concern, arguing that literacy schools would perpetuate class differences. The children of the rich, he predicted, would come to dominate enrolment in the primary schools while the children of the poor would be permanently consigned to the literacy schools.[86] Zhuang Yu thus anticipated the criticism that was to be levelled at Yuan Shikai's dual-track scheme in the early years of the Republic (see Chapter Four).

The Board of Education reacted to these concerns by informing the provinces in early 1911 that priority must be given to the creation of lower primary schools and that such schools had to be clearly distinguished from literacy schools, which were designed for adults only.[87] (This had not been so stipulated in the 1909 regulations.) Clearly, however, the Board of Education was in two minds about this since it soon afterwards issued revised regulations on literacy schools that permitted graduates of either the one- or two-year course to transfer to a primary school provided they were of primary school age. The revised regulations also prescribed a more specific curriculum for literacy schools, comprising Chinese (six hours per week), moral training (two hours per week) and arithmetic (three hours per week), with physical education as an optional subject.[88]

The Board of Education's reluctance to slow down the establishment of literacy schools anticipated the views of those who were to argue after both 1911 and 1949 that the creation of a wide network of popular educational facilities took priority over the construction of a more formal school system. By providing the opportunity to children of primary school age to enter primary schools via literacy schools quicker than previously, the Board of

Education may have hoped to solve the problem. This apparently did not work since in July 1911 it informed the provincial commissioners of education that henceforth literacy schools were to accept only adults because local authorities had ceased building lower primary schools.[89]

VOCATIONAL EDUCATION

A significant feature of the campaign to promote education during the last years of the dynasty was the attempt to provide vocational training facilities for the poor and unemployed. Writing in 1931, Huang Yanpei, who founded the Chinese Vocational Education Association in 1917 (see Chapter Five) argued that vocational education in the late nineteenth century had been exclusively concerned with the enhancement of state wealth rather than with the improvement of the individual's standard of living.[90] He hailed the 1904 regulations on supplementary vocational education as the first sign of a shift in focus from the state to the individual.

In fact, after 1900 the two became inextricably linked in the eyes of educators. Whereas the earlier Self Strengthening Movement had pinned its hopes on the creation of a few specialised training schools to increase China's military and economic strength, a recurrent theme in the promotion of vocational education during the early years of the twentieth century was the emphasis on making everyone economically self-sufficient as a prerequisite for a strong nation. Officials increasingly insisted, in contrast to the *laissez-faire* attitude towards the unemployed earlier exhibited by Qing authorities, that it was the state's duty to ensure everyone was equipped with appropriate skills in order to earn a livelihood.

Not only would this guarantee law and order by keeping potential discontents off the streets, but would also enable China, with a more skilled and productive workforce, to compete successfully with foreign industry in what was perceived as a crucial struggle for economic survival. Once again, officials and local elites could draw inspiration from *both* western example and native precedent. While the system of industrial and vocational training in such countries as Germany was praised as a key factor in national strength, the tradition of Confucian paternalism could be cited as justification for vigorous action to 'ensure the people's livelihood'.

As with other aspects of popular education, the initial urgency with which officials and gentry grappled with vocational training was motivated by their alarm at the destruction wrought by the Boxers in 1900. Unemployment and vagrancy were seen as the root of the problem. Thus the Beijing official, Huang Zhonghui, helped found the Beijing Industrial Training Bureau (*shanhou gongyi ju*) at the end of 1900 to provide people with the means and know-how to earn a living. For Huang, industrial training bureaux represented a wise investment for long term benefits. They would not only bring vagrants off the streets and teach them a skill, thus eliminating the potential for crime and 'expanding the people's knowledge' (*kaitong minzhi*) but also, by providing handicraft workers with materials and assistance in marketing their products and in promoting machine-made manufactures, would help stem the tide of foreign imports and enhance the position of Chinese industry. Huang's enthusiasm also extended to the 'old and infirm', who could be trained in simple skills such as weaving and basketwork.[91] Crucially, Huang assumed that non-official funds would play a significant role in the promotion of vocational training.

The Beijing model was soon adopted in Tianjin, where Governor-General Yuan Shikai established the Beiyang Industrial Training Bureau in 1903. The Bureau opened a training factory (*shixi gongchang*) and supervised the running of several apprentice schools.[92] The training factory recruited two hundred students on government grants and over four hundred privately-financed students (with ages ranging from twelve to twenty-two) and taught a wide variety of skills that included machine-making, printing, dyeing, carpentry, embroidery, spinning, and soap manufacture.[93] Students were also taught Chinese, history, geography and arithmetic. Goods produced at the factory were put on sale at two exhibitions organised in 1905 and 1906. Interestingly, the Bureau also created an Office for the Manufacture of Educational Products (*jiaoyupin zhizaosuo*) to encourage native production of goods required by schools from furniture and equipment to exercise books and ink.

Both Yuan Shikai and Zhou Xuexi, who managed the Bureau, emphasised the duty of the state in training a skilled work force, thereby rescuing the poor and unemployed and equipping the country with the means to compete economically with the foreign powers. Exhibiting the same boundless confidence that others had expressed in the potential of general education, Zhou predicted that: 'In the future, as factories are set up everywhere and manufacturing daily becomes more skilled and proficient, naturally the number of people condemned to idleness and aimlessness will decrease... This will not only eliminate anxieties about livelihood, but will also establish the foundation for a strong and wealthy state.'[94]

The importance now given to vocational education was symbolised by the coining of a new term, borrowed from the Japanese, *zhiye jiaoyu* (Japanese: *shokugyo kyōiku*),[95] apparently first used in a letter written by the director of the Shaanxi Agricultural School, Yao Wendong, in 1904: 'As for the main principles of education, then what is most relevant for the people is, firstly, general education and, secondly, vocational education (*zhiye jiaoyu*). The two should be co-ordinated and not be mutually exclusive.'[96] The idea of assigning vocational training an importance equal to that of general education (as well as the notion that the two should be carried out in conjunction with one another) was a radical departure from traditional concepts of education that equated it with moral cultivation; it also contrasted with opinions voiced in the West, where debates on educational reform often centred on the need to keep general and vocational education separate.

As was noted in Chapter One, the court issued regulations in 1904 on vocational education and in 1906 it again urged the provinces to speed up the creation of higher- and lower-level vocational schools.[97] In 1907 the court also issued more detailed regulations on apprentice schools. As with literacy schools the possibility was left open for students from apprentice schools to transfer to primary school. The curriculum was expanded to include moral training, Chinese, arithmetic, general science, history, drawing and physical education, as well as specialised courses on wood carving, metallurgy and lacquer work.[98] The main emphasis was on giving students practical knowledge and skills. Moral training, for example, was only to be taught one hour a week.[99] Like half-day schools, apprentice schools were not to levy tuition fees.[100] (Lower primary schools and vocational schools could charge reduced fees – set at 30 cents a month – or waive them if circumstances permitted.)

Although the Board of Education instructed the provinces to set up vocational teacher training institutes, vocational schools were plagued from the beginning by a shortage of qualified teachers. Many of the higher-level vocational schools employed foreigners, while teachers in lower-level schools were very often not school graduates. Thus in 1909, out of a total of ninety-four teachers in Zhili's various vocational schools, six were foreigners and thirty-two were non-graduates. In Xinjiang, seventy-two out of the seventy-three teachers in vocational schools were non-graduates.[101]

The plethora of examples cited in the contemporary periodical press of attempts by officials, gentry, and entrepreneurs to establish facilities for vocational training should also be seen in the context of the court's promotion of industry and commerce after 1900 and its sanction of new merchant institutions like the Chambers of Commerce. As in the case of the gentry-dominated education associations, the new chambers of commerce played an important role in the promotion of new forms of education.

As part of its administrative reform, the Qing government had set up the Ministry of Commerce (*shangbu*) in 1903, which became the Ministry of Agriculture, Industry and Commerce (*nonggongshangbu*) in 1906. Between 1903 and 1911 these ministries introduced new ideas and pioneered new institutions to encourage industrial development and innovation.[102] Thus a Commercial Law Office (created in 1903) drew up commercial legal codes and company registration laws; a system of awards and merits was outlined to provide incentives for entrepreneurs, inventors, and potential investors in industry;[103] and trade fairs and exhibitions were organised to display industrial products. The central government's efforts were paralleled in the provinces, where officials had already begun to create commercial institutions of their own. In 1895, for example, Zhang Zhidong, while Governor of Jiangsu, had established the first provincial Bureau of Commercial Affairs (*shangwu ju*). Other provinces followed suit and in 1904 the court officially recognised these provincial bureaux as branches of the Ministry of Commerce.

In 1904 also the court sanctioned the creation of merchant-organised chambers of commerce (*shangwu hui*), the first of which appeared in Shanghai later that same year. As with education associations, they rapidly became an institution through which provincial and local elites could expand their public activities, including education.[104] The number of chambers of commerce increased from 281 in 1908 to 794 in 1912. In addition to involving themselves in civic activities such as the installation of street lights and the organisation of fire-fighting services,[105] many chambers of commerce gave public lectures on commerce and industry as well as organising evening classes and half-day schools for shop hands and apprentices. It may well be that chambers of commerce ultimately failed to establish modern enterprises and to form the nucleus of a vigorous bourgeoisie,[106] but their contribution to education, in theory and practice, should not be overlooked. They helped in securing a wider acceptance by elites and people alike that education was no longer to be exclusively identified with the moral and literary cultivation of the scholar.

Following the establishment of provincial bureaux of commerce and industry, industrial training centres (*gongyiju, zhuanxisuo, shixi gongchang*) were created by both officials and gentry to promote vocational education. In Zhili, eighty-seven such centres appeared between 1904 and 1910 (only nine of which were specifically established by officials.) The average number of trainees was thirty-eight and the skills taught included spinning, lacquerwork, soap manufacture, carpentry, ceramics, metalwork, sugar refining, match manufacture, carpet weaving, brewing and the making of straw headwear.[107] In Shandong, 113 training centres were established between 1900 and 1911, where one of the skills taught was the weaving of 'patriotic' cotton cloth (*aiguobu*) to compete with foreign textiles.[108] In 1911 the Governor of Guangdong reported the existence of thirty training centres. Such centres, he noted, would be the most effective solution to the problem of widespread gambling in the province.[109]

Many of these training centres were initially set up with official funds but were managed by gentry and entrepreneurs who also contributed funds for the ongoing operation of such centres. Some, like the industrial training centre in Deyang, Sichuan, were financed by local taxes, in this case a tax on opium dens.[110] Many of the products made were sold and profits were used for operation expenses. (Such a practice was to be applied to formal vocational schools, where administrators encouraged the sale of handicraft goods made by students.) In many cases industrial training centres were located, as in the case of half-day and literacy schools, in temples, former academies and charitable halls.[111]

No member of society was to escape the attention of officials and elites. The unemployed, vagrants, beggars, criminals, the infirm, and even the 'undisciplined and profligate offspring of good households' (*liangjia buxiao zidi*) were all suitable candidates who, with the appropriate training, could contribute to the economic well-being of the country. Thus, the training centre in the Shandong provincial capital instructed up to five hundred local beggars and vagrants in the skills of shoemaking and cloth weaving.[112] In Chongqing, Sichuan, workshops were opened for beggars and orphans.[113] The training centre set up by the Governor of Jiangxi in 1903 had separate workshops teaching skilled work to unemployed artisans, and unskilled work to beggars, petty criminals and labourers. Only the teaching of industrial skills, the Governor claimed, could solve the problems of crime, vagrancy and idleness.[114] Such a view was echoed by the Governor of Sichuan in 1903 when he founded a Bureau to Encourage Industry (*guanggong ju*), which comprised factory workshops training the unemployed and petty criminals. While the forces of law and order might prevent disorder (*luan*), he surmised, only the provision of vocational skills for the people could guarantee an absence of crime and violence.[115]

Special vocational training centres (*zuifan xiyisuo*) were also opened within prisons.[116] In Zhili, between 1904 and 1908, twenty-five training centres were set up in prisons, where skills taught included food processing.[117] One such prison centre in Yuanshi taught prisoners reading and writing, arithmetic and handicraft skills.[118] Others in Jiangsu, Sichuan, and Anhui taught spinning and weaving.[119] In a Zhejiang district, two artisans were employed to teach prisoners how to weave garments and belts.[120] More frequently, prisoners were recruited to attend nearby industrial training centres. Thus the one in Deyang district, Sichuan, enlisted twenty prisoners from a nearby prison and trained them in the making of fans, towels and cloth shoes.[121] In Suzhou, Jiangsu, the training centre purchased textile machinery from Shanghai and selected prisoners from surrounding areas to attend a training course in its operation.[122] At the training centre in the Sichuan provincial capital, prisoners were graded and awarded prizes for their work. Superior workers among them had their sentences reduced or were released.[123]

The campaign to promote vocational training was not only motivated by a desire to 'secure the people's livelihood' and strengthen the country economically. Reflecting the growing sense of *provincial* identity among officials and gentry that was to be greatly stimulated by the creation of provincial assemblies in 1909, provincial officials expressed alarm that outsiders (both Chinese and foreign) were profiting excessively from their own provinces' natural resources. As the Governor of Shaanxi remarked in 1905:

> The knowledge of the people of Shaanxi is limited and industry is at a rudimentary stage. Modern equipment and machinery is a rarity. Everything produced in our province serves as raw material for outsiders to process and manufacture. Foreigners buy our animal products (e.g. fur, hides) and by a sleight of hand obtain huge profits (from the processing of these raw materials). Cotton and medicinal herbs are purchased by neighbouring provinces, processed and then sold to us at high prices. Everything we have flows into the hands of outsiders, whereas we have to obtain everything we cannot manu-

facture from outside. The province thus has a considerable trade imbalance. This can all be attributed to the dull-witted nature of the people and official neglect in educating and guiding them.[124] Other provinces such as Guizhou, Heilongjiang, Jilin and Xinjiang also expressed the fear that they might remain the hewers of wood and drawers of water.[125] Vocational training that would promote handicraft production and the processing of raw materials would thus equip the provinces to compete successfully with their neighbours as well as with foreign imports.

In addition to the industrial training centres, a wide variety of vocational schools were established by gentry and merchant elites throughout this period. They included agricultural night schools;[126] night schools for shopkeepers' children, illiterate traders and peddlers;[127] spare-time classes for fishermen and illiterate local constabulary.[128] As noted before, chambers of commerce were particularly active – the Fuzhou Chamber of Commerce funded an industrial training centre that instructed 160 students,[129] while local chambers of commerce in Jiangsu, Shandong, Zhili and Anhui opened spare-time schools for shop apprentices.[130]

Individual entrepreneurs were also energetic in promoting vocational training. Zhang Jian not only established normal and primary schools in his native district of Nantong in Jiangsu, but also opened an apprentice school for the children of his textile workers as well as a sericulture and silk-weaving school for women.[131] Yu Zhimo (1866-1907) opened an apprentice school in 1903 for the forty workers of his towel factory in Changsha, Hunan. Yu, later to be executed for his anti-Manchu political activities, came from a merchant family and had studied industry in Japan. He showed a paternalistic concern for his workers reminiscent of that of the early nineteenth-century English reformer Robert Owen at his New Lanark mill. As one contemporary remembered: 'He [Yu Zhimo] slept and ate with the workers, rose and went to work with them, and talked and laughed with them. The relationship was as close as that between father and children, and there was certainly no difference of labour and capital between them.'[132]

Finally, it might be noted that it was during the last years of the dynasty that the first attempts were made to provide vocational instruction for girls and women. Although official 1907 regulations stated that the principal aim of women's education was to train 'virtuous mothers and good wives'[133] some preferred to advocate vocational education for women as a means to utilise their skills in the economy.[134] In Fengtian, for example, the Governor-General opened a training centre for banner women in 1909 where embroidery and weaving skills, in addition to general knowledge, were taught.[135] In the same year, the Ministry of Agriculture, Industry and Commerce in Beijing established a women's industrial training workshop. The project received 17 000 *taels* from official and non-official sources and students were instructed in machine spinning and embroidery as well as being taught Chinese and arithmetic. Over one thousand girls were recruited and the Ministry expressed the hope that graduates might become instructors in women's factories that would be set up in the future.[136] Private schools for girls' vocational training were also opened, such as a school for sericulture in Shanghai (1904) and a vocational school in Changzhou, Jiangsu (1906) that taught Chinese, art, applied science, arithmetic and handicrafts.[137]

CHANGES IN THE PRIMARY SCHOOL CURRICULUM

Changes introduced to the primary school curriculum during the last years of the dynasty revealed a tendency to downplay the importance of the Confucian Classics and co-ordinate the teaching of general and vocational subjects. Whereas the 1902 school regulations had prescribed a primary-school curriculum that comprised moral training, Chinese, the Classics, history, geography and arithmetic, in 1904 one hour of science per week was added to the lower-primary-school curriculum (with handicrafts as an optional subject) and two hours a week of science for higher primary schools (with agriculture and commerce as optional subjects).[138]

By 1909 the number of courses at lower primary schools had been reduced, including the amount of time spent on the Classics. In that year the Jiangsu education association complained that too many hours a week (twelve out of thirty) were being spent on the Confucian Classics in lower primary schools,[139] suggesting that more attention be paid to Chinese and arithmetic, which would be 'more of a preparation for earning a livelihood'.[140] The preservation of the 'national essence' (*guocui*), the association commented, had to be combined with practical everyday matters. Some educators even argued against teaching some of the Classics on moral grounds. Not only were they irrelevant for children, but some, like the *Zuozhuan* (Zuo Commentary on the Spring and Autumn Annals) and the *Shijing* (Classic of Odes), were harmful to the child's moral upbringing because they dealt with 'promiscuous affairs' (*yinluan zhi shi*) and 'pornography' (*nan'nü xiangyue*).[141]

Formal regulations in 1910 took into account this criticism by prescribing only five hours per week (out of thirty) for the Classics at lower primary school[142] and eleven hours per week (out of thirty-six) at higher primary schools. [143] Singing was also added to the curriculum to stimulate patriotism, while for higher primary schools, English was added as an optional subject.[144]

The changes in the primary-school curriculum thus reflected a widespread belief that education needed to be adapted to the current needs of society. A 1910 article in *The Educational Review* boldly asserted that values and morality were relative and changed over time. In an increasingly complex society in which the need for different professional and economic skills was becoming more urgent it was, at best, impractical and, at worst, irrelevant to teach Confucian morality with its praise of frugality, its contempt for entrepreneurship and professionalism, and its adherence to outdated notions of a moral way (*dao*). The ideas of non-Confucian thinkers needed to be incorporated into moral training, the article continued, while non-official literature such as novels should be used as texts in the teaching of Chinese.[145]

Another article in the same journal pointed out in 1911 that society now comprised a growing number of professional groups (*jia*), including educators, lawyers, doctors, agronomists, industrialists and artists. All were indispensable and thus general education needed to incorporate the teaching of professional and vocational skills. General education, the article maintained, should not cater solely to the scholar class (*shi*), neither should it be separated from vocational education, thus perpetuating hierarchical distinctions.[146] These were radical ideas, implying the need to dismantle the centuries-old Confucian monopoly over education that had preserved the classical moral and literary tradition as the very core and *raison d'être* of education. The regulations of 1910 had not gone quite as far, but they had begun a process whereby the Confucian Classics would be totally eliminated from the school curriculum.

The Qing government also hoped to use the new schools to impose a unified standard national language. Educators like Chen Zibao, of course, had already begun to use vernacular readers in his school at Macao in 1899 (see Chapter Two). But whereas Chen had proposed the use of local dialects, the Qing government decided to adopt the official Beijing dialect, *guanhua* ('officials' speech', so-called because it had originally been associated with the standard official language at the capital). In 1910 the Board of Education ordered the compilation of *guanhua* textbooks and requested all primary and middle schools to add *guanhua* to their curricula.[147] The shortage of qualified Chinese teachers, particularly in the south, meant that Manchus often had to be drafted to teach *guanhua*. This sometimes led to unfortunate results, as in the case of a school in Fujian where a Manchu teacher aroused the hostility of the students when he asked them to recite the word *nucai* (slave), a term that Manchus always used of themselves when addressing the Emperor.[148]

Changes in the primary school curriculum were accompanied by government attempts to increase its control over textbooks.[149] In 1906 the Board of Education issued its first guidelines on lower-primary-school textbooks, and a textbook bureau was established under the Board's direction.[150] A provisional list of books that the Board deemed suitable was issued, along with the injunction that students should not have to pay more than six *yuan* over a five-year period for text books.[151] All other text-books produced by such publishing firms as the Shanghai Commercial Press and the Nanyang Book Company had to be sent to the Board for approval.[152] As Zhuang Yu later recalled, this did not prevent a flurry of bogus textbooks being published in the last years of the dynasty in the cause of quick and easy profits.[153] Interestingly, this half-way measure as far as government control of textbooks was concerned contrasted with developments in Japan where a gradual process of administrative control culminated in the Ministry of Education (*Mombushō*) assuming sole responsibility in 1902 to compile elementary school textbooks.[154]

The implementation of a nationwide school system and increasing official control over textbooks also necessitated greater state supervision of educational endeavours that had traditionally been the responsibility of local communities. The 1904 school regulations, for example, called for the conversion of traditional charitable and village schools (*xixue*, *shexue*) into modern elementary and primary schools.[155] In one district in Shandong, twenty-four charitable schools were converted into primary schools. The curriculum had to conform to official standards and teachers were expected to send copies of the students' work to local officials, who were empowered to conduct a personal investigation of the schools every month.[156]

A similar trend may have occurred with the traditional private schools (*sishu*), usually run by one scholar to tutor boys in the Confucian classics. In 1905 a censor, Xia Shufu, proposed that students from these schools be examined and that the successful ones be admitted into modern schools.[157] In 1906 the Board of Education directed that *all* traditional schools with over thirty students be converted into primary schools.[158] The gentry were also enlisted in the cause and in 1906 the court sanctioned the organisation of the Society for the Reform of Traditional Schools by a member of the Shanghai gentry elite, Shen Liangqi. The society, which had branches in neighbouring provinces, was to investigate traditional schools and ensure they were teaching Chinese, arithmetic and physical education. Teaching methods had to stress comprehension rather than rote memorisation and examinations were to be held regularly.[159] In 1910 the Board of Education formally transferred the duty of supervising reformed traditional schools from Shen Liangqi's society to the provincial education commissioners and the Education Promotion Bureaux.[160] Unreformed traditional schools, however, continued to exist despite the government's attempt to change their nature. As late as 1935 it was reported that 101 027 such schools existed, with a total enrolment of 1 757 014 students.[161]

Another traditional educational institution, the clan or lineage school (schools financed by an endowment that primarily aimed to prepare the better-off members of the clan for the civil service examinations),[162] may have undergone change after 1900 as clans, particularly in the south where they were most prevalent, enthusiastically responded to the government's call for the expansion of education.[163] In Shandong, for example, the Yu clan school in 1905 was converted into a primary school that taught writing, history and geography.[164] In Chenping, Guangdong, Xie Longzhang requested permission to open a clan primary school in 1906, the expenses of which would be met by the Xie clan.[165] Whereas in the past clan schools more often than not had catered to the well-off amongst clan members, many schools were now opened for poorer members. Clan ancestral temples, for example, were used to house schools for the benefit of a wider group of people.¹⁶⁶ A school located in the Zhang clan ancestral temple in Guangdong allowed everyone over the age of thirteen to attend.¹⁶⁷ In Chaoyang district, Guangdong, although all the teachers and administrators of a clan elementary school belonged to the clan in question, not all of the eighty pupils were necessarily from the same clan, since they were reported to have come from 'far and wide'.¹⁶⁸ Finally, a revealing incident took place in Shaoxing, Zhejiang in 1910, when a mob destroyed a school (opened by a certain Liu Yinfeng), not because extra taxes on salt and bamboo had been imposed for the school's upkeep, but rather because the school had only served the Liu clan and had not allowed others to enrol.¹⁶⁹ It seemed to be assumed that clan schools should serve a wider populace.

Two important features of educational reform during the last years of the dynasty need to be underlined. Firstly, the process of reform itself followed two courses. On the one hand, modern primary and secondary schools were built; they were expensive, generally concentrated in administrative and urban centres, and catered to a minority of school-age children.¹⁷⁰ Many of them were the targets of mob wrath as increased taxes for their upkeep fell on the shoulders of those who benefited least from modern education. Sometimes even conservative gentry, who perceived modern schools as a threat to their own status, would lead mob attacks on the schools.¹⁷¹ On the other hand, attempts were made during this period to spread education to a wider audience, a result of changing attitudes towards the role and function of education. The importance of part-time education, vocational training and literacy education as a means to improve individual welfare and offset the high costs of modern education was perceived and acted upon.¹⁷² Furthermore, it might be noted that the motivation for the promotion of popular education in the last years of the dynasty sprang from the desire to create a strong, united and wealthy nation, a desire that was both inspired by the examples of the West and Japan and encouraged by the traditional belief that everyone could benefit from education. It did not stem from an urge to combat the challenge of missionary schools.¹⁷³

Secondly, the initiative of local elites (gentry, merchants, entrepreneurs) in the promotion of education signified an increased participation in public activities that had been evident since the eighteenth century. This local elite involvement in education (whether it be funding or the establishment and supervision of schools) was a feature of what Max Weber has termed the 'liturgical' structures of local government whereby local elites were called upon to perform public services on the state's behalf at their own expense.¹⁷⁴ This was, of course, a double-edged sword as far as the Qing authorities were concerned. Just as the dynasty had lost its monopoly of military force with the sanctioning of gentry-led militia armies from the late eighteenth century onwards, so it lost its monopoly of education.¹⁷⁵ Debate over the function and purposes of education, as well as its practical implementation, now belonged to a wider audience. Despite the dynasty's attempt to bring gentry organisations such as the education associations under closer bureaucratic supervision, it had begun a process, that was to continue after 1912, in which increasing numbers of groups and organisations assumed the right to discuss educational policy.

NOTES

1. S. Naquin, E. Rawski, *Chinese Society in the Eighteenth Century* (New Haven, 1987), pp. 45-6; M. Elvin, 'The Gentry Democracy in Chinese Shanghai 1905-1914' in J. Gray (ed.), *Modern China's Search For a Political Form* (London, 1969); M. Elvin 'The Administration of Shanghai 1905-1914' in M. Elvin, W. Skinner (eds.), *The Chinese City Between Two Worlds* (Stanford, 1974). For a study of local elite political mobilisation in Zhejiang and the ensuing clash with the bureaucracy, see M. Rankin, *Elite Activism and Political Transformation in China* (Stanford, 1986).
2. *Xuebu guanbao*, no. 13 (1907), *fulu*, p. 287.
3. Kuo Ping-wen, *The Chinese System of Public Education*, p. 96, translates *quanxuesuo* as the 'Education Exhortation Office'; D. Buck, *Urban Change in China*, p. 62, renders the term as the 'Education Promotion Office'. H. Brunnert, V. Hagelstrom, *Present Day Political Organization of China* (Shanghai, 1912), p. 408, erroneously translate the term as the 'Association for the Fostering of Public Education', hence obscuring the fact that the *quanxuesuo* was a government institution.
4. Regulations on the *quanxuesuo* are in Taga Akigorō (comp.), *Shiryō*, 1: 423-5; and DYJN, 1: 30-1. The regulations for the Beijing *quanxuesuo* are in *Xuebu guanbao*, no. 7 (1906), *jingwai xuewu baogao*, pp. 27-9. In 1911 the Board of Education permitted self-governing councils at the prefectural and district levels (created in accordance with the court's plans for local autonomy) to establish middle, primary, and literacy schools. Below the district level, the court also sanctioned the creation of 'joint educational federations', which were permitted to establish primary schools. All residents of an educational district, the court insisted, were to contribute to the upkeep of the schools. Such an idea echoed the proposal put forward by Liang Qichao in 1902, whereby the state would supervise (*jiandu*) primary schools but the local populace would be responsible for financing them. For the Board of Education's regulations see JYZZ, 3: 4 (1911), *faling*, pp. 41-7. Liang's proposal is in Shu Xincheng (ed.) *Zilao*, 3: 947-54.
5. For a discussion of the clash between the bureaucracy and the gentry over the control of educational reform, see M. Bastid, *Aspects de la Réforme de l'Enseignement*, pp. 57-82.
6. The Beijing Education Promotion Bureau organized two-month training courses to instruct gentry assistants in pedagogy, administration, and school management. *Xuebu guanbao*, no. 7 (1906), *jingwai xuewu baogao*, pp. 27-9.
7. *Xuebu guanbao*, no. 22 (1907), *jingwai xuewu baogao*, p. 154.

8. *Xuebu guanbao*, no. 7 (1906), *jingwai xuewu baogao*, p. 38.
9. *Zhonghua baihua bao*, no. 2 (1903), p. 79.
10. The term used for popular education – *tongsu jiaoyu* – had already been used in the regulations for the Board of Education. It was used interchangeably with the term for 'social education' (*shehui jiaoyu*) and referred to all educational activity outside the formal schools. See DFZZ, 3: 5 (1906), *jiaoyu*, p. 65; DFZZ, 4: 7 (1907), *jiaoyu*, p. 169.
11. Taga Akigorō (comp.), *Shiryō*, 1: 535-7. *Uncle Tom's Cabin* and *Robinson Crusoe* had been translated by the classical scholar Lin Shu in 1901 and 1905 respectively. H. Boorman, R. Howard (eds.), *A Biographical Dictionary of Republican China*, 2: 384. The use of *Uncle Tom's Cabin* was potentially ambiguous as far as the court was concerned. Lectures on it were supposed to warn the people that they might also become enslaved by the whites. Yet Chinese revolutionaries were arguing that the Han Chinese were already the slaves of the Manchus.
12. Although the lectures were meant to foster patriotism, the court attempted to separate this from politics. The regulations of the Beijing Education Promotion Bureau specifically forbade lecturers from broaching the subject of politics and stipulated that the local constabulary should always be present at lectures ready to call a halt to the proceedings at any time law and order seemed threatened. *Xuebu guanbao*, no. 7 (1906), *jingwai xuewu baogao*, p. 38.
13. Some lectures went even further than this. Thus the head of an Education Promotion Bureau in Zhili encouraged school attendance by pointing out that a student's chances of becoming an official were now better under the new school system than they had been under the traditional civil service examination system. See *Jinghua xinbao*, nos. 245, 246 (1906).
14. See, for example, the report on the Henan Education Promotion Bureaux in *Xuebu guanbao*, no. 28 (1907), *jingwai xuewu baogao*, p. 204. Out of 34 Education Promotion Bureaux in Henan in 1907, 3 were located in former academies, 4 in Confucian temples, 2 in former examination halls, and 1 in a temple to the God of War.
15. Chen Qitian, *Zuijin sanshinian Zhongguo jiaoyushi*, pp. 76-8.
16. Kuo Ping-wen, *The Chinese System of Public Education*, p. 109. This was out of a total of 3 867 lecture halls. In 1907 Shandong had the highest number of such halls, a position it retained during the early years of the Republic.
17. *Xuebu guanbao*, no. 9 (1906), *fulu*.
18. The regulations are in Taga Akigorō (comp.), *Shiryō*, 1: 430-3; Shu Xincheng (ed.), *Ziliao*, 1: 361-5.
19. For a list of study societies from 1895 to 1910, see Wang Erh-min, 'Qingji xuehui huibiao' (A Record of Study Societies in the Late Qing), *Dalu Zazhi*, 26: 2 (31 January 1962), pp. 14-20; 26: 3 (15 February 1962), pp. 16-24. Reformist gentry had already anticipated the Board of Education's directive. Thus in 1904 over one hundred members of the local gentry elite had created the Zhejiang Educa-

tion Association, while in early 1906 Zhang Jian and others had set up the Jiangsu General Education Association (*xuewu zonghui*). DFZZ, 1: 1 (1904), *jiaoyu*, p. 136; Ding Zhipin, *Zhongguo jin qishinian lai jiaoyu jishi* (Taibei, 1961), p. 16; M. Bastid, *Aspects de la Réforme de l'Enseignement*, pp. 164-5-

20. Huang Yanpei, *Zhongguo jiaoyu shiyao* (Shanghai, 1930), p. 108. In fact, the members of the pre-1906 study societies often formed the core of the new education associations. The gentry founders of the Jiangsu General Education Asociation (including Huang Yanpei) were all prominent in the new association after 1906. M. Bastid, *Aspects de la Réforme de l'Enseignement*, p. 72.
21. Taga Akigorō (comp.), *Shiryō*, 1: 432.
22. *Dalu Zazhi*, 26: 3 (15 February 1962), pp. 19-20.
23. Kuo Ping-wen, *The Chinese System of Public Education*, p. 108; M. Bastid, *Aspects de la Réforme de l'Enseignement*, pp. 70-1.
24. M. Bastid, *Aspects de la Réforme de l'Enseignement*, pp. 73, 89.
25. *Xuebu guanbao*, no. 25 (1907) *jingwai xuewu baogao*, pp. 175–81; DFZZ, 4: 2 (1907), *jiaoyu*, p. 23
26. DYJN, 2: 458.
27. Regulations for the Physical Education Lecture Bureau are in *Jingzhong ribao*, no. 18 (1904), *zhuanjian*. The bureau apparently also allowed visitors, on payment of an entrance fee, to use their facilities for target practice. The first sports day held by a Chinese school occurred in 1903 at one of Zhang Zhidong's new schools in Wuchang. S. Borthwick, *Education and Social Change in China*, p. 138.
28. Taga Akigorō (comp.), *Shiryō*, 1: 409.
29. JYZZ, 1: 7 (1909).
30. This is the first use I have come across in the Chinese sources of the term *minzhong jiaoyu* (people's education), which came to mean 'mass education' in the 1920s and 1930s.
31. One half-day school in Henan included Japanese in its curriculum. DFZZ, 1: 10 (1904), *jiaoyu*, p. 236.
32. M. Bastid, *Aspects de la Réforme de l'Enseignement*, p. 46; DFZZ, 1: 8 (1904), *jiaoyu*, p. 193. There are also constant references to nonofficial establishment of schools for poorer children after 1904. In the capital of Fujian, for example, two residents founded a school of their own for those who could not afford to go to the provincial primary school. DFZZ, 1: 4 (1904), *jiaoyu*, p. 101. For a similar school in Hanyang, Hubei, see DFZZ, 1: 9 (1904), *jiaoyu*, p. 215. For other examples, see DFZZ, 1: 10 (1904), *jiaoyu*, p. 235; 2: 8 (1905), *jiaoyu*, p. 199 .
33. Taga Akigorō (comp.), *Shiryō*, 1: 458-9; S. Borthwick, *Education and Social Change in China*, pp. 105-9.
34. Non-official schools were even more expensive.
35. It should be stressed again that these figures are not always complete. Thus we simply do not know whether the fact that Hunan only reported fifteen half-day schools in 1907 (whereas in 1904 it reported a total of twenty-four) is due to the non-reporting of

schools or to the closure of schools. Also, figures very often do not distinguish between official and non-official schools. Thus Tianjin in 1906 had nineteen half-day schools with an enrolment of 1 258 pupils, but we do not know which ones were public and which were private. *Xuebu guanbao*, no. 14 (1906), *jingwai xuewu baogao*, p. 300.

36. A study of Zhili indicates, however, that lower primary schools – unlike higher primary schools, which were often converted academies – were widely distributed and not necessarily located in district capitals or market towns. R. Orb, 'Chihli Academies and Other Schools in the Late Ch'ing: An Institutional Survey' in P. Cohen, J. Schrecker (eds.), *Reform in Nineteenth Century China* (Cambridge, Mass., 1976), pp. 231–40. For a list of lower and higher primary schools in Zhili, see *Xuebu guanbao*, no. 14 (1906), *jingwai xuewu baogao*, pp. 91-4; no. 15 (1906), *jingwai xuewu baogao*, pp. 95-100; no. 16 (1906), *jingwai xuewu baogao*, pp. 101-5; no. 17 (1906), *jingwai xuewu baogao*, pp. 106-13.

37. DYJN, 2: 460.

38. *Diyici jiaoyu tongji tubiao* (Beijing, 1909), pp. 23, 35.

39. D. Buck, *Urban Change in China*, p. 56. By 1915, twenty-four of the thirty-six officially supported primary schools in Shandong were located in the provincial capital of Jinan. D. Buck, 'Educational Modernization in Tsinan 1892-1937' in M. Elvin, G. Skinner (eds.), *The Chinese City Between Two Worlds*, p. 189. For educational reform in Guangdong, Hunan and Hubei, see E. Rhoads, *China's Republican Revolution*, pp. 18–19, 51–6, 73–6, 124–8; J. Esherick, *Reform and Revolution in China*, pp. 231-40.

40. *Diyici jiaoyu tongji tubiao*, pp. 73-84.

41. *Ibid.*, pp. 12–14. Funds for the Board of Education came from the interest on stock in the Sino-Russian Bank, the Board of Revenue, and provincial contributions.

42. Some Education Promotion Bureaux were not financed by officials at all but rather were funded by voluntary subscriptions by gentry. In Henan, four out of the thirty-four Bureaux were 'voluntarily' (*yiwu*) established, and one was directly financed by the local education association. *Xuebu guanbao*, no. 28, (1906), *jingwai xuewu baogao*, pp. 204-5.

43. *Diyici jiaoyu tongji tubiao*, pp. 49, 51, 53. Sources for provincial expenditures came from special taxes, contributions and tuition fees. It should be noted, however, that expenditures on primary schools constituted the largest single item for most provincial educational budgets.

44. The regulations are in Taga Akigorō (comp.), *Shiryō*, 1: 627; Shu Xincheng (ed.), *Zilao*, 2: 446-9; JYZZ, 2: 1 (1910), *faling*, pp. 9-10. See also Chen Qingzhi, *Zhongguo jiaoyushi*, p. 614.

45. The Board of Education confidently predicted that 'the more there is one additional person in school, then that area has one more person who understands moral propriety, and is truly a huge benefit for the development of constitutional government.' JYZZ, 2: 1 (1910), *faling*, p. 9.

46. E. Rawski, *Education and Popular Literacy in Ch'ing China* (p. 4) defines the lowest level of literacy as the recognition of several hundred characters, while a mastery of up to 2 000 characters could provide a 'functional literacy of a specialised sort'.
47. Zhang Jinglu, 'Qingmo Minqu duiyu minzhong duwu bianfan zhi jingguo' (The Changes in Mass Reading Material in the Late Qing and Early Republic) in Zhang Jinglu (ed.), *Zhongguo quban shiliao bubian* (Shanghai, 1957), pp. 145-8.
48. Unlike Japan, where the primary schools were *not* perceived as a natural feeder for middle schools, the primary schools in China were linked to middle schools.
49. The Board of Education's proposed graduation certificate is in *Liangguang guanbao*, no. 3 (1911), 26a-28a.
50. DFZZ, 1: 4 (1904), *jiaoyu*, p. 80; JYZZ, 1: 10 (1909), *jishi* p. 76; JYZZ, 1: 11 (1910), *jishi*, p. 88.
51. Sichuan also had 7 504 reformed traditional schools that gave literacy classes.
52. JYZZ, 3: 6 (1911), *jishi*, p. 91. Henan had 2 500 literacy schools with 59 000 students. Hubei, Shandong, Guangdong, Zhejiang, Fujian, Shaanxi and Hunan all had over 500 literacy schools.
53. *Zhengzhi guanbao*, 32: 909 (1910), p. 83. In May 1911 the Governor-General reported a total of 601 literacy schools in the province with an enrolment of 16 615. *Zhengzhi guanbao*, 44: 1260 (1911), p. 135.
54. *Zhengzhi guanbao*, 43: 1234 (1911), pp. 207-9. Sun had a rather more blunt appraisal of the benefits of literacy schools, remarking that 'the more the people's knowledge daily advances, the easier it will be for government orders to be carried out'.
55. *Zhengzhi guanbao*, 43: 1253 (1911), p. 533.
56. *Zhengzhi guanbao*, 45: 1289 (1911), p. 125.
57. *Zhengzhi guanbao*, 45: 1291 (1911), pp. 157-8. For reports by the governors of Jilin and Hunan, see *ibid.*, 43: 1237, p. 253; 43: 1251, p. 501.
58. *Zhengzhi guanbao*, 32: 910 (1910), p. 102. See also *Xuebu guanbao*, no. 130 (1910), *jingwai zoudu*, p. 4; Taga Akigorō (comp.), *Shiryō*, 1: 98.
59. JYZZ, 2: 1 (1910), *jishi*, pp. 3-4. Literacy classes in Nanjing also taught arithmetic. JYZZ, 1: 11 (1910), *jishi*, p. 88.
60. JYZZ, 2: 1 (1910), *jishi*, pp. 3-4. Literacy classes were also held in lower and higher primary schools in Hangzhou, Zhejiang. JYZZ, 2: 2 (1910), *jishi*, pp. 14-15.
61. DFZZ, 3: 6 (1907), *jiaoyu*, p. 136.
62. On Chinese religion, see C. Yang, *Religion In Chinese Society* (Berkeley, 1961); R. Smith, *China's Cultural Heritage* (Boulder, 1983), pp. 124–155.
63. On the City God, see S. Feuchtwang, 'School-Temple and City God' in G. William Skinner (ed.), *The City in Late Imperial China* (Stanford, 1977), pp. 581–608; A. Zito, 'City Gods, Filiality and Hegemony in Late Imperial China', *Modern China*, 13: 3 (July 1987), pp. 333-71.

64. JYZZ, 2: 1 (1910), jishi, p. 3; JYZZ, 2: 5 (1910), jishi, p. 39. City God temples were not only used to house spare-time classes. In Zhili, one such temple was used in 1905 to stage an educational exhibition which displayed scientific equipment and textbooks. DFZZ, 2: 3 (1905), jiaoyu, pp. 49-50.
65. Chan Sin-wai, *Buddhism in Late Ch'ing Political Thought* (Hong Kong, 1985), p. 15.
66. Of the 80 000 Buddhist temples existing in 1668, more than 12 000 had been founded by imperial order since the Manchu conquest.
67. Chan Sin-wai, *Buddhism in Late Ch'ing Political Thought* argues that Kang Youwei, Liang Qichao, Tan Sitong, and Zhang Binglin all had a keen interest in Buddhism, which they saw as compatible with western learning. For a good example of what Chan sees as a utilitarian and politically-oriented approach towards Buddhism at this time see Liang Qichao, 'Lun fojiao yu qunzhi zhi guanxi' (On the Relationship Between Buddhism and Popular Rule), *Yinbing shi quanji, zhuan* 3, pp. 26-31.
68. DFZZ, 1: 5 (1904), jiaoyu, p. 121.
69. DFZZ, 1: 7 (1904), jiaoyu, p. 172. See also DFZZ, 1: 12 (1905), shiping, p. 88.
70. Wang Fenggang, *Japanese Influence on Educational Reform in China from 1895 to 1911*, p. 92. Japanese Buddhism had come to China in 1876 with the establishment of a branch temple of the Higashi Honganji chapter of the Jōdō Shinshū sect in Shanghai. surprisingly little has been written on the Japanese Buddhist missionary enterprise in China. M. Peattie, 'The Japanese Treaty Port Settlements in China 1895-1937' in P. Duus, R. Myers, M. Peattie (eds.), *The Japanese Informal Empire in China 1895–1937* (Princeton, 1989), simply remarks (p. 197) that a Buddhist temple was a 'ubiquitous' feature of Japanese communities in treaty-port China.
71. *Jingzhong ribao*, no. 75 (1904), *difang jiwen*.
72. DFZZ, 2: 1 (1905), jiaoyu, p. 19.
73. DFZZ, 2: 3 (1905), jiaoyu, p. 49. Another temple in Guangzhou contributed 60 000 taels for education. *Jingzhong ribao*, no. 2 (1905), *xuejie jiwen*.
74. DFZZ, 1: 9 (1904), jiaoyu, p. 214.
75. DFZZ, 1: 6 (1904), jiaoyu, p. 145. For other examples in Hunan and Guangdong, see DFZZ, 1: 3 (1904), jiaoyu, p. 72.
76. For example, in Shuntian district, Zhili, a group of middle-school graduates opened a half-day school in 1906 and recruited twenty volunteer teachers. A half-day school in the Shandong provincial capital had fourteen voluntary teachers who came to the school at different times of the day. DFZZ, 1: 7 (1904), jiaoyu, p. 168.
77. JYZZ, 2: 5 (1910), jishi, p. 39. There was, of course, great variation in salaries paid. A half-day school in Tianjin paid its teacher the princely sum of 20 yuan a month. *Xuebu guanbao*, no. 9 (1906), *fulu*.
78. *Jiaoyu yu shiye*, no. 22 (October 1920).
79. *Xuebu guanbao*, no. 36 (1907), *jingwai xuewu baogao*, p. 314. For the salaries of primary school teachers in Zhili, see *Xuebu guanbao*, nos.

22, 23.
80. See, for example, information on teachers' salaries at the Jiangxi Higher Normal School in *Xuebu guanbao*, no. 35 (1907), *jingwai xuewu baogao*, pp. 305-7. At Shanxi University teachers were paid from 60 to 100 *taels* a month. The teacher of physical education, however, was paid a relatively low salary of 12 *taels* a month. *Xuebu guanbao*, no. 10 (1906), *jingwai xuewu baogao*, pp. 56-7.
81. J. Tobar, 'La Réforme des Etudes en Chine', *Etudes*, vol. 97 (1903), pp. 711-16. On Japanese teachers in China, see Sanetō Keishū, *Chugokujin Nihon Ryūgaku Shi*, pp. 93-104; Hiroshi Abe, 'Borrowing from Japan: China's First Modern Educational System' in R. Hayhoe, M. Bastid (eds.), *China's Education and the Industrial World* (New York, 1987), pp. 67-73. In 1905 there were up to 500 Japanese teachers and educational advisers in China. They taught at all levels and were distributed widely throughout China (although Zhili had the highest number – 114 – in 1909). The majority of Japanese teachers in China, however, were employed in normal and vocational schools.
82. *Xuebu guanbao*, no. 35 (1907), *jingwai xuewu baogao*, p. 309. Another revealing example is that of the Japanese employed at the Beijing Lecture Training Institute (*jiangxisuo*), who earned 300 dollars a month. *Jinghua xinbao*, no. 238 (1906). Chinese lecturers in Tianjin were paid 20 dollars a month. *Xuebu guanbao*, no. 9 (1906), *fulu*.
83. C. Gluck, *Japan's Modern Myths* (Princeton, 1985), pp. 151, 353. In the late 1890s teachers' salaries in Japan were lower than those of artisans and labourers. For example, an elementary school teacher earned 13 *yen* a month, while a middle-rank labourer could earn just over 16 *yen*.
84. JYZZ, 2: 9, *jishi*, p. 74.
85. JYZZ, 2: 11 (1910), *zhangcheng wendu*, pp. 51-2.
86. JYZZ, 2: 5 (1910), *sheshuo*, pp. 23-9.
87. JYZZ, 2: 12 (1911), *jishi*, p. 99.
88. JYZZ, 3: 3 (1911), *faling*, pp. 38-9; *jishi*, pp. 19-20.
89. JYZZ, 3: 9 (1911), *faling*, p. 91.
90. Huang Yanpei, 'Sanshiwunian Zhongguo zhi zhiye jiaoyu' (Vocational Education in China in the Last Thirty-five Years) in Zhuang Yu (ed.), *Zuijin sanshinian zhi Zhongguo jiaoyu*, p. 136.
91. Peng Zeyi (comp.), *Zhongguo jindai shougongyeshi ziliao* (Beijing, 1957), 2: 515–8.
92. Ibid., 2: 521. By 1907 training factories were also being set up for unemployed bannermen in the metropolitan region.
93. Between 1903 and 1907, 476 students apparently graduated from the spinning and weaving course, and 101 from the dyeing course.
94. Peng Zeyi (comp.), *Zhongguo jindai shougongyeshi ziliao*, 2: 524. See also the memorial from the Governor of Zhejiang in 1905 on the establishment of industrial training bureaux, which showed as much concern for individual welfare as for state wealth. DFZZ, 2: 7 (1905), *shiye*, p. 111.

95. The Japanese term was itself a translation from the German (*Gewerbeerziehung*). *Jiaoyu cihui*, p. 164.
96. Cited in Huang Yanpei, 'Sanshiwunian Zhongguo zhi zhiye jiaoyu', p. 138.
97. Taga Akigorō(comp.), *Shiryō*, 1: 427.
98. *Ibid.*, 1: 519-20. Unfortunately, it is not possible to calculate the number of either apprentice schools or supplementary vocational schools since they are not listed as a separate category in the Board of Education statistics for 1907, 1908 and 1909. The Governor of Hunan in 1911 referred to seventeen apprentice schools in his province, while the Governor of Xinjiang referred to an increasing number of such schools there without giving a specific figure. *Zhengzhi guanbao*, 32: 910 (1911), p. 103; 43: 1224 (1911), p. 29.
99. The curriculum for the Guizhou provincial apprentice school stipulated 5 hours per week for Chinese, 1 hour for writing, 3 hours for physical education, 1 hour for drawing and 21 hours for metallurgy, carpentry, weaving, and dyeing. The school was financed by taxes on kerosene lamps and meat. *Guizhou jiaoyu guanbao*, no. 3 (1907), *guizhi*, pp . 1–2.
100. It is important to remember the non-existence or permitted waiving of fees for half-day, literacy, apprentice, vocational and lower primary schools when considering M. Bastid's conclusion that the costs of modern eucation exceeded those of traditional education. *Aspects de la Réforme de l'Enseignement*, pp. 223-4. It is significant that Bastid only focuses on modern primary and normal schools to illustrate the higher costs of education. Even in the case of modern primary schools, as was noted in Chapter One, fees were not always charged, sometimes forcing them to close down.
101. Chen Qitan, *Zuijin sanshinian Zhongguo jiaoyushi*, pp. 132-4.
102. On this, see W. Ch'an, *Merchants, Mandarins and Modern Enterprise in Late Ch'ing China*, pp. 175-233.
103. For the regulations on rewards and merits for entrepreneurs, industrialists and inventors, see Wang Jingyu (comp.), *Zhongguo jindai gongye shi ziliao* (Beijing, 1957), 2.1: 638-47. First-class awards went to those involved in shipping and railways; second-class awards for those involved in mining and steam engines; third-class awards for those pioneering textile and agricultural technology; fourth-class awards for improving handicraft production; and fifth-class awards for those successfully imitating foreign products for the domestic market. W. Ch'an, *Merchants, Mandarins, and Modern Enterprise in Late Ch'ing China*, p. 190.
104. Local chambers of commerce also assumed political roles, becoming leaders in commercial tax protests and local defence organisations. S. Mann, *Local Merchants and the Chinese Bureaucracy 1750-1950* (Stanford, 1987), pp. 153-5. On the increasing public role of chambers of commerce in Zhejiang, see R. Keith Schoppa, *Chinese Elites and Political Change: Zhejiang Province in the Early Twentieth Century* (Cambridge, Mass., 1982), pp. 65-6.
105. W. Ch'an, *Merchants, Mandarins and Modern Enterprise in Late*

Ch'ing China, pp. 226-32.
106. This is the view adopted by W. Ch'an, *ibid.*, p. 237. S. Mann, *Local Merchants and the Chinese Bureaucracy 1750-1950*, p. 154, also points out, however, that the widespread distribution of local chambers of commerce provided a unique organisational structure for expressing a new political consciousness.
107. Peng Zeyi (comp.), *Zhongguo jindai shougongye shi ziliao*, 2: 527.
108. *Ibid.*, 2: 535-8.
109. *Ibid.*, 2: 558. Reflecting also the prevalence of clan organisation in the province, the Governor also proposed the creation of clan industrial training centres (*jiazu gongyi zhuanxi suo*) to help combat problems of 'idleness and unemployment' within clans. *Zhengzhi guanbao* 44: 1259 (1911), p. 115.
110. Peng Zeyi (comp.), *Zhongguo jindai shougongye shi ziliao*, 2: 556.
111. For example, the industrial training centre in Lianzhou prefecture, Guangdong, which taught the unemployed and petty criminals, was located in a temple, as was the training centre in the Shandong provincial capital. DFZZ, 2: 5 (1905) *shiye*, p. 94; DFZZ, 1: 6 (1904) *shiye*, pp. 101, 103; *Jingzhong ribao*, no. 115 (19 June 1904), *difang jiwen*.
112. *Jingzhong ribao*, no. 115 (19 June 1904), *difang jiwen*.
113. Peng Zeyi (comp.), *Zhongguo jindai shougongye shi ziliao*, 2: 556.
114. *Ibid.*, 2: 539.
115. *Ibid.*, 2: 554. What is especially striking about the Governor's view is that he made no reference to the necessity of moral indoctrination as the most important guarantor of a law-abiding people.
116. For memorials from the Governor of Shandong, Yuan Shikai, and the Governor-General of Yunnan and Guizhou on the importance of training prisoners, see DFZZ, 1: 10 (1904), *shiye*, pp. 170-1, 175-7; 2: 5 (1905), *shiye*, pp. 64-72; 2: 7 (1905), *shiye*, pp. 113-4. In 1911, China sent a representative to the Eighth World Congress of Prison Associations. For his report, see *Zhengzhi guanbao*, vol. 40, pp. 474-92.
117. Peng Zeyi (comp.), *Zhongguo jindai shougongye shi ziliao*, 2: 533.
118. Gao Jiansi, 'Sanshiwu nian lai zhi minzhong jiaoyu', pp. 159-160; DFZZ, 3: 3 (1906), *jiaoyu*, p. 52.
119. DFZZ, 3: 10 (1906), *shiye*, p. 196; 3: 11 (1906), *jiaoyu*, p. 331; 3: 12 (1907), *shiye*, p. 238.
120. DFZZ, 2: 7 (1905), *shiye*, p. 129.
121. Peng Zeyi (comp.), *Zhongguo jindai shougongye shi ziliao*, 2: 556.
122. DFZZ, 1: 4 (1904), *shiye*, p. 16.
123. Peng Zeyi (comp.), *Zhongguo jindai shougongye shi ziliao*, 2: 554. In Lijin, Shandong, even a former academy was converted into a 'self-renewal training centre' (*zixin xiyi suo*) for local prisoners. DFZZ, 2: 9 (1905), *shiye*, p. 164.
124. Peng Zeyi (comp.), *Zhongguo jindai shougongye shi ziliao*, 2: 563.
125. *Ibid.*, 2: 559, 569, 571. A memorial from the Governor of Xinjiang underlining the importance of vocational education for provincial self-sufficiency and the prevention of raw materials flowing outside

the province is in *Xuebu guanbao*, no. 129 (1910), *jingwai coudou*, pp. 1-2.
126. For example, in Jianglu, Sichuan and Gaoyang, Zhili. Gao Jiansi, 'Sanshiwu nian lai zhi minzhong jiaoyu', p. 157; DFZZ, 2: 2 (1905), *jiaoyu*, p. 29.
127. In Tianjin, a night school for shopkeepers' children was opened, while in Chengdu, Sichuan, a night school with the grandiose name of the Enlightenment Night Class Institute (*qiwu yekeguan*) catered for traders and peddlers. DFZZ, 2: 2 (1905), *jiaoyu*, p. 27; DFZZ, 2: 12 (1906), p. 347.
128. DFZZ, 4: 7 (1907), *jiaoyu*, p. 169; JYZZ, 2: 10 (1910), *jishi*, p. 79; Gao Jiansi, 'Sanshiwu nian lai zhi minzhong jiaoyu', p. 159.
129. Peng Zeyi (comp.), *Zhongguo jindai shougongye shi ziliao*, 2: 560.
130. For example, the chambers of commerce in Wuyang (Jiangsu), Zhoucun (Shandong), Tianjin (Zhili), and Wuhu (Anhui). DFZZ, 2: 2 (1905), *jiaoyu*, pp. 27, 28; 2: 12 (1906), *jiaoyu*, p. 345; 3: 1 (1906), *jiaoyu*, p. 25.
131. Qu Lihe, *Zhang Jian di jiaoyu sixiang* (n.p., n.d.), p. 64; S. Chu, *Chang Chien: Reformer in Modern China* (New York, 1965), p. 96; M. Bastid, *Aspects de la Réforme*, p. 46.
132. Peng Zhongwei, 'Huiyi Yu Zhimo' (Remembering Yu Zhimo) in *Xinhai geming huiyi lu*, 2: 217. On Yu Zhimo, see Chen Xinxian et al. (eds.), *Yu Zhimo shiliao* (Changsha, 1981); Feng Ziyou, *Geming yishi* (Shanghai, 1947), 2: 180-7; *Xinhai geming*, 2: 533-7; Nakamura Tadashi, 'Chūgoku ni okeru kakumeiteki minshū shugika no to' (The Career of a Revolutionary Democrat in China), in *Higashi Ajia Kindaishi no Kenkyū* (Tokyo, 1967); J. Esherick, *Reform and Revolution*, pp. 53-8. Other examples include the owner of a spinning factory in Lincheng, Shandong, who opened two spare-time schools for his workers and poorer members of the local community. DFZZ, 3: 1 (1906), *jiaoyu*, p. 25. In Cixi, Jiangsu, a certain Wang Mutang opened a vocational school in 1909 that taught silkworm breeding to three hundred students. Operating expenditures were met from the sale of crops grown on school land. JYZZ, 3: 6 (1911), *zazuan*, pp. 31-2. See also Gao Jiansi, 'Sanshiwu nian lai zhi minzhong jiaoyu', p. 158; DFZZ, 2: 3 (1905), *jiaoyu*, p. 51; 3: 12 (1907), *jiaoyu*, pp. 369-70.
133. Taga Akigorō (ed.), *Shiryō*, 1: 459-68; Shu Xincheng (ed.), *Ziliao*, 3: 800-19. In 1908 the first official normal school for girls was opened in Beijing, although women had already begun going to Japan from 1905 onwards for normal school training. Taga Akigorō (ed.), *Shiryō*, 1: 74. The number of women students in modern schools grew only modestly in the years preceding the 1911 Revolution, increasing from 306 in 1906 to 12 614 in 1912. By 1915-16 the total had increased to 180 940. Lin Paotchin, *L'Instruction Féminine en Chine* (Paris, 1926), pp. 14, 22.
134. Even the Empress-Dowager showed an interest in promoting vocational training for women. In 1905 skilled Chinese women workers were employed by the Imperial Household Department to

teach Manchu girls. Peng Zeyi (comp.), *Zhongguo jindai shougongye shi ziliao*, 2: 515.
135. *Ibid.*, 2: 568. See also *Xuebu guanbao*, no. 130 (1910), *jingwai coudou*, p. 2.
136. For a report on the Beijing women's vocational training workshop, see *Xuebu guanbao*, no. 137 (1910), *jingwai coudou*, p. 1.
137. Taga Akigorō (ed.), *Shiryō*, 1: 74; DFZZ, 3: 10 (1906), *jiaoyu*, p. 278.
138. Wu Yanyin, 'Sanshiwunian lai Zhongguo zhi xiaoxue jiaoyu' (Primary Education in China in the last Thirty-five Years) in Zhuang Yu (ed.), *Zuijin sanshinian zhi Zhongguo jiaoyu*, pp. 12-3. The 1902 and 1904 curricula for lower and higher primary schools can also be found in Shu Xincheng (ed.), *Ziliao*, 2: 406-9, 421-4, 437-8; and M. Bastid, *Aspects de la Réforme*, pp. 42-3.
139. This represented an increase over the schedule prescribed in the 1902 regulations, which had proposed that twelve hours (out of seventy-two hours in a twelve day week) be spent on the Confucian classics.
140. Shu Xincheng (ed.), *Ziliao*, 2: 445 .
141. DFZZ, 2: 10 (1905), *jiaoyu*, p. 194; JYZZ, 3: 5 (1911), *yanlun*, p. 51. Not everyone agreed with this view. A 1904 article in *Anhui suhua bao* rejected the notion that the Classic of Odes was pornographic, arguing that it was progressive for its time because the poems advocated free choice in marriage. Xue Cong, 'Zai lun hunyin' (A Further Discussion of Marriage), *Anhui suhua bao*, no. 16 (1904). The *Spring and Autumn Annals* was a chronicle of events from 722-481 BC traditionally believed to have been compiled and edited by Confucius to indicate his value judgements on historical events and personalities. The *Zuo* commentary, of unidentifiable origin, was an elaboration of the Annals. The *Classic of Odes* was a collection of three hundred-odd poems, again reportedly selected by Confucius from a collection of more than three thousand songs gathered by the music master in Confucius' own state of Lu.
142. In the first two years of lower primary school they were not to be studied at all. The last two years were to teach just two of the Confucian Classics - the *Analects* (a collection of Confucius' homilies noted down by his disciples) and the *Classic of Filial Piety* (*Xiaojing*), a work dating from the early Han dynasty 202 BC–9 AD) which extolled filial piety as the root of all other virtues.
143. JYZZ, 3: 3 (1911), *faling*, pp. 9-13; Taga Akigorō (ed.), *Shiryō*, 1: 652-3; Chen Qingzhi, *Zhongguo jiaoyushi*, pp. 614–6. In the final year only ten hours per week were to be spent on the Classics. In 1904 it had been stipulated that higher primary schools spend twelve (out of thirty-six) hours on the Classics.
144. Taga Akigorō (ed.), *Shiryō*, 1: 65–8.
145. Miao Wengong, 'Lun xiushen jiaoshou buke zhuanyong rujia yan' (The Teaching of Morality Should not Just be Confined to Confucianism), JYZZ, 1: 12 (1910), *sheshuo*, pp. 149-55. Another attack on Confucian morality appeared in an article on the link between aestheticism and manufactured goods. The article main-

tained that foreign goods always looked better than Chinese ones because the natural aesthetic sense of the Chinese child was stifled by the Confucian stress on plainness and frugality. *Jinghua xinbao*, nos. 236, 237 (1906).
146. Gu Shi, 'Lun putong jiaoyu yu shiye jiaoyu zhi fentu' (On the Separation of General and Practical Education), JYZZ, 3: 3 (1911), *yanlun*, pp. 33-46. Gu used the term *jia*, borrowed from the Japanese *ka* to indicate a professional specialist. In praising the educational systems of France and Germany which, in his view, stressed practical education overall, Gu overlooked the sharp divisions between general and vocational upper primary schools in France and the clear distinction between the two kinds of secondary school in Germany.
147. JYZZ, 3: 1 (1911), *jishi*, p. 4.
148. Li Jinxi, 'Sanshiwunian lai zhi guoyu yundong' (The National Speech Movement in the Last Thirty-five Years) in Zhuang Yu (ed.), *Zuijin sanshinian zhi Zhongguo jiaoyu*, p. 71. In 1911 the term *guanhua* was replaced by *guoyu* (national speech). The attempt to use Manchus to teach *guanhua* may also have had its successes. Already, in 1904, the Fuzhou Normal School had employed a Manchu teacher in the hope of improving Chinese–Manchu harmony. He was reportedly a conscientious teacher. *Jingzhong ribao*, no. 20 (16 March 1904), *difang jiwen*.
149. Zhang Zhidong had earlier been much impressed with the western practice of having primary school texts checked and edited by the authorities.
150. Taga Akigorō (ed.), *Shiryō*, 1: 534-5; Shu xincheng (ed.), *Shiliao*, 2: 259.
151. The Board also pointed out that unlike other education ministries in the world, which charged fees for approval and certification, it would not do so in the interests of promoting education.
152. Taga Akigorō (ed.), *Shiryō*, 1: 67.
153. In 1912 the new republican Education Ministry was to order the provinces to organise 'textbook examining committees' (*dushu fanchahui*) to check educational texts. Shu Xincheng (ed.), *Shiliao*, 4: 179. It also took time for the Board to impose its will on schools. Thus a Board inspector in Henan noted in 1908 that not all primary schools were using the recommended textbooks. *Xuebu guanbao*, no. 53 (1908), *jingwai xuewu baogao*, p. 722.
154. C. Gluck, *Japan's Modern Myths*, p. 147.
155. E. Rawski, *Education and Popular Literacy in Ch'ing China*, p. 138.
156. *Linqing xianzhi* (1934), p. 478. In the Shanghai area, 25 out of the 32 charitable schools established during the Qing were converted into primary schools between 1902 and 1910. Ogawa Yoshiko, 'Shindai ni okeru gigaku setsuritsu no kiban' (The Foundations for the Establishment of Charitable Schools in the Qing), in Hayashi Tomohara (ed.), *Kindai Chūgoku Kyōikushi Kenkyū* (Tokyo, 1958), pp. 275-7.
157. Taga Akigorō (ed.), *Shiryō*, 1: 63.

158. Wu Qiping, *Gailiang sishu* (Shanghai, 1935), pp. 3-5.
159. Superior students were to be promoted to modern primary schools.
160. Shu Xincheng (ed.), *Ziliao*, 1: 109-13.
161. Wu Qiping, *Gailiang sishu*, p. 6. See also T'ai-ch'u Liao, 'Rural Education in Transition', *Yenching Journal of Social Studies*, 4: 2 (February 1949), pp. 19–67.
162. On clan education, see Hui-chen Wang Liu, *The Traditional Chinese Clan Rules* (New York, 1959), p. 107, 127-9. A recent study of a Guangdong lineage notes that the proceeds of education land (*xuetian*) up until the early twentieth century were used to encourage scholarly success in the examinations and hence win prestige for the lineage. Such funds benefeted the wealthier members at the expense of the poorer ones. Yuen-fong Woon, *Social Organization in South China 1911-1949: The Case of the Kuan Lineage in K'ai-p'ing County* (Michigan, 1984), p. 31.
163. On clan schools in the early twentieth century, see Taga Akigorō, 'Kindai Chūgoku ni okeru zokujuku no seikaku' (The Nature of the Clan School in Modern China), *Kindai Chūgoku Kenkyū*, no. 4 (1960), pp. 207-54. Taga shows that after 1905 the nature of the clan school gradually changed as it accepted for the first time both girls and outsiders to the clan.
164. DFZZ, 2: 9 (1905), *jiaoyu*, p. 242.
165. DFZZ, 2: 11 (1906), *jiaoyu*, p. 292.
166. M. Bastid's assertion (*Aspects de la Réforme*, pp. 84-5) that clan schools were often abandoned by wealthy families who sought to place their sons in modern schools (thus depriving poorer members of any potential access to education) may therefore not be valid in all cases.
167. DFZZ, 1: 1 (1904), *jiaoyu*, p. 34.
168. DFZZ, 1: 2 (1904), *jiaoyu*, p. 44.
169. DFZZ, 7: 5 (1910), *jidai*, pp. 27-8.
170. Although again it must be noted that many of these 'modern' schools were either located in temples or were converted traditional schools. In Henan, for example, out of the reported 2 603 primary schools in 1906, 2 274 were reformed traditonal schools. Abe Hiroshi, 'Shinmatsu no kindai gakkō, kōsei-sho o chūshin ni' (Modern Schools at the end of the Qing, with reference to Jiangxi Province), in *Rekishi Hyōron*, no. 1 (January 1965), p. 54.
171. In Guang'an Sichuan, for example, disgruntled gentry stirred up mob anger against the modern school in 1904 by spreading rumours that disastrous changes in the weather were due to the school's presence. DFZZ, 1: 9 (1904), *sheshuo*, p. 217. For a useful discussion of the reasons behind popular anger against the modern schools, see Nakamura Tsune, 'Shinmatsu gakudo setsuritsu o meguru, Kōsetsu nōson shakai no ichi danmen' (A Look at Rural Society In Jiangsu and Zhejiang, based on the Establishment of Schools at the End of the Qing) in *Rekishi Kyōiku*, 10: 11 (1962), pp. 72-85. Nakamura calculates that there were forty-nine cases of school destruction between 1902 and 1910 in Jiangsu and Zhejiang

(of which thirty occurred in 1910 alone). Nineteen of these incidents were due to increased taxes and fifteen were associated with the arrival of population census teams in the area, which provoked popular fear of more increased taxes.

172. Previous studies have concentrated solely on the new schooling in the cities and the tendency for reformers to start anew rather than build upon traditional foundations. G. Rozman (ed.), *The Modernization of China*, pp. 187, 403-7. Many of the ideas and innovations that the contributors to this volume attribute to the May Fourth period and after (e.g. exhibitions of Chinese-made educational products, the experiments with shorter courses, and the encouragement of manual labour) were, in fact, raised and acted upon in the 1910s and before.

173. The reverse was probably true. Thus the renewed interest in education amongst missionaries in China was partly prompted by the fear that if they did not pool their resources, missionary schools would be swamped by native ones. In 1915 the China Christian Education Association was specifically founded to meet competition from Chinese government schools. J. Lutz, *China and the Christian Colleges* (Ithaca, 1971), pp. 105, 180. In fact, the number of Chinese students in missionary schools was always a small proportion of the total number of students in government and private schools at this time. As late as 1921 only 6.5 per cent of Chinese primary-school students were enrolled in missionary primary schools. (The proportion for middle and higher schools was a little higher, 12.5 per cent and 11.7 per cent respectively). Shu Xincheng (ed.) *Ziliao*, 1: 376-80; *Christian Education in China* (Shanghai, 1922), pp. 26-32.

174. M. Weber, *The Religion of China* (New York, 1951), p. 19. For a discussion of how liturgical governance affected merchants, see S. Mann, *Local Merchants and Chinese Bureaucracy 1750–1950*, pp. 12-25. Mann points out that merchants, trade organisations and gentry lineages with commercial investments assumed tax-collecting roles in the marketplace to compensate for the limits of bureaucratic control. Their importance in liturgical governance greatly increased after 1853.

175. On militarisation in the late Qing and the emergence of gentry-led militia armies, see P. Kuhn, *Rebellion and Its Enemies in Late Imperial China* (Cambridge, Mass., 1970).

4. The 1912 School System

The Manchu reform effort after 1901 ultimately failed to stem the growing tide of opposition to Qing rule. The series of political, educational and military reforms through which the dynasty hoped to enlist gentry support and stifle the vociferous anti-Manchu clamour amongst radical Chinese students in Japan merely exacerbated the growing alienation of provincial and local elites from the central government, while providing grist for the mill of anti-Manchu republication revolutionaries.

Attempts at constitutional reform, such as the creation of provincial assemblies, simply whetted the appetite of gentry elites, whose initial enthusiasm soon turned to frustration and anger as the Qing government attempted to restrict the process. The encouragement of overseas study (primarily in Japan) exposed thousands of Chinese students to concepts of nationalism and democracy. Many returned to take up teaching posts in the new schools set up by the Qing, where they spread and distributed anti-Manchu revolutionary propaganda. Military reform, whereby the Qing hoped to create a new modernised national army under the control of a central ministry of war, revived Han Chinese fears that the court was attempting to centralise control in the hands of Manchus. Finally, the increased taxes needed to finance reform incurred the wrath of rural and urban masses who vented their anger by attacking the visible manifestations of reform, whether they be local government bureaux, new police bureaux or modern schools.

Amidst growing discontent and alienation, the court's decision to nationalise railways by taking over provincial-financed lines was the spark that ignited the revolutionary flame. Riots led by provincial gentry elites in Sichuan in early 1911 were followed by an army mutiny in Wuchang, Hubei, in October. Provinces soon began to declare their independence from Beijing, spearheaded by gentry-dominated provincial assemblies and new army units. In desperation the court recalled Yuan Shikai (who had been forced to retire from official life in 1908) to head a cabinet and command the imperial army.

A stalemate soon ensued as imperial and revolutionary forces remained locked in combat around Hankou. It was at this point that Sun Yatsen, who had returned from the United States in December 1911 and been elected provisional President by an assembly in Nanjing comprising hand-picked delegates from the southern provinces, decided to reach an agreement with Yuan Shikai. Sun feared that continued civil war might lead to intervention by the powers to protect their economic interests. In return for the presidency Yuan guaranteed the peaceful abdication of the dynasty[1] and his adherence to a republican constitution. In February 1912, the Empress-Dowager Longyu, acting on behalf of the six-year-old Emperor Puyi,[2] formally proclaimed the abdication of the Qing dynasty and in March 1912 Yuan Shikai became provisional President of a new Chinese Republic. Although the revolutionaries had expected the site of the new capital to be in Nanjing, Yuan insisted that it remain in Beijing, the centre of his power base.[3]

Despite misgivings by some about Yuan's credentials to be president of a republic – he had, after all, served the *ancien régime* in important provincial and central government posts – there was general optimism about the future. Yuan's reputation as a modernising official when he was Governor-General of Zhili (1901-8) and his promise that national elections would be held at the end of 1912 held out the hope that the transition to a republic would be a smooth one. Although Yuan, under the provisional constitution of 1912, had considerable executive power (e.g. he was Commander-in-Chief of the army and had broad powers of appointment), the provisional parliament in Beijing, comprising five representatives from each province, was able to go ahead and make arrangements for the election of a bicameral parliament and new provincial assemblies.[4] Furthermore, Sun's pre-1911 revolutionary organisation, the *Tongmenghui* (Alliance League) had four adherents appointed to the first cabinet, including Cai Yuanpei, who became education minister.[5]

The early years of the republic were to see a continuation of efforts begun in the last years of the monarchy to promote popular education. There was, in fact, a real continuity, in both ideas and personnel, that cut across the political change in 1912. The public debate on education widened in the last months of the dynasty, with the convening of national education conferences to discuss policy. This set a precedent that was followed during the early republic and beyond. Many of the educators involved in the debate before 1912 were active participants in early republican developments, while proposals put forward before the fall of the dynasty were to be adopted in 1912.

In the aftermath of the 1911 Revolution education was a crucial topic in debates over the post-imperial order, just as it had been after the French and Russian revolutions.[6] The educational debate that culminated in the 1912 school system (which was to remain in effect until 1922) was a complex affair, and cannot simply be viewed in terms of a struggle between 'liberal' educators like Cai Yuanpei and his conservative opponents wanting to use education as a means of moral indoctrination.[7] Before analysing this debate, it is necessary to describe developments during the last months of the dynasty, since so many of the ideas raised at this time anticipated those of post-imperial China.

THE WIDENING PUBLIC DEBATE

Growing numbers of people became involved in the educational debate in 1911. In the early part of the year representatives from various schools in

Shanghai organised a Federation of Educational Circles (*xuejie lianhehui*), which called for the promotion of military education.[8] In April, on the recommendation of the Jiangsu Education Association, a nationwide federation of provincial education associations was organised. It convened a meeting in Shanghai, and it is a measure of how the state's monopoly over the setting of the educational agenda had been infringed upon that this conference of provincial education associations assumed the right to discuss educational reform measures. Each education association was to submit its proposals one month ahead of time and each delegation (two or three representatives) would have one vote. A presiding chairman, who had the casting vote, was elected at each session.[9]

When the conference opened at the end of April 1911, eleven provinces were represented (Anhui, Fujian, Guangxi, Henan, Hubei, Hunan, Jiangsu, Jiangxi, Shandong, Zhejiang, Zhili).[10] The representatives were given a welcoming banquet by the Shanghai Commercial Press, another indication of the fact that an increasing number of non-official groups and organisations were concerning themselves with educational reform.[11] On the opening day, Zhang Jian, vice-chairman of the Jiangsu Education Association, made it clear that all the provinces needed to join together to discuss educational plans for the country. The court's attempt to enlist gentry support for its reform programme had thus led to an unforeseen development – non-official elites had now assumed the right to discuss policy, a right heretofore never conceded by the imperial state.

The conference addressed five proposals to the Board of Education. All were concerned with changes in educational practice or reiteration of ideas already raised in the periodical press. Firstly, the conference advised the government that schools needed to emphasise a 'militant citizenry education' (*junguomin jiaoyu zhuyi*). In a constitutional country where everyone would have to perform military service, the conference reasoned, a martial spirit would have to be encouraged at school. Interestingly, not only was it suggested that physical education be a compulsory subject at school[12] and that military drill be carried out in all higher primary schools and above,[13] but also that firing practice (using live ammunition) be carried out in all middle schools. The idea itself was not new. A Hunanese normal school student in 1904 had petitioned the Governor requesting that students be provided with firearms for military drill – forty Remington (*linmingdun*) rifles were in fact issued by the provincial armaments bureau.[14] The Governor-General of the three north-eastern provinces, Xi Liang, had also proposed this for his area in April 1911.[15] Now, however, the conference suggested that this should be standard practice for all middle schools.[16]

Secondly, the conference proposed changes in the primary-school curriculum. In general it stressed the importance of using textbook material relevant to local needs and conditions rather than uniformly prescribed material. More specifically, the conference urged that handicrafts (*shougong*) be made compulsory so that the child would be trained in the 'habit of labour' (*laodong zhi xiguan*).[17] In sharp contrast to traditional attitudes, it was stressed that a dexterity in manual skills was intimately linked with intellectual, moral and physical education. At the same time the conference took up the question of the relevance of the Confucian Classics and suggested that they be entirely eliminated from the primary school curriculum. The conference also supported the idea of coeducation (up to the age of ten); if segregated elementary education continued, it noted, girls' education would inevitably suffer since the building of boys' schools would always take priority.

The remaining three proposals addressed to the Board of Education included the more equitable distribution of higher-level educational institutions rather than being concentrated in Beijing and other important cities, and that their courses should meet the needs of the province in which they were situated; the unification of the national language (*guoyu*) using the Beijing pronunciation as the standard;[18] and the abolition of the practice of awarding traditional civil service degrees to school graduates, which was seen to perpetuate the link between education and the gaining of official posts.[19]

The conference also discussed the need to organise federations of professional teachers. Ignoring both the state's traditional role in deciding the content of education (through the civil service examination system) and the prestige that had traditionally accrued to the Confucian 'generalist', the conference asserted that only *professionals* were equipped to deal with matters concerning curricula, school administration, and teaching methods. The importance of professionalism in education had already been perceived with the creation of normal schools, and the process was accelerated in the early years of the Republic. Thus by 1913, out of the sixty-one heads of provincial education offices and their departments, twenty were normal school graduates.[20] In 1918 twenty-eight of Anhui's sixty district education inspectors (whose average age was 37) were normal school graduates, with the majority of them having had previous experience in teaching or education administration.[21]

In the wake of this widening debate the Qing government itself came to accept the need to call upon a larger body of opinion in the formulation of educational policy. In July 1911 the Board of Education thus sanctioned the creation of a central educational council (*zhongyang jiaoyu hui*) under its jurisdiction, whose members would include education inspectors, government school supervisers, representatives from education associations, and experienced educators chosen by the Board.[22] The members of the council were to have a three-year term and meet once a year for thirty days. They were empowered to submit resolutions to the Board of Education, which would implement those it considered appropriate.[23] The Board expressed the hope that the creation of the council would enable the government to benefit from the ideas of a wide range of people (including professional educators), noting that since education was becoming increasingly complicated, it could no longer be managed by just a few people.[24]

The council met between July and August 1911 and there were over one hundred participants, most of whom had already been actively involved in education as officials, publicists or teachers.[25] They included prominent contributors to *The Educational Review* such as Lu Feigui, Meng Zhaochang and Jia Dianzhi, educational reformers such as Huang Yanpei, Luo Zhenyu and Shen Liangqi, and reforming officials within the Board of Education such as Fan Yuanlian, Chen Baoquan and Yan Xiu. Fan, Chen and Yan had all studied in Japan and all three were to remain involved in education during the early republic. Fan Yuanlian was to be education minister three times (1912-13, 1916-7, 1920-21); Chen Baoquan was to become head of the general education department in the education ministry as well as a vice-minister of education; Yan Xiu later became one of the founders of Nankai Middle School in Tianjin (a school that Zhou Enlai was to attend).[26]

Like the previous conference of education associations, the central education council focused on primary education. In particular it criticised extravagant spending on new school buildings and the salaries of superfluous administrators which, it was felt, hindered the spread of primary education to a wider populace. The Board of Education, in fact, was proceeding to respond to this criticism when it issued new regulations on primary-school expenditures in the same month the council met.[27] In order to prevent tuition fees from becoming excessively high expenditures were to be kept to a minimum by utilising existing buildings and ensuring that all menial jobs in schools be performed by students rather than servants. This latter directive was supported by educators not only on economic grounds, but also on the assumption that it would acquaint students with manual labour and hence dispel their elitist attitudes. The Board also suggested that, apart from tea, schools should not provide free food – another indication that at the beginning of educational reform attempts were made to continue traditional practices such as not charging tuition fees and providing board and lodging.

In their discussions of 'militant citizenry education'[28] the council was not as bold as the conference of education associations since it did not think the use of live ammunition for firing drill in middle schools was necessary because of the expense involved.[29] The council did, however, put forward two additional proposals concerning 'militant citizenry education': firstly, it suggested that all normal school graduates perform three months' compulsory military service to equip them to teach military drill at school and, secondly, the council proposed that all soldiers leaving the army who were of 'good character' be awarded a certificate that would enable them to teach physical education at schools. This latter suggestion, a radical departure from the traditional Confucian attitude towards the military, aroused some opposition within the council. Some representatives argued that, since most soldiers were uneducated, they would have a harmful effect on children's morals and character development. Others thought that too much importance was being attached to physical education. Supporters responded by pointing out that with the expansion of popular education there would be fewer uneducated soldiers, as well as reiterating the opinion increasingly held by educators in this period that both intellectual and physical prowess had to be cultivated at school.[30]

How the Qing government would have responded to these proposals will, of course, never be known since the worsening political situation in the summer of 1911 diverted the government's attention from reform to confronting unrest and opposition. Before the outbreak of the army mutiny at Wuchang in October 1911 the Board of Education was only able to implement one reform proposal when it abolished the practice of awarding traditional civil service degrees to school graduates. Henceforth there was to be no special title for primary- and middle-school graduates, while graduates of higher-level schools were simply to be given the title of 'graduate' (*yeshi* or *xueshi*), following Japanese practice.[31]

Nevertheless, the developments that had taken place in the summer of 1911 were highly significant. Not only had the Qing government called on provincial and local elites to assist in the expansion of education but it had also, for the first time in China's imperial history, accepted the premise that a larger input was required in the making of educational policy. The recruitment of the bureaucracy from those who had passed civil service examinations based on the officially prescribed canon had meant that education was inextricably linked with, and controlled, by the Confucian imperial state. The abolition of the examination system in 1905 had begun the process of severing the links between education and the state. With the government-approved gentry initiative in holding a conference of education associations and the creation of a central educational council, the court now publicly sanctioned the right of educators to discuss and debate all aspects of education as well as accepting the state's need to draw on a wide body of expert opinion to oversee a process that was no longer seen to be solely concerned with the preservation of the Confucian classical tradition or training a loyal bureaucracy.

THE REPUBLICAN MINISTRY OF EDUCATION

When republican revolutionaries established a provisional government in Nanjing in January 1912[32] education was quickly seen as a priority. Cai Yuanpei was appointed education minister[33] and he issued temporary guidelines on schools pending a future conference that would be held to formulate a republican school system. Cai's guidelines included the proscription of all textbooks that did not accord with republican ideals, the elimination of the Confucian Classics from the primary-school curriculum, the introduction of coeducation in lower primary schools, and the compulsory teaching of handicrafts. The accompanying primary-school curricu-

Table 8. Primary School Curricula for 1904, 1910 and 1912 (in hours per week)

	First year	Second year	Third year	Fourth year
1904				
Lower Primary				
Classics	12 (40)	12 (40)	12 (40)	12 (40)
Moral training	2 (6·7)	2 (6·7)	2 (6·7)	2 (6·7)
Chinese literature	4 (13·3)	4 (13·3)	4 (13·3)	4 (13·3)
Arithmetic	6 (20)	6 (20)	6 (20)	6 (20)
History	1 (3·3)	1 (3·3)	1 (3·3)	1 (3·3)
Geography	1 (3·3)	1 (3·3)	1 (3·3)	1 (3·3)
Physical education	3 (10)	3 (10)	3 (10)	3 (10)
Science	1 (3·3)	1 (3·3)	1 (3·3)	1 (3·3)
(Drawing and handicrafts optional)				
Higher Primary				
Classics	12 (33.3)	12 (33.3)	12 (33.3)	12 (33.3)
Moral training	2 (5·5)	2 (5·5)	2 (5·5)	2 (5·5)
Chinese literature	8 (22·2)	8 (22·2)	8 (22·2)	8 (22·2)
Arithmetic	3 (8·3)	3 (8·3)	3 (8·3)	3 (8·3)
Chinese history	2 (5·5)	2 (5·5)	2 (5·5)	2 (5·5)
Geography	2 (5·5)	2 (5·5)	2 (5·5)	2 (5·5)
Science	2 (5·5)	2 (5·5)	2 (5·5)	2 (5·5)
Physical education and Handicrafts	3 (8·3)	3 (8·3)	3 (8·3)	3 (8·3)
Drawing	2 (5·5)	2 (5·5)	2 (5·5)	2 (5·5)
(Agriculture and commerce optional)				

Note: Percentage of total hours per week in brackets.
Source: Zhuang Yu (ed.), *Zuijin sanshinian zhi Zhongguo jiaoyu*, pp. 12-13.

	First year	Second year	Third year	Fourth year
1910				
Lower Primary				
Classics	0	0	0	0
Moral training	2 (8.3)	2 (8.3)	2 (8)	2 (8)
Writing and Composition (*Guowen*)	14 (58·3)	14 (58·3)	14 (56)	14 (56)
Arithmetic	4 (16·7)	4 (16·7)	5 (20)	5 (20)
Physical education	4 (16·7)	4 (16·7)	4 (16)	4 (16)
(Drawing, handicrafts, singing optional)				
Higher Primary				
Classics	11 (30·5)	11 (30·5)	11 (29·7)	11 (29·7)
Moral training	2 (5·5)	2 (5·5)	2 (5·4)	2 (5·4)
Guowen	8 (22·2)	8 (22·2)	8 (21·6)	8 (21·6)
Arithmetic	4 (11·1)	4 (11·1)	5 (13·5)	5 (13·5)
History	2 (5·5)	2 (5·5)	2 (5·4)	2 (5·4)
Geography	2 (5·5)	2 (5·5)	2 (5·4)	2 (5·4)
Science	2 (5·5)	2 (5·5)	2 (5·4)	2 (5·4)
Drawing	2 (5·5)	2 (5·5)	2 (5·4)	2 (5·4)
Physical education	3 (8·3)	3 (8·3)	3 (8·1)	3 (8·1)
(Agriculture, commerce, singing, handicrafts, English optional)				

Source: Zhuang Yu (ed.), *Zuijin sanshinian zhi Zhongguo jiaoyu*, pp. 14-15.

The 1912 School System

	First year	Second year	Third year	Fourth year
1912 (January)				
Lower Primary				
Moral training	2 (8)	2 (7·1)	2 (6·5)	2 (6·5)
Guowen (Chinese)	10 (40)	12 (42·8)	15 (48·4)	15 (48·4)
Arithmetic	5 (20)	6 (21·4)	6 (19·4)	6 (19·4)
Physical education	4 (16)	4 (14·3)	4 (12·9)	4 (12·9)
Handicrafts	1 (4)	1 (3·6)	1 (3·2)	1 (3·2)
Drawing	1 (4)	1 (3·6)	1 (3·2)	1 (3·2)
Singing	1 (4)	1 (3·6)	1 (3·2)	1 (3·2)
Sewing (for girls)	1 (4)	1 (3·6)	1 (3·2)	1 (3·2)
Higher Primary				
Moral training	2 (6·2)	2 (6·2)	2 (5·5)	2 (5·5)
Guowen (Chinese)	10 (31·2)	10 (31·2)	10 (27·8)	10 (27·8)
Arithmetic	4 (12·5)	4 (12·5)	4 (11·1)	4 (11·1)
Chinese hist/geogr.	5 (15·6)	5 (15·6)	5 (13·9)	5 (13·9)
Biol/phys/chem.	2 (6·2)	2 (6·2)	2 (5·5)	2 (5·5)
Drawing	1 (3·1)	1 (3·1)	2 (5·5)	2 (5·5)
Handicrafts	1 (3·1)	1 (3·1)	2 - B (5·5)	2 - B (5·5)
			1 - G (2·9)	1 - G (2·9)
Singing	2 (6·2)	2 (6·2)	2 (5·5)	2 (5·5)
Sewing (for girls)	2 (6·2)	2 (6·2)	2 (5·5)	2 (5·5)
Physical education	3 - B (9·4)	3 - B)9·4)	3 - B (8·3)	3 - B (8·3)
	2 - G (6·3)	2 - G (6·3)	2 - G (5·9)	2 - G (5·9)
(English, agriculture, commerce optional)				

Note: B: Boys; G: Girls   Source: *Jiaoyu zazhi*, 3 : 10 (1912), *faling*, pp. 100-1.

	First year	Second year	Third year	Fourth year
1912 (November)				
Lower Primary				
Guowen (Chinese)	10 (45·4)	12 (46·1)	14 (50)	14 (50)
Moral training	2 (9·1)	2 (7·7)	2 (7·1)	2 (7·1)
Arithmetic	5 (22·7)	6 (23)	6 (21·4)	5 (17·8)
Handicrafts	1 (4·5)	1 (3·8)	1 (3·6)	1 (3·6)
Drawing	–	1 (3·8)	1 (3·6)	2 - B (7·1)
				1 - G (3·4)
Singing/Phys ed.	4 (18·2)	4 (15·4)	4 (14·3)	4 (14·3)
Sewing (for girls)	–	–	1 (3·4)	2 (6·9)
Higher Primary				
Moral training	2 (6·7)	2 (6·7)	2 (6·7)	No Fourth Year
Guowen (Chinese)	10 (33·3)	12 (26·7)	14 (26·7)	
Arithmetic	4 (13·3)	4 (13·3)	4 (13·3)	
Chinese hist/geog.	3 (10)	3 (10)	3 (10)	
Science	2 (6·7)	2 (6·7)	2 (6·7)	
Handicrafts	2 - B (6·7)	2 - B (6·7)	2 - B (6·7)	
	2 - G (3·1)	2 - G (3·1)	2 - G (3·1)	
Drawing	2 - B (6·7)	2 - B (6·7)	2 - B (6·7)	
	2 - G (3·1)	2 - G (3·1)	2 - G (3·1)	
Singing	2 (6·7)	2 (6·7)	2 (6·7)	
Physical education	3 (10)	3 (10)	3 (10)	
Agriculture	2 (6·7)	2 (6·7)	2 (6·7)	
English	–	–	3 (Optional)	
Sewing (for girls)	2 (6·7)	2 (6·7)	2 (6·7)	

Source: Shu Xincheng (ed.), *Ziliao*, 2: 460-2.

lum was, in fact, little different from that of 1910 (see Table 8). The elimination of the Confucian Classics continued the trend begun in the last years of the dynasty when the number of hours devoted to their study had been gradually reduced. Drawing, handicrafts and singing were now compulsory rather than optional (*suike*) subjects. As an indication of the changing attitudes towards manual work, handicrafts were also introduced into the normal school curriculum.[34] The new curriculum closely followed that of the Japanese primary school curriculum of 1900 except that handicrafts did not form part of the latter.[35] Unfortunately, the Nanjing education ministry had neither the funds nor the facilities to implement its guidelines. Jiang Weiqiao, a counsellor in the ministry, has left an account of its makeshift character.[36] Sun Yatsen was apparently too preoccupied even to concern himself with where the ministry was to be located, and Cai Yuanpei was obliged to lease three rooms from the Jiangsu provincial government's internal affairs bureau, hardly an auspicious beginning for the new republican Ministry of Education. The staff totalled thirty (while other ministries had staffs of one hundred and more) and the ministry itself disposed of limited funds (see Table 9).

Furthermore, many schools had been destroyed or damaged during the fighting since the previous October. Undisciplined troops frequently occupied school buildings, destroying equipment and burning books. Local officials themselves often persuaded unruly groups of soldiers to occupy school buildings in order to avert possible danger to official residences.[37]

With this in mind, the Education Ministry directed the provinces to promote social education, which was now described as equally important as school education.[38] Public lectures were seen as the principal tool of social education since, the Ministry noted, they would provide the quickest way to inform people of their rights and duties. Response may have been overenthusiastic since the Ministry had to reproach one public lecture society organised by a middle-school administrator in Jiangsu for being too overbearing and dogmatic. One should lecture to the people, the Ministry advised, in a spirit of prudence and conciliation.[39]

For the first time also film (*huodong hua*) was referred to as a potentially beneficial aspect of social education.[40] Film had been introduced to China in 1896 and in 1903 the first Chinese-owned film company had been formed, which specialised in showing imported foreign films in Beijing's theatre district. In 1905 the first Chinese-made film was produced.[41] If regulations imposed by the Shanghai municipal council in 1911 are anything to go by, however, concern was also beginning to be shown about the possible harmful effects of the cinema. The regulations stipulated that no 'immoral' films were to be shown, that men and women should sit separately, and that films were to finish before midnight.[42]

The new ministry's preoccupation with inculcating republican principles among the people was also accompanied by a stated commitment to the expansion of educational opportunities for China's ethnic and religious

Table 9. Expenditures of the Nanjing Government, March 1912 (in *yuan*)

Army	8 935 892
Internal Affairs	270 701
Navy	197 036
Justice	11 401
Communications	8 846
Finance	7 268
Industry	4 991
Education	4 854
Foreign affairs	4 590

Source: *Linshi zhengfu gongbao*, 3: 45 (22 March 1912), pp. 998-9.

minorities. 'Equal education' (*tongdeng jiaoyu*), the Ministry declared, would ensure that Mongols, Tibetans and Chinese Moslems would have access to their own education previously denied them under the Qing.[43] The ministry accordingly sanctioned the creation of an Association for the Unity of China's Races (*Zhonghua minzu datonghui*), which proposed organising a special teachers' training school for the study of minority languages.[44] Clearly the ministry hoped to avoid the hostility and suspicion towards modern schools that had prevailed among minorities during the last years of the Qing. In Kashgar, Xinjiang, for example, angry residents had protested against official directives in 1911 ordering their children to attend school because of the fear that schools were being used to eradicate Moslem culture.[45]

The increasing penury of the Nanjing government, which obliged it to resort to increased sales taxes, brought it into increasing conflict with merchants and businessmen and no doubt made them more amenable to the idea of a strong unified central government under Yuan Shikai in Beijing.[46] The compromise worked out between Sun Yatsen and Yuan Shikai led to a unified government based in Beijing in March 1912. As part of an initially conciliatory atmosphere that prevailed at this time – Sun, for example, publicly expressed his confidence in Yuan Shikai as President of the Republic[47] – Yuan allowed several *Tongmenghui* members to join his cabinet. One such member was Cai Yuanpei, who was allowed to retain his post as Education Minister. The *Tongmenghui* itself now reorganised itself as the *Guomindang* (Nationalist Party) in preparation for parliamentary elections scheduled for the end of 1912.

The new unified republican Education Ministry comprised textbook committees as well as departments overseeing general education, specialist education and, for the first time, social education.[48] The department of general education was placed in charge of elementary and primary schools, middle schools, normal schools and vocational schools. The department was also responsible for ensuring the reform of traditional schools[49] and supervising education for Mongols, Tibetans and Chinese Moslems.

The latter responsibility was felt to be particularly important since both Tibet and Outer Mongolia (encouraged respectively by Britain and Russia) had broken free from Chinese control during the 1911 disorders. In 1913 a specialist school for Mongols and Tibetans was founded in the capital to offer instruction in the Mongol and Tibetan languages as well as in international and commercial law, politics and finance. The Education Ministry hoped such a school would help dispel the 'ignorance' prevalent among Mongols and Tibetans during the Qing, a state of affairs, it ruefully added, that had enabled the Russians and British to deceive them so easily.[50] Yuan Shikai's attempts, however, to regain control over Tibet and Outer Mongolia ultimately failed since he was compelled to recognise their autonomy in return for British and Russian recognition of the new Chinese Republic.[51]

The creation of the department of social education (*shehui jiaoyu ke*) reflected the growing importance educators attached to overseeing all forms of popular culture. During the early years of the republic the department's remit gradually widened. Initially it comprised three sections dealing with religion and rites, science and art, and popular education. By the end of 1912 museums and libraries came under its jurisdiction.[52] In 1914 the department was made responsible for all matters pertaining to popular ceremonies and customs (*tongsu liyi*), literature, music, theatre, recreational facilities, zoos and parks.[53] Inspectors appointed by the Education Ministry were to supervise social education in the eight education districts in which the country was now divided.[54] The Ministry also enjoined education associations to become actively involved in the promotion of social education.[55]

One member of the social education department was Wu Bochun (Wu Da), who had studied education in Japan and helped organise in 1912 the China Popular Education Association. His views reflect the growing attention to *techniques* as well as the content of popular education. Wu was perhaps the first Chinese educator to stress the importance of professionalism in public lecturing.[56] Referring to other countries where public speaking was an art, Wu insisted that lecturing was a skill that required extensive training. In contrast to the traditional view of public lecturing as the part-time moral obligation of the Confucian scholar, Wu pointed out that lecturers needed to be professionals whose tone of voice and ability to stimulate audiences and use words in a lively way (all of which would have been condemned by Confucian gentry as 'vulgar techniques') would be as invaluable as their knowledge in enhancing the efficacy of public lectures. With this in mind, he proposed the creation of training institutes to teach rhetoric and psychology.[57]

The personnel of the new republic's Ministry of Education represented a continuity of attitudes towards the role of education since many of them had been educated in Japan and/or worked for the Board of Education during the last years of the Qing.[58] They included not only Cai Yuanpei and Fan Yuanlian but also Dong Hongwei, secretary to the Ministry, and Lin Qi, head of the specialist education department.[59] Others had been involved in provincial education administration before the revolution, like Yuan Xitao, head of the general education department, who had previously served as director of the Zhili provincial education office. In 1913, out of the sixty-one directors of *provincial* education offices and their departments, twenty-six had been educated in Japan during the last years of the Qing.[60] The influence of Japan on Chinese educational thought, therefore, did not wane after the establishment of the republic in 1912[61] and the notion (inspired by Japan's example) that had taken hold during the last years of the *ancien régime* attributing to education the power to forge a powerful nation by reforming customs and training a patriotic and hard-working citizenry continued to underpin educational debates during the early years of the republic.[62]

THE ROLE OF EDUCATION IN THE NEW REPUBLIC

In May 1912 the Education Ministry declared its intention to hold a conference in July to help devise a new school system. This, however, did not preclude a vigorous debate on the future aims and direction of education during the months that led up to the conference. Issues included the desirability of creating a single- or multi-track system, whether resources should be concentrated in general or higher-level education, the structure of educational administration as well as the very nature of education itself in a republic. The participants in the debate were all associated with educational reform during the last years of the Qing, particularly members of gentry education associations and contributors to educational journals such as *The Educational Review*.

At the end of 1911 Guangdong 'educational circles' posited a choice between the Japanese system in which, it was assumed, there was close co-ordination between primary and secondary schools, the latter being undifferentiated and regarded as general education, and the French and German systems in which there was little connection between primary and specialised secondary schools, regarded as preparation for university.[63] The Guangdong educators had in mind the existence of elementary classes attached to prestigious French *lycées*, which obviated the need for children from the middle and upper classes to attend primary schools,[64] as well as the gulf that separated German *Volksschulen* (elementary schools), which the majority of children attended, from the *Gymnasien* (secondary schools), which drew their students from preparatory schools and prepared them for university and the professions.[65]

Curiously, the reference to Japan as the model of a single-track system did not accurately reflect recent developments there. Although the Japanese Ministry of Education had defined secondary education in 1872 as one in which general education was extended to primary-school graduates, by the 1880s moves were made to establish a dual-track system. Mori Arinori, Education Minister from 1885 to 1889, asserted that secondary education was the privilege of a few[66], and secondary schools were redefined as places that offered a higher level of education necessary for entry into universities and the professions. The middle-school ordinance of 1899 effected a final split between secondary and vocational education, with the latter consigned to an inferior position. Gradually, in fact, Japan adopted a multi-track system with very little opportunity to transfer from one track to another. Notwithstanding their misunderstanding of the Japanese system, the Guangdong educators clearly favoured a single-track system, which was, in fact, to be adopted in 1912.

Another issue involved where resources were to be concentrated. Gao Fengqian, a regular contributor to *The Educational Review*, argued that exaggerated attention had been paid in the last years of the dynasty to devising a uniform education system. The result had been rigidity, overabundance of regulations, and excessive government interference, all of which had aroused opposition to modern education.[67] Gao insisted that the current priority was to make some kind of education available to all. Rather than concentrating on building modern schools which fit all the required standards (*wanquan xuexiao*) within a centralised and uniform system, Gao suggested that the new republic encourage flexibility and local initiative so that some education, no matter how rudimentary, was provided for everyone. Anticipating future trends, he warned that if attention was paid only to building a network of well-equipped regular schools, only the urban areas would benefit.

This issue also divided Cai Yuanpei and his deputy, Fan Yuanlian. While studying in Germany before 1911 Cai had been much impressed with the quality of German universities. In 1912 his stated priority was to improve higher-level education in China and he proposed to abolish all provincial higher-level schools (which he thought did not meet required academic standards) and replace them with five well-endowed national universities in Beijing, Nanjing, Hankou, Guangzhou and Chongqing. Fan Yuanlian opposed the project, arguing that the republic's most pressing task was to establish a wide network of primary schools.[68] It might be noted, also, that while Cai Yuanpei particularly admired higher-level education in Germany, other Chinese educators preferred to focus on other aspects of German education. Of the thirteen articles devoted to the subject which appeared in *The Educational Review* between 1909 and 1913, for example, eight were concerned with primary, vocational, and popular education in Germany. In fact, the German system of widespread elementary and vocational education continued to be praised as a worthwhile model for China throughout the 1910s, despite massive allied propaganda in China during the First World War that portrayed Germany as a barbaric and militaristic nation.[69]

The issue of where to concentrate resources was to be debated in strikingly similar terms during the early years of the People's Republic after 1949. Mao Zedong's strategy has been described as rural-oriented and egalitarian, in contrast to that of Liu Shaoqi, which was urban-oriented and elitist.[70] While the distinction is perhaps a little overdrawn, it does point to an important difference in policy favoured by the two Communist leaders. Mao and his supporters, like Gao Fengqian, preferred to see a widespread system of elementary, spare-time, and supplementary education (e.g. the *minban* school) as the priority, while Liu Shaoqi had scant respect for the educational value of such part-time institutions and preferred to underline the importance of a network of modern, well-equipped and full-time schools.[71]

Lu Feigui, editor of *The Educational Review*, focused on the question of educational policy formulation in the new republic. In late 1911 he proposed the adoption of the French model, symbolised by the Higher Council on Education (*Conseil Supérieur de l'Instruction Publique*), which had been created in 1901 and which for Lu embodied the republican spirit.[72] Lu reasoned that the twice-yearly meeting of the Council, which comprised representatives from the National Assembly, schools and universities and which laid down policy guidelines and oversaw teaching material allowed for a wider input in the decision-making process as well as ensuring a more uniform education system.[73] He proposed that China have a similar council, whose members would include officials, parliamentarians, education associaton members and school principals. Lu's proposal was not entirely new since the convening of the Central Educational Council by the Qing in 1911 had already set the precedent of a government advisory body on education.

By far the most crucial issue, however, concerned the aim and nature of education in the new republic. Many Chinese educators were concerned about the need to guarantee 'equality in education' (*pingdeng jiaoyu*). Shen Buzhou, another contributor to *The Educational Review*, for example, opposed the suggestion that tuition fees be charged at lower primary schools as in Japan. This, in Shen's view, would inevitably lead to the monopoly of education by the upper and middle classes (*shangzhong liu shehui*).[74] Far better, he argued, that the rich be taxed to ensure free education for everyone at the elementary level. Although Shen proposed the creation of two-year supplementary classes for those who were unable or unqualified to to go on to upper primary school he still insisted that graduates of such classes be eligible to enter the first year of upper primary school, indicating once again the reluctance of some Chinese educators to see a rigid dual-track system.

Shen's concerns were echoed by Jiang Kanghu, the founder of China's first socialist party in November 1911.[75] Jiang, like so many other educators, came from a scholar-official family and had studied in Japan before 1911. In 1901 he had briefly worked for Yuan Shikai's educational administration in Zhili compiling primary- and middle-school textbooks. Jiang was also an active proponent of women's education, founding several private schools.[76] In contrast to many officials and educators who had underlined the contribution of universal education to western strength and prosperity, Jiang argued that equality of educational opportunity in the West was a fiction since so many factors (parental background, costs) militated against its realisation. He was particularly critical of higher education in the West which, in his view, was merely the monopoly of 'rich bourgeoisie and aristocrats' (*fuhao guizu*).[77] Like conservative officials in the last years of the Qing who had sought to rationalise educational reform by citing ancient precedents, Jiang himself wistfully harked back to the Zhou dynasty, when education had been a genuine community affair in which everyone had participated.[78]

To ensure that the new republic did not neglect the educational needs of the poor, the Hunan education association suggested a closer co-ordination between the economy and education. Poor people's schools might be opened and funded by factories and other economic enterprises, while educational officials were enjoined to form joint-stock companies to create training factories for the poor in which local products could be produced and spare time education carried out.[79]

Cai Yuanpei preferred to focus on the *content* of education rather than its intended audience. In February 1912 he called for both a militant and utilitarian education to ensure a strong state.[80] This would be balanced by a training in 'citizen morality' (*gongmin daode*), which would ensure the preservation of social harmony by training everyone to respect the interests and well-being of others. However, this was not, in Cai's view, the final aim of education. He anticipated a future education that would transcend national and racial barriers, an education in which genuine internationalism and an appreciation of pure beauty would prevail. The curriculum for the new republic, Cai concluded, should therefore also introduce aesthetic training and inculcation of a world outlook.[81]

Cai Yuanpei was not the first to promote a cosmopolitan outlook in education. A year before, a certain Gu Shi, writing to Zhang Jian during the meeting of the Central Education Council in July 1911, had given his own unique definition of social education.[82] In a world that was becoming smaller and in which national barriers were breaking down, Gu claimed, education that either stressed the importance of the state (*guojia zhuyi jiaoyu*) or encouraged people to pursue their own individual interests (*geren zhuyi jiaoyu*: literally 'individualistic education')[83] was fast becoming irrelevant. Since interdependence was increasing among nations as well as among groups within society, social or collective education (*tuanti jiaoyu*) was required that would develop a sense of community beyond the family or the state.

The idea of a world outlook in education was not taken up by other Chinese educators; instead they criticised Cai Yuanpei's views on the grounds they were not relevant to China's situation and needs. Zhuang Yu, who was to be one of the most prolific textbook compilers during the early Republic, answered Cai's call for an education that would transcend politics by insisting that educational policy had to be always co-ordinated with the situation of the state.[84] Jia Dianzhi, noting that under a republic educators had to decide everything from 'the people's viewpoint' observed that Cai Yuanpei's approach to education had nothing to do with the people's needs and desires. Just as the Qing educational aims of 'honouring the monarch' and 'honouring Confucius' had been irrelevant, so Cai's ideals of aestheticism and a world outlook (in Jia's view indiscriminately borrowed from ancient Greece and Rome anyway) offered few concrete educational benefits for the majority of school-age children.[85]

The most important problem facing China, one writer noted, was that the upper classes of society were parasites, incapable of productive work, while the lower classes, although having the perseverance, lacked the necessary knowledge to earn a livelihood. If too much attention were paid to aesthetic education, the danger would arise of a return to the dilettante and literary Confucian tradition.[86] A similar fear was expressed by Shen Shidong, who argued that a republic should concern itself with educating the majority of its people rather than cultivating a scholarly elite.[87] Shen evidently heard in Cai's reference to aestheticism and cosmopolitanism an echo of the traditional 'amateur ideal' of the Confucian gentleman-scholar. Republican education, in Shen's view, should give everyone the chance of acquiring a skill or trade rather than produce a leisured generalist. Another writer reduced the argument to a fundamental choice: should education under the republic be used to train a majority of citizens or to cultivate an elite minority of academic philosophers?[88]

The debate over education preceding the conference of July 1912 was therefore a complex one and cannot simply be viewed as a struggle between the progressive Cai Yuanpei and his more conservative opponents. There was genuine concern that Cai's views were potentially elitist, unsuited to the people's needs and to the development of the economy. It was concerns such as these, as much as the desire to see education create a united and patriotic citizenry, that were to play a role in the 1912 education conference. Other aspects of the debate – such as whether to give priority to a widespread system of supplementary education or to concentrate resources on a well-structured formal school system and/or higher-level educational institutions – were even to have relevance beyond the early republic in the educational debates of post-1949 China.

The educational debate in China at this time also needs to be placed in a wider context since many of the issues addressed were, and continued to be, topics of debate in the West. While Chinese educators stressed the need for common primary schooling and a unified education system, for example, it was not until after the First World War that there arose in Europe a concerted movement to establish a single, national system of primary education.[89] In France a reform campaign began in 1918 that advocated greater co-ordination of the primary and secondary sectors and the creation of the *école unique* (one primary school for all), which would replace the hitherto socially divisive system symbolised by the preparatory elementary classes attached to the elitist *lycées*.[90] In Germany, the Weimar Constitution of 1919 finally prescribed a common four-year elementary school for all (*Grundschule*) and abolished the elementary classes at secondary schools (*Vorschulen*) in line with the principle of *Einheitschule* (co-ordinated system of schooling).[91]

It has often been remarked that the ambitious plans for compulsory education that Chinese officials and educators proposed from the late Qing onwards were hopelessly unrealistic,[92] yet in the West also there was a long time-gap between the creation of a national primary school system and the enactment of free compulsory education. In France it was not until 1882 that the ideals of free, secular, and compulsory education first advocated during the Revolution were finally implemented, even though an 1833 law had established a national system of primary schools.[93] England, the greatest industrial power throughout most of the nineteenth century, did not provide for a national primary school system until 1870 and it was not until 1891 that a law was passed providing for free elementary education (and even then it was not until 1918 that the complete abolition of fees in public elementary schools was finally enforced).[94] An extreme case of discrepancy between theory and reality occurred in Italy where, despite the passing of laws in 1877, 1906 and 1911 allowing for a system of schools with compulsory attendance, it was discovered in Calabria in 1923 that less than half the number of school-age children were attending school.[95]

The Chinese debate over the desirability of teaching the Confucian Classics also has its parallels in Europe, where supporters and opponents of the classics had been locked in fierce debate since the end of the nineteenth century. Although the complete dominance of the classics in the secondary school curriculum was brought to an end after 1900,[96] German educators in the early twentieth century, for example, continued to rail against the excessive teaching of Latin and Greek which, they thought, 'denationalised' German students.[97] (In a similar way, Chinese educators were to express the fear that Chinese students might be 'denationalised' because of the excessive teaching of English in Chinese schools.)[98] In France the debate continues to this day over the necessity to teach the classics.[99] Yet while Latin still occupies an important place in both the English public school and the French *lycée*, in China the Confucian classics were to be systematically eliminated from both the primary- and secondary-school curricula within the space of two years (1910-12).[100]

Finally, the question of vocational education and its importance in the curriculum, a subject being discussed by Chinese educators from the turn of the century onwards, occupied an important place in educational debates in the West, where 'generalists' strove to prevent the incursion of more vocationally-oriented subjects into the school curriculum. While Chinese educators in the early twentieth century criticised the excessively literary and classical emphasis of traditional education and called for a general education that would include 'practical subjects', as late as 1956 a commission of inquiry in France criticised the secondary school system for not being relevant to everyday needs, concluding that technical education was not esteemed enough.[101]

The kind of problems that Chinese educators focused on, and the solutions they proposed, therefore, were very much part of world-wide educational trends. (It might even be argued, as in the case of the elimination of the Confucian classics, that Chinese educators showed a willingness for change in advance of their English or French counterparts.) It must also be emphasised that the educational debate in China did not take place in a vacuum. With the proliferation of the periodical press after 1900, especially of journals devoted to education, Chinese educators were able to draw on a more extensive knowledge of educational developments in the West than had hitherto been possible.

THE SCHOOL SYSTEM OF 1912

The education conference called for by the Education Ministry met in July 1912. The Ministry, affirming the need to elicit a wide range of opinion concerning educational policy, stipulated that all measures decided upon by the conference were to be put into effect. There were eighty-one participants present.[102] All the provinces were represented, with Jiangsu and Zhejiang having the largest contingents (see Table 10).

Among the participants were contributors to *The Educational Review* such as Lu Feigui, Zhuang Yu, Jia Dianzhi and Hou Hongjian, as well as other educators noted for their promotion of popular and vocational education such as Huang Yanpei, Chen Baoquan, and Wu Da. Fifteen of those present (i.e. approximately 20% of the participants) had been members of the Central Education Council convened by the Qing on the eve of the Wuchang uprising.[103] This continuity of personnel involved in educational discussion and administration continued throughout the early years of the republic. Thus, in 1917, six out of the twenty-one directors of the provincial education bureaux (*jiaoyu ting*) had participated in the 1912 conference. (Of these, two – Huang Yanpei and Hu Jiaqi – had been members of the Central Education Council, as had the director of the Hunan education bureau, Shen Enfu.) Four others had been employed in educational administration in 1912 at central and provincial levels. This meant that nearly 50% of the directors of provincial education bureaux in 1917 had been involved with education just before and after the 1911 Revolution.

The conference met nineteen times, although it never had its full complement of representatives, the average attendance being fifty. Resolutions were adopted on a wide range of topics that included educational aims, a school system, administration, teachers' salaries, a national anthem, and the creation of a phonetic alphabet. Although Zhuang Yu gave a negative assessment of the conference, remarking that too much time had been wasted because participants had simply discussed their own province's point of view,[104] the conference was unique in Chinese history. For the first time a large group of people (many of whom were not officials) was convened not only to advise the government but also to propose a new system and policy in the realm of education. Many of the resolutions, in fact, were implemented soon afterwards by the Education Ministry.

The most important debate concerned educational aims. As originally presented to the conference by the Education Ministry, the aims were described as: 'An attention to moral education, accompanied by a stress on utilitarian and martial values, with cosmopolitanism and aesthetic training to provide a higher form of education and complete the citizen's morality.' In Cai Yuanpei's opening address to the conference, however, he focused on the inculcation of patriotism as the core of educational strategy.[105] The conference participants agreed with the emphasis on nationalism, arguing, as had been done during the French Revolution, that the new republic needed to train citizens aware of the importance of the *patrie*. One participant, Liu Yizhong, had earlier observed that all advanced countries since the days of Napoleon had ensured their educational systems promote the national interest. The weakness of the Qing education system, he noted, was that it had allowed everyone to pursue excessively their own selfish interests.[106] Yet although the conference unanimously endorsed the principle of nationalism it also added that such a focus should not obstruct 'the principle of world progress or hinder the development of the individual', indicating that other views were expressed.

The educational aims issued by the Education Ministry (now headed by Fan Yuanlian who had succeeded Cai Yuanpei at the end of July)[107] in September 1912, in fact, omitted the specific reference to nationalism recommended by the conference: 'Educational aims should involve a stress on moral education with utilitarian and militant-citizenry education to supplement it. Furthermore, aesthetic training will be given to complete the citizen's morality.'[108] A practical concern with promoting nationalism, however, was evident in other regulations issued in the same month. Thus those on school uniforms for lower and higher primary schools stipulated that caps and shoes be Chinese-made.[109] Such a requirement, of course, also made sound economic sense. (In 1916, at the second conference of education associations in Beijing, one of the resolutions called for the use of Chinese-produced paper in the manufacture of textbooks.)[110] Regulations on school ceremonies stipulated that the national day (the day of the founding of the Republic) be celebrated by raising the flag and singing the national anthem.[111] (Allowance was also made for celebrating Confucius' birthday, although such practices as kneeling and bowing were forbidden.)[112]

The conference also proposed the organisation of a central education council (*zhongyang jiaoyu huiyi*). Like Lu Feigui earlier, it cited French practice as the model, insisting that such a council not only advise

Table 10. Provincial Origin of Delegates to the 1912 Education Conference

Jiangsu	14
Zhejiang	10
Zhili	8
Fujian	6
Anhui	4
Hubei	4
Sichuan	3
Fengtian	3
Inner Mongolia	2
Guangdong	2
Jiangxi	2
Heilongjiang	2
Hunan	2
Henan	2
Shandong	2
Yunnan	2
Shaanxi	2
Gansu	2
Shanxi	2
Guizhou	2
Guangxi	2
Jilin	1
Xinjiang	1
Overseas Chinese	1
Total	81

Source: Jiaoyu zazhi, 4: 6 (1912), tebie jishi, pp. 15-16.

government but also assist in administration. The conference suggested a wide membership, which would have included representatives from primary and vocational schools as well as delegates from national libraries and museums. Nothing came of this ambitious proposal, but the conference itself set a precedent for a number of conferences that were held during the early years of the Republic to discuss educational policy. In addition to the national conference of education associations that met annually between 1915 and 1919,[113] the Education Ministry convened a conference of normal school principals in 1915, a conference of vocational school principals in 1917, and a conference of secondary school principals in 1918.[114]

The school system, incorporating the proposals of the education conference, was announced on September 3, 1912 and was to remain in force until 1922. Unlike the tortuous process that characterised debates over a new educational system during the French Revolution, when fierce divisions of opinion had led to various schemes being successively adopted and abandoned,[115] the adoption of the Chinese school system so soon after the education conference of July–August 1912 had been a remarkably smooth affair in which Chinese educators had been unanimous in their desire to see an emphasis on general education within a fully co-ordinated system that would train a patriotic, hard-working and economically independent citizenry. Neither had the educational debate of 1912 witnessed the division of opinion that was to occur in the aftermath of the Bolshevik revolution, when A. Lunarcharsky, the first Commissar of Education, who favoured a unified and comprehensive school offering general education for all 7-to-12-year-olds, was opposed by those who wanted to see early vocational and technical training in order to man the factories. [116]

The 1912 system involved a shorter period of schooling than the 1904 one, with two years eliminated from the primary school level and one year from the secondary level (see Figure 2). After four years of lower primary school for the 6-to-10-year-olds (which were to be considered compulsory), a student could enter either a higher primary school (10-to-14-year-old group) or a lower vocational school. After graduation a student could choose between normal school, secondary school, or a higher vocational school (for the 14-to-18-year-olds). One important difference from the 1904 system was the establishment of two-year supplementary courses for graduates of lower and higher primary schools who could not continue in the regular system. They were to provide vocational training or more general instruction in the event that the student desired to re-enter the regular system at a later date.[117] The 1912 system also permitted coeducation for the first time (for ages 6 to 10) and provided for middle, vocational and higher normal schools for girls.[118] Just as the ambitious plans for free schooling proposed in the aftermath of both the French and Bolshevik revolutions had been dropped in the face of stark reality,[119] so the Education Ministry confirmed earlier trends by issuing formal regulations on school fees at all levels. Monthly tuition fees for lower primary schools were now set at 30 cents and for higher primary schools at one dollar. [120]

Primary schools were to 'cultivate the foundation of citizen morality and to teach the necessary knowledge and skills needed to earn a livelihood'.[121] Citizen morality was to comprise love towards one's family, love and respect towards one's friends, sincerity and honesty, boldness and initiative, cleanliness, diligence and frugality (*qinlian*).[122] As for girls, the regulations stressed that they must be taught 'chastity and purity' (*zhenjie*) and how to be 'independent', a curious combination of traditional and modern ideals.[123] The teaching of handicrafts was to nourish the habit of 'industriousness' (*qinlao*).[124] The curriculum was generally the same as that issued in January 1912, except that in higher primary schools agriculture was now to be a regular, instead of an optional subject. Military drill was also to be part of physical education for boys at higher primary schools.[125]

Lower primary schools could be established by district governments, as well as by rural townships (*xiang*), towns (*shi*) and cities (*cheng*), which were administrative units below the district level, while higher primary schools were to be established by the districts. The regulations also allowed lower and higher primary schools to be established privately.[126] In most provinces non-official funds continued to play an important role in the spread of education, as the number of 'privately-established' primary schools indicate. In Hubei in 1916 there were 1 549 district lower primary schools and 2 443 'private' lower primary schools (this figure probably includes those schools established by rural townships and towns).[127] Huang Yanpei discovered in 1915 that a district in Shandong had twelve primary schools opened by the district government and 250 primary schools that were established by towns, rural townships, or private individuals.[128] Even if privately-created primary schools did not outnumber official ones, they still represented a considerable proportion of the total. Thus in 1915 out of a total of 1 111 143 lower primary schools, 33 840 (3%) were privately established, and out of a total of 8 623 higher primary schools, 2 232 (26%) were privately established.[129]

Regulations for lower and higher vocational schools stipulated that 'practice' was to occupy at least two-fifths of the schedule although other subjects like Chinese, history, geography, physical education, singing and, for higher vocational schools, foreign languages could be taught.[130] Provincial governments were to establish higher-level vocational schools, while district governments, rural townships and trade guilds could establish lower-level vocational schools.[131] During the early years of the Republic more lower-level vocational schools were opened. Thus Sichuan province in 1916 had two higher vocational schools and twenty-eight lower vocational schools.[132] In 1916, throughout China, there were 84 higher vocational schools (with 10 524 students) and 441 lower vocational schools (with 19 535 students).[133] Significantly, most of them were agricultural. In 1915 all but two of Shandong's fifty-five lower vocational schools specialised in agriculture or sericulture.[134] Of Sichuan's twenty-eight lower vocational schools in 1916, sixteen were agricultural, eleven were industrial and one was commercial,[135] while forty-two of Henan's fifty lower vocational schools in the same year were agricultural.[136] These lower-level agricultural schools often concentrated on the teaching of one particular skill. Thus the one in Yanghu, Jiangsu, which had been established by a tea merchant, specialised in the cultivation of tea.[137]

The regulations on middle schools continued the approach adopted since the revolution of stressing their role as part of general education. Their aim was 'to complete general knowledge and create an all-round citizen'.[138] They could be established by the province, district or privately. Thus, of the eleven middle schools in Hubei province in 1916, five had been established by district governments, three by the provincial government and three had been privately opened.[139] As with primary schools, handicrafts were to be part of the curriculum so that students would be trained to have 'an interest in manual work'. English also occupied an important place in the curriculum (eight hours a week for boys and four hours a week for girls).

Normal schools could also be established by the province or district. Out

Figure 2: The 1912 School System

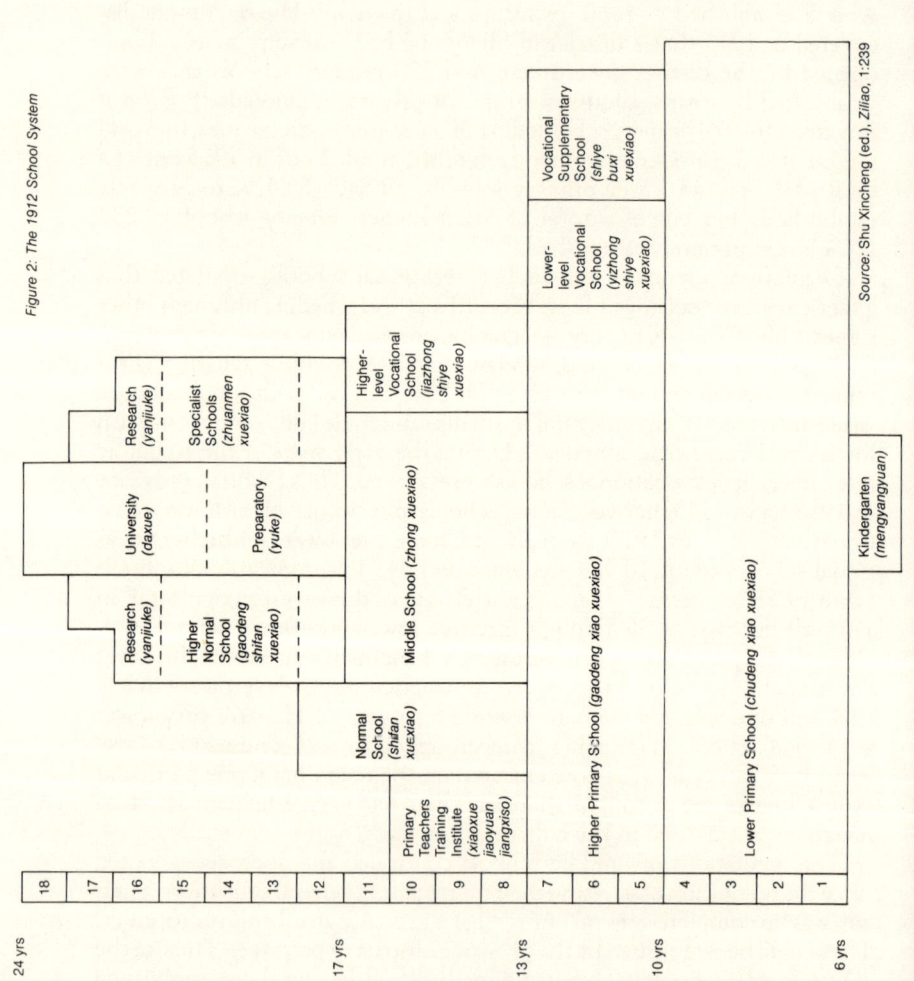

of 194 normal schools that existed in 1917, 135 had been created by provincial governments, fifty by district governments and nine privately.[140]

Handicrafts, English and physical education were included in the curriculum, as were the Confucian classics (even though they had been eliminated from the middle-school curriculum). Higher normal schools came under the direct control of the Education Ministry – in 1917 there were eight such schools, one of which was for women – and were the only kind of school that could not be established privately.[141]

The 1912 system also attempted to clarify lines of responsibility for the schools. Specialist education (universities, higher normal and specialist schools)[142] was to be under the direct control of the Education Ministry and financed by central government. The Ministry was also to lay down policy (*guiding*) and methods (*jinxing fangfa*) for general education (middle, primary and vocational schools), while it was the responsibility of the provinces and districts to manage (*zhixing*) and finance these schools. Education Ministry inspectors were to supervise (*jiandu*) the schools and ensure central government regulations were being implemented.[143]

In practice, however, education increasingly came under the jurisdiction of the provinces, reflecting the diminution of central government influence after 1912 as provincial military governors blocked Yuan Shikai's ambitious attempts to recentralise power that were to culminate in his desperate ploy to revive the monarchy with himself as Emperor. In 1913 the provincial education bureaux (*jiaoyuting*), nominally under the control of the Education Ministry, were subordinated to the provincial governor's administrative office and in 1914 were abolished altogether. With any semblance of central government influence over the provinces fast disappearing after Yuan's death in 1916, even the brief revival of the provincial education bureaux under Beijing's jurisdiction in 1917 could not halt the trend towards provincial control of education.[144]

It is not surprising, therefore, that provincial and district governments bore the brunt of educational expenditures, as Table 11 indicates. Sources for central government expenditures on education came from government property rent, admission fees for the central observatory and metropolitan libraries, the annual interest from Sino-Russian Bank stocks, and miscellaneous fees.[145] Sources for provincial expenditures came from taxes on land and grain transport, as well as from contributions and fines.[146] District expenditures continued to come from specially-imposed taxes and surcharges on existing taxes. Thus in Jiangsu, between 1912 and 1921, 71·5 per cent of district expenditures came from supplementary taxes (on reed marshes, fish and the slaughter of livestock) and surcharges (principally on the land tax), 9 per cent from school land rent,[147] 9 per cent from contributions, and 8·7 per cent from tuition fees.[148] Other districts, like Tai'an in Shandong, relied on special taxes on wine, hemp and oil,[149] while some districts in Fengtian levied taxes on marriages.[150]

District governments consistently spent more money on education than

Table 11. Sources of School Funds 1915-16 (in Chinese dollars)

	Central government	Province/District	Other
Primary Schools		18 843 992	5 037 738
Secondary Schools	123 718	8 059 715	658 186
Higher Schools	1 432 849	10 005 914	987 732

Source: Chai-Hsuan Chuang, *Tendencies Toward a Democratic System of Education in China* (Shanghai, 1922), p. 33.

the provincial governments. In Jiangsu district expenditures on education ranged from 2 380 329 dollars in 1912 to 3 581 350 dollars in 1920, while provincial expenditures ranged from 796 833 dollars to 1 384 283 dollars during the same period.[151] In 1913 the education inspector for Shaanxi reported that provincial expenditures on schools amounted to 129 500 dollars while district expenditures totalled 237 500 dollars.[152] It has been calculated that by 1930-31 the proportion of the total cost of all public schools borne by the central government was 11·05 per cent, by provincial governments 28·25 per cent and by district governments 60·7 per cent.[153]

As during the last years of the Qing, there was a rapid increase of general educational facilities compared to secondary and higher levels of education during the early years of the Republic. Thus from 1912 to 1915 the number of lower-level schools (primary and vocational) increased from 86 318 to 129 425, middle-level schools (secondary, normal, vocational) from 832 to 1 110, while higher-level schools actually decreased from 122 to 86 (see Table 12).[154] The contrast was so great that in 1913 even Lu Feigui, the champion of literacy schools and primary education during the last years of the Qing dynasty, bewailed the imbalance he felt had occurred since 1912 as a result of the enthusiasm for general education.[155] Figures for the province of Zhejiang provide a further illustration of educational development in the early years of the Republic. Between 1912 and 1916 there was an increase in lower-level education (both in the number of schools and students) and stagnation or reduction in secondary and higher levels of education. This situation is also borne out by the expenditures involved. Expenditures on lower primary schools (or 'citizen schools' as they were called after 1916) increased from 1 230 080 dollars in 1912 to 1 581 965 dollars in 1916, while expenditures on middle schools increased from only 231 648 dollars to 272 802 dollars during the same period (see Tables 13 and 14).

A recent study of Yuan Shikai has drawn attention to the increase of primary schools at the expense of higher education between 1912 and 1915 as an example of both Yuan's conservative reformism and his anti-elitist inclination to go against gentry interests, which were centred on higher education.[156] Such a view is misleading for three reasons. Firstly, it fails to take into account the prevailing view among many Chinese educators and officials since the end of the Qing that general education had to be given

Table 12. Number of Schools and Students 1912–16[a], 1922[b]

	1912	1913	1914	1915	1916	1922
Lower Level	86 318 (2 793,633)	107 287 (3 485 807)	121 080 (3 921 727)	128 525 (4 140 060)	120 103 (3 843 455)	177 755 (6 601 802)
Middle Level	832 (103 045)	1 039 (117 313)	1 079 (119 057)	1 110 (126 455)	932 (111 078)	1 096 (182 804)
Higher Level	122 (41 716)	122 (40 086)	109 (34 554)	104 (27 730)	84 (19 921)	125 (34 880)
Total	87 272 (2 938 394)	108 448 (3 643 206)	122 246 (4 175 338)	129 739 (4 294 245)	121,119 (3 974 454)	178,976 (6 819 486)

Note: Number of students are in brackets.
Sources: a. *Zhonghua Minguo disanci jiaoyu tongji tu* (Beijing, 1915), *gesheng xuewu linian bijiaobiao*, p. 148; *Zhonghua Minguo disici jiaoyu tongji tu* (Beijing, 1916), *quanguo xuewu tongji zongbiao*, pp. 1-2; *Zhonghua Minguo diwuci jiaoyu tongji tu* (Beijing, 1917), *quanguo tongji zongbiao*, pp. 1-2.
b. Huang Yanpei, 'Zhongguo ershiwunianjian quanguo jiaoyu tongji de zong jiancha', *Renwen*, 4: 5 (June 1933), pp. 13-20.

Table 13. Number of Schools and Students in Zhejiang 1912–16

	1912	1913	1914	1915	1916
Citizen Schools	5 358 (231 925)	5 817 (253 449)	5 789 (263 988)	6 621 (288 644)	7 426 (290 822)
Higher Primary	733 (29 682)	779 (33 588)	759 (31 596)	720 (31 143)	734 (33 570)
Lower-level Vocational Schools:					
Agricultural	6 (270)	7 (249)	6 (284)	11 (373)	14 (569)
Industrial	2 (114)	1 (48)	1 (47)	–	–
Commercial	4 (304)	5 (568)	5 (432)	8 (627)	9 (523)
Elementary Schools, Supplementary Schools, Half-day Schools	–	–	44 (1 210)	67 (1 896)	59 (1 972)
Middle Schools	24 (4 505)	23 (4 581)	24 (4 695)	25 (4 930)	23 (5 110)
Normal Schools	11 (1 136)	14 (2 015)	12 (1 572)	12 (1 433)	12 (1 708)
Higher-level Vocational Schools:					
Agricultural	3 (272)	2 (266)	2 (224)	3 (309)	3 (400)
Industrial	3 (345)	3 (653)	3 (544)	3 (538)	3 (534)
Commercial	3 (261)	3 (309)	4 (295)	5 (359)	6 (451)
Law Schools	6 (4 219)	2 (1 405)	2 (1 007)	2 (409)	2 (142)
Medical Schools	1 (45)	1 (112)	1 (157)	1 (184)	1 (171)

Note: Number of students are in brackets.
Source: *Jiaoyu chao*, 1: 1 (1919), *diaocha baogao*, pp. 87-9.

Table 14. School Expenditures in Zhejiang 1912–16 (in Chinese dollars)

	1912	1913	1914	1915	1916
Citizen Schools	1 230 080	1 245 800	1 286 816	1 448 147	1 581 965
Higher Primary	698 210	681 216	692 721	667 561	571 487
Lower-level Vocational Schools:					
Agricultural	6 896	8 544	9 154	12 801	17 155
Industrial	1 784	517	508	–	–
Commercial	5 741	8 169	9 653	11 922	13 186
Elementary Schools, Supplementary Schools, Half-day Schools	–	–	3 286	8 227	10 176
Middle Schools	244 685	269 469	257 391	282 095	272 802
Normal Schools	66 484	154 238	168 259	180 902	168 932
Higher-level Vocational Schools:					
Agricultural	24 213	32 646	35 206	41 010	51 702
Industrial	74 744	64 108	54 133	68 635	86 904
Commercial	13 572	23 264	22 884	30 894	46 400
Law Schools	101 141	43 939	34 347	26 143	22 592
Medical Schools	16 101	33 118	41 289	62 966	63,380

Sources: *Jiaoyu chao*, 1: 2 (1919), *diaocha baogao*, pp. 79-80.

Table 15. Number of Schools and Students in Guangdong Province 1912–18

	1912	1913	1914	1915	1916	1917	1918
Lower Primary (Citizen Schools)	2 396 (106 842)	2 805 (132 491)	3 901 (165 513)	4 093 (161 003)	3 869 (168 183)	4 481 (183 418)	4 746 (191 677)
Higher Primary	786 (36 269)	510 (56 060)	1 074 (44 587)	1 100 (45 998)	960 (39 140)	1 012 (45 286)	1 076 (47 448)
Middle Schools	29 (4 917)	33 (5 523)	42 (5 739)	49 (6 796)	53 (7 704)	60 (7 943)	61 (8 440)
Normal Schools	10 (1 199)	13 (1 249)	12 (1 212)	14 (1 050)	17 (1 201)	27 (1 806)	34 (2 203)
Higher Specialist	3 (549)	2 (624)	3 (1 048)	4 (980)	4 (660)	5 (717)	5 (630)

Note: Number of students are in brackets.
Source: *Guangdong jiaoyu tongji tubiao* (Guangzhou 1918), *quansheng gexiang xuexiao xueshi linian bijiaobiao*, p. 1.

priority. Furthermore, as will be noted later, the fierce opposition to Yuan's dual-track scheme in 1915 arose precisely because it was felt to be elitist. Secondly, it was not Yuan's central government in Beijing that financed the increase in general education after 1912, but provincial and district governments. Thirdly, the emphasis on general education continued after Yuan's death in 1916, as Table 12 illustrates. In 1916-17, for example, while total expenditures on lower primary schools had increased to 15 615 517 dollars (from 10 964 398 dollars in 1912-13), expenditures on middle schools had increased to only 3 651 870 dollars (from 3 034 703 dollars in 1912-13), and those on higher-level schools had actually decreased to 3 673 155 dollars (from 3 971 352 dollars in 1912-13).[157] By 1918-19, out of a total of 4 987 647 students in public and private schools, 4 852 642 were in primary schools.[158] Figures for the province of Guangdong are also revealing (see Table 15). The number of middle schools in the province increased from only fifty-three to sixty-one between 1916 and 1918 and that of higher specialist schools from four to five. On the other hand, the number of citizen schools (lower primary) during the same period increased from 3 869 (with 168 183 students) to 4 746 (with 191 677 students).[159]

THE FUNCTION OF THE NEW SCHOOLS: HOPES AND MISGIVINGS

The day before the promulgation of the republican school system in September 1912, the Education Ministry declared to school administrators, teachers and students: 'We should know that our people are not foolish or lazy. The only reason we have not as yet been able to attain the same level as other more advanced countries is that our education is lacking. There are no means to develop the people's morality and ability.'[160] Education was to be considered, in the ministry's words, a 'holy task' (*shensheng zhi shiye*); the schools were not only to train productive citizens but also to forge a unity among the people that was considered to be lacking.

The importance attributed to this latter role was as evident from attitudes toward the seemingly trivial question of school uniforms as it was from reaction to Yuan Shikai's attempt to introduce a double-track system in 1915. The Education Ministry justified its strict guidelines on school uniforms in 1912 on the basis that if all students looked the same the difference between rich and poor would be eliminated. In 1913 the provincial education bureau in Guangdong reprimanded female students influenced by foreign fashion who were wearing 'long red stockings and trousers that did not go below the knees'. It insisted that they all wear black cotton skirts so that 'rich and poor would look the same'.[161] Similarly, an education journal in 1913 argued that schools could play the crucial role of unifying the people and eliminating the 'rich-poor difference'. It hoped that schools would become 'solid units' (*qunti*) and that their influence would spread throughout society.[162]

This same concern to see schools produce a united citizenry explains the rejection by many Chinese educators of Yuan Shikai's schemes for education in 1915. After 1913, in line with his attempts to recentralise power and impose bureaucratic order, which involved the proscription of the Guomindang, the abolition of parliament and all provincial and district assemblies, and the appointment of his followers to key provincial posts,[163] Yuan Shikai increasingly resorted to traditional values to buttress his position. At the end of 1913 a presidential mandate was issued praising Confucius and stressing the importance of the Confucian cult. By early 1914 another mandate instructed schools to carry out ritual ceremonies on Confucius' birthday.[164] In January 1915 Yuan made known his intention to reintroduce the Confucian classics into the school curriculum, insisting that educational aims needed to promote the traditional virtues of 'loyalty, filial piety, and uprightness' (*zhong, xiao, jieyi*) and thus combat the 'heretical theories, greed, and impetuosity' he felt were being encouraged in the schools.[165]

More significantly, in his 'Principles of Education' (*jiaoyu gangyao*) issued the following month, Yuan proposed the adoption of the German dual track system.[166] Preparatory schools, attached to middle schools, would supply their students, leaving the majority of children to study in primary school. It was not practical, Yuan declared, for the children of the common folk to have the same education as those coming from scholarly or better-off families. The idea was firmly rejected by most Chinese educators, continuing a tradition that was evident in the 1909 regulations for literacy schools which had attempted to avoid rigid stratification of education. Zhu Yuanshan, writing in *The Educational Review*, feared that a system of preparatory schools would only lead to the consolidation of class differences and he cited German critics of the dual-track system within Germany itself as support for his case.[167] The Hunan provincial education association noted that critics condemned the scheme on egalitarian grounds, warning that it would widen the gulf between the well-to-do and the ordinary people.[168] The rejection of Yuan's scheme attests to a basic egalitarianism in Chinese educational thought, an egalitarianism that has often been overlooked in studies of early-twentieth-century Chinese education.

In September 1916, following Yuan Shikai's abortive attempt to restore the monarchy and his death shortly afterwards, the regulations on preparatory schools were abolished, Yuan's 'Principles of Education' were declared redundant, and the Confucian Classics were once again removed from the curriculum. It is significant, however, that with the revised regulations on lower primary schools (now called 'citizen schools'), more emphasis was placed on the inculcation of patriotic ideals than had been evident in the 1912 regulations. The aim of such schools now was to train students to understand 'their responsibilities to society and country' so that 'their determination will be stimulated and a spirit of love for the state and collectivity will be nourished'.[169]

The concern with unity was also evident in reactions to student disturbances in the schools. The last years of the Qing dynasty and early months of the Republic witnessed many disturbances as discipline increasingly broke down, a phenomenon referred to as 'the student tide'. It had begun in 1902 when students withdrew from the Nanyang School in Shanghai in protest against the arbitrary and intolerant attitudes of their teachers. Those students who took part in the protest later recalled that the teachers' 'crimes' ranged from forbidding students to read copies of Liang Qichao's *New People's Miscellany* to reprimanding them for wearing black jackets and white gym shoes.[170] At other schools in the last years of the dynasty students disrupted classes when they felt teachers to be academically incompetent. (Guo Moruo recalls that the geography teacher in his middle school claimed that Japan was to the south of China and Korea lay to the east of Japan.)[171] Students might also protest over more mundane matters such as the tastelessness of school food or the rule insisting on Saturday afternoon classes.[172] It was not uncommon either for students to play truant, visiting 'places of entertainment' *(xichang)* or desecrating temple idols.[173] School examinations were also a problem. A Jesuit missionary at the Nanyang School in 1911 recounted how his students had boycotted class because he had refused to give them the examination questions beforehand.[174] In November 1911 the minister of education in Beijing expressed concern at the behaviour of Beijing students, who formed into groups and 'indulged in unruly behaviour on the streets'.[175]

Even after the formal establishment of the Republic in February 1912, disturbances continued. Students at a Suzhou middle school went on strike in March 1912 when a new principal disciplined a student for quarrelling with the supervisor.[176] Students from a middle school in Anqing, Anhui, issued pamphlets denouncing the incompetence of the teachers and petitioned the governor to look into the matter.[177] In a middle school in Wu district, Jiangsu, it was reported that students had abused the school principal, while one student apparently assaulted the supervisor and vandalised the school building at will.[178] Fathers of students were also a source of disturbance. Thus in Yixing, Jiangsu, in March 1912, an irate father whose son had been expelled from the local primary school for breaking school rules assembled a mob and marched on the school, where they assaulted the teacher responsible and destroyed school furniture and equipment.[179]

In the wake of this unrest the Education Ministry in September 1912 exhorted teachers to build close relationships with their students, while at the same time warning students that they must not misunderstand the term 'equality' and disobey school regulations. One month later the ministry ordered schools to compile report cards on students, which were to record student behaviour and be taken into consideration when promotion or graduation was decided.[180]

What were the reactions of other Chinese educators? Some responded by insisting on severe discipline. Zhang Jian, for example, cited the examples of Europe and the United States where, according to Zhang, educators had abandoned Rousseau's philosophy of a libertarian education and were now insisting on strict discipline in the schools.[181] Others, however, attributed the disturbances to a lack of unity in the schools as a result of teachers' attitudes and behaviour. A frequent complaint made at this time was that teachers were not close enough to their students. Jia Dianzhi in 1912 argued that one could not simply blame the students' abuse of equality and freedom. On the contrary, he asserted, the disturbances stemmed from a genuine lack of confidence in the teachers. 'To love the students', Jia continued, 'is the teachers' foremost duty.'[182] Teachers were not only criticised for being incompetent but also for lacking personal feelings towards their students. (It is significant, for example, that although Chinese educators praised American schools for the inculcation of patriotic ideals at an early stage, they also drew attention to the absence of harmony and 'close feelings' between teachers and students.)[183] At a conference of school principals in Jiangsu, in 1914, teachers were reprimanded for laziness and insincerity.[184] It urged them to be more hard-working and to identify more with their students.

Finally, it is significant that two people as far apart as Shu Xincheng, the Presbyterian teacher of pedagogy and educational psychology,[185] and Mao Zedong, the Marxist revolutionary, expressed a certain nostalgia for the traditional academy (*shuyuan*) precisely because, in their view, the teacher-student relationship had been close, in contrast to the modern schools. Shu contrasted the aloofness of teachers in modern schools with the relaxed atmosphere of the traditional academy where the teacher had been regarded as a family member.[186] He recalled in his autobiography that at the higher primary school he attended in 1908 teachers and students were like strangers, while never-ending rules and regulations added to the over-formalised character of the school.[187] In 1921 Mao criticised modern education because students and teachers had no personal rapport (*ganqing*).[188] While Shu described modern education as a marketplace where knowledge was bought and sold, Mao referred to it as a 'commercial transaction'.

A number of solutions were proposed. Formal regulations attempted to change teachers' attitudes. The 1912 regulations on primary schools, for example, forbade the use of corporal punishment and laid down strict rules concerning teachers' behaviour.[189] In Hubei, in 1914, the education bureau, expressing concern at the high rate of teacher absenteeism, ordered that henceforth a daily 'report card' was to be kept for all teachers.[190]

Some educators proposed that a combination of two or more classes of different levels be taught by the same teacher in the hope that co-operation between teachers and students would be thereby encouraged.[191] Unlike a school arranged in one-year classes where, it was thought, competition was fierce, such a teaching method would foster harmony and unity. Another writer advocated organising the class like a family, where the teacher should regard himself as the parent and students should be like elder and younger brothers and sisters. Such an approach would moderate the competition and strict discipline that seemed to characterise modern education.[192]

The educational debates that took place during the early republic had continued to grapple with issues first raised during the last years of the Qing. Officials and educators were unanimous in their desire to see a unified education system that would produce a dynamic and patriotic citizenry. In the process new questions were raised about the role of schools. Thus, whereas some educators wanted schools to encourage 'boldness and initiative', others feared that too much stress on competition and individual ambition would threaten harmony and unity. Some would even question the value of a purely academic education itself. It was in this context that social, or popular, education would come to be regarded as an alternative, as well as a complement, to formal school education.

NOTES

1. The eventual abdication arrangements allowed the Emperor to retain certain privileges and to continue residing in the imperial palace in Beijing. His private property was to be protected and an annual subsidy would be granted by the new republican government for the maintenance of the imperial family and the upkeep of imperial temples and mausolea.
2. Puyi had succeeded his uncle the Guangxu emperor in 1908. Longyu, the niece of Empress-dowager Cixi who had also died in 1908, was the former consort of Guangxu.
3. For an analysis of the events in 1911, see F. Wakeman, *The Fall of Imperial China* (New York, 1975), pp. 247-51; R. Scalapino, G. Yu, *Modern China and its Revolutionary Process*, pp. 260-320. The railway dispute is summarised in R. Huenemann, *The Dragon and the Iron Horse* (Cambridge, Mass., 1984), pp. 58-82. On the compromise of 1912, see E. Young, 'Yuan Shih-k'ai's Rise to the Presidency' in M. Wright (ed.), *China in Revolution: The First Phase 1900-1913*, pp. 419-42; H. Schiffrin, 'The Enigma of Sun Yat-sen' in *ibid*, pp. 462-74.
4. On political developments in the early republic, see E. Young, 'Politics in the Aftermath of Revolution: The Era of Yuan Shih-k'ai 1912-1916' in J. Fairbank (ed.), *The Cambridge History of China*, vol. 12 (Cambridge, Mass., 1983), pp. 208-55.
5. R. Scalapino, G. Yu, *Modern China and its Revolutionary Process*, p. 352.
6. For the debates on education during the French Revolution, see H. Barnard, *Education and the French Revolution* (Cambridge, 1969); K. Baker, *Condorcet: From Natural Philosophy to Social Mathematics* (Chicago, 1975); R. Palmer, *The Improvement of Humanity: Education and the French Revolution* (Princeton, 1985). For the debate in Russia after the revolution, see R. Price, *Marx and Education in Russia and China* (London, 1977); S. Fitzpatrick, *The Commissariat of Enlightenment* (Cambridge, 1970), pp.26-34; J. Bowen, *Soviet Education: Anton Makarenko and the Years of Experiment* (Madison, 1962),

pp. 27-45
7. See, for example, the discussion of the 1912 debate in M. Bastid, *Aspects de la Réforme*, pp. 94-7.
8. JYZZ, 3: 5 (1911), *jishi*, pp. 36-7
9. JYZZ, 3: 3 (1911), *jishi*, pp. 23-4.
10. A report of the conference is in JYZZ, 3: 6 (1911), *fulu*, pp. 1-12. Fengtian also chose a representative but did not attend because of illness. A total of twenty-two delegates attended the conference, half of whom came from the four provinces of Jiangsu, Hunan, Jiangxi and Anhui. *Minli Bao*, no. 195 (30 April 1911).
11. *Minli bao*, no. 195 (30 April 1911).
12. Physical education was already being taught in some primary schools before 1911, although the Board of Education inspector who went to a primary school in Tianjin thought that teaching martial arts *(wuqi)* to young children was going too far. *Xuebu guanbao*, no. 19 (1907), *jingwai xuewu baogao*, pp. 125-9.
13. Again, this was already being carried out by some schools before 1911. The French Consul at Chongqing, on a visit to Chengdu in 1905, reported on military exercises performed by 2 000 students from local schools, all of whom wore military-style uniforms. Letter from French Consul to the Beijing Legation (27 December 1905), *Archives du Ministère des Affaires Etrangères: Nouvelle Série 582*.
14. *Jingzhong ribao*, no. 9 (5 March 1904), *difang jiwen*.
15. In reply the Board of Education noted that only physical exercise should be taught in schools. It did, however, make an exception in the case of Fengtian which, because of its 'special position' (presumably a reference to potential Russian encroachment), could allow its schools one day a term to be devoted to firing drill supervised by army graduates. *Zhengzhi guanbao*, 43: 1230 (1911), pp. 135-6.
16. A month after the conference, an association to promote military training in schools was launched in Hangzhou, Zhejiang. Over two hundred people attended the inaugural meeting where it was proposed that each district organise merchant, artisan and peasant groups amongst which military training would take place. *Minli bao*, no. 258 (2 July 1911).
17. Reports by Board of Education inspectors before 1911 indicate that handicrafts was already flourishing in some schools. One inspector reported on a Tianjin primary school in 1906 where the students had become adept at making 'exquisite bowls' *(xidou)*. *Xuebu guanbao*, no. 9 (1906), *fulu*.
18. For a study of language reform in China, see J. DeFrancis, *Nationalism and Language Reform in China* (Princeton, 1950). As early as 1900 Wang Zhao had devised a Mandarin phonetic alphabet, while Lao Naixuan, influenced by earlier missionary efforts, created the phonetic symbols for the Shanghai and Guangzhou dialects. At the conference of education associations it was suggested that phonetic symbols (taking the Beijing dialect as the standard) be used alongside characters. What is significant, however, is that Chinese

educators aimed to devise a *unified* national language. Missionary attempts to create separate scripts for the various dialects were generally condemned.
19. One educator had earlier criticised this practice because it perpetuated class differences between 'aristocrat' and 'commoner'. JYZZ, 2: 5 (1910), *sheshuo*, pp. 50-1.
20. *Jiaoyubu bianzuanqu yuekan*, no. 6 (1913), *fulu*, pp. 1-6.
21. *Anhui jiaoyu yuekan*, no. 8 (1918), *biaoce*, pp. 1-5. The beginnings of professionalism in education thus *antedate* the May Fourth period. Studies which describe the period 1919-22, when the influence of the American educator, John Dewey, was at its height, as a time when professionalism in education first began to be emphasised are therefore misleading. See, for example, Chow Tse-tsung, *The May Fourth Movement* (Cambridge, Mass., 1960), and B. Keenan, *The Dewey Experiment in China* (Cambridge, Mass., 1977).
22. The regulations for the council are in JYZZ, 3: 6 (1911), *faling*, pp.67-72; *Zhengzhi guanbao*, 45: 1295 (1911), pp. 221-2; Taga Akigorō (ed.), *Shiryō*, 1: 688-91.
23. JYZZ, 3: 6 (1911), *faling*, p. 69. Zhang Jian was recommended as chairman.
24. JYZZ, 3: 6 (1911), *faling*, p. 67. At the opening meeting of the council, the Minister of Education, Tang Jingzong, repeated the assertion that educational reform had to be discussed by as wide a range of people as possible. *Minli bao*, no. 264 (28 July 1911).
25. My information on the central educational council is based on reports in JYZZ and *Minli bao*.
26. For information on Fan Yuanlian, see H. Boorman, R. Howard (eds.), *Biographical Dictionary*, 2: 14-5; for Chen Baoquan, see *Tuisi zhai wencun* (Taibei , 1971), 1: 23-4; for Yan Xiu, see H. Boorman, R.Howard (eds.), *Biographical Dictionary*, 1: 100-5. Yan had also worked for Yuan Shikai's educational administration while Yuan was Governor-General of Zhili. For a complete list of council members, see *Minli bao*, no. 278 (22 July 1911), no. 279 (23 July 1911).
27. JYZZ, 3: 7 (1911), *faling*, pp. 73-7. The Board also laid down guidelines concerning teachers' salaries. Primary-school teachers were divided into three categories among which were several salary grade-scales. The category of 'regular' teacher comprised nine grades, ranging from 30 *yuan* to 6 *yuan* a month. The Board allowed for an increase of up to 60 *yuan* a month for higher primary-school teachers. One of the criticisms to be levelled at primary education during the early republic was the gulf that separated lower and higher primary schools in terms of their prestige and salaries paid to teachers.
28. Council members frequently distinguished 'military education' (*junshi jiaoyu*), designed to train an army for war, from 'militant citizenry education', designed to inculcate martial attitudes among the people on a long-term basis. The latter, therefore, had to remain under the control of the Board of Education, although some

members like Huang Yanpei felt it appropriate that the Board work with the Army Ministry on this matter. France and Germany were cited as examples of countries where the Education Ministry retained links with the service ministries. *Minli bao*, no. 285 (29 July 1911).
29. This caution may be explained by the fact that the council was more under the control of the Board of Education. According to Lu Feigui, the decision to drop the idea was close (a majority of nine). See his report on the meeting in JYZZ, 3: 8 (1911), *yanlun*, pp. 69-74.
30. *Minli bao*, no. 283 (27 July 1911).
31. JYZZ, 3: 9 (1911), *faling*, pp. 95-6.
32. For a discussion of Sun Yatsen and the provisional Nanjing government, see Chen Xiqi, 'Sun Yat-sen and the Founding of the Provisional Nanjing Government' in Etō Shinkichi, H. Schiffrin (eds.), *The 1911 Revolution in China*, pp. 209-23; and Hu Shengwu, Jin Chongji, 'Sun Zhongshan zai linshi zhengfu shiqi di douzheng' (Sun Yatsen's Struggles at the Time of the Provisional Government) in *Xinhai geming lunwenji* (Guangzhou, 1980), pp. 37-81.
33. *Linshi zhengfu gongbao*, 1: 3 (31 January 1912), pp. 60-1. Sun's first choice for Education Minister was Zhang Binglin, but the provisional assembly rejected the nomination. Hu Shengwu, Jin Chongji, 'Sun Zhongshan zai linshi zhengfu shiqi di douzheng', p. 50. Until May 1912 there were, in fact, two Education Ministers since Yuan Shikai appointed Tang Jingzong (in charge of the Board of Education at the time of the Wuchang uprising) as Education Minister in the cabinet he formed in Beijing. *Linshi gongbao* (26 December 1911).
34. The guidelines and curricula are in JYZZ, 3: 10 (1912), *faling*, pp. 99-103; *Linshi zhengfu gongbao*, 1: 4 (February 1912), pp. 67-73, Taga Akigorō (ed.), *Shiryō*, 2: 571-4. See also Tsang Chiu-sam, *Nationalism in School Education in China* (Shanghai, 1933), pp. 57-8 for a comparison of the 1904 and 1912 primary-school curricula.
35 Taga Akigorō (ed.), *Shiryō* 2: 47. The Vice-Minister of education, Jing Yaoyue, was Japanese-educated, as was his successor Fan Yuanlian.
36. Jiang Weiqiao, 'Minguo jiaoyubu qushe shi zhi zhuangkuang' (An Account of the Republican Education Ministry at the time of its Creation), *Zhuanji wenxue*, 32: 1 (January 1978), pp. 31-2.
37. See, for example, the complaint made by the primary school of Guiche district, Anhui, in *Linshi zhengfu gongbao*, 1:12 (10 February 1912), pp. 231-2. See also JYZZ, 3: 11 (1912) *jishi*, pp. 78-9, for a report on the destruction of schools in Nanjing.
38. JYZZ, 3: 10 (1912), *jishi*, pp. 69-70.
39. *Linshi zhengfu gongbao*, 3: 51 (29 March 1912).
40. The 1906 regulations on education associations had recommended the use of 'shadow lantern' (*jingding*) performances as a method of popular education. Shu Xincheng (ed.), *Ziliao*, 1: 361-5.
41. For information on the beginnings of cinema in China, see the volume produced by the Centre Nationale d'Art et de Culture Georges Pompidou, *Le Cinéma Chinois* (Paris, 1985); Cheng Jihua,

Zhongguo dianying fazhan shi (Beijing, 1963), 1: 8-10; R. Bergeron, *Le Cinéma Chinois 1905-1949* (Lausanne, 1977), 1: 21-33; J. Leyda, *Dianying: An Account of Films and the Film Audience in China* (Cambridge, Mass., 1972), pp. 7-10; P. Clark, *Chinese Cinema: Culture and Politics since 1949* (Cambridge, 1987), pp. 6-7.

42. Cheng Jihua, *Zhongguo dianying fazhan shi*, 1:11. These regulations were maintained in force after the revolution but apparently with little effect. In 1914 a French observer, Jean Rodes, commenting on cinema in Hong Kong remarked: 'In front of this extremely mixed audience, the cinemas showed comedies and dramas in which sometimes virtue was rewarded but, most often, in which vice triumphed and which gave the Chinese, avid to receive them, some strange lessons. In Hong Kong, thanks to the vigilance of the British police one did not see too much the consequences of this, but in Shanghai some films of crime and robbery had to be banned since the illegal acts portrayed in these films were often tried out successfully in real life soon afterwards.' Cited in R. Bergeron, *Le Cinéma Chinois 1905-1949*, 1: 42.

43. Yuan Shikai also sent a telegram to northern governors informing them that the future republic would extend equal opportunities to minorities. *Linshi gongbao* (27 December 1911).

44. *Linshi zhengfu gongbao*, 3: 54 (1 April 1912). Despite its approval and interest, nevertheless, the Ministry was unable to offer the funds requested by the association. Significantly, the Ministry also approved of an all-China Buddhist Association *(Zhonghua fojiao zonghui)* on the grounds that it would contribute to general education, unlike previous Buddhist organisations, the Ministry declared, which had been concerned solely with the propagation of 'superstitious obscurantism'. *Linshi zhengfu gongbao*, 2: 37 (13 March 1912).

45. JYZZ, 3: 7 (1911), *jishi*, p. 52.

46. M-C Bergère, *La Bourgeoisie Chinoise et la Révolution de 1911* (Paris, 1968), p. 88.

47. M. Wilbur, *Sun Yatsen: Frustrated Patriot* (New York, 1976), pp. 22-3. Sun was not the only one who had confidence in Yuan. Congratulatory telegrams were sent to Yuan Shikai from Beijing women teachers and from the Shanghai Women's Martial Arts Society. *Linshi gongbao* (26, 29 February 1912).

48. The Education Ministry in Nanjing had also set up a bureau of social education, dealing with art, religion, and publications. JYZZ, 3: 11 (1912), *jishi*, p. 79.

49. As noted in Chapter Three, traditional schools, particularly in rural areas (where their activities were shrouded in secret) continued to flourish until the 1940s. It might be noted, however, that even in France, which had the most complete government-controlled education system of any country, private education (mostly Catholic) continued to occupy an important place. As late as 1958-9 there were 202 000 students in private primary schools (compared to 1 081 000 in state schools) and 1 072 000 in private secondary schools (compared to 5 254 000 in state schools). W. Fraser, 'Edu-

cation and Society in Modern France' in R. Havighurst (ed.), *Comparative Perspectives on Education* (Boston, 1968), p. 18.
50. Taga Akigorō (ed.), *Shiryō*, 2: 149; Shu Xincheng (ed.), *Ziliao*, 3: 637-9.
51. In 1913 a Sino-Russian convention extended full autonomy to Outer Mongolia. By 1924 it had become a republic (very much within the Soviet sphere of influence) and no longer recognised Chinese suzerainty. Likewise, in 1914 the Sino-British Simla Convention provided for Tibetan autonomy. The question of ultimate control was to remain in abeyance until 1950. On Yuan Shikai's dealings with Russia and Britain over Mongolia and Tibet, see Shinkichi Etō, 'China's International Relations 1911-1931' in J. Fairbank (ed.), *The Cambridge History of China: vol.13* (Cambridge, 1986) pp. 77-80; R. Scalapino, G. Yu, *Modern China and its Revolutionary Process*, pp. 391-400; M. Mancall, *China at the Center* (New York, 1984), pp. 189-200; E. Young, *The Presidency of Yuan Shih-k'ai* (Michigan, 1977), pp. 43-4, 182-5.
52. Jiang Jianbai, *Zhongguo shehui jiaoyu xingzheng*, pp. 31-2.
53. Taga Akigorō (ed) *Shiryō*, 2: 382-3; Chen Qingzhi, *Zhongguo jiaoyushi*, p. 665. In 1913 the department of social education had also been placed in charge of collecting old documents of historical value and of protecting ancient monuments, but these responsibilities were omitted in the 1914 regulations. By 1933 a special department of social education had been created at Daxia University in Shanghai. Ma Zongrong, one of the teachers there, wrote a lecture manual for the department. *Bijiao shehui jiaoyu* (Shanghai, 1933).
54. The regulations are in Taga Akigorō (ed.), *Shiryō*, 2: 387-8. The eight districts were (1) Zhili, Fengtian, Jilin, Heilongjiang; (2) Shandong, Shanxi, Henan; (3) Jiangsu, Anhui, Zhejiang; (4) Hubei, Hunan, Jiangxi; (5) Shaanxi, Sichuan; (6) Gansu, Xinjiang; (7) Fujian, Guangdong; (8) Yunnan, Guizhou.
55. Regulations for education associations, which specifically charged them with promoting social education were issued in September 1912. Taga Akigorō (ed.), *Shiryō*, 2: 403. As with the 1906 regulations, the 1912 ones stipulated that education associations were *not* to interfere with administration. This, in fact, may very well have happened in the aftermath of the Revolution. In Suzhou, for example, it was the local education association which decided that funds continue to be spent on primary and half-day schools and that middle schools temporarily close. JYZZ, 3: 10 (1911), *jishi*, p. 72.
56. Wu used the term *jia* (borrowed from the Japanese *ka*) meaning 'specialist', for all those involved in education on a long-term basis.
57. Wu Da, 'Niban tongsu jiaoyu jiangyan lianxisuo yijian' (My Opinion on Setting Up Training Institutes for Lecturers) in *Minguo jingshi wenbian* (n.p., 1914; reprint Taibei, 1970), 5: 4298-303. Lu Xun also joined the social education department of the Education Ministry in 1912, working in the science and art section (eventually becoming section head). He helped in the setting up of the Historical Museum *(lishi bowuguan)* in 1913 and in the development of the

The 1912 School System 173

Beijing Library, originally established in 1909. In 1914 Lu Xun was also involved in the organisation of a two-month children's exhibition which displayed primary-school children's drawings, paintings, and handicrafts. On Lu Xun's activities in the Education Ministry, where he remained formally employed until 1926, see Gu Mingyuan, *Lu Xun di jiaoyu sixiang he shixian* (Beijing, 1981), pp. 24-30.

58. Information on the background of Education Ministry officials is obtained from Taga Akigorō (ed.), *Shiryō*, 2: 49-51.
59. Other officials who had studied in Japan included Xu Choutang and Wu Zongxue, both in the general education department, and Tang Zhong, a member of the compilation committee. Ma Linyi (counsellor), Chen Wenxian (accounts section) and Lu Xiazhi (department of specialist education) were all former officials in the Qing Board of Education. Cai Yuanpei himself had been employed by the Board of Education working in the translation bureau.
60. *Jiaoyubu bianzuanqu yuekan*, no. 6 (1913), *fulu*, pp. 1-6. A contemporary also remembers that in the early years of the Republic many of the teachers were Japanese-educated who impressed upon their students the need to learn from the success of the Meiji Restoration. Lai Jinghu, 'Minchu shidai de Hunan qingnian' (Hunan Youth in the Early Republic), *Zhuanji wenxue*, 16: 3 (March 1970), p. 37.
61. Earlier studies in the 1920s and 1930s misleadingly argued that the period of 'Japanisation' before 1912 gave way to one in which the new republic looked to the democratic model of the United States. Wang Feng-gang, *Japanese Influence on Educational Reform in China from 1895 to 1911*, pp. 142-3; H. Galt, 'Oriental and Occidental Elements in China's Modern Educational System', *Chinese Social and Political Science Review*, 12: 4 (July 1928), pp. 19-21; 13: 1 (January 1929), pp. 1-5.
62. Of course, this is not to say that Chinese educators did not focus on other aspects of Japanese education such as vocational training and supplementary education. It should also be reiterated that Chinese educators' attraction to western education systems had as much to do with perceived success in achieving uniformity, discipline, centralisation and the inculcation of patriotic ideals as it was to any form of democracy within those systems.
63. JYZZ, 3: 10 (1911), *fulu*, pp. 42-5.
64. W. Fraser, 'Education and Society in Modern France', pp. 16-7.
65. A. Peterson, *A Hundred Years of Education*, pp. 21-3. A recent study argues that the educational systems which emerged in Germany, France and England at the turn of the twentieth century ended by perpetuating and reinforcing the hierarchic organisation of their societies. F. Ringer, 'Introduction' in D. Muller, F. Ringer, B. Simon (eds.) *The Rise of the Modern Education System* (Cambridge, 1987), pp. 1-12. For specific analyses of Germany and France, see D. Muller, 'The Process of Systemisation: The Case of German Secondary Education' in *ibid.*, pp. 15-52; F. Ringer, 'On Segmentation in Modern European Educational Systems: The Case of French

Secondary Education 1865-1920' in *ibid.*, pp. 53-87.
66. I. Hall, *Mori Arinori*, pp. 415-16.
67. JYZZ 3: 11 (1911), *yanlun*, pp. 15-18. The idea that the Qing had devoted all their attention to regular school education and had neglected social and supplementary education was a prevalent one in the early years of the Republic. See, for example, JYZZ, 3: 12 (1912), *yanlun*, p. 34. Such a view overlooked the Qing encouragement of half-day and literacy schools.
68. *Cai Yuanpei zishu* (Taibei, 1967), pp. 9, 41; *Cai Yuanpei xuanji* (Hong Kong, n.d.), p. 50. It is indicative of the scant attention western scholars pay to the actual content of the educational debate during these years that W. Duiker can refer to both Cai and Fan as 'reform-minded educators' without mentioning this important difference. W. Duiker, *Ts'ai Yuan-p'ei: Educator of Modern China* (University Park, Pa., 1977), p. 60.
69. Such a phenomenon warns us against a simplistic approach to understanding foreign influences on Chinese educators. Not only did different countries exert influence at the same time, but also quite different aspects of each country's system were focused upon by Chinese educators.
70. J. Gardner, 'Educated Youth and Urban-Rural Inequalities 1958-1966' in J. Lewis (ed.), *The City in Communist China* (Stanford, 1971), pp. 236-7.
71. For spare-time education and educational debates in the 1950s and 1960s, see M. Abe, 'Spare-time Education in Communist China: A General survey' in S. Fraser (ed.), *Education and Communism in China* (London, 1971), pp. 239-53; P. Harper, 'Problems of Industrial Spare-time Schools' in S. Fraser (ed.), *ibid*, pp. 255-73; R. Barendson, 'Half-work, Half-study Schools in Communist China', *US Office of Education Bulletin*, no. 24 (1965), pp. 1-56; P. Seybolt, *Revolutionary Education in China* (New York, 1973), pp. 15-17, 19-20, 48, 203, 212, 214; T. Chen, *The Maoist Educational Revolution* (New York, 1974), pp. 16, 27-9, 39-42, 79-81; R. Price, *Education in Communist China* (New York, 1970), pp 36, 192-7, 211-8.
72. JYZZ, 3: 10 (1911), *yanlun*, pp. 1-4. A report on the French Higher Council on Education appears in JYZZ, 3: 6 (1911), *diaocha*, pp. 70-1. It is interesting to note that some Chinese writers also argued that China should emulate the French *political* model. One writer maintained that it was superior to the American model because the French president was far less powerful than his American counterpart. Unlike France, therefore, the United States was always likely to develop into an autocracy. DFZZ, 8: 10 (1912), *neiwai shibao*, pp. 7-11. Since the establishment of the Fifth Republic in 1958, of course, the power of the French president has increased considerably.
73. In another article Lu Feigui stressed the necessity of having a co-ordinated school system, with equal attention paid to general, vocational, and specialist education. JYZZ, 3: 10 (1911), *yanlun*, pp. 4-13.
74. JYZZ, 4: 1 (1912), *yanlun*, pp. 11-20.

75. *Minli bao*, no. 533 (9 April 1912).
76. On Jiang Kanghu, see H. Boorman, R. Howard (eds.), *Biographical Dictionary of Republican China*, 1: 338-44. The Chinese Socialist Party was proscribed in 1913. For an analysis of Jiang's socialist thought, see A. Dirlik, E. Krebs, 'Socialism and Anarchism in Early Republican China', *Modern China* 7: 2 (April 1981), pp. 117-51. As the authors point out, Jiang's socialism emphasised equality of opportunity rather than egalitarianism.
77. Jiang's attack on western education on the grounds of inequality reached a climax with Yang Xianzhang's ferocious criticism of American education in 1929. JYZZ, 21: 12 (1929), *lunping*, pp. 1-12. See Conclusion.
78. Other writers referred to the existence of social education during Zhou times, when people were extolled to behave virtuously and work hard as well as being instructed in the ways of earning a livelihood. JYZZ, 6: 10 (1914), *yanlun*, p. 187.
79. JYZZ, 4: 2 (1912), *fulu*, pp. 7-11. The association also proposed that children from rich families pay higher tuition fees at primary school.
80. *Cai Yuanpei xuanji*, pp. 20-8.
81. Cai suggested that militant-citizenry education should occupy 10 per cent of the curriculum, utilitarian education 40 per cent, moral education 20 per cent, aesthetic training 25 per cent, and training in a world outlook 5 per cent.
82. *Minli bao*, no. 287 (31 July 1911).
83. Chinese educators in the early twentieth century criticised traditional education precisely because, they felt, it had been too 'individualistic' (i.e. the civil service examination system had merely encouraged the selfish ambitions of individuals).
84. JYZZ, 4: 1 (1912), *yanlun*, pp. 1-11. For a similar view, see *Minguo jingshi wenbian*, 5: 4091. Although Cai's views on education have been described as a forthright attack on traditional concepts, it is also true that the view put forward by Cai's critics - that educational aims should always accord with present circumstances - was equally untraditional in its rejection of the Confucian assumption of never-changing moral norms in education.
85. *Minguo jingshi wenbian*, 5: 4094-9.
86. *Minli bao*, no. 540 (16 April 1912). Other writers gave a more pragmatic rationale for aesthetic education than Cai perhaps intended. One article attributed the domination of foreign goods in China to the fact that they looked so much better than Chinese goods. Such a lamentable situation had arisen, the article bewailed, because Chinese workers and peasants lacked aesthetic training. *Minli bao*, no. 651 (5 August 1912).
87. *Minguo jingshi wenbian*, 5: 4140-4.
88. *Ibid.*, 5: 4102. A parallel debate occurred over the role of universities. Many educators argued, as Mao Zedong was to in the 1960s, that such institutions needed to be more responsive to the social and economic needs of the regions in which they were located. Cai Yuanpei took a different view, insisting that universities should be

centres of pure research and should not become too involved with local society. *Cai Yuanpei zishu*, pp. 28-9.
89. A. Peterson, *A Hundred Years of Education*, p. 123.
90. J. Talbott, *The Politics of Educational Reform in France 1918-1940* (Princeton, 1969), pp. 34-42. Most of the reform proposals were implemented with the victory of the left in 1924 elections.
91. R. Samuel, R. Thomas, *Education and Society in Modern Germany*, p. 38.
92. As has been noted previously, however, some modern schools initially attempted to maintain the traditional practice of waiving fees.
93. During the radical phase of the Revolution in 1793 a free and compulsory system of primary instruction was adopted. R. Palmer, *The Improvement of Humanity*, pp. 135-6; H. Barnard, *Education and the French Revolution*, pp. 109-31.
94. A. Peterson, *A Hundred Years of Education*, p. 40.
95. *Ibid*, pp. 13-15, 33.
96. *Ibid*, p. 122.
97. Chinese educators were well aware of this development. See the article on the opposition of German educators to the secondary school curriculum, which produced, in their view, an elite of impractical, 'denationalised' graduates, in JYZZ, 4: 10 (1912), *diaocha*, pp. 99-108.
98. In 1908 the Jiangsu education commissioner observed that Jiangsu students were not as competent writing Chinese as they were English. He forecast that in another ten years there would be no-one competent enough to teach Chinese or edit official documents. Cited in J. Rodes, *La Chine Nouvelle* (Paris, 1910), p. 14. This concern was shared by the Board of Education and in 1911 it felt obliged to warn teachers of Chinese language not to use foreign (i.e. English) expressions and explanations when teaching the subject. JYZZ, 3: 7 (1911), *jishi*, pp. 54-5. See also an article by Gao Zhuo in JYZZ, 16: 12 (1925), pp. 1-7, which expressed the fear that Chinese students would inevitably lose contact with their culture as a result of the dominance of English. Such critics faced an uphill task. As early as 1907 a rural school was teaching English to its students on the grounds that 'it would help them earn money in the future'. Former graduates who were doing well in neighbouring Shanghai were hailed as models to emulate. See Yu Zili's recollections of the school in JYZZ, 19: 12 (1927), pp. 1-13.
99. The debate in France *reverses* the position adopted in Germany. While the teaching of Latin was condemned in Germany, it was supported in France precisely because it was seen to preserve the roots of French culture. Like Chinese educators, French educators and writers have continued to warn of the danger to the French language as a result of the increasing influence of English. For the contemporary debate, see *Le Monde*, 9 December 1979; 15 March 1980. The French also feared 'denationalisation' among their nationals in China because of the dominance of English there. *Asie*

Française, no. 127 (October 1911), p. 471.
100. In late 1911 Lu Feigui proposed that the Confucian classics be entirely eliminated from the primary and secondary school curricula. JYZZ, 3: 10 (1911), yanlun, pp. 1-4.
101. W. Fraser, 'Education and Society in Modern France' p. 21.
102. This figure is obtained from a list of those present in JYZZ, 4: 6 (1912), tebie jishi, pp. 15-16. Members of the conference were to include two representatives from each of the provinces, two representatives from among Mongols and Tibetans, one representative of the oversees Chinese, representatives from the ministries of agriculture-industry-commerce, finance, army and navy, and those especially invited by the Education Ministry.
103. A list of the members of the Central Education Council is in *Minli bao*, nos. 279, 280. Among the fifteen were Yan Fu, Chen Baoquan, Jia Dianzhi and Huang Yanpei.
104. Shu Xincheng (ed.), *Shiliao*, 4: 176. One example to which Zhuang may have been referring was the discussion over school holidays, which were to be in the spring and summer. Delegates from Jilin, Heilongjiang and Xinjiang insisted that because of the severe winter climates in their provinces there should be additional holidays in the winter.
105. JYZZ, 4: 6 (1912), tebie jishi, pp. 104. Cai did not discuss the ideal, ultimate form of education that he had outlined in his February article. It is clear from Cai's speech to the conference that he equated 'citizen morality' with nationalism.
106. *Minguo jingshi wenbian*, 5: 4156-66. Shu Xincheng refers to Liu's article and notes that it was written some time after Cai Yuanpei's February article. *Jindai Zhongguo jiaoyu sixiangshi* (Shanghai, 1929), p. 328. Liu, a graduate of the Higher Normal School in Tokyo, was deputy director of the Fujian education bureau. *Zhengfu gongbao* (26 May 1912), 1: 299. In 1917 Liu was appointed head of the Zhejiang education bureau.
107. In the summer of 1912 all the Tongmenghui members of Yuan Shikai's government (including Cai Yuanpei) had resigned in protest against the loan conditions imposed by the six power Banking Consortium on Yuan Shikai, conditions that precluded the Chinese government from seeking large-scale loans elsewhere and which would have involved foreign supervision of any loan disbursement. Yuan eventually signed a loan agreement with the Banking Consortium, without parliamentary approval, in April 1913. R. Scalapino, G. Yu, *Modern China and its Revolutionary Process*, pp. 353-79.
108. Taga Akigorō (ed.) *Shiryō*, 2: 403.
109. *Ibid.*, 2: 408. In December 1914 the Office for Manufacturing Educational Equipment (*jiaoyupin zhuangzaosuo*) was created under the jurisdiction of the Education Ministry. Ding Zhipin, *Zhongguo jin qishinian lai.jiaoyu jishi*, p. 56.
110. *Ibid.*, p. 65.
111. Taga Akigorō (ed) *Shiryō*, 2: 404. For an account of the process

whereby a national anthem was created, see Shu Xincheng (ed.), *Shiliao*, 4: 186-95. During the last years of the Qing each school had composed its own version of a national anthem. It was not until September 1911 that the court issued its own version. At the education conference of 1912 Zhang Binglin had presented his own version of a national anthem but it was not considered suitably 'modern'. Thereupon schools once again reverted to their own compositions. It was not until 1915, in fact, that an official national anthem was composed, the words of which were:

> China stands proudly in the world,
> And stretches to the eight regions.
> The Chinese race comes from the summit
> of Kunlun [mountains north of Tibet]
> Immense are the country's rivers and
> Its mountains without end.
> The republican union combines the five races
> At the start of an eternal era, worthy of Yao.

See *Bulletin de l'Association Amicale Franco-Chinoise*, vol. 7, no. 2 (1915), pp. 115-19.

112. At the education conference a proposal calling for the abolition of the school ceremony honouring Confucius was rejected, although some participants thought that the decision could be left to the individual schools concerned. In practice most schools simply gave a day off on Confucius' birthday. 'Confucéisme sous la République 1911-1922', *La Chine*, no. 28 (15 October 1922), pp. 1533-43.

113. Reports on the national conferences of education associations appear in JYZZ, 7: 6 (1915), *tebie jishi*, pp. 37-41; 8: 12 (1917), *tebie jishi*, pp. 59-65; 9: 11 (1917), *tebie jishi*, pp. 108-11; 10: 11 (1918), *tebie jishi*, pp. 23-6; 11: 11 (1919), *zhuanjian*, pp. 47-53; 11: 12 (1920), *tebie jishi*, pp. 17-24. The conferences met in Tianjin, Beijing, Hangzhou, Shanghai and Taiyuan respectively. At the first conference the Education Minister, Tang Hualong, called for the promotion of *qinlao zhuyi* (the philosophy of hard and diligent work). On this, see Chapter Five. The fifth conference called for the introduction of the vernacular (*guoyu*) into the primary school curriculum and proposed that schools organise Boy Scout groups to train students in 'civic morality'.

114. Chai-Hsuan Chuang, *Tendencies Toward a Democratic System of Education in China* (Shanghai, 1922), p. 35.

115. Between 1789 and 1795 there were at least five schemes of national education put before the constituent and legislative assemblies. Two of them, the Talleyrand plan (1791) and Condorcet plan (1792) were condemned as elitist. A radical phase (1793-1795), during which a free and compulsory system of primary instruction was adopted, was succeeded by the more cautious Daunou scheme in 1795 which brought back fees and ended compulsory education. R. Palmer, *The Improvement of Humanity*, pp. 81-191.

116. S. Fitzpatrick, *Education and Social Mobility in the Soviet Union 1921-1934* (Cambridge, 1979), pp. 5-10; S. Fitzpatrick, *The*

Commissariat of Enlightenment, pp. 26-34.
117. DYJN, 1: 24. See also Zheng Shixing, Zhongguo xiandai jiaoyu shi (Taibei, 1981), pp. 125-6.
118. Lu Feigui in late 1911 had already advocated coeducation at the lower primary level. JYZZ, 3: 10 (1911), yanlun, pp. 4-13.
119. School fees were reintroduced in the Soviet Union in 1921 and it was not until 1936 that primary schooling once again became free. R. Price, Marx and Education in Russia and China, pp. 77-87.
120. Taga Akigorō (ed.), Shiryō, 2: 409. Middle schools were to charge 1-2 dollars per month, while universities were to charge 3 dollars. The regulations did provide for the waiving of fees at lower primary schools in special circumstances.
121. Shu Xincheng (ed.), Ziliao, 2: 449.
122. Such an expression was to gain importance in the work-study movement after 1912.
123. Shu Xincheng (ed.), Ziliao, 2: 456.
124. It was also to perform another function. In April 1914 the Education Ministry organised an all-China exhibition of primary school handicrafts, which it regarded as a useful contribution to 'industrial development'. Many provinces contributed to the exhibition, including Xinjiang and Gansu. JYZZ, 6: 2 (1914), jishi, p. 14. Zhuang Yu reported on the exhibition in JYZZ, 6: 3 (1914), tebie jishi, pp. 1-6. It was held in the same building that had housed the 1912 education conference. In 1913 various provinces such as Jiangsu, Zhejiang and Jiangxi had already organised provincial exhibitions in their respective capitals. JYZZ, 5: 1 (1913), jishi, p. 6.
125. An interesting aspect of the regulations concerning the teaching of geography was the reference to the use of film (jingpian) as a useful aid.
126. Shu Xincheng (ed.), Ziliao, 2: 459-60. Whereas before 1911 schools were divided into three categories - official (maintained by central or provincial funds), public (managed and maintained by district governments or local communities), and private (established by individuals) - after 1912 schools were simply categorised as either public (established by people in official positions) or private.
127. 'Linshi zengkan' (Temporary Supplement), Jiaoyu gongbao (December 1916), p. 2.
128. Huang Yanpei kaocha jiaoyu riji (Shanghai, 1914-15), 2: 82.
129. Taga Akigorō (ed.), Shiryō, 2: 590.
130. Ibid., 2: 444-8; Shu Xincheng (ed.), Ziliao, 2: 785-95.
131. Shu Xincheng (ed.), Ziliao, 2: 785. Thus the lower commercial school at Wuhu, Jiangsu, was founded by the local chamber of commerce. It taught the writing of letters, accountancy and commercial vocabulary. Huang Yanpei kaocha jiaoyu riji, 1: 11.
132. Taga Akigorō (ed.) Shiryō,, 2: 361.
133. DYJN, 2: 375.
134. Jiaoyu gongbao, 2: 5 (September 1915), jidai, pp. 4-10.
135. Taga Akigorō (ed.), Shiryō, 2: 365-6.
136. 'Linshi zengkan', Jiaoyu gongbao (December 1916), pp. 1-2.

137. Huang Yanpei kaocha jiaoyu riji, 1: 148.
138. Shu Xincheng (ed.), Ziliao, 2: 526.
139. 'Linshi zengkan', Jiaoyu gongbao (December 1916), p. 2. In Sichuan, in 1916, out of a total of 63 middle schools, 5 were established by the province, 54 by district governments, and 4 privately. Taga Akigorō (ed.), Shiryō, 2: 361.
140. Chai-Hsuan Chuang, Tendencies Toward a Democratic System of Education in China, p. 106.
141. Ibid., p. 119. There were, in fact, five private universities in existence in 1916. Chen Qingzhi, Zhongguo jiaoyushi, p. 683. There were also a number of private, denominational institutions of higher learning. See A. Li, The History of Privately Controlled Higher Education in the Republic of China (Westport, Conn., 1977).
142. It is interesting to note how the expression rencai (talent) was used in different ways in China and Japan (in Japanese, jinzai). In China, rencai jiaoyu (specialist education) was used in contrast to the term for general education (putong jiaoyu) and had elitist connotations. In Japan jinzai was used by reformers before the Meiji Restoration in 1868 in their call for a more widespread education and had more of a populist connotation.
143. JYZZ, 4: 5 (1912), yanlun, p. 93. The distinction between management (guanli) and supervision was also made at the district level. Thus schools established by authorities below the district level were to be managed and financed by them, while the district magistrate had the authority to supervise them. Shu Xincheng (ed.), Ziliao, 2: 469. In 1919 a special handbook was published for school inspectors, which stressed the specialised nature of their work. Wang Guangsong, Shexue gangyao (Shanghai, 1919).
144. DYJN, 1: 38; Chen Qingzhi, Zhongguo jiaoyushi, p. 666; Chen Qitian, Zuijin sanshinian Zhongguo jiaoyushi, p. 211. E. Young, The Presidency of Yuan Shih-k'ai (Michigan, 1977) argues that in the aftermath of his crushing the Guomindang-inspired revolt in 1913 by southern military governors, Yuan was able to impose greater central control than at any time in the 1912-49 period. He dissolved the national parliament and provincial assemblies and was able to place civilian governors in the provinces to counterbalance the military ones. It would seem, however, that this process did not extend to education.
145. Chiling Yin, Reconstruction of Modern Educational Organizations in China (Shanghai, 1926), pp. 38-9.
146. After 1923 in Jiangsu a special tax on rolled tobacco was imposed specifically to finance education. Jiang Weiqiao, Jiangsu jiaoyu xingzheng gaikuang (Shanghai, 1924), p. 17. On educational finances during the early 1920s, see Ka-che Yip, 'Warlordism and Educational Finances 1916-1927' in J. Fogel, W. Rowe (eds.), Perspectives on a Changing China (New York, 1981), pp. 183-95.
147. The system of setting aside land to be used to finance schools had originated during the Sung dynasty. See T'ai-ch'u Liao, 'School Land: A Problem of Educational Finance', Yenching Journal of Social

Studies, 2: 2 (February 1940), pp. 212-33. By 1753 there were 1 158 615 mou of school land, which was tax exempt and, in theory, used to finance local schools. It comprised land reclaimed by district governments or contributed by individuals, temple land owned jointly by villages, old river beds and dry lakes. After 1912 school land tended to merge with other land and was less used to finance education. It was still important, however, in certain provinces. In Yunnan, 55 per cent of educational expenditures in 1934 came from school land.
148. DYJN, 2: 424.
149. Huang Yanpei kaocha jiaoyu riji, 2: 82.
150. Taga Akigorō (ed.), Shiryō, 2: 288.
151. Jiang Weiqiao, Jiangsu jiaoyu xingzheng gaikuang, pp. 19-20, 23-4.
152. Taga Akigorō (ed.) Shiryō, 2: 306.
153. R. Yu Soong Cheng, The Financing of Public Education in China (Shanghai, 1935), p. 35.
154. Shu Xincheng (ed.), Ziliao, 1: 368. See also Huang Yanpei, 'Zhongguo ershiwu nianjian quanguo jiaoyu tongji de tong jiancha' (An Overview of the Country's Educational Statistics in the last Twenty-Five Years), Renwen, 4: 5 (15 June 1933), pp. 13-20, where the figures are slightly different.
155. Lu Feigui, 'Lun rencai jiaoyu zhiye jiaoyu dang yu guomin jiaoyu bingzhong' (Education for Talent and Professional Education Should Receive Equal Emphasis as Citizen Education) in Jiaoyu wencun (Shanghai, 1922), zhuan 1, pp. 11-18.
156. E. Young, The Presidency of Yuan Shih-k'ai (Michigan, 1977), pp. 195-9. See also his 'Politics in the Aftermath of Revolution: The Era of Yuan Shih-k'ai 1912-1916' in J. Fairbank (ed.), The Cambridge History of China, vol. 12, p. 245.
157. Zhonghua Minguo diyici jiaoyu tongji tu (Beijing, 1913), zhisheng zongbiao, p. 5; Zhonghua Minguo diwuci jiaoyu tongji tu (Beijing, 1917), quanguo gexiang xuexiao suichu linian bijiaobiao, p. 70.
158. Shu Xincheng (ed.), Ziliao, 1: 381. This figure excludes those in missionary primary schools, of whom there were 179 045. The number of girl students had increased only modestly since the end of the Qing. In 1909 there had been 722 girls schools with 26 465 pupils. By 1917 the total had increased to 3 533 with an enrolment of 170 789. Most girls were in primary schools. Thus in 1916-17 out of a total of 172 724 students, 160 539 were in primary schools. In 1918-19 out of a total of 180 949 girl students 168 234 were in primary schools. Shu Xincheng (ed.), Ziliao, 1: 370; Diwuci jiaoyu tongji tu (1917) quanguo xuewu tongji, p. 2; I. Lewis, The Education of Girls in China, pp. 30, 34, 41. Lewis notes that in 1918 only 5 per cent of girls of school age were attending school.
159. It is significant also that even in 1916-17, when the turmoil and conflicts accompanying Yuan Shikai's attempt to restore the monarchy and the ensuing opposition in the south in 1915-16 led to an overall drop in the number of schools and students, some provinces still registered a sizeable increase in general education.

Thus in 1913 Jiangsu had 4 740 lower primary schools (200 260 students) and 25 middle schools (3 056 students). By 1917 the number of lower primary schools had increased to 6 169 (287 029 students) while the number of middle schools had fallen to 24. A similar phenomenon occurred in Zhili. In 1913 it had 10 657 lower primary schools (243 302 students) and 22 middle schools (3 810 students). By 1917 the respective numbers totalled 16 059 (479 093 students) and 24 (5 670 students). *Diyici jiaoyu tongji tu* (1913), *zhisheng gebiao*, pp. 6, 41; *Diwuci jiaoyu tongji tu* (1917), *shengqu gebiao*, pp. 21-2, 181-2.
160. Taga Akigorō (ed.), *Shiryō* 2: 141.
161. JYZZ, 5: 4 (1913), *jishi*, p. 30.
162. *Zhongguo xuebao*, no. 6 (April 1913), p. 10.
163. All of which has led E. Young to describe Yuan's regime as a 'republican dictatorship... constructed around the principles of administrative centralisation and bureaucratic order'. 'Politics in the Aftermath of Revolution: The Era of Yuan Shih-k'ai 1912-1916' in J. Fairbank (ed.), *The Cambridge History of China*, vol. 12, p. 238.
164. 'Le Confucéisme sous la République 1911-1922', *La Chine*, no. 28 (15 October 1922), pp. 1536-8.
165. Shu Xincheng (ed.), *Ziliao*, 1: 248-57.
166. Yuan's 'Principles of Education' are in *ibid.*, 1: 257-69. Yuan's praise of the German dual-track system contrasted with Chinese educators' praise of other aspects of German education such as compulsory primary and supplementary education.
167. JYZZ, 7: 4 (1915), *zhuzhuang*, pp. 7-10. Another article argued that Yuan's proposal was part of his wider campaign to destroy democratic education in China. ZHJYJ, 5: 7 (1916), *lunshuo*, pp. 1-8.
168. Shu Xincheng (ed.), *Shiliao*, 2: 64-75. The Hunan education association itself supported the scheme but judging from the space it devoted in its letter to other provincial associations to rebut the critics it is clear that opposition to the proposal was widespread.
169. Shu Xincheng (ed.), *Ziliao*, 2: 476-7.
170. For an account of the Nanyang 'student tide' based on personal remembrances of those who took part, see *Xinhai geming huiyi lu* , 4: 63-77. Teachers reproached the students for looking like hooligans *(liumang)* and pickpockets.
171. *Moruo zizhuan*, 1: 95. Guo also claims that the maths teacher in his upper primary school simply got the students to copy out roman numerals from texts and that he even got the additions wrong when he went through the answers to exercises. *Ibid*, 1: 64. At least Guo's teacher had attended a crash teachers' training course in Japan. Students at a school in Zhejiang complained that their maths teacher was merely a local shopkeeper. JZRB, no. 99 (June 1904), *difang jiwen*. In a school in Hubei, the students' ridicule of the history teacher, who apparently claimed that the Qin statesman Shang Yang (4th century bc) lived during the Later Han dynasty (25-200 ad), forced the hapless teacher to leave the school.

JZRB, no. 84 (May 1904), *difang jiwen*.
172. At schools in Henan and Jiangsu students went on strike to demand change of school food. JZRB, no. 58 (April 1904), *difang jiwen*; no. 93 (May 1904), *difang jiwen*. Guo Moruo helped organise a boycott of classes at his middle school to demand Saturday afternoons off. *Moruo zizhuan*, 1: 85-6.
173. *Moruo zizhuan*, 1: 66, 95. Some students protested for more puritanical reasons. Thus students at a school in Zhili objected to the school being located next door to a wine shop, where drunk clients brought prostitutes. When the authorities did nothing to improve the situation the students withdrew from the school. JZRB, no. 112 (June 1904), *difang jiwen*.
174. A. Brou, 'Les réformes scolaires en Chine' *Etudes*, vol. 128 (1911), p. 35. Brou remarked that he would have been disloyal to his profession as a teacher if he had agreed to the students' request. The students would have seen Brou's action in another light - as an arrogant refusal to be 'sincere' with his students. It may appear strange that Chinese students protested so much about examinations when China had had a long tradition of formal examinations. The difference was that now exams took place *within* the schools and not in an official examination hall which housed literally hundreds of students. The idea of a teacher strictly and impartially setting exams for his students would have seemed to many Chinese students inappropriate to a harmonious teacher – student relationship. It is significant to note that, according to Brou, the Chinese government tried to avoid employing European and American teachers precisely because they were supposed to be stricter than their Chinese or Japanese counterparts.
175. JYZZ, 3: 8 (1911), *jishi*, p. 61.
176. JYZZ, 4: 1 (1912), *jishi*, p. 5.
177 JYZZ, 4: 3 (1912), *jishi*, p. 21.
178. JYZZ, 4: 3 (1912), *jishi*, p. 21.
179. JYZZ, 4: 1 (1912), *jishi*, p. 5. Other schools affected by the 'student tide' included the middle school at Nanchang, Jiangxi (JYZZ, 4: 3, *jishi*, p. 38), the middle school at Hangzhou, Zhejiang (JYZZ, 4: 7, *jishi*, pp. 45-6), and the normal school at Baoding, Zhili (JYZZ, 4: 8, *jishi*, p. 55). An account of the unrest at the Hangzhou middle school, based on the diary of the future poet Xu Zhimo is in Saito Akio, 'Chūgoku gakusei kaikaku no shisō to genjitsu' (Thought and Practice in China's Educational Reform), *Senshū Jimbun Ronshū*, no. 4 (December 1969), pp. 8-18.
180. Taga Akigorō (ed.), *Shiryō*, 2: 410.
181. *Minguo jingshi wenbian*, 5: 4103-4. A French translation of Zhang's article, written at the end of 1912, is in M. Bastid, *Aspects de la Réforme de l'Enseignement*, pp. 207-8.
182. JYZZ, 4: 4 (1912), *shilian*, pp. 25-8.
183. JYZZ, 4: 4 (1912), *shilian*, pp. 25-8. Others drew attention to the harmful effects of constant examinations on children in American schools. JYZZ, 3: 11 (1912), *diaocha*, pp. 123-6. Strict proscription

of smoking and the consumption of alcohol in American schools was, however, praised. JYZZ, 2: 8 (1910), *jiaoyu xingzheng*, pp. 1-4. During the last years of the Qing the Board of Education had repeatedly issued regulations proscribing the habit of smoking among school students, apparently with little success.
184. JYZZ, 5: 10 (1914), *jishi*, pp. 88-9.
185. Shu Xincheng (1893-1960) attended the Hunan Higher Normal School from 1913 to 1917 and afterwards taught pedagogy at a Presbyterian girls' school. In 1921 he became a middle school director in Wusong, where he attempted to implement the Dalton Plan, a pedagogic method of gearing teaching to individual requirements and ability. In 1924-5 he was a professor of educational psychology at Chengdu Higher Normal School. The author of many books on education and educational theory, Shu became a delegate to the National People's Congress after 1949. H. Boorman, R. Howard (eds.), *Biographical Dictionary of Republican China*, 3: 135-7.
186. Shu Xincheng, *Jiaoyu tonglun*, pp. 32-3. Shu's hostile views of modern, western-style education were reiterated in *Zhongguo jiaoyu jianshe fangzhen* (Shanghai, 1932), pp. 1-18, and *Jindai Zhongguo jiaoyushi gaoxuancun* (Shanghai, 1936), pp. 4-5. Shu argued that the new education had not accorded with China's needs and had brought in its wake conflict and division within Chinese society.
187. Shu Xincheng, *Wo he jiaoyu*, pp. 42-52. Shu also criticised the American teachers at the Presbyterian Girls' School where he taught in 1918-19. They were not only conservative and intolerant but lacked compassion in their dealings with students.
188. 'Hunan zixiu daxue chuangli xuanyan' (Declaration on the Inauguration of the Hunan Self-Study University) in Takeuchi Minoru (ed.), *Mao Zedong Ji* (Tokyo, 1970-2), 1: 81. A translation appears in M. Henri Day, *Mao Zedong 1917-1927: Documents*, pp. 140-3.
189. Taga Akigorō (ed.) *Shiryō*, 2: 143.
190. JYZZ, 6: 1 (1914), *jishi*, p. 6.
191. JYZZ, 6: 1, *yanlun*, pp. 1-10.
192. JYZZ, 6:6 (1914), *yanlun*, pp. 144-6. A 1920 article even proposed that teachers should conduct a daily 'self-examination' (*zisheng*), much in the same manner that traditional neo-Confucianists had done. The teacher should ask himself such questions as 'Am I lazy or energetic?', 'Is my voice friendly or severe?', or 'Do I encourage or discourage my students?' and to note each time that he had failed in his duties. Cited in L. Wieger, *Chine Moderne*, vol. 2 (Hebei, 1920), pp. 196-208.

5. Popular Education Developments in the Early Republic

The political history of the Chinese republic after 1912 was one of failure and turmoil.[1] The experiment with parliamentary politics soon foundered on the rocks of corruption, factionalism, and the growing conflict between Yuan Shikai and the Guomindang. Emerging as the dominant political party after national elections in 1912-13, the Guomindang insisted that the locus of executive power lie in a cabinet responsible to parliament. At the same time it favoured the continued development of local self-government as realised in the city, district, and provincial assemblies originally sanctioned during the last years of the Qing.[2] Yuan Shikai, never fully committed to parliamentary politics, saw the Guomindang as a threat to his presidential ambitions, and all forms of local self government as obstacles to the creation of centralised bureaucratic power.

Relying on coercion, as well as on the bribery and manipulation of other political groupings and factions, Yuan was able to outmanoeuvre the Guomindang in parliament. When a revolt broke out among pro-Guomindang southern military governors in 1913 Yuan used his superior military force to crush insurrection and enhance his own power. After being affirmed as President for life he proceeded to ban the Guomindang, abolish parliament and all other elected assemblies, and impose greater centralised control in the form of stricter press censorship. Yuan was also able to appoint civilian provincial governors to counteract the influence of military governors entrenched in the provinces since the 1911 Revolution.[3] His centralising policies, however, alienated both provincial military leaders, hostile to Beijing's incursions into their domains, and merchants and gentry, resentful at the sweeping away of elected assemblies they had largely dominated, and suspicious of Yuan's new tax schemes. In the summer of 1915, in a desperate attempt to impose his control over an increasingly disaffected polity, Yuan stage-managed a public campaign calling for the restoration of the monarchy with himself as Emperor. A military uprising, originating once again in the south, led to provinces declaring their independence from Beijing, just as they had done in 1911. Yuan was forced to abandon his scheme in March 1916 and died a few months later.

Although the trappings of a republic were restored on Yuan's death with the revival of the 1912 Constitution and the reconvening of the 1913 parliament, political power quickly gravitated towards military leaders who jostled for control and influence over the Beijing civilian government. A republic continued in name only. Cabinets and parliaments continued to exist in Beijing after 1916 but they simply became tools in the hands of whichever military 'warlord' was controlling Beijing at the time. At the same time central control from Beijing gradually diminished as the provinces themselves came under the domination of warlord cliques. Since the foreign powers continued to recognise the Beijing government as the sole legitimate government of China, the fiction of a civilian government was preserved so that the military faction ensconced in Beijing might acquire legitimacy and the customs revenue remitted by the powers to the central government. It was not until after the Guomindang (which had set up a separate government in the south after 1917), in alliance with the Chinese Communist Party (created in 1921), had embarked on a military campaign to defeat the warlords in 1926 that any semblance of a central government reappeared.

The political confusion and turmoil of this period, however, did not mean that the educational debate suddenly ceased. Education ministers in Beijing may have come and gone with bewildering frequency (in all, thirty-eight were appointed between 1912 and 1926), but educational issues continued to be discussed and debated in the press and practical measures, no matter how scattered and poorly co-ordinated, were still implemented. An awareness of this debate and the measures proposed, particularly as they relate to popular education, is crucial to our understanding how Chinese perceptions of, and attitudes towards, education evolved in the twentieth century, from the last years of the monarchy to the People's Republic after 1949.

THE REFORM OF POPULAR CULTURE

The creation of a special department of social education within the Education Ministry in 1912 heralded a renewed commitment to reform popular culture. Numerous private and semi-official organisations to promote popular education were also established. Several educators in Shanghai, for example, formed the Enlightenment Society (*kaimingshe*) with the specific aim of writing plays for popular consumption that would not only be 'colourful' but would also 'develop the people's knowledge' and 'reform customs'.[4] Another group calling itself the Society for Revitalising Customs and Improving Entertainment requested funds from the Education Ministry in May 1912 so that it could 'improve drama'.[5]

In April 1912 a popular education research association (*tongsu jiaoyu yanjiu hui*) was created under the auspices of the Jiangsu education association. (Wu Da and Huang Yanpei were elected executive officers.)[6] During the education conference in July-August 1912 it changed its name to the China Popular Education Association and proposed that local associations be set up in the provinces to promote the teaching of hygiene, vocational skills, public morality and patriotism.[7] Between 1912 and 1915 popular education associations were established in most of the provinces. Henan had the highest number with thirty, which had nearly 2 000 members (see Table 16). These associations often received official subsidies or were headed by educational officials. Thus the chairman of the Jiangxi pro-

Table 16. Number of Popular Education Associations in 1915

Province	No. of associations	No. of members
Henan	30	1 956
Yunnan	24	1 441
Sichuan	24	1 022
Shandong	20	1 571
Hubei	19	1 441
Jiangxi	18	923
Liaoning	16	356
Jiangsu	12	1 012
Shaanxi	12	299
Gansu	9	166
Shanxi	8	155
Fujian	6	453
Guangdong	4	410
Hunan	4	230
Hebei	3	292
Jilin	3	90
Guizhou	2	823
Heilongjiang	2	158
Xinjiang	2	58
Guangxi	2	50
Anhui	2	30
Total	222	12 936

Source: DYJN, 3: 696-7

vincial association in 1912 was the director of the provincial education bureau,[8] while the chairman of the Heilongjiang provincial association in 1915 was concurrently the head of the education section in the governor's office.[9]

The emphasis Chinese educators and officials placed on the connection between popular education and the supervision of popular culture and recreation was clearly evident in the Education Ministry's request in 1913 that the provinces compile information on all establishments and organisations that might contribute to popular education.[10] The ministry's list was wide-ranging in its scope, including spare-time schools and libraries as well as museums, theatres, cinemas, tea-houses, parks, and associations to ban alcohol (see Table 17).[11] Educators in the early Republic were to envisage a more thorough surveillance of popular culture than had been the case under the Empire.

Taking the lead from private and semi-official organisations, the Education Ministry decided to establish a popular education research association of its own in 1915 whose aim would be to 'reform society and universalise education'.[12] In addition to representatives from the education ministry and

Table 17. Items Considered Beneficial for Popular Education by the Education Ministry, 1913

Popular libraries
Museums
Art galleries
Newspaper reading rooms
Lecture institutes
Public reading rooms
Industrial exhibitions
Music training centres
Supplementary schools
Half-day schools
Literacy schools
Night schools
Vocational schools
Associations to reform drama, novels and songs
Physical education associations
Associations against alcohol and tobacco
Youth associations
Parks
Zoos/botanical gardens
Theatres
Cinemas

Source: *Zhengfu gongbao* (1913), 12: 431-38

the Beijing Police Bureau, association members included administrators from various higher institutions of learning such as Beijing University, Beijing Women's Normal School and the Beijing Higher Industrial School.[13] Its remit was to investigate novels, plays and songs, and public lectures. All forms of popular entertainment and reading material were therefore to be strictly supervised.

In 1916, for example, the association drew up a list of 247 novels and assigned them grades of superior, average and inferior (*shang, zhong, xia*). 37 were classified as 'superior',[14] 146 as 'average', and 49 as 'inferior' (novels in this category were to have their sales severely restricted.) The remaining fifteen were to be banned outright.[15] In 1917 the association published another list of 387 books, of which 63 were deemed superior, 237 average, 82 inferior, and five deserving to be banned.[16] At the same time the association suggested that the Internal Affairs Ministry crack down more on street peddlers who sold 'lewd' material.[17] In addition to popular literature, the association attempted to supervise drama.[18] It was claimed, just as it had been during the last years of the Qing, that the corrupting influences of popular drama had encouraged the Boxers and contributed to the deterioration of morals.[19] Theatres were requested to submit to the association detailed descriptions of their plays before they were performed, while officials from the Beijing Police Bureau were issued with special tickets to enable them to attend plays as censors.²⁰

One of the most common themes in discussions of popular entertainment and reading material was the fear expressed by Chinese educators that sexual corruption was spreading throughout society.²¹ Many of the books listed by the popular education research association in 1916 as 'inferior' and deserving to be banned concerned stories of sexual adventures. In 1915 the Education Ministry had already proscribed a number of books whose titles included *Free Marriage, A History of Love in the Republic, Women Students, A Recent Account of the True Face of Womanhood, Strange Stories of Conspiracies Between Men and Women,* and *Songs of Beautiful Women of Leisure*.²² Although there were references to other kinds of reprehensible literature (for example, the Guangzhou education bureau proscribed all books dealing with 'superstition and omens'),²³ for the most part criticism was levelled at material that was considered pornographic, lewd or obscene.²⁴ In 1919 the association recommended that the Education Ministry ban the sale of three kinds of 'harmful novel' - those describing the 'public world of sex, the secret and corrupt (*heimu*) world of the family, and the intimate adventures of women students'.²⁵

This concern over sexual corruption had already emerged during the last years of the Qing. In an article entitled 'Sex and education' Lu Feigui in 1911 attributed the corruption of society to the flaunting of sexual mores among students as a result of the combination of modern ideas of freedom taught in the new schools and traditional decadent influences in Chinese society.²⁶ This ultimately boded ill for education, Lu warned, since it would 'drain the students' energy and health'. Expressing dissatisfaction with current solutions to the problem such as the proscription of student visits to brothels and different rest days for boys' and girls' schools, Lu suggested that schools teach hygiene, stress the morality of 'one husband, one wife', and offer suitable extra-curricular activities like sports to distract students from any unseemly desires.²⁷ Another example of late Qing puritanism can be seen in educators' objections to some of the Confucian Classics, such as the Classic of Odes, being taught at primary school because they contained too many 'pornographic references' (*nan'nü xiangle zhi ci*).²⁸

The increasing popularity of urban popular fiction, especially 'scandal fiction' (*heimu xiaoshuo*), during the last years of the Qing and early years of the republic was further evidence to educators that society was becoming increasingly corrupt.²⁹ This 'Mandarin Duck and Butterfly' fiction, as it was pejoratively called, often took the form of serialised short stories appearing in such journals as *The Novel Monthly* (founded in 1909), *The Amusement Review* (founded in 1912) and *The Saturday Magazine* (founded in 1913), many of which were themselves published by the major presses (like the Commercial Press) as a lucrative sideline to their main business of producing textbooks and other more serious works.³⁰ The circulation of these 'butterfly' novels, such as Xu Zhenya's *Jade Pear Spirit* (*Yuli hun*) composed between 1912 and 1914, ran into the hundreds of thousands and herein, as one scholar has remarked, lays the irony of the spread of education during this period. Increased literacy gave growing numbers of people, especially those in urban areas, the opportunity to read this fiction so much decried by educators.[31] A further irony was that Liang Qichao's call at the turn of the century for a new popular fiction that would 'elevate' the lower classes was lost amidst the rush by publishers and authors to produce more diversionary and escapist literature.[32]

There were, of course, many different types of popular fiction, ranging from satirical novels to the knight-errant yarn, which combined traditional themes with those from western popular fiction. Yet while later May Fourth intellectuals would condemn 'butterfly' fiction *in toto* as reactionary and decadent, Chinese educators from 1912 to 1918 generally focused only on those novels which were felt to have a damaging effect on sexual morality.[33]

It is not surprising, therefore, to find Lu Feigui expressing dismay in 1913 over the increasing number of published stories describing the 'sexual affairs of men and women' (*ziyou nanzi yu nü jishi*) which, in his view, reflected the current decadence of society.[34] As in 1911 Lu blamed modern education: boys and girls studying together, which encouraged sexual desires; the slack supervision of school dormitories, which led to homosexuality; the nefarious influence of morally-deficient male teachers who frequented brothels or had illicit sexual relations with their female students; and the fashionable idea of freedom, which had deteriorated into an orgy of libertinism and hedonism. At the same time, however, Lu condemned traditional practices such as concubinage for corrupting young boys and girls.[35] As in 1911 Lu suggested that youthful energies be channelled into sports and other forms of exercise, and that personal hygiene be taught at school. He also advised students to eat and drink modestly at home, not to masturbate in bed, and to wear thin rather than thick clothing.[36] For Lu and many others, the excessive sexual freedom and activity they saw being encouraged by modern education and reflected in popular literature and drama would eventually lead to the physical and moral degeneration of the population as a whole, as the followlng comment from a contemporary observer illustrates: 'If the sexual desire is not curbed, the sexual organs will weaken through wear and tear. This in turn will affect the physical strength of our sons and grandsons, eventually leading to the disappearance of our race.'[37]

It was this fear that added urgency to educators' calls for the censorship of popular literature and drama. In addition to this, however, intellectuals were encouraged to produce novels, dramas and songs of their own which would contribute to education. In response to the confident assertion by the Governor of Zhili in May 1912 that the people were now ready to forsake 'outmoded and corrupt customs'[38] the Tianjin education bureau created a training institute for would-be playwrights.[39] In 1916 the Education Ministry declared that all those writing plays and novels 'beneficial to society' were to be awarded certificates.[40]

Other aspects of popular culture also came under close scrutiny. The social education department of the Education Ministry maintained contact with oral storytellers and helped organise a guild among them in Beijing with the aim of 'improving the old stories that have been told for years and adding new and modern material, thereby advancing the morality and education of the people'.[41] The popular education association in Fujian also concerned itself with the 'improvement' of professional storytelling, holding regular discussion meetings attended by officials, school teachers, and administrators.[42] In Shaanxi, New Year pictorial posters (*nianhua*) were condemned as 'absurd and despicable' and the authorities set about producing 'reformed' ones.[43] In 1913 the Zhili education inspector reported that 6 000 *nianhua* had been examined and that some had been proscribed.[44] The popular education research association in Beijing also ordered the police to collect all *nianhua* for inspection and, according to its second yearly report in 1917, 780 had been so checked by the end of the previous year.[45] Finally, even paper cutouts (*huazhi*) and pictorial stories (*huazhang*) traditionally bought for children on their birthdays, were condemned as 'lewd and indecent'.[46]

As well as drawing inspiration from Japan's example - the Education Ministry, in setting up its popular education research association in 1915, pointed to the considerable investment in popular education by the Japanese government,[47] while Chinese educational journals frequently published Japanese articles on the importance of social education in reforming the lower classes[48] - Chinese educators often cited western practice to support their claim that popular culture needed to be supervised. In a 1913 article in *The Chinese Educational World* Qin Wenhuan contrasted the strict censorship of popular drama and fiction in the West with the slackness of the authorities in China, which had allowed 'lewd and vulgar amusements' (*yinbi zhi yule*) to flourish.[49] In France, Qin noted, the buying and selling of pornographic material was punishable by law. (A translation of an 1811 French law prescribing prison sentences for anyone printing material 'detrimental to moral behaviour' had in fact appeared in a Chinese educational journal in 1906)[50]. Qin also referred to the examples of Germany and Austria, where committees edited popular literature and sold the products at reduced prices.[51] In China, on the other hand, educators were paying too much attention to school textbooks and not enough to popular publications. Qin maintained that theatres, concert halls and museums were taken seriously in the West as educational institutions and were not simply regarded as amusement centres as in China. Finally, he approvingly referred to western practice such as the ban on cinema attendance for children in the evening and the strict enforcement of film censorship to prevent undue emphasis on sex and violence.

Cai Yuanpei, in a speech to the popular education research association in 1917, also drew attention to the strict supervision of cinema entertainment in Germany and contrasted this with the *laissez-faire* attitude in China.[52] Other articles referred to government film censorship committees in England and the vigilance of the United States government in banning unsuitable films.[53] Huang Yanpei, reporting on his visit to the United States in 1916, also praised the beneficial influence cinema attendance had on the American working class. Before each performance, Huang noted, the national anthem was played and the audience had to 'take off their hats and stand up'.[54]

Government paternalism in Germany was particularly admired. A 1914 article noted that although the German lower classes were more orderly and disciplined than in China the government still maintained a vigilant surveillance over popular culture in order to prevent the people from becoming corrupted.[55] It ensured, for example, that popular songs and drama combined entertainment and educational value. Unlike popular songs in China, the article concluded, which were lewd and immoral, those in Germany were 'pure and lofty', stimulating love for the motherland and encouraging respect for public order.[56]

Finally, it might be noted that it was during this period that Chinese educators became aware of the importance western governments attached to the Boy Scout movement. Such a movement, it was noted in China, was seen as a positive development by the authorities because it channelled young males' free time into useful activities and acquainted them with patriotism, obedience, discipline and hard work.[57]

Just as officials in the late Qing located the source of western strength in their formal school systems, with their stress on government control, uniformity, discipline and strict supervision of curricula, so Chinese educators now highlighted the scrupulous attention western governments paid to overseeing popular culture. For them it seemed a far cry from the situation in China where the Beijing Police Bureau could complain in 1918 that immoral literature was still to be found everywhere[58] and the ineffectiveness of film censorship was to remain a cause for concern throughout the 1920s.[59]

Simply concentrating on the existence or non-existence of western 'liberal' influence on Chinese education, as some scholars do, is to ignore the fact that Chinese educators were impressed with other aspects of western education that had little to do with abstract ideas of liberalism or democracy. Cai Yuanpei's western liberal ideas on education, for example, have been contrasted with those of the 'traditionalists'.[60] Such an approach overlooks the fact that those very traditionalists were able to cite western practice as support for their own ideas.[61] It also does not take into account the fact that 'progressive' educators like Cai Yuanpei were just as impressed as their more conservative colleagues with the efficient and wide-ranging surveillance of popular culture which they assumed to exist in the West. It is all very well to claim, as one scholar does, that Cai Yuanpei 'was probably atypical in giving greater weight to the inherent value of education as a way to individual self-realization and freedom',[62] but Cai shared a common concern evident since Kang Youwei's 1898 memorial on establishing Confucianism as a state religion - how to emulate the West (and Japan) and transform the weakly-organised, ignorant and superstitious Chinese people into a patriotic, disciplined and morally-upright citizenry.

It was as a result of this concern that officials and educators envisaged a more extensive official and elite supervison of popular culture than had been the case under the Confucian monarchy. The representatives of the classical Confucian tradition, of course, had always railed against the corrupting influences of popular culture. Sometimes, harsh measures were prescribed. In the Yuan dynasty (1264-1368), for example, those who wrote 'evil' plays inciting people to crime or who 'wasted their time' in the marketplace performing plays and telling stories of a 'lewd nature' were subject to the death penalty.[63] In the seventeenth century a prefectural magistrate condemned the appearance of women's theatre troupes in his region because they outraged social mores (i.e. men and women mixing socially together) and encouraged people to spend money instead of working.[64] The more puritanical amongst the gentry frequently resorted to censorship campaigns against 'decadent literature', destroying all books considered detrimental to moral well-being.[65] Others, like the Ming dynasty scholar Lü Kun, attempted to change the content of popular songs.[66]

Very often, however, it seemed as if the champions of Confucian moral propriety were fighting a losing battle. The prefectural magistrate who complained about women's theatre troupes also noted sadly that officials did nothing to prohibit such activities but, rather, frequently went out into the streets to join in the fun. The sons of gentry and other local notables were often taken to task for indulging in 'immoral extravagance'.[67] When an official memorialised the throne in 1781 proposing that the authorities clamp down on people's extravagant and wasteful spending in inns and teahouses, the Qianlong Emperor replied that in a period of peace and prosperity it would be impractical to turn the clock back to a more frugal and simple lifestyle:[68]

> I labour night and day; it is not that I do not desire that the people's mores become simple and pure ... but customs daily become more extravagant and the situation cannot be altered by law; just as the waters of the rivers flow east, who can block them and turn them westward? ... Liu Tiancheng's memorial is acceptable as good counsel, but it is not a good method for ruling in today's world.[69]

Three new elements, however, explained the *increased* concern of Chinese educators after the turn of the century to see a more effective and wide-ranging surveillance of popular culture. Firstly, the concept of social education, borrowed from Japan, had underlined the importance of 're-forming' the people as a means to attain national strength. Secondly, Chinese educators and officials now feared that the decadence they felt had always characterised popular culture in China (abetted by an ineffective or nonexistent official censorship) would become more pervasive with the introduction (via the modern schools) of western ideas of freedom and libertarianism. Thirdly, whereas in the late nineteenth century Chinese reformers had focused on western superiority in technology and political institutions, many now attributed the West's superiority to the character of its peoples. Paradoxically, while Chinese educators warned about the potentially harmful effects of importing western ideas of freedom, they praised the strict supervision of popular culture by western governments to ensure their peoples were suitably disciplined and morally upright.

PUBLIC LECTURES

In October 1915 the Education Ministry issued regulations on popular lecture institutes (*tongsu jiaoyu jiangyansuo*). It hoped that at least four would be opened in each provincial capital and that others would be set up in smaller towns and villages. Private individuals, including primary school teachers, normal school graduates and 'those experienced in public speaking', were encouraged to participate in public lectures (provided they obtained government authorisation), as well as members of education associations and 'leading local gentry' (*difang shendong*).[70] In theory, all lecture material was to be submitted beforehand to local authorities and the Education Ministry.[71]

The official aim of public lectures was to 'enlighten the people and reform society'. More specifically, lectures were to stimulate patriotism, encourage respect for the laws, promote moral behaviour and industry, and stress the importance of physical fitness and hygiene. Other lectures were to keep the people informed on current events, both domestic and foreign. Shortly after issuing its regulations on public lectures, the Education Ministry opened a 'model popular education lecture institute' (*mofan tongsu jiaoyu jiangyansuo*) in Beijing.[72] Reflecting the growing acceptance of public lecturing as a specialised skill, the institute offered training courses for would-be lecturers. Candidates were to be taught the principles of sociology, psychology and rhetoric (*xiongbian fa*: literally 'the method of arguing vociferously'), in addition to being offered courses on the world situation, law, and economics.[73]

As with most educational developments during the late Qing and early Republic, government regulations merely sanctioned an existing situation or process. Many of the lecture halls (*xuanjiangsuo*) established at the end of the Qing continued to function after 1912,[74] while provincial and district authorities took the initiative in establishing new ones. In Taiqiang district, Jiangsu, for example, a popular lecture institute was created in 1913. It organised mobile lectures (*xunhui jiangyan*) in tea-houses and temples; as well as promoting the virtues laid down in the 1915 regulations, the Taiqiang lecture institute also promoted what it called 'family education', exhorting people to cut down on extravagance (e.g. marriage or funeral ceremonies) and stressing the benefits of vocational training for women.[75]

By 1916-7 there were 2 131 lecture institutes, with Shandong province having the highest number (see Table 18). Most lecture institutes gave an

Table 18. Number of Lecture Institutes in 1916-17

Province	No. of Institutes	Average Attendance
Shandong	655	30
Hubei	239	90
Guangxi	177	30
Zhejiang	168	30
Fengtian	150	40
Shanxi	109	30
Zhili	100	40
Gansu	88	20
Jiangsu	69	30
Jiangxi	60	30
Guangdong	52	.30
Henan	51	30
Yunnan	47	20
Sichuan	37	30
Fujian	23	30
Anhui	21	30
Jilin	20	20
Hunan	18	30
Shaanxi	13	20
Beijing Metropolitan Region	17	113
Heilongjiang	13	20
Xinjiang	2	20
Guizhou	2	20
Total	2 131[a]	

Sources: *Zhonghua Minguo diwuci jiaoyu tongji tu* (Beijing, 1917), *shehui jiaoyu*, pp. 7-8; *Jiaoyubu xingzheng jiyao* (Beijing, 1916), *shehui jiaoyu*, pp. 13-17; DYJN, 3: 691
a. By 1918 the total number of lecture institutes was 2 579. *Shehui jiaoyu yanjiu* (Taibei, 1968), p. 201.

average of three lectures a week, and the average attendance ranged from thirty to forty.[76] If one compares the number of lecture institutes in 1916 with that of lecture halls in 1909 it is apparent that the internal conflicts of the intervening years had taken their toll. Only seven provinces (Zhili/ Hebei, Shandong, Jilin, Heilongjiang, Fujian, Hubei and Guangdong) had more lecture institutes in 1916 than in 1909. Other provinces registered a drastic decline. Guizhou and Shaanxi, for example, had had 1 167 and 327 lecture halls respectively in 1909,[77] while in 1916 they had two and eighteen lecture institutes respectively.

On the other hand, Beijing had eleven lecture institutes in 1916, seven of which dated from 1911.[78] According to an education ministry report in 1916, daily attendance at the lectures ranged from 30 to 160[79] (see Table 19). Lectures usually took place in the afternoon and lasted three hours. Each lecture institute had a team of three or four lecturers, who were paid

Table 19. Beijing Lecture Institutes in 1916

Lecture Institute	No. of Staff	Monthly expenditures (in Chinese dollars)	Daily Attendance
No. 1	4	62	150
No. 2	3	45	120
No. 3	3	38	40
No. 4	3	41	78
No. 5	3	30	50-60
No. 6	4	30	30
No. 7	3	40	90
No. 8	3	47	60
No. 9	3	47	160
No. 10	4	51	–
No. 11	–	–	–

Source: *Jiaoyubu xingzheng jiyao* (Beijing, 1916), *shehui jiaoyu*, pp. 12-13.

an average of ten dollars per month.[80] There was also a mobile lecturing team that visited temples during the afternoons. Attendance at lectures was sometimes quite considerable. In April 1916 over 3 000 attended lectures given at a temple in the southern suburbs, while in May of the same year over 1 000 attended lectures given over a period of two days at a temple in the eastern suburbs.[81] Most lecture institutes in Beijing also ran libraries and newspaper reading rooms, which were open to the public from early morning to afternoon (see also Table 20 for newspaper reading rooms in the provinces). Such newspaper reading rooms attracted considerable interest; the two attached to the model lecture institute in the Shandong provincial capital, for example, recorded 200 visitors daily.[82]

It is important to remember that the attention paid to public lectures during the early years of the Republic was essentially a continuation of developments during the last years of the Qing, and was not the result of missionary influence upon Chinese educators as some writers have maintained. It has been claimed, for example, that the Chinese YMCA exerted a dominant influence on the development of, and interest in, public lectures.[83] Quite apart from the fact that the Chinese YMCA tended to concentrate its educational efforts on students and businessmen,[84] such a claim overlooks the tradition of public lecturing performed by the Chinese gentry.[85] It is also significant that most promoters of popular education, such as Chen Baoquan and Wu Da, were Japanese-educated, and there is no evidence to show they were influenced by missionaries. While it is true that the secretary of the Chinese YMCA education department, David Yui (Yu Zhichang) held a series of conferences in the Yangzi provinces during 1915-16 highlighting the importance of popular education and lectures,[86] such activities would have merely confirmed Chinese educators' views

Popular Education in the Early Republic

Table 20. Number of Newspaper Reading Rooms in 1916

Province	No. of reading rooms	No. of newspapers	No. of readers daily
Jiangsu	187	18	50
Zhejiang	170	14	30
Sichuan	156	12	30
Guangdong	149	17	50
Henan	139	12	30
Zhili	124	14	40
Shandong	113	14	60
Jiangxi	106	10	20
Hubei	103	16	50
Yunnan	99	8	30
Gansu	91	5	20
Shanxi	77	10	30
Guangxi	54	5	20
Fujian	52	8	40
Fengtian	45	10	50
Hunan	39	11	40
Anhui	30	8	20
Beijing Metropolitan Region	19	22	40
Jilin	17	5	60
Guizhou	16	4	20
Shaanxi	15	9	30
Rehe	6	5	30
Heilongjiang	5	4	50
Xinjiang	5	4	20
Total	1 817		

Sources: *Zhonghua Minguo, diwuci jiaoyu tongji tu* (Beijing, 1917), *shehui jiaoyu*, pp. 7-8; *Jiaoyubu xingzheng jiyao* (Beijing, 1916), *shehui jiaoyu*, pp. 47-8.

without inspiring or directly engendering new interest in the subject.[87]

What *was* new after 1912, however, was the emergence of a vigorous debate over what exactly the role of public lectures was to be. The debate centred on two related issues: firstly, whether public lectures should be identified with the values being inculcated in modern schools or whether they should champion alternative ones and, secondly, whether public lectures were to encourage social harmony and concern for the collective interest or individual ambition and betterment.

One of the official aims of public lectures was to persuade the people of the benefits of a school education. In 1915 the Vice-Minister of Education, Yuan Xichou, asserted that the most serious obstacle to educational development was the lack of public confidence in the schools,[88] a theme that was echoed by many educators during this period.[89] Evidently, the popular distrust of modern schools so apparent in the last years of the dynasty had not disappeared with the Revolution. There were reports of officials resorting to material incentives in order to prompt unwilling parents to send their children to school.[90] Schools, as in the last years of the dynasty, were often the target of public anger when census teams investigating the number of school-age children entered villages.[91] Furthermore, even if parents had been willing to send their children to school there was always the danger of bandits. While touring Jiangsu in 1914, Hou Hongjian discovered that as soon as primary schools were opened pupils would be kidnapped in order to obtain a ransom from their parents.[92] (At one primary school a teacher's twelve-year-old son was abducted by bandits to serve as their 'secretary', presumably to aid them with the drafting of pamphlets.)[93]

Educators themselves, however, were often extremely critical of the new schools, although sometimes for differing reasons. In *The Chinese Educational World* two contrasting views were advanced on schools. In 1914 Gu Shusen compared modern schools to prisons because they stifled creativity and freedom; teachers were likened to 'hatchet men' who destroyed pupils' natural enthusiasm and energy.[94] In the same year Fan Yuanlian condemned the new schools for their excessive promotion of freedom. According to Fan, the lack of discipline had made students rebellious and unruly.[95] For the most part, nevertheless, schools were critcised for fostering division and elitism. A 1918 article argued that schools did not allow all students to develop equally; too much attention was paid to cultivating a talented few, the article continued, and thus the majority of slower students were ignored.[96] The same point was made by the future Marxist educator, Yang Xianzhang, in 1919 when he observed that modern schools lacked a 'spirit of equality' (*pingdeng jingshen*) because of the undue attention paid to 'superior' students.[97] Another article in 1919 commented that schools only served the rich and were therefore carrying out 'class education'.[98]

A journal founded in 1919 entitled *Pingmin jiaoyu* (Popular Education) condemned the system of school examinations (which encouraged students to 'hanker after empty glory') as well as the tendency of some schools to discriminate against the poor, thus reinforcing social inequality.[99] Popular education would, the journal declared, 'equalise (*pingdenghua*) society' by being available to everyone.[100] By 1920 one writer, Xiang Zhutan, was maintaining that only social, or popular, education could ensure cooperation, solidarity, and equality.[101] Popular education, with its aim of reaching a wider audience and promoting solidarity, thus increasingly came to be regarded as a corrective to the formal school system, which fostered social division and stimulated individual ambition.[102] Public lectures, paradoxically, were therefore expected to encourage school attendance, while at the same time instilling among the people values felt to be missing in the schools.

Yet the content of lectures themselves revealed different priorities. In 1917 the Education Ministry issued a list of appropriate works from among which lecturers were to choose their material.¹⁰³ Such works included biographies of patriotic heroes like Washington and Nelson and military heroes like the Song dynasty general Yue Fei; a history of China's relations with the foreign powers (literally 'A history of the national shame'); a Chinese translation of Samuel Smiles' *Self Help*; a study of the causes of Germany's wealth and strength; a book on commercial ethics (*shangye daode*), and biographies of ten wealthy American capitalists.¹⁰⁴ The Ministry's list suggested that an overall aim of public lectures was to promote patriotism and economic development. Lectures given in Beijing in 1914, for example, were already calling on people to support national products and thereby reduce foreign imports.¹⁰⁵ The Beijing popular education research association itself organised a series of lectures between 1913 and 1915, at which attendance ranged from 700 to 2 000, exhorting people to support national goods and invest in government bonds.

What is more significant, however, is the importance some educators attributed to inculcating what might be called a 'capitalist mentality' among the population. One lecture given at the No. 4 lecture institute in Beijing emphasised that the best way for the poor to become rich was to enter industry, recounting the life of the American oil baron (*meiyou dawang*), Rockefeller, as an inspirational model.¹⁰⁶ Many lectures also stated bluntly that study was useful because it was the basic way to 'make money' (*facai*).¹⁰⁷ Hou Hongjian in 1914 suggested that public lectures stress the advantages of machines as opposed to manpower, as well as the efficacy of joint-stock companies which would allow for greater accumulation of capital.¹⁰⁸

Related to this theme was the novel emphasis now placed on time and punctuality. Shanghai authorities in 1914 recommended that lectures emphasise the virtue of 'loving time'. Such a virtue, it was claimed, was 'the mother of success and the basis for wealth and strength'.¹⁰⁹ Li Yanhan in 1915 bemoaned the fact that traditionally too much time had been wasted in China; punctuality and efficient use of time, he argued, were essential to create a wealthy country.¹¹⁰ Articles in the educational press insisted that education among workers not only inculcate habits of hard work but also convince them that earning and saving money was beneficial for future wealth.¹¹¹

At the same time some educators felt that too much emphasis on enonomic initiative and the pursuit of wealth would adversely affect social harmony, particularly harmony within the family. A lecture in Beijing warned that co-operation and friendship among brothers were breaking down due to concern with their own selfish economic interests. Only a harmonious family, it concluded, could form the basis for a strong country.¹¹² An article In *The Chinese Educational World* claimed that 'competition for wealth and goods' was leading to disputes between brothers, sisters-in-law, and husbands and wives.¹¹³ Reports on the No. 1 and No. 6 lecture institutes in Beijing in 1915 show that much emphasis was placed on family co-operation,[114] while in 1917 the Beijing popular education research association insisted that public lectures extol the morality of co-operation and harmony amongst friends.[115]

Whether educators chose to stress wealth creation or social harmony, however, most continued to echo the other important theme in discussions of popular education. Public lectures were to contribute to the ongoing 'reform' of the people's behaviour and habits. Lectures compiled by the popular education research association focused on the concept of *gongde* (civic morality). In contrast to 'private morality'(*side*), which guided people's behaviour within the family or in personal relationships, civic morality was to improve people's behaviour within the community at large.[116] The lectures are a fascinating insight into what Chinese educators assumed needed to be 'improved'. Thus they exhorted local communities to arrange their houses and roads in an organised manner so as not to inconvenience visitors or passers-by; strictures against public vandalism particularly condemned garbage being thrown out on the street, walls being covered with graffiti, and people urinating in the streets; references to personal behaviour included insistence on people forming orderly queues in public (with no pushing or shoving when getting on trains) and on refraining from shouting in public, talking during theatrical performances, and spitting in other people's homes.[117] (It is interesting to note that a 1919 article on the benefits of public parks not only observed, as William Morris in the nineteenth century might have done, that they would stimulate among the people an appreciation of beauty, but also that they would train the Chinese in habits of public hygiene, such as not urinating in public places.)[118]

Finally, against the background of increasing concern over sexual libertarianism noted earlier, some educators felt that lectures on public hygiene should include 'sex education' (*xingyu jiaoyu*), which meant nothing more than warning the populace against the harmful effects of promiscuity.[119] *The Educational Review* in 1915 noted that such measures were being taken in Germany so as to ensure that the physical and mental health of the lower classes would not deteriorate.[120] Lu Feigui stated baldly in 1918 that sex education should be aimed at restraining the sexual urges before they got out of hand.[121] Typically, enormous confidence was expressed in the role public lectures would play in transforming an 'uncivilised' populace into a suitably public-spirited and well-behaved citizenry.[122]

SPARE-TIME SCHOOLS AND LIBRARIES

Half-day and literacy schools, which had begun to be established in the last years of the Qing, continued in existence after 1912. In 1914 the Education Ministry issued new regulations on half-day schools, noting that they were designed for 12-16-year-olds who had not received a primary school education.[123] Courses were to last three years and the curriculum included writing (twelve hours a week), arithmetic (three hours a week), physical

Table 21. Number of Half-Day Schools and Literacy Schools in 1916

Province	Half-Day Schools[a]		Literacy Schools[b]	
Sichuan	345	(20 700)	160	(9 600)
Shanxi	314	(12 560)	250	(10 400)
Zhili	118	(9 240)	1 511	(120 880)
Hubei	73	(8 760)	165	(19 800)
Guangdong	53	(6 360)	54	(6 480)
Jiangxi	42	(2 520)	108	(6 480)
Gansu	33	(660)	230	(4 600)
Hunan	29	(1 740)	8	(480)
Shandong	29	(2 610)	73	(6 570)
Guangxi	28	(1 120)	224	(8 960)
Zhejiang	28	(3,360)	84	(10 080)
Fujian	21	(1 890)	13	(1 170)
Henan	17	(1 530)	932	(55 920)
Jiangsu	17	(2 040)	33	(3 960)
Jilin	13	(780)	86	(5 160)
Xinjiang	11	(220)	20	(400)
Anhui	10	(400)	69	(2 760)
Yunnan	7	(630)	28	(2 520)
Shaanxi	6	(360)	14	(840)
Fengtian	1	(90)	5	(450)
Guizhou	–		6	(240)
Heilongjiang	–		4	(80)
Total	1 195	(67 570)	4 087	(277 830)

Note: Numbers of students are in brackets.
Sources: a. Jiaoyubu xingzheng jiyao (Beijing, 1916), shehui jiaoyu, pp. 42-7.
b. DYJN, 3: 602.

education (two hours a week) and moral training (only one hour a week). Although the new school system of 1912 had allowed coeducation at the lower primary school level, the regulations stated that girls were to have their own half-day schools.[124] The overwhelming majority of half-day schools, in fact, were established for boys. Some of the first half-day schools for girls were opened in the provincial capital of Hubei; four such schools opened in 1914, each employing teachers who were students from the provincial women's normal school.[125] In addition to the curriculum laid down in the official regulations, half-day schools sometimes gave a more practical training. The one opened by the Beijing model lecture institute in 1917 taught boys how to make soap, ink-slabs, and slate pencils.[126] The half-day school attached to a lecture institute in the Shandong provincial capital organised a 'trading department' (fanmai bu) among the students. They sold local products, some of the proceeds of which were distributed among students' families.[127] By 1916 there were over one thousand half-day schools, Sichuan having the highest number (345), and over four thousand literacy schools, with Zhili having the highest number (1 511) (see Table 21).

Another kind of spare-time school that was created during this period was the open-air school (*lutian xuexiao*). Such schools appeared in Beijing in 1914, giving classes once or twice a week for boys and girls aged between six and fourteen years. By 1915 the Beijing popular education research association had established seven open-air schools, while the Beijing education bureau had opened six, all of which were set up within the vicinity of primary schools.[128] Singing and recreational activities (*yuxi*) were usually added to the curriculum of writing, arithmetic and moral training. As with many other aspects of education, Germany was cited as a model. A five-part article in *The Educational Review* on open-air schools in Europe and the United States in 1915 noted that they were first established in Berlin in 1904.[129]

Huang Yanpei, on a tour of Tianjin, wrote of the existence of seven open-air schools. One such school he visited was attended by about one hundred pupils. Teachers were usually volunteers from local schools and for writing lessons the school used paper and writing instruments discarded by the schools. Lessons always began with singing in order to attract potential pupils.[130] Unlike the half-day schools, there seemed to be no segregation of the sexes at open-air schools. A report on the one near the No. 4 primary school in Beijing recorded an attendance of thirty boys and forty-five girls.[131] In the Shandong provincial capital, one of the twelve open-air schools had an equal attendance of boys and girls. Average attendance at the schools was about twenty, although there were many 'spectators' as well. Blackboards were hung on walls and the trees 'served as roofs'. The teachers, who were all full-time school teachers, were paid from 2 to 10 dollars a month.[132]

There are also references in this period to 'public supplementary schools' (*gongzhong puxi xuexiao*), primarily designed for primary-school graduates unable to proceed further up the educational ladder. They were established in most provinces, although unfortunately little information exists on the running and nature of these schools.[133] Beijing reportedly had three such schools which initially attracted about 1 000 students.[134] The main subjects taught were writing and arithmetic. Most of the students at the No. 2 public supplementary school were petty traders, while those at the No. 1 school included labourers and handicraft workers. Ages ranged from 15 to 20.[135]

Since it was not until 1928 that educational statistics specifically recorded provincial and district expenditures on popular education, a precise picture of popular education funding in the early years of the republic is difficult to obtain. From the information that is available, however, it would appear that the trend begun in the last years of the Qing of *increasing* official expenditure on popular education continued after 1912.[136] In Zhejiang, for example, official expenditures on lecture institutes increased from 9 506 dollars to 14 976 dollars between 1913 and 1914, and

Table 22. School Attendance in 1919

Province	No. of school-age children	No. in school	Percentage attendance
Zhili	2 093 000	489 396	23.38
Shandong	3 824 790	476 182	12.45
Shanxi	1 220 000	699 913	57.37
Henan	2 531 700	223 383	8.82
Shaanxi	840 000	136 756	16.28
Gansu	1 038 600	60 503	5.25
Sichuan	6 870 000	470 213	6.84
Hubei	3 528 000	208 358	5.90
Hunan	2 216 900	204 349	9.22
Jiangxi	2 653 200	112 819	4.25
Anhui	2 367 000	53 672	2.27
Jiangsu	2 398 000	320 436	13.36
Zhejiang	1 158 000	282 510	24.39
Fujian	2 287 000	87 169	3.85
Guangdong	3 186 500	167 950	5.20
Guangxi	514 000	144 357	28.09
Yunnan	1 272 000	166 961	13.12
Guizhou	765 000	50 129	6.55
Xinjiang	120 000	2 988	2.49
Three north-eastern provinces	1 500 000	325 835	21.72

Source: Chen Baoquan, *Zhongguo jindai xuezhi bianyi shi*, (Beijing, 1927), pp.56-7

from 7 142 to 11 622 dollars on libraries during the same period.[137] In Beijing official funds spent on middle schools decreased from 84 811 dollars in 1915 to 82 288 dollars in 1916, whereas those spent on primary schools increased from 209 331 to 212 638 dollars and those spent on popular education increased from 12 417 to 13 421 dollars in the same period.[138]

Significantly, also, whereas during the early years of educational reform the amount of funds spent on higher and specialist education dwarfed all others, in Fengtian, in 1916, while 70 749 dollars were spent on specialist education, 50 420 dollars were devoted to popular education (2 375 000 dollars also went towards general education, that is primary and middle schools).[139] The trend continued through the 1920s. In 1932 Jiangsu reported spending 541 212 dollars on social/popular education, while only 279 912 were spent on higher-level education.[140]

Clearly, public lectures, spare-time schools, and supplementary schools were helping to fill the huge gaps left by the formal school system. Throughout the early years of the Republic attendance at formal schools was low. By 1919 the percentage of school-age children attending school ranged from 57 per cent in Shanxi to 2 per cent in Xinjiang (see Table 22).[141] The drop-out rate was also considerable. In 1915, for example, 134 550 boys dropped out of official lower primary schools (out of a total of 2 388 264) (see Table 23). Furthermore, in Beijing, only one quarter of the 2 291 students who graduated from lower primary schools in 1916 were able to enter higher primary school, while only one-fifth of those who graduated from higher primary schools went on to middle school.[142] The turmoil of these years meant also that primary and middle schools often ceased functioning as a result of war. Hou Hongjian noted that in Anhui over fifty middle and primary schools had been closed down in December 1913, leaving over 6 000 children of school-age without access to formal education.[143]

In any event, the necessity of spare-time and supplementary education was continually emphasised in Chinese educational journals and once again Germany was held up for emulation. A 1918 article described Germany's system as the best in the world, one which England and the United States strove to imitate.[144] Supplementary education in Germany, it was noted, had led to economic prosperity and a skilled and patriotic workforce. Another article in the same year argued that Germany, unlike England, had no 'young layabouts' because its widespread system of supplementary education ensured that school drop-outs, workers and apprentices were both skilled and suitably disciplined.[145] Chinese educators also began in this period to turn their attention to supplementary education in rural areas and for this they often cited Denmark's system of 'folk high schools' (*pingmin zhongxuexiao*) as a model. The first Danish folk high school had been founded in 1844 with the aim of giving short winter or summer courses to rural youth. The emphasis was not so much on the teaching of vocational skills *per se* but rather on instilling patriotic pride through the teaching of history, literature and national songs.[146] Articles on these schools first appeared in the Chinese educational press in 1910, and thereafter Chinese educators continued to express their admiration for Denmark's success in educating its rural population.[147]

Another significant development in the early republic was the attempt to create libraries for a wider populace. Public libraries had begun to be founded during the last years of the Qing[148] and by 1914 most provinces had opened libraries in their respective capitals.[149] In 1922 there were forty-two public libraries in all (see Table 24). Some libraries, as in Fengtian, were housed in former official buildings while others, as in Jiangsu and Fujian, made use of former academies (*shuyuan*). The library in Anhui's capital was located in a Confucian temple.[150] Some provinces recorded the number of visitors. Figures for 1916 indicate that libraries in Yunnan and Guangxi received 3 000 and 1 800 visitors a month respectively, while Fujian and Zhili recorded figures of 12 000 and 8 560 visitors a year respectively.[151] During 1915 the Beijing library had 3 443 visitors.[152]

Although the creation of libraries at the end of the Qing had been an important innovation, in the sense that what had existed previously were private book collections in individual wealthy households, the aim had

Table 23. School Drop-out Rate in 1915

	Total in school		No. of those dropping out	
	Boys	Girls	Boys	Girls
Lower Primary (official)	2 388 264	117 255	134 550 (5·6%)	8 866 (7·5%)
Lower Primary (private)	930 842	24 952	44 119 (4·7%)	1 808 (7·2%)
Higher Primary (Official)	327 058	15 826	25 743 (7·8%)	1 438 (9·08%)
Higher Primary (private)	67 290	3 806	5 379 (7·9%)	369 (9·7%)

Source: Taga Akigorō (ed.) Shiryō, 2: 590-1

been primarily to preserve classic texts and provide facilities for scholars rather than extend reading privileges to a wider public. In 1909 Zhang Zhidong emphasised the importance of libraries for keeping precious books in China and thus putting an end to the 'increasing practice of scholars selling rare editions abroad for high profits'.[153] Regulations on libaries in 1910 stipulated that they were to be established 'in order to preserve the national essence [guocui] , help create talent, provide study facilities for scholars and students, and to collect materials from far and wide for people to look over'.[154] No books could be borrowed from these libraries and reading fees were charged.[155] In 1913 the Guangdong education inspector could complain that the provincial library, whose officials were mostly 'old Confucian scholars', was more concerned with preserving old manuscripts than with opening up to the public.[156]

After 1912 attempts were made to remedy the situation. In 1913 the Beijing popular library (tongsu tushuguan) was opened, to which was later attached a public recreation ground and a children's reading room. The library contained over 1 400 volumes; no reading fees were charged and borowing was permitted. It was estimated that about 620 people visited the library daily.[157] In 1915 the Education Ministry ordered the provinces to open similar libraries in order to benefit 'the ordinary people', insisting that no reading fees be charged.[158] Popular libraries were, in fact, established by most provinces after 1915 with Hubei and Fengtian having the most in 1916 (forty-four and thirty-five respectively, see Table 24). The popular library in Nanjing, which opened in February 1916, comprised a museum, lecture-hall and physical recreation hall, as well as a reading room. By the end of 1916 over 13 000 people were reported to have visited the library.[159] The popular library in the Shandong provincial capital, which had over 2 000 books, received 1 000 visitors a day, most of them coming to read the newspapers and magazines (of which there were seventy kinds).[160]

The public libraries also began to expand their facilities at this time.

Table 24. Popular Libraries in 1916, 1922 and 1930

Province	1916[a] No.	No. of books	Visitors per year	1922[b] No.	No. of books	1930[c] No.
Zhili	4 (2)	900	34 675	5 (4)	2 300	119 (94)
Fengtian	35 (2)	7 500	328 500	35 (4)	7 500	17 (31)
Heilongjiang	4 (1)	650	31 025	3 (2)	650	4 (3)
Jilin	3 (1)	700	32 850	3 (1)	700	– (12)
Shandong	23 (1)	10 000	547 500	23 (1)	10 000	45 (61)
Shanxi	9 (–)	2 700	109 500	9 (7)	2 700	5 (33)
Henan	22 (1)	9 000	373 250	22 (1)	9 000	93 (132)
Jiangsu	5 (3)	1 600	65 740	5 (11)	1 600	27 (65)
Jiangxi	5 (1)	1 500	45 625	5 (1)	1 500	4 (32)
Anhui	4 (1)	1 200	43 900	4 (1)	1 200	7 (37)
Fujian	21 (1)	600	21 900	21 (1)	600	20 (49)
Zhejiang	21 (1)	5 350	219 000	21 (6)	5 350	70 (44)
Hubei	44 (1)	18 000	357 000	44 (1)	18 000	33 (20)
Hunan	14 (1)	3 500	13 870	14 (1)	3 500	77 (3)
Shaanxi	– (1)			Figures not available		
Gansu	2 (–)			2 (2)		– (52)
Xinjiang	4 (–)	500	18 250	4 (–)	500	
Sichuan	4 (1)	1 200	36 500	4 (1)	1 200	9 (45)
Guangdong	6 (1)	1 600	54 750	6 (1)	1 600	72 (88)
Guangxi	1 (1)	1 800	73 000	1 (1)	1 800	4 (1)
Yunnan	6 (1)	300	10 950	6 (1)	300	40 (50)
Guizhou	– (1)	1 500	35 700		1 500	
Beijing Metropolitan Area	1 (2)	1 400	246 300			
Total	238			237		646

Note: Number of general libraries are in brackets.
Sources: a. *Zhonghua minguo diwuci jiaoyu tongji tu* (Beijing, 1917), *shehui jiaoyu*, pp. 7-8.
b. R. Pelissier, *Les bibliothèques en Chine Pendant la Première Moitié du XXème Siècle*, pp. 35-6.

Table 25. Number of Readers in the Shaanxi Public Library (June 1918-May 1919)

	No. per month
Soldiers	1 196
Scholars and students	364
Workers and traders	186
Politicians	165
Women	134
Others	169

Source: Jiaoyu gongbao 6: 10 (October 1919), baogao, pp. 1-12.

Some now allowed borrowing, while others had special reading rooms for children.[161] The library in Jilin also had a reading room for women; in Shandong the public library reserved certain days for women readers, suggesting that they had originally not been allowed to enter.[162] An intriguing report in 1919 on the public library in Shaanxi gave the occupational background of readers visiting the library between June 1918 and May 1919, using the categories of 'politicians' (zheng) 'scholars and students' (xue), 'soldiers' (jun), 'workers and traders' (gongshang), women, and 'others'. According to the report soldiers constituted the highest number of readers, followed by scholars and students (see Table 25). The most popular reading material comprised novels and scientific works.[163]

One writer, Shen Shaoqi, summed up the changes in attitude towards libraries in 1917 when he remarked that they were no longer to be merely places where old books were preserved for the benefit of a scholarly elite.[164] Popular libraries were welcomed precisely because they would be free, books would be available to all and people from all social groups and levels would be able to assemble in one place.[165] Shen also underlined the connection between a wide network of libraries and economic development. Citing the example of the American capitalist, Carnegie, who contributed funds to the establishment of libraries, Shen argued that libraries should be seen as a productive investment, which would increase workers' knowledge and hence improve Chinese industry.

VOCATIONAL EDUCATION AND THE PROMOTION OF
'HARD AND DILIGENT WORK'

In 1920 a student reportedly complained that teachers were continually harping on the abstract themes of 'emancipation', 'reconstruction' and 'building a future for the young'. Instead of this 'verbiage', the student continued, what was required was more 'practical and instructive lessons'.[166] Such an attitude is indicative of a general concern during this period to see education serve the people in a more practical way by preparing them for a livelihood. In 1913 Huang Yanpei delivered a stinging attack on existing education, which he regarded as useless and irrelevant.

He advocated a more 'pragmatic' approach to education (*shiyong zhuyi*), which ideally should permeate all subjects.[167] History, for example, according to Huang, should deal with those who had been successful in industry or who had contributed to practical knowledge.

Huang's call for pragmatic education was echoed by other educators who insisted that education should 'prepare students for life'.[168] One warned that if primary school students were not taught appropriate skills their 'intrinsic lazy and pleasure-seeking natures' would ill-equip them to survive in society.[169] Only a pragmatic approach, it was declared, would transform the people from a 'consumer' to a 'productive' one.[170] In 1917 Huang Yanpei, Zhuang Yu, Lu Feigui, Jiang Weiqiao, Chen Baoquan and Cai Yuanpei founded the Chinese Vocational Education Association (*Zhonghua zhiye jiaoyushe*) in Shanghai.[171] Its manifesto called for an education that would directly solve the 'problem of livelihood' (*shengji wenti*) and hence avoid the prospect of a surfeit of 'higher-level vagrants' unable to apply their knowledge to the practical problems of Chinese society.[172]

Accompanying the call for a more pragmatic education was the insistence by many educators that schools stress the importance of manual work, an idea first raised in the last years of the Qing. At that time modern schools had often been criticised for producing a lazy and non-productive elite. An article in 1904 noted that whereas in the past students had been treated as slaves, the prestige now attached to westernisation and modern education had given them an elevated view of themselves. Not only do students have no concept of public service, the article complained, 'but at times they throw away their food, beat up servants, and are haughty and arrogant like rich people'.[173] Another writer observed in 1910 that even in middle and primary schools, where over half the students came from 'middle-level families or below', laziness and elitist attitudes were being encouraged. Upon graduation they would spread this 'spirit of idleness and hedonism' (*duoyi zhi feng*) throughout society.[174] It was suggested that students perform all the menial tasks at school, traditionally allotted to servants. The very imagery used to refer to education during the last years of the Qing and early years of the Republic reflected the changing emphasis on the *raison d'être* of education. Traditionally, it had been described in terms of 'gardening' or 'cultivation' (of the moral nature). By 1910 education was being referred to as a 'factory that produces citizens'.[175] In 1912 the Education Ministry was referred to as a 'manufacturing plant' and students as the 'manufactured products'. Officials in the ministry were compared to 'technicians' (*jishu*) who, if they did not do their jobs properly, would be like 'useless machinery producing defective goods'.[176] The whole thrust of education was now perceived as the training of economically productive and hard-working citizens, an aim that was encapsulated in a phrase frequently referred to in the educational press after 1912, *qinlao zhuyi* (the philosophy of hard and diligent work).

A person's worth was now seen in terms of how economically productive and hardworking the person was. Thus a 1916 article on vocational education argued that it did not distinguish between 'aristocrat and commoner' (*guijian*). No one occupation, the article continued, should be regarded as inferior to another; the only criterion was whether the job was diligently done and whether it contributed to the country's economic development. The article concluded by asking, 'How can the tasks carried out by the worker and the government minister not be considered of equal importance?'[177]

There were also constant references in this period to the importance of 'productive ability' (*shengchan zhi nengli*).[178] One educator in 1916 demanded that social education teach people 'to regard labour as sacred in order that production be developed'.[179] The key function of education, Zhuang Yu noted in the same year, was to 'develop the people's productive power'.[180] The virtues instilled by vocational education, according to another educator in 1917, would be patience, and love of labour and productive work.[181] The necessity of such an education was felt to be especially urgent by some educators because of what they perceived as the lazy and indolent nature of the Chinese people. Zhuang Yu, for example, pessimistically claimed that the Chinese nature was inclined to passivity rather than activity and that people preferred to avoid hard work.[182] Another writer expressed alarm that the influence of western material civilisation in China would produce an extravagant rich class on the one hand and a lazy class of poor people intent on making quick profits on the other unless education promoted the virtue of hard work.[183]

Educators even went on to insist that there was nothing morally wrong in the active and diligent pursuit of wealth, pouring scorn on the traditional Confucian aversion to such activities. Huang Yanpei claimed that the prosperity of the overseas Chinese (particularly in South-East Asia) was due to the fact they were unfettered by outdated moral taboos on the acquisition of wealth.[184] Since vocational training was now more relevant than traditional moral education, one educator wrote in 1919, the traditional antithesis of *yi* (righteousness) and *li* (self-interest) should be rejected; self-interest, in fact should be the order of the day.[185]

It was no coincidence, therefore, that educational journals frequently contained accounts of people who had worked hard both to increase their knowledge and enhance their material situation. One referred to a twenty-nine-year-old peddler, Dai Yuanfa, who saved money to study at a Shanghai primary school because he wanted to be more knowledgeable and earn more money.[186] It was also suggested that role models in school textbooks should be those who had worked to become successful industrialists and entrepreneurs.[187] At the same time, in an intriguing anticipation of later Maoist practice, it was proposed that students who excelled in vocational training and labour be honoured at ceremonies and designated 'model personages'.[188]

Students thus had to become accustomed to thinking in 'economic' terms, whether they were attending general, vocational or spare-time schools. Wu Da's 1913 proposed curriculum of extra-curricular activities included 'commercial practice' and the organisation of a savings society.[189] In Wujin, Jiangsu, the education association in 1914 proposed that students organise into 'traders' groups' (*fufantuan*) in order to sell local goods or handicrafts produced at their schools.[190] A 1917 article confidently predicted that all schools could run themselves by setting up 'factories' (*gongchang*) in their largest classroom to produce handicrafts, which would then be sold in retail stores set up on school premises.[191] By 1918 Anhui educational authorities ordered all half-day and vocational schools to sell the handicrafts students produced, the proceeds to be used to run the school and help needy students.[192]

These ideas were put into practice by some schools. The Anhui No. 2 normal school, for example, added a trading department and a workshop to its attached primary school in 1918.[193] A higher primary school, also in Anhui, taught handicrafts so that students, by making use of local raw materials and creating useful products, could 'expand the country's economy'.[194] In some cases school-produced goods were meant to substitute for foreign imports. Thus, the students of the primary school attached to the Nantong normal school in Jiangsu produced and sold mounted cloth substitutes for foreign brands of writing paper.[195] Finally, agricultural schools in this period began to sell the crops grown on experimental plots.[196]

Accompanying this development was the idea that school students should be encouraged to 'save money' (*zhujin*). As the education bureau in a Fujian district argued, such an activity might cultivate an 'economic outlook', which would spread to 'labouring society' (*laodong shehui*).[197] Since the lower classes lacked the 'habit of saving', one article declared (in line with the prevalent view that people frittered away their money on gambling and decadent entertainment) there was no accumulation of capital, and industry therefore could not develop. Frugality and thriftiness should thus be taught first in the schools, after which such habits would gradually become widespread in society.[198] Although the idea of encouraging students to save money was to make them think of their own long-term interest, one article in 1915 suggested it would help foster a public spirit. The money saved from the proceeds of selling school handicraft goods could be used to purchase national bonds, contribute to local needs, subsidise poorer students or add extra facilities to the school.[199]

Nevertheless, some educators feared that too much emphasis on vocational training and the need to acquire skills to better oneself materially would lead to individualism and selfishness (*liyi zhuyi*).[200] An excessively pragmatic approach to education, one journal claimed in 1914, would result in the neglect of a student's moral character.[201] Without attention to the development of moral character, Zhu Yuanshan warned in 1917, vocational education might simply encourage people to seek individual gain, thus harming the collectivity and endangering the existence of the state. He referred to the English working classes who continually went on strike for more money as an example of what happened when people were only concerned with their own welfare.[202]

It was to conciliate these two views that many Chinese educators at this time discussed the educational philosophy of Georg Kerschensteiner (1854-1932) and his concept of the *Arbeitsschule* (labour school).[203] Director of Education in Munich from 1895 to 1919, Kerschensteiner was a keen supporter of compulsory supplementary education, while also stressing the interdependence of moral and vocational training. His proposed *Arbeitsschule* in 1912 emphasised practical work (such as handicrafts), which would inculcate qualities of diligence, industry, cleanliness, punctuality and honesty. Students would also learn the value of doing a job well, no matter how insignificant. The first aim of the school was thus to train an efficient worker (what Kerschensteiner called the 'egoistic stage'). The second aim was to 'accustom the pupil to put his trade efficiency and joy in work to the service of fellow pupils and fellow citizens'.[204] This 'altruistic stage' would make the student aware of the citizen's obligations to the state, while group work at school would accustom the student to devote his labour to the collectivity.

As one writer has noted, Kerschensteiner's educational ideal was ultimately to educate individuals 'to form a community of thinking, selfless, efficient people all working willingly and joyfully together for the betterment and progress of the state'.[205] It was Kerschensteiner's emphasis on the importance of training hard-working and diligent citzens,[206] fully aware of their duties towards the collectivity and the state, that most attracted Chinese educators. In addition to the numerous articles on Kerschensteiner in the educational press during the early years of the republic,[207] a full-length work on his educational philosophy was published in 1916.[208]

Kerschensteiner's concept of the *Arbeitsschule* was often described as a manifestation of *qinlao zhuyi* (philosophy of hard and diligent work).[209] Not only would the scourge of idleness be eliminated but moral qualities, such as a sense of duty, would be enhanced if such a philosophy permeated education.[210] Industrialisation, Zhuang Yu declared in 1915, would never be achieved in China unless the people were industrious and diligent.[211] There was, however, another significant rationale for promoting *qinlao zhuyi*. An article in 1915 observed that an education which championed the importance of manual work would help bring about a change in attitudes towards labouring people. Such a change was especially needed in China, it continued, where contempt for manual work was rife.[212] Once again, Germany was hailed as a model. Whereas children in England were trained to become 'gentlemen' (*shenshi*), one educator maintained in 1915, in Germany more prestige was attributed to manual or mechanical work.[213] Germany was praised as a country where 'labour was held sacred' throughout society.[214]

The early years of the Republic had been depressingly bleak as far as political development was concerned. The initial hopes of republicans had turned to disappointment and disillusion as constitutionalism withered and the unity of the country became fragmented by a bewildering array of competing warlord cliques. Intellectuals after 1915, in what became known as the New Culture Movement, turned their attention to the underlying cultural reasons for the failure of republicanism, arguing that an entrenched Confucian tradition had prevented the emergence of dynamic, autonomous, and public-minded citizens. Yet many of the issues thrown up in this movement were already being debated by Chinese educators from the end of the Qing onwards. Significantly, also, the importance educators placed on manual labour, which was to play a crucial part in the work-study movement (to be discussed in the next chapter), antedated the campaign by radical intellectuals in the wake of the May Fourth Movement in 1919 to champion the cause of labour.

NOTES

1. For a general history of the period, see J. Sheridan, *China In Disintegration* (New York, 1977).
2. On the politics of the early Republic, see R. Scalapino, G. Yu, *Modern China and its Revolutionary Process*, pp. 321-404; G. Yu, *Party Politics in Republican China* (Berkeley, 1966).
3. E. Young, *The Presidency of Yuan Shih-k'ai*, pp. 139-68.
4. JYZZ, 3: 12 (1912), *jishi*, pp. 93-4. See also W. Dolby, *A History of Chinese Drama* (London, 1976) p. 203.
5. *Zhengfu gongbao* (26 May 1912), 1: 111. In the same month the Education Ministry approved a request from another organisation, the Shanghai Association to Advance Citizen Education, to compile vernacular (*baihua*) materials for specific use among army units.
6. JYZZ, 4: 3 (1912), *jishi*, p. 22. The association later decided to create a 'film bureau' that would produce films and lantern slides for educational use. JYZZ, 4: 10 (1912), *jishi*, p. 71.
7. JYZZ, 4: 5 (1912), *jishi*, p. 39.
8. JYZZ, 4: 10 (1912), (jishi), p. 71.
9. JYZZ, 7: 2 (1915), *zhuanjian*, pp. 1-8. The association had a corps of fifty lecturers and ran a music training institute (*yinyue zhuanxisuo*).
10. The Jiangsu education inspector in 1913 specifically defined popular education as 'the reform of plays and novels'. Shu Xincheng (ed.) *Ziliao*, 1: 325.
11. *Zhengfu gongbao* (1913), 12: 432-8. The Education Ministry later noted that most provinces sent in the requested reports but unfortunately there are no details concerning the reports themselves. *Jiaoyubu xingzheng jiyao* (Beijing, 1916), *shehui jiaoyu*, pp. 18-20.
12. *Tongsu jiaoyu yanjiu hui diyici baogaoshu* (Beijing, 1916), *zhangcheng*, p. 1. See also Shu Xincheng (ed.), *Ziliao*, 3: 820-2.
13. *Tongsu jiaoyu yanjiu hui diyici baogaoshu*, *wendu*, pp. 6-8. See also S. Gamble, *Peking: A Social Survey* (New York 1921), pp. 156-7. Another member of the association was Lu Xun. Gu Mingyuan, *Lu Xun di jiaoyu, sixiang he shixian*, p. 26. Chen Baoquan was in charge of investigating books.

14. Two of the books classified as superior were Chinese translations of *Uncle Tom's Cabin* and *Robinson Crusoe*.
15. *Tongsu jiaoyu yanjiu hui dierci baogaoshu* (Bejing, 1917), *fubiao*, pp. 1-19. See also DYJN, 3: 670; Zhang Zhinglu (ed.), *Zhongguo chuban shiliao bubian* (Shanghai, 1957), pp. 146-7. In 1922 the Shanghai Book Company organised a censorship committee (*chuye zhengxin tuan*) of its own to prevent the publication of pornographic novels. Ibid., pp. 147-8.
16. *Tongsu jiaoyu yanjiu hui disanci baogaoshu* (Beijing, 1918), *biao*, pp. 1-28. One of the books classified as superior was a life of Napoleon, presumably one that omitted details of his amorous as opposed to his military adventures.
17. *Tongsu jiaoyu yanjiu hui dierci baogaoshu*, *wendu*, p. 15.
18. Those in charge of investigating drama were also responsible for films and phonograph records.
19. See, for example, *Jiaoyu gongbao*, no. 94 (August 1915), *jijian*, p. 20. See also the speech by Education Minister Cai Heqing in December 1916 in *Tongsu jiaoyu yanjiu hui dierci baogaoshu*, *zhuanjian*, pp. 4-5. Cai argued that the Boxers had been influenced by the supernatural elements of traditional theatre.
20. *Tongsu jiaoyu yanjiu hui dierci baogaoshu*, *wendu*, pp. 5, 14. See also S. Gamble, *Peking: A Social Survey*, p. 227. Provincial authorities were also critical of popular drama. In 1918 the Anhui governor ordered magistrates to keep a closer watch over the theatre because of its 'indecent' and 'obscene' content. *Anhui jiaoyu yuekan*, no. 12 (1918), *gongwen*, pp. 38-9.
21. In the early years of the twentieth century opium seemed to be the principal concern. Thus a 1906 article condemned the widespread existence of brothels because, it was felt, their clients (most of whom were merchants and students) became infected with the 'opium habit'. *Jinghua xinbao*, no. 223 (June 1906).
22. *Jiaoyu zhoubao* (August 1915), no. 93, *fulu*, pp. 47-8.
23. Shu Xincheng (ed.), *Ziliao*, 1: 320.
24. Differences of opinion, however, sometimes arose over whether certain books were suitable or not. Thus in 1915, at a meeting of the popular education research association, the Education Minister condemned the popular Ming novel *The Water Margin* (*Shui hu zhuan*) for having a bad effect on society (i.e. it propagated sex and violence). Yet in 1917 another education minister maintained that the novel was useful because it contained 'some revolutionary thought'. *Jiaoyu zhoubao*, no. 108 (October 1915), *jijian*, p. 13; *Jingshi jiaoyubao*, no. 23 (November 1915), *zhuanjian*, p. 28; *Jingshi jiaoyubao*, no. 38 (February 1917), *yanshuo*, p. 2; JYZZ, 9: 3 (1917), *zhuanjian*, pp. 1-5.
25. Taga Akigorō (ed.), *Shiryō*, 2: 252.
26. JYZZ, 3: 9 (1911), *yanlun*, pp. 75-8. Lu's article is reprinted in *Jiaoyu wencun*, *zhuan* 4, pp. 67-72.
27. Lu also suggested that prostitutes be given regular medical examinations and that an age limit be imposed on potential clients.

28. JYZZ, 3: 5 (1911), *yanlun*, p. 51.
29. Wei Shaochang (comp.), *Yuanyang hudiepai yanjiu ziliao* (Shanghai, 1962) p. 86. A recent study from the People's Republic is specifically devoted to the 'corruption of society' during the Republic, focusing in particular on gambling, opium, and prostitution. Wu Yu et al., *Minguo heishehui* (Nanjing, 1988).
30. Wei Shaochang (comp.), *Yuanyang hudiepai yanjiu shiliao*, pp. 108-16; P. Link, *Mandarin Ducks and Butterflies* (Berkeley, 1981), p. 93.
31. P. Link, *ibid.* p. 10.
32. Leo Ou-fan Lee, A. Nathan, 'The Beginnings of Mass Culture: Journalism and Fiction in the Late Ch'ing and Beyond', pp. 382-8.
33. For example, Jade Pear Spirit, one of the most popular of butterfly novels, was not mentioned at all in the Education Ministry's classification of books. P. Link sees particular tastes for popular fiction advancing in 'waves' during this period. Thus in the early 1910s the craze was for 'love stories', in the late 1910s satirical social novels, western-style detective stories, and scandal fiction were popular, and in the 1920s 'knight-errant' fiction was fashionable. *Mandarin Ducks and Butterflies*, p. 22.
34. ZHJYJ, 2: 4 (1913), *jishi*, pp. 45-50. Reprinted in *Jiaoyu wencun*, *zhuan* 4, pp. 58-66.
35. Lu also condemned the family practices of having young boys and girls sleep in the same room and of employing young male and female servants which, he maintained, encouraged licentious behaviour.
36. Lu's advice on how to solve the 'sex problem' bears a striking similarity to that of current sex manuals published recently in China. Examples include *Jianshen yu xing* (Beijing, 1980) and *Xing de zhishi* (Beijing 1980).
37. Cited in J. Ch'en, *China and the West* (London, 1979), p. 388. Some educators attributed the source of the problem to the traditional custom of early marriage, which distracted boys and girls from the serious task of study and affected their physical and mental health. L. Wieger, *Chine Moderne*, vol. 2 (1921): *Le Flot Montant*, pp. 191-5, 208-14. In 1915, in fact, the Education Ministry felt it necessary to prohibit girls at school from marrying. *Zhongguo jiaoyu cidian* (Shanghai, 1930), p. 30.
38. JYZZ, 4: 4 (1912), *jishi*, p. 26. In addition to plays and songs the Governor also referred to the educational value of paintings. He cited the example of France where paintings depicting the French defeat at the hands of the Prussians in 1871 were displayed everywhere to stimulate the people's patriotism.
39. Shu Xincheng (ed.), *Ziliao*, 1: 315. At the same time the bureau apparently banned thirty-three 'immoral' plays.
40. *Tongsu jiaoyu yanjiu hui dierci baogaoshu*, *wendu*, pp. 1, 24; *zhangcheng*, pp. 1-6. See also DYJN, 3: 1005; ZHJYJ, 5: 3 (1916), pp. 5-6. In 1919 the popular education research association reported that it had created over thirty plays between 1916 and 1918. *Tongsu jiaoyu yanjiu hui disici baogaoshu*, *biaoce*, pp. 1-2.

41. S. Gamble, *Peking: A Social Survey*, pp. 227-8.
42. Taga Akigorō (ed.), *Shiryō*, 2: 309.
43. *Tongsu jiaoyu yanjiu hui dierci baogaoshu, wendu*, p. 2.
44. Shu Xincheng (ed.), *Ziliao*, 1: 315.
45. *Tongsu jiaoyu yanjiu hui dierci baogaoshu, wendu*, pp. 4, 24.
46. ZHJYJ, 8: 4 (1919), *lunzhu*, p. 41.
47. *Tongsu jiaoyu yanjiu hui diyici baogaoshu, zhuanjian*, pp. 102. The Ministry noted that the Japanese government spent 75 000 dollars annually on popular education.
48. See, for example, *Jiaoyu gongbao*, 2: 4 (1915), *yishu*, pp. 8-14; 5:1 (1919), *yishu*, pp. 13-21.
49. ZHJYJ, 2: 4 (1913), *tongsu jiaoyu*, pp. 1-9.
50. *Jiaoyu shijie*, no. 125 (1906), *fulu*, p. 9.
51. See also JYZZ, 4: 6 (1912), *xueshu*, pp. 57-84, for an account of popular education in Germany. The article made special mention of the popular education associations that were formed to oversee popular literature.
52. L. Wieger, *Chine Moderne*, 2: 227-31.
53. *Jingshi jiaoyubao*, no. 4 (1914), *lunshuo*, pp. 9-11. JYZZ, 4: 6 (1912), *diaocha*, pp. 59-68. The latter article also approvingly referred to government attempts in the United States to 'educate' immigrants so that they became suitably well-behaved and loyal.
54. *Jingshi jiaoyubao*, no. 27 (1916), *jiangyan*, p. 14.
55. JYZZ, 6: 2 (1914), *diaocha*, pp. 11-19.
56. In 1914 the Shanghai popular education association condemned 'immoral' flower-drum songs (*yanchang huagu*). ZHJYJ, 3: 4 (1914), *jishi*, p. 6. Hou Hongjian argued in 1914 that if youngsters from the lower classes were taught 'reformed' popular songs this might make them immune from picking up bad habits from their unemployed or vagrant parents. JYZZ, 6: 3 (1914), *yanlun*, pp. 46-58.
57. JYZZ, 4: 5 (1912), *zazu*, pp. 23-7. See also JYZZ, 7: 8 (1915), *yanlun*, pp. 13-4, for an account of the Boy Scout movement and its usefulness as a supplement to school education. See also JYZZ, 7: 8 (1915), *diaocha*, pp. 75-86; *Xin qingnian*, 2: 2 (October 1916), pp. 5-6; *Jiaoyu zhoubao*, no. 138 (1916), *yanlun*, pp. 1-12. A six-part article on the Boy Scout movement also appears in ZJHJY, 4: 10, 4: 11, 5: 1, 5: 3, 5: 4, 5: 5, (1915-16).
58. *Tongsu jiaoyu yanjiu hui disici baogaoshu, wendu*, pp. 25-6.
59. In 1922, for example, police authorities complained about the proliferation of pornographic films in Beijing and Tianjin. *Tongsu jiaoyu zongkan*, no. 14 (1922), *shijian*, pp. 8, 18. One of the reasons for ineffective censorship may have been lack of funds. Although the Education Ministry, on setting up the popular education research association, planned to spend 1 200 dollars a month on running expenses, Gao Buying (the secretary of the association) noted in his annual report that the association had received only 1 000 dollars between January and April of 1916, while between May and June it had received nothing. From July to October the association received 500 dollars a month. *Tongsu jiaoyu yanjiu hui*

dierci baogaoshu, jishi, p. 2. This contradicts official government figures which showed that expenditures for the popular education research association in 1916 amounted to 14 400 dollars. Jia Shiyi, *Minguo caizheng shi* (Shanghai, 1917), 1: 140-1.
60. J. Ch'en, *China and the West*, p. 402.
61. Mention has already been made (Chapter Four) of Zhang Jian's praise of the strict discipline carried out in European and American schools.
62. M. Rankin, *Early Chinese Revolutionaries*, p. 57. Such a view, I believe, is due to the fact that too much attention has been paid to Cai's thought on the role of universities. As chancellor of Beijing University in 1917 he had remarkably progressive things to say about academic freedom and the need to encourage a diversity of opinions, but this should not obscure the fact that Cai was just as concerned as other Chinese educators to see more government supervision of popular culture.
63. Wang Xiaochuan (comp.), *Yuanmingqing sandai jinhui xiaoshuo xiqu shiliao* (Beijing, 1958), p. 3.
64. Tanaka Issei (comp.), *Shindai Chihōgeki Shiryō Shū* (Tokyo, 1968), 1: 2.
65. Ibid., 2: 14-5. Many book publishers often escaped official censorship by covering the book with a seal indicating official approval, or by even changing the book's title. Wang Xiaoquan (comp.), *Yuanmingqing sandai jinhui xiaoshuo xiqu shiliao*, p. 15. Such ploys were also carried out during the early republic.
66. J. Handlin, *Action in Late Ming Thought*, p. 157.
67. Tanaka Issei (comp.), *Shindai Chihōgeki Shiryō Shū*, 1: 6.
68. *Daqing Gaozong chun huangdi shilu* (Taibei, 1964), 1143: 29-30.
69. Translation from S. Naquin, E. Rawski, *Chinese Society in the Eighteenth* Century, p. 63.
70. Shu Xincheng (ed.), *Ziliao*, 3: 822-4; Taga Akigorō (ed.), *Shiryō*, 2: 165-6; *Jiaoyu fagui huibian* (Beijing, 1919), pp. 468-9.
71. There is evidence that the Education Ministry did, in fact, check over public lecture material sent in by the provinces. In 1915 it apparently sent back material to the Hunan education office for revision. *Jiaoyu gongbao*, no. 1 (June 1915), *gongdu*, pp. 39-40. However, the Ministry noted later on in the same year that, with the exception of Shandong and Shaanxi, the provinces did not adopt a unified approach to public lectures. It complained that districts compiled their own material without having it checked by higher authorities. *Jiaoyu gongbao*, no. 3 (July 1915), *gongdu*, p. 29.
72. Ding Zhipin, *Zhongguo jin qishinian lai jaoyu jishi*, p. 61.
73. DYJN, 3: 690-1. Articles in the educational press frequently underlined the importance of professionalism in public lecturing. ZHJYJ, 5: 3 (March 1916), pp. 1-8; JYZZ, 11: 2 (1919), *yanlun*, p. 32.
74. In 1913, for example, the Governor of Zhejiang ordered district officials to give detailed information on lecture halls (*xuanjiangsuo*), an indication they were still in existence. JYZZ, 5: 2 (1913), *jishi*, p. 13.

75. JYZZ, 5: 8 (1913), jishi, pp. 69-70. In Nantong, Jiangsu, a women's lecture association was created in order to promote women's education. JYZZ, 4: 12 (1914), jishi, p. 90. In 1917 the model lecture institute in the Shandong provincial capital reserved certain lecture days for female audiences and invited women to give talks on 'practical knowledge and skills'. Taga Akigorō (ed.), Shiryō, 2: 236.
76. Jiaoyubu xingzheng jiyao (Beijing, 1916), shehui jiaoyu, pp. 13.
77. Disanci jiaoyu tongji tubiao (Beijing, 1911), pp. 40-1.
78. Jiaoyubu xingzheng jiyao, shehui jiaoyu, pp. 12-3.
79. Ibid., pp. 12-3. S. Gamble, Peking: A Social Survey, p. 424, noted that audiences generally comprised merchants and labourers. At the model lecture institute there was apparently a daily attendance of 300. DYJN, 3: 692.
80. Lecturers in Beijing were primary and normal school teachers, members of the education association, and scholars. 'Roving lecturers' who talked at temple markets were paid 20 dollars a month, evidently because this was considered more difficult than lecturing in a hall. S. Gamble, Peking: A Social Survey, pp. 151-3. Some idea of the funds spent on lecture institutes by the Beijing education office can be obtained from Jingshi jiaoyubao. The average amount spent increased from about 600 dollars a month in 1914 to 1 000 in 1918. The model lecture institute, which was funded directly by the Education Ministry had a monthly budget of 700 dollars.
81. Jingshi jiaoyubao, no. 33 (1916), gongdu, pp. 2-3. In the Shandong provincial capital the daily attendance at lectures organised by the model lecture institute was reported to be about 1 500. Attendance was recorded and each individual who came to more than one hundred lectures was awarded money and a badge. Taga Akigorō (ed.), Shiryō, 2: 236.
82. Ibid., 2: 236. S. Gamble, Peking: A Social Survey, p. 427, gives the number and classification of books in Beijing reading rooms. Fiction and magazines constituted most of the reading matter.
83. S. Garrett, Social Reformers in Urban China: The Chinese YMCA 1895-1926 (Cambridge, Mass. 1970), pp. 136, 140.
84. At an 1877 conference of Protestant missionaries in Shanghai it was agreed that more effort had to be made to establish links with the upper classes as a way to influence the population. J. Ch'en, China and the West, pp. 122, 134.
85. S. Garrett also remarks that Chinese students developed an interest in educating the poor before 1919 partly because of YMCA enlistment of students in social service work (Social Reformers in Urban China, p. 133). Again, it should be emphasised that Chinese students were aware of the importance of popular education before 1911, independently of missionary influence. Many of the students who returned from study in Japan, for example, established half-day and literacy schools for the poor. See DFZZ, 2: 6 (1905), jiaoyu, p. 160. Enough evidence has also been given (Chapter Three), I believe, to refute the rather bald statement (p. 88) that Chinese educators were not concerned with vocational education and

therefore the YMCA 'had the field to itself'.
86. R. Pelissier, *Les Bibliothèques en Chine pendant la Première Moitié du XXème Siècle*, p. 27; S. Garrett, *Social Reformers in Urban China*, p. 140.
87. M. Bastid, *Aspects de la Réforme de l'Enseignement*, has convincingly shown that educational reform during the last years of the Qing had little to do with missionary influence.
88. JYZZ, 7: 12 (1915), *jishi*, p. 105.
89. Liang Qichao even claimed in 1917 that people had been much more enthusiastic about education during the last years of the Qing than they were during the early years of the republic. DFZZ, 14: 3 (1917), *neiwai shibao*, pp. 176-7.
90. JYZZ, 5: 3 (1913), *zazu*, pp. 23-4.
91. In Qinhua, Jiangsu, for example, several hundred villagers in 1914 set fire to prominent gentry residences, schools and the police bureau following the spread of alarmist rumours concerning a recently arrived census team. JYZZ, 6: 6 (1914), *jishi*, p. 53. In Wuxing district, Zhejiang, people thought a census team was counting school–age children in order to recruit them to build a railway bridge. JYZZ, 6: 6 (1914), *jishi*, p. 53.
92. JYZZ, 6: 5 (1914), *diaocha*, p. 42. Since traditional schools were less conspicuous (e.g. most of them were located in private homes) and thus were less likely to be attacked by bandits, Hou noted that many parents preferred to send their children to traditional schools.
93. *Ibid.*, *diaocha*, p. 42.
94. ZHYJY, 3: 13 (1914), p. 5.
95. ZHJYJ, 3: 17 (1914), pp. 1-8.
96. *Anhui jiaoyu yuekan*, no. 12 (1918), p. 14.
97. *Jiaoyu chao*, 1: 4 (1919), pp. 12-3.
98. *Jiaoyu*, no. 4 (1919), p. 12.
99. *Pingmin jiaoyu*, no. 25 (1920), no. 26 (1920), pp. 12-4.
100. *Pingmin jiaoyu*, no. 29 (1921), pp. 1-4.
101. L. Wieger, *Chine Moderne*, vol. 2. In a study of social education that Xiang wrote years later he noted that it had corrected three defects in the school system, namely its 'promotionalism' (encouragement of competition among students for promotion), 'formalism' and 'isolationism' (lack of relevance for the society and country). Xiang Zhutan, *Shehui jiaoyu* (Taibei, 1958), p. 15.
102. Popular education was often contrasted with 'individualist education'. *Jiaoyu gongbao*, 5: 1 (1918), *yishu*, pp. 13-21. Lectures later compiled by the Henan education bureau in the 1920s claimed that popular education would rectify the shortcomings of previous formal education, which had been 'individualistic' and 'aristocratic' *Shehui jiaoyu jiangyan dagang* (Loyang, 1929), pp. 60-1, 69.
103. *Tongsu jiaoyu yanjiu hui disanci baogaoshu, biao*, pp. 1-7; DYJN, 3: 692. In 1913 the Education Ministry had already informed the Beijing education bureau that public lectures were to encourage 'self-help, patriotism, and a hard working and frugal attitude'. *Jingshi jiaoyubao*, no. 1 (1914), p. 7.

104. Another appropriate biography deemed worthy of public lecture material was that of the Ming official and scholar, Wang Yangming. There was a revival of interest in Wang's philosophy in this period and it was often cited in support for a more 'practical' education. Thus an article in *Jiaoyu gongbao*, no. 110 (December 1915), *yanlun*, pp. 1-4, argued that Japan had become prosperous because, unlike China, the country had enthusiastically embraced Wang Yangming's philosophy, with its stress on the unity of knowledge and practice.
105. *Jingshi jiaoyubao*, no. 1 (1914). Lectures also campaigned against the import of such 'evil' foreign goods as champagne and cigarettes. *Jingshi jiaoyubao*, no. 2 (1914), *jiangyan*, pp. 1-6.
106. *Jingshi jiaoyubao*, no. 28 (1915), *chaxue baogao*, p. 18.
107. *Jingshi jiaoyubao*, no. 31 (1916), pp. 25, 28; no. 32 (1916), p. 16; no. 34 (1916), p. 3. At one spare-time school in Beijing a teacher reportedly emphasised that the 'capital' required for earning money was study. Morality was also needed, he remarked, but it is significant that the morality to which he referred was one of 'not selling false goods'. *Jingshi jiaoyubao*, no. 30 (1916), p. 20.
108. JYZZ, 6: 5 (1914), *yanlun*, pp. 88-99.
109. ZHJYJ, 3: 4 (1914), pp. 6-7.
110. 'Xunyu tan' (A Discussion of Training), in *Jiaoyu conggao*, p. 35.
111. *Jiaoyu yu shiye*, no. 14 (April 1919).
112. *Jingshi jiaoyubao*, no. 1 (1914), *tongsu jiangyan*, pp. 1-3.
113. ZHJYJ, 4: 2 (1915), p. 6. Another writer bewailed the lack of family harmony in China due to competition and the quest for wealth. A harmonious family, he concluded, was the foundation for a healthy state. Jiang Zhuocheng, *Daode jiaoyulun* (Shanghai, 1925), pp. 2-7. At the same time the Education Minister Tang Hualong in 1915 was urging the replacement of family loyalties with loyalty to the country, suggesting that schools teach children 'to love the country and forget the family' (*aiguo wangjia*). Shu Xincheng (ed.), *Shiliao*, 3: 215. In descriptions of those who contributed their wealth to the establishment of schools, the common phrase used to describe their action was *huijia xingxue* (lit. 'breaking up the home to set up schools'), that is to say they forewent the opportunity to expand ancestral or lineage institutions in order to create schools for a wider populace. For two examples, see Shu Xincheng (ed.), *Shiliao*, 3: 233-5; *Xin jiaoyu*, 1: 5 (1919), pp. 456-60.
114. *Jingshi jiaoyubao*, no. 22 (1915), p. 30; no. 24 (1915), p. 37.
115. JYZZ, 8: 6 (1917), *jishi*, p. 40. The principal of a primary school in Baoshan, by way of contrast, recommended that schools cultivate a 'spirit of competition' amongst pupils in order to channel their energy into useful outlets. JYZZ, 7: 10 (1916), *jishi*, p. 91.
116. See the discussion of civic morality by the popular education research association in *Jingshi jiaoyubao*, no. 23 (1915), *zhuanjian*, pp. 26-7.
117. *Gongde jianghua* (Beijing, n.d.), pp. 2-29.
118. JYZZ, 11: 2 (1919), *yanlun*, pp. 32-3.

119. L. Wieger, *Chine Moderne*, vol. 2, pp. 326-9.
120. JYZZ, 6: 12 (1915), *zaxuan*, pp. 61-6. See also ZHJYJ, 8: 2 (1918), p. 19.
121. Lu Feigui, *Jiaoyu wencun, zhuan* 4, pp. 48-58.
122. ZHJYJ, 2: 6 (1913), *tongsu jiaoyu*, pp. 14-6; 5: 3 (1916), p. 1.
123. *Jiaoyu gongbao* (June 1914), *fagui*, pp. 9-11; Shu Xincheng (ed.)., *Ziliao*, 3: 819-20.
124. It is also apparent that girls had their own lower primary schools since educational statistics at this time always distinguish boys' and girls' primary schools.
125. JYZZ, 5: 9 (1914), *jishi*, p. 75. Each school had about sixty pupils.
126. S. Gamble, *Peking; A Social Survey*, p. 152.
127. Taga Akigorō (ed.), *Shiryō*, 2: 236. Other government organisations were involved in opening half-day schools. Thus the Tianjin police bureau established twenty-seven such schools, with an estimated enrollment of 2 000. Two hours of instruction (writing, arithmetic, physical education) were given every day and it was hoped to recruit the brighter students into the police or army. ZHJYJ, 4: 11 (1915), pp. 2-4.
128. *Jiaoyubu xingzheng jiyao, shehui jiaoyu*, pp. 39-40; Shu Xincheng (ed.), *Ziliao*, 3: 825-6.
129. JYZZ, 7: 3 (1915), *diaocha*, pp. 28-35; 7: 7 (1915), *diaocha*, pp. 69-74; 7: 10 (1915), *diaocha*, pp. 93-102, 7: 11 (1915), *diaocha*, pp. 112-8; 7: 12 (1915), *diaocha*, pp. 119-27.
130. JYZZ, 7: 1 (1915), *tebie jishi*, pp. 1-3. See also the report on the open-air school in Beijing's southern district in *Jingshi jiaoyubao*, no. 20 (1915), *zongzai*, pp. 1-3.
131. *Jingshi jiaoyubao*, no. 31 (1916), *chaxue baogao*, pp. 17-8.
132. Taga Akigorō (ed.), *Shiryō*, 2: 235.
133. DYJN, 3: 601, 642. Guangxi was reported to have forty-five such schools.
134. 'Linshi zengkan', *Jiaoyu gongbao* (1916), *jingtao*, p. 12. Scattered information on these schools also appear in *Jingshi jiaoyubao*, no. 5 (1914), *chaxue baogao*, p. 20; no. 13 (1915), *chaxue baogao*, pp. 26-7; no. 17 (1915), *chaxue baogao*, p. 28; no. 19 (1915), *chaxue baogao*, p. 49; no. 22 (1915), *chaxue baogao*, pp. 28-30; no. 25 (1916), *chaxue baogao*, p. 42; no. 28 (1916), *chaxue baogao*, p. 16; no. 29 (1916), *chaxue baogao*, p. 12; no. 30 (1916), *chaxue baogao*, p. 20.
135. One student at the no. 1 school was 69 years old.
136. As noted in Chapter Three, expenditures on spare-time schools did not have to be high. Teachers were often volunteers, while the schools themselves often made use of existing buildings such as charitable halls or primary schools. JYZZ, 5: 18 (1913), *jishi*, pp. 67-8.
137. 'Linshi zengkan', *Jiaoyu gongbao* (1916), *Zhejiang*, pp. 12-15.
138. Ibid., *jingtao*, p. 2.
139. Ibid., *Fengtian*, pp. 2-3.
140. *Jiangsu jiaoyu gailan*, 1: 155-7. In 1928 the Education Ministry

insisted that expenditures on social education should always constitute between 10 and 20 per cent of total educational budgets. R. Yu Soong Cheng, *The Financing of Public Education in China*, p. 53.
141. Chen Baoquan, *Zhongguo jindai xuezhi bianyi shi* (Beijing, 1927), pp. 56-7. In 1920 Shanxi recorded a figure of 57 per cent. For details on specific provinces, see *Jiaoyu gongbao*, 3: 3 (April 1916), *jinzai*, pp. 21-37 for school attendance in Zhili; Taga Akigorō (ed.), *Shiryō*, 2: 360 for school attendance in Xinjiang in 1916; *Jiaoyu yanjiu*, no. 13 (1914), *zazuan*, pp. 12-14 for school attendance in Jiangsu in 1913. The figures for Zhili are interesting in that they specify the number of boys and girls at school, and also give separate totals for both modern and traditional schools. The percentage of children at school *within* the province ranged from 4 to 15 per cent.
142. 'Linshi zengkan', *Jiaoyu gongbao* (1916), *jingtao*, p . 7 .
143. JYZZ, 6: 5 (1914), *yanlun*, p. 96.
144. JYZZ, 10: 6 (1918), *zhiwen*, pp. 39-56. See also JYZZ, 4: 5 (1912), *diaocha*, pp. 50-6 and 4: 7 (1912), *diaocha*, pp. 69-80 for reports on supplementary education in Germany. Chinese educators from 1910 onwards were noting that Germany was beginning to overtake Britain economically. It was precisely for this reason that the German educational system was much discussed and praised.
145. JYZZ 9: 1 (1917), *diaocha*, pp . 1-8 . See also the article, translated from English, on the problem of uneducated school leavers in England forming a 'vagrant class' and on the successful way Germany was dealing with the problem with her system of compulsory supplementary education, in *Jiaoyu gongbao*, 6: 12 (December 1919), *yishu*, pp. 1-22.
146. A. Peterson, *A Hundred Years of Education*, pp. 199-214.
147. JYZZ, 2: 3 (1910), *diaocha*, pp. 21-5; 6: 3 (1914), *diaocha*, pp. 21-5; *Jiaoyu yanjiu*, no. 2 (1913), *diaocha*, pp. 12-5; ZHJYJ, 10:1 (1921), pp. 72-8. Danish folk high schools continued to attract the interest of Chinese educators in the 1920s and 1930s. See Ma Zongrong, *Bijiao shehui jiaoyu* (Shanghai, 1933), pp. 79-98; Gan Cao, *Xingcun jiaoyu* (Shanghai, 1939), pp. 37-40.
148. Li Duanfen in 1896 and Luo Zhenyu in 1902 had recommended establishing libraries in all the provinces.
149. In chronological order, libraries were opened in Hunan (1907), Fengtian (1908), Zhili (1909), Heilongjiang (1909), Henan (1909), Shaanxi (1909), Guangxi (1910), Zhejiang (1910), Jiangsu (1910), Shandong (1910), Yunnan (1910), Fujian (1911), Anhui (1912), Hubei (1912), Guangdong (1912), Guizhou (1913), Sichuan (1914). *Jiaoyubu xingzheng jiyao, shehui jiaoyu*, pp. 4-7. Zhili had another public library in Baoding (established in 1910), Fengtian had another one in Xinmin (established in 1909), while Jiangsu had two other public libraries.
150. DYJN, 3: 800-1, 809. Many popular libraries in Yunnan were also housed in Confucian temples. See also Shu Xincheng (ed.), *Ziliao*, 1: 299-308.

151. *Jiaoyubu xingzheng jiyao, shehui jiaoyu*, pp. 4-7. Other figures recorded included 300 visitors a month in Guizhou, 900 a month in Hubei, and 1 200 a year in Henan.
152. *Jiaoyu gongbao*, 3: 1. (February 1916), *baogao*, pp. 5-6.
153. Chen Baoquan, *Zhongguo jindai xuezhi bianyi shi*, p. 112.
154. *Ibid.*, p. 113; DYJN, 3: 787. In 1916 the Education Ministry was to rule that a copy of every publication be deposited in the Beijing library.
155. The Shandong public library, for example, charged three coppers as a reading fee. *Huang Yanpei kaocha jiaoyu riji*, 2: 25. The Beijing library charged one copper, while the Tianjin library charged two coppers. JYZZ, 10: 8 (1918), *fulu*, pp. 37-45.
156. Shu Xincheng (ed.), *Ziliao*, 1: 318.
157. *Jiaoyubu xingzheng jiyao, shehui jiaoyu*, p. 8
158. DYJN, 3: 788; Taga Akigorō (ed.), *Shiryō*, 2: 165, 498; JYZZ, 7: 12 (1916), *faling*, p. 25.
159. Taga Akigorō (ed.), *Shiryō*, 2: 338; JYZZ, 8:8 (1916), *jishi*, p. 50-1.
160. Taga Akigorō (ed.), *Shiryō*, 2: 237; *Jiaoyu gongbao*, 2: 4 (August 1915), p. 52.
161. Gaimushō (comp.), *Chuka Minkoku Kyōiku Sono ta no Shiretsu Gaiyō* (Tokyo, 1931), pp. 784, 788. The Liaoning provincial library had been the first to provide facilities for children in 1908. Borrowing was allowed at the Beijing library, while in Tianjin books of a 'general nature' were allowed to be borrowed. JYZZ, 10: 8 (1918), *fulu*, pp. 37-45.
162. Gaimushō (comp.), *Chuka Minkoku Kyōiku Sono ta no Shiretsu Gaiyō*, p. 788; *Huang Yanpei kaocha jiaoyu riji*, 2: 7, 25.
163. *Jiaoyu gongbao*, 6: 10 (October 1919), *baogao*, pp. 1-12.
164. DFZZ, 14: 6 (1917), *neiwai shibao*, p. 190. Chinese educators were also quick to point out that popular libraries were only a recent phenomenon in the West. *Jiaoyu gongbao*, 2: 4 (August 1915), *fulu*, pp. 1-8. Even the task of preserving old books was now given a more 'popular' rationale. Thus in 1912 Ma Xiangbo, the brother of the late-nineteenth-century economic reformer Ma Jianzhong, advocated the creation of a cultural academy on the model of the French Academy. Such an academy, Ma suggested, would be charged with producing dictionaries, searching for old texts and publishing them on a mass scale. Fang Hao, 'Ma Xiangbo xiansheng choushe hanxia kaowenyuan shimo' (Ma Xiangbo's Proposal To Establish a Research Academy) in *Fang Hao liushij ziding gao* (Taibei, 1970), 2: 1995-6.
165. See the article on popular libraries in DFZZ, 15: 9 (1918), pp. 157-62. For a similar observation, see JYZZ, 10: 10 (1918) *yanlun*, pp. 142-3.
166. JYZZ, 12: 1 (1920), cited in L. Wieger, *Chine Moderne*, 1: 196.
167. Huang's article is in JYZZ, 5: 7 (1913), *fulu*, pp. 55-82; ZHJYJ, 2: 11 (1913), *yanjiu*, pp. 155-70; 2: 12 (1913), *yanjiu*, pp. 177-88; *Minguo jingshi wenbian*, 5: 4167-73.
168. JYZZ, 5: 7 (1913), *yanlun*, p. 88.

169. *Minguo jingshi wenbian*, 5: 4209.
170. *Ibid.*, 5: 4221.
171. The manifesto of the association is in JYZZ, 9: 7 (1917), *zhuanjian*, pp. 7-17; DFZZ, 14: 7 (1917), *neiwai shibao*, pp. 163-6; Shu Xincheng (ed.), *Shiliao*, 2: 238-43.
172. On the vocational education association, see M. Gewurtz, 'Social Reality and Educational Reform: The Case of the Chinese Vocational Education Association 1917-1927', *Modern China*, 4: 2 (April 1978). In seeking to emphasise the novelty of this enterprise, Gewurtz posits a misleading contrast between Chinese education and that in the West where 'western culture has never so sharply separated mental and manual labour, nor so avidly disparaged specialisation while championing the "amateur ideal"' (p. 159). In fact, just that *has* been a feature of western education, as the example of England testifies.
173. *Jingzhong ribao*, no. 43 (April 1904), *shiping*.
174. JYZZ, 2: 6 (1910), *sheshuo*, pp. 69-72.
175. JYZZ, 2: 1 (1910), *sheshuo*, p. 9.
176. JYZZ, 3: 12 (1912), *yanlun*, p. 33.
177. *Jingshi jiaoyubao*, no. 26 (1916), *zuanshu*, pp. 14-20. In the same issue, Huang Yanpei, in a discussion of vocational education in the United States, noted that an agricultural or industrial worker could earn more than a 'mental' worker, such as a school teacher. *Ibid.*, no. 26, *jiangyan*, p. 4.
178. See, for example, Zhu Yuanshan, *Zhiye jiaoyu zhenyi* (Shanghai, 1917), p. 174, where the author warns that if workers have low 'productive ability' the country would suffer.
179. ZHJYJ, 4: 8 (1915), pp. 8-9. This is the first reference I have found to the slogan 'the sacredness of labour', thus anticipating the later campaign during the May Fourth movement by intellectuals such as Li Dazhao to promote the virtues of manual labour.
180. JYZZ, 8: 9 (1916), *yanlun*, pp. 129-37.
181. Zhu Yuanshan, *Zhiye jiaoyu zhenyi*, p. 60.
182. JYZZ, 9: 7 (1917), *yanlun*, p. 126. It may be the case that the increasing importance attached to vocational education may have even led to the conversion of general schools into vocational schools. Huang Yanpei reported in 1915 that the no. 2 agricultural school in Anhui was originally a middle school. *Huang Yanpei kaocha jiaoyu riji*, 1: 12-13.
183. DFZZ, 14: 10 (1917), pp. 1-6. One article suggested that an education promoting hard and diligent work first be implemented in the towns and cities since the people there were less accustomed to hard work than in the rural areas. JYZZ, 7: 11 (1916) *cilun*, p. 134.
184. ZHJYJ, 4: 12 (1915), p. 10; *Jiaoyu yu shiye*, no. 7 (June 1918).
185. *Anhui jiaoyu yuekan*, no. 15 (1919), *lunshuo*, pp. 1-10. The author supported his case by citing the philosophy of Hobbes.
186. ZHJYJ, 2: 4 (1913), pp. 5-6. For another example, see *Jingshi jiaoyubao*, no. 8 (1914), *biji*, pp. 1-2. Such students were called

'hardship students' *(ku xuesheng)*. Interestingly, there was a fashion at this time to underline the poor beginnings of prominent people in order to promote the ideals of self-help and hard work. In 1911, for example, Zhang Jian was specifically described as someone who had come from an 'ordinary background' and his father was pointedly referred to as being a street peddler by origin, even though he had been a fairly well-to-do farmer. Wang Jingyu (comp.), *Zhongguo jindai gongye shi ziliao*, 2.2: 938.
187. JYZZ, 10: 6 (1918), *zhengwen*, p. 31.
188. *Ibid.* In 1917 the Education Ministry did, in fact, suggest that 'model workers' *(mofan zhigong)* be chosen among students in vocational schools. Taga Akigorō (ed.), *Shiryō*, 2: 240.
189. JYZZ, 4: 11 (1913), *yanlun*, pp. 201-12.
190. JYZZ, 5: 10 (1914), *jishi*, pp. 89-90.
191. JYZZ, 9:13 (1917), *zazuan*, pp. 5-8. See also *Jingshi jioyubao*, 5: 6 (1918), *zhuanjian*, p. 14 for the suggestion that all primary schools organise trading departments to market goods produced at the schools.
192. *Anhui jiaoyu yuekan*, no. 15 (1919), *zhuanjian*, p. 6.
193. *Jiaoyu yu shiye*, no. 3 (January 1918). Nos. 10 and 14 of *Jiaoyu yu shiye* give details of handicrafts produced by students. In Chuansha, table-tennis bats were sold for 7 cents, while ink-slabs were sold for 34 cents. The Wujin industrial school produced lacquer chairs for 8 dollars each.
194. *Jiaoyu yu shiye*, no. 4 (February 1918).
195. ZHJYJ, 4: 10 (1915). The Education Ministry in 1917 and 1920 ordered all primary and middle schools to market the handicrafts produced at the schools. Taga Akigorō (ed.), *Shiryō*, 2: 240, ZHJYJ, 9: 4 (1920), *faling*, p. 4.
196. See, for example, the reports on the Nanqing agricultural school and the Suzhou no. 2 agricultural school, in Jiangsu, in *Jiaoyu yu shiye*, no. 3 (January 1918). Another interesting experiment carried out in Jiangsu was the promotion of reforestation. Schools were to be encouraged to plant trees and given funds as a reward. The first school chosen was an agricultural school in Jiangpu district which reportedly planted an area of 20 000 *mu* (1 *mu* = 0·067 hectares). *Jiangsu sheng jiaoyutuan gongyoulin baogaoshu* (Shanghai, 1916).
197. JYZZ, 8: 12 (1917), *jishi*, p. 80. See also ZHJYJ, 5: 9 (1916), *lunshuo*, pp. 1-9 for an article on the necessity for training an 'economic citizenry' *(jingji zhi guomin)*. The idea of producing handicrafts at school and encouraging the saving of money was frequently referred to by Chinese educators who visted Japan. See, for example, a report on rural primary schools in Japan in JYZZ, 8: 9 (1916), *tebie jishi*, p. 47, and a report by the principal of Jiangsu's no. 2 agricultural school on vocational education in Japan in *Jiaoyu yu shiye*, no. 3 (January 1918).
198. *Anhui jiaoyu yuekan*, no. 15 (1919), *zhuanjian*, p. 6. See also *Jiaoyu gongbao*, no. 197 (April 1918), *jijian*, p. 19.

199. ZHJYJ, 4: 2 (1915), pp. 11-12.
200. *Jiaoyu yu shiye*, no. 8 (August 1918).
201. *Jingshi jiaoyubao*, no. 1 (1914), *lunzhu*, pp. 1-3. The article rather speciously cited the cases of the Phoenicians, who 'were skilled at maritime endeavours' , and the Jews, who 'were skilled at money matters', but who both perished because they lacked 'morality' (i.e. concern for the collectivity).
202. Zhu Yuanshan, *Zhiye jiaoyu zhenyi*, p. 257.
203. D. Simon, *Georg Kerschensteiner* (London, 1966), p. 41, prefers to translate *Arbeitsschule* as 'activity school' since by *Arbeit* Kerschensteiner meant the students' active and intellectual participation in the learning process. The Chinese, however, particularly stressed the benefit of *physical* work, hence I have translated the term as 'labour school'. A 1931 article in *The Educational Review* did, in fact, render the term *Arbeitsschule* as 'labour school' (*laodong xuexiao*) and such education given in these schools as 'labour education' (*laodong jiaoyu*). As in the early republic, the writer praised what he assumed to be Kerschensteiner's emphasis on group labour and the fostering of a patriotic spirit. JYZZ, 23: 2 (1931), pp. 61-72.
204. D. Simon, *Georg Kerschensteiner*, p. 55. See also R. Savioz, 'Georg Kerschensteiner', in J. Chateau (ed.), *Les Grands Pedagogues* (Paris, 1980), pp. 259-74.
205. D. Simon, *Georg Kerschensteiner*, p. 29.
206. In 1908 Kerschensteiner remarked that 'education of the people means leading them systematically to take a common pleasure in work'. D. Simon, *ibid.*, p. 50.
207. For articles on Kerschensteiner and German education, see JYZZ, 4: 5 (1912), *diaocha*, pp. 50-6; 5: 10 (1914), *xueshu*, pp. 71-84; 5: 11 (1914), *xueshu*, pp. 85-96; 5: 12 (1914), *xueshu*, pp. 97-111; 7: 3 (1915), *shilun*, pp. 21-30; 8: 5 (1916), *cilun*, pp. 43-50; 8: 7 (1916), *diaocha*, pp. 51-6; 10:6 (1918), *zhiwen*, p. 59. See also the article on Kerschensteiner and the promotion of continuation schools in *Jingshi jiaoyubao*, no. 41 (1917), *shishu*, pp. 9-17; an article on Kerschensteiner and the concept of the labour school in ZHJYJ, 5: 8 (1916), *xueshuo*, pp. 1-5; a two-part article on Kerschensteiner and supplementary vocational education in Bavaria in *Jiaoyu zhoubao*, no. 161 (1917), *jijian*, pp. 21-2; no. 162 (1917), *jijian*, pp. 16-17. Zhu Yuanshan's 1917 work on vocational education (*Zhiye jiaoyu zhenyi*) made frequent references to Kerschensteiner. See also *Jiaoyu yu shiye*, nos. 3 (January 1918), 5 (March 1918), 10 (December 1918).
208. The work was Fan Bingqing, *Kaishanxinaishi jiaoyushuo* (The Educational Theory of Kerschensteiner). See W. Bauer, Shen-chan Hwang, *German Impact on Modern Chinese Intellectual History* (Wiesbaden, 1982). Kerschensteiner's 1912 work *Begriff der Arbeitsschule*, however, was not fully translated into Chinese until 1935.
209. At this time, *Arbeitsschule* was frequently translated as *qinlao*

xuexiao (industrious schools). *Qin* was to be used in the expression 'half-work half-study' (*qingong jianxue*), to be discussed in the next chapter. The first specific reference I have found to the term 'labour education' (*laodong jiaoyu*) is in an article by Zhang Zouhan in *Jiaoyujie*, no. 10 (June 1916), p. 2. For an account of the history of the labour school in Germany, see *Jiaoyu yanjiu*, no. 2 (1913), pp. 9-14. The author noted that the idea originated with handicrafts being made a school subject in the eighteenth century. On this, see T. Dietrich, *La Pedagogie Socialiste* (Paris, 1973), pp. 17-19.
210. JYZZ, 10: 1 (1918), *zhuzhang*, pp. 5-7. See also JYZZ, 5: 10 (1914), *yanlun*, pp. 116-19.
211. JYZZ, 7: 1 (1915), *yanlun*, p. 21. For a six-part article on the connection between labour education and industrialisation, see JYZZ, 7: 1 (1915), *cilun*, pp. 1-8; 7: 4 (1915), *cilun*, pp. 31-44; 7: 6 (1915), *cilun*, pp. 61-72; 7: 9 (1915), *cilun*, pp. 99-108; 7: 10 (1916), *diaocha*, pp. 109-21; 7: 11 (1916), *cilun*, pp. 123-34.
212. JYZZ, 7: 1 (1915), *cilun*, pp. 1-8. The article pointed out that *qinlao zhuyi* was being promoted in the West in order to 'harmonise' class differences by teaching people to respect hard work and not to look down on workers.
213. JYZZ, 7: 5 (1915), *cilun*, pp. 50-1.
214. *Jiaoyu yanjiu*, no. 18 (1914), *diaocha*, pp. 10-14. See also *Jiaoyu zhoubao*, no. 147 (1916), p. 4; *Jiaoyu gongbao*, no. 1 (June 1914), *fulu*, pp. 1-9 for references to the frugality and hardiness of the Germans.

6. The Work-Study Movement

The rationale behind the work-study movement promoted in the 1910s by Chinese anarchists reflected many of the concerns Chinese educators had expressed during the early years of the Republic: the need for students to divest themselves of their elitism; the stress on a more practical education that would prepare students for life and contribute to economic development; the hope that education could create social unity; and the demand that labour be endowed with moral worth.

It began as a campaign to educate the large numbers of Chinese workers who were contracted to work in France during the First World War; the principal concern was to raise the cultural level of the workers and in the process to 'reform' their habits and behaviour. After 1918 work-study was associated primarily with students anxious to study abroad. Since some of these students later became prominent members of the Chinese Communist Party, the movement has hitherto attracted interest because of its political significance.[1] Yet the episode deserves to be viewed within the larger context of educational thought and practice in the early twentieth century. A Chinese journal published in France noted in 1921 that it had been a 'great social movement' whose aims were to provide a way for the 'sons of the proletariat' to study and to bring together the intellectual and labouring classes.[2] As such the work-study movement, and the ideas behind it, represent an important stage in the ongoing debate since the turn of the century over the aims of education.[3]

LI SHIZENG AND THE FRENCH CONNECTION

The key figure in the work-study movement was Li Shizeng (1881–1973),[4] whose father, Li Hongcao, had been a Grand Councillor and tutor to the Tongzhi Emperor in the 1860s.[5] Introduced to western studies at an early stage, Li was able to take advantage of his father's important connections and gain the chance of studying abroad in 1902 when he accompanied Sun Baoqi, newly appointed Minister to France, as an embassy student.[6] Li was joined by his friend Zhang Jingjiang (1877-1950), who came from a family of wealthy silk merchants and was to serve for a time as commercial attaché at the Paris consulate.[7] Another student in the group was Chen Lu (1876-1939), who was to become Chinese Minister to France from 1920 to 1927.

Li's decision to go to France was an early indication of his radical inclinations. Chinese government students had first gone to Europe in early 1875, when Prosper Giquel (1835-86), a former French naval officer hired by the Chinese government to oversee the Fuzhou shipyard, was allowed to take five students from the shipyard's training schools when he returned to

France to recruit foreign specialists for the shipyard. In 1875 a further educational mission from the Fuzhou shipyard training schools, comprising thirty students under Giquel's supervision, went to France and England to study shipbuilding and navigation.[8] After 1890, also, Chinese Ministers to England, France, Germany and Russia were requested to take up to four 'embassy students' (*suiyuan xuesheng*) to study foreign languages.[9] In 1903 another fifty-two students were sent to Belgium, Germany, England and Russia primarily to acquire industrial training.[10]

Nevertheless, most students going abroad in the late nineteenth and early twentieth centuries went to either the United States or Japan. Between 1872 and 1877, for example, 120 government students went to the United States with the ultimate aim of studying military science, navigation, and shipbuilding. Following the decision by the United States in 1910 to remit its share of the Boxer indemnity to fund Chinese overseas study in the United States, the number of Chinese government students there totalled 847 by 1914.[11] Chinese students first began to go to Japan in 1896 and by 1902 numbered 280. Thereafter the total increased dramatically, reaching a peak in 1905-6 when there were reportedly 8 000 to 10 000 Chinese students in Japan.[12] As Li Shizeng was to recall in 1925, France at the turn of the century was very much associated in the Chinese official mind with dangerous political radicalism, and anyone going there to study was vulnerable to the charge of being an extremist.[13]

Sun Baoqi apparently allowed Li Shizeng not to come into the consulate every day,[14] but it is clear that Li absented himself permanently, since he studied at the École Pratique d'Agriculture in Montargis, just south of Paris. After graduating in 1905, he studied chemistry and biology at the Institut Pasteur in Paris. Li very soon became a fervent Francophile and his admiration for French culture and education never wavered throughout his life. In his view, France was the centre of humanism and he was continually to contrast French culture, which he characterised as one that extolled freedom, creativity and pacifism, with German culture, which he associated with autocracy, utilitarianism and militarism.[15] During the following years Li established a wide network of contacts among French politicians and intellectuals, which was to be of considerable benefit when he set up the work-study scheme.[16] Zhang Jingjiang, also, was evidently in a position to build contacts since he was listed by the Bulletin of the Association Amicale Franco-Chinoise (published between 1907 and 1916) – an association that included important French politicians, diplomats, and bankers among its membership – as a member of its editorial committee.

At the same time, through his acquaintance with Paul Reclus, the nephew of the French geographer and utopian anarchist Elisée Reclus (1830-1905), Li was introduced to the anarchist thought of Proudhon and Kropotkin, who had extolled the virtues of mutual assistance and cooperative endeavour free of state interference.[17] Li also became attracted to the utopian ideals of Elisée Reclus himself and, in particular, the faith

Reclus had in evolutionary progress, during which science and education would sweep away all the prejudices of the established order and create a new society based on co-operation and mutual help.[18] In 1906 Li and Zhang Jingjiang formed the World Society (*shijie she*), a publishing venture to promote both science and anarchism. It was financed by Zhang's trading company that he had created in 1902 to import Chinese curios, tea and silk.[19] Significantly, one of its first publications was a pictorial magazine giving information on famous scientists and philosophers, including Elisée Reclus.[20]

Li and Zhang were soon joined by Wu Zhihui (1864-1953), who came from a scholar–official family and who had gained the provincial level civil service degree (*juren*) in 1891. Increasingly hostile to the Manchu regime, Wu had originally gone to Britain to study in 1903 (where he attended lectures at Edinburgh University) before arriving in Paris.[21] Other members of this emerging Chinese anarchist group included Zhang Ji (Puchuan) and Chu Minyi. Zhang Ji had stayed for a time at the Aiglemont communal village (on the Franco-Belgian frontier), apparently on the invitation of French anarchists,[22] while Chu Minyi (1884-1946), who also came from a scholar–official family, helped manage the group's publication venture.[23] Local ties, as well as a developing interest in anarchism, also drew some of the group together. Chu Minyi, for example, came from Zhang Jingjiang's own village. Such local ties were also to be utilised when Li Shizeng first brought Chinese workers over to France.

In 1907 this group began to publish New Century (*xin shiji*), which took its French title from the prominent anarchist journal, Les Temps Nouveaux.[24] Although the journal supported the anti-Manchu stance of Sun Yatsen's *Tongmenghui* (Li Shizeng, Wu Zhihui, and Zhang Jingjiang had all joined the organisation in 1906), attacking the backwardness and corruption of the dynasty, it did not endorse Sun's revolutionary strategy, which anticipated a period of military tutelage once the dynasty was overthrown and the imposition of state socialism.[25] The journal, in fact, became a forum for the group's anarchist beliefs and condemned all kinds of state control. The ideas of Bakunin and Kropotkin were given special prominence and the latter's *Mutual Aid* was translated into Chinese.[26] Traditional institutions like the family were condemned for stifling the unfettered development of the individual, one article even suggesting that marriage itself be abolished.[27]

Furthermore, unlike the Chinese anarchist group which emerged in Tokyo at the same time, Li Shizeng and the others in Paris did not advocate a return to an idealised rural past untainted by the material values of the modern world.[28] Rather, taking inspiration from Reclus and Kropotkin, they expressed confidence in the power of science and education to bring about a new society free of material want and social division. Wu Zhihui, for example, claimed in 1908 that the only education worth the name was in the physical, chemical and mechanical sciences and industries, which would constantly press for new inventions thereby 'creating the happiness of mankind and bringing about the progress of mankind'.[29] Li Shizeng, in contrast to contemporary Chinese thinkers who were drawn to social Darwinism, insisted that violent struggle was not a permanent feature of evolution and that mutual aid and coexistence were the logical end-products of evolutionary progress.

In a series of articles on anarchism that appeared in *New Century* in 1908 Li defined 'anarchist revolution' in terms of an education that would end all divisions within society by encouraging equality and harmony (as opposed to an education imposed by the state, which would simply be the bulwark of militarism, an oppressive legal system, and obscurantist religion).[30] In addition to the division between the rich and powerful on the one hand, and the poor and weak on the other, Li particularly underlined the gulf that separated the educated from the uneducated *(zhiyu)*. He disputed the notion that the lower classes were permanently to accept subordination to the educated and worthy, arguing that once everyone was educated there would be no need for one section of society to defer automatically to another. Furthermore, Li claimed, the lower classes were more hard-working and potentially more intelligent than the well-to-do since they had constantly to use their wits in a daily struggle for survival whereas the wealthy, with no challenges to exercise their ingenuity, spent their lives in idleness.[31] Thus, despite the numerous articles appearing in *New Century* praising the individual acts of violence carried out by European anarchists in the late nineteenth and early twentieth centuries, Li Shizeng and Wu Zhihui continued to insist that only education would bring about positive and lasting change. While a radical Shanghai journal in 1904 complained that education was unable to promote rapid change and advocated widespread acts of violence against officials,[32] Wu Zhihui declared that education itself constituted revolution.[33]

For the Chinese anarchists in Paris, France, a republic *par excellence* free of the baleful influences of monarchy and religion, provided the ideal environment in which to promote education. (Chu Minyi also pointed to the beneficial influence of French trade unions because they trained their members to work together and become aware of their collective interest.)[34] Li Shizeng's first experiment with worker education occurred in 1908 when he employed thirty Chinese workers, all of whom came from his native home town in Gaoyang, Zhili, to work in his recently opened beancurd factory *(Usine Caseo-Sojaine)* in Colombes, near Paris.[35] Li, like his anarchist colleagues, had become a strict vegetarian and was confident that the French would appreciate the beancurd's nutritional value;[36] in 1910 copies of his pamphlet on the benefits of the beancurd were to be distributed at the Universal Exhibition in Bruxelles.[37]

The Chinese workers were brought over to France by Qi Rushan (1876-1962), whose father had been one of Li Hongcao's protégés, while Rushan's brother, Qi Zhushan, managed the beancurd factory. Significantly, the Qi family, like the family of Li Shizeng, were natives of Gaoyang.[38] Li's official contacts also proved useful in setting up the project. On a return trip to China in 1910 he was able to secure an interview with the Zhili Governor-General, Yang Lianpu, through the services of his nephew, who was Yang's secretary.[39] Yang Lianpu was apparently enthusiastic about the project and contributed funds, illustrating the ease with which anti-Manchu radicals like Li Shizeng could move within both revolutionary and official circles.

It was among these Chinese workers at both the beancurd factory and Zhang Jingjiang's publishing house (some of whom came from Singapore), totalling one hundred in all, that 'diligent work and frugal study' (*qingong jianxue*) was first carried out. A workers' school was opened in which Li and Wu taught Chinese, French and general scientific knowledge. Another prominent radical who taught at the school was Cai Yuanpei, who was in Paris briefly *en route* to Germany where he was to study European philosophy. Li, like so many other Chinese educators of the time, was concerned that workers not only should become knowledgeable but also that they should divest themselves of their 'undesirable' habits and backward customs. Accordingly, a strict regimen was imposed; no smoking, gambling or alcohol were permitted, and the workers were constantly exhorted to devote their spare time to study.[40] Furthermore, the workers slept, ate and studied in the same building so as to create the patterns of a communal life.[41]

Having begun Chinese worker education in Paris, Li Shizeng was now keen that more Chinese students go to France. After the establishment of the Republic in 1912 and the appointment of Cai Yuanpei as Education Minister, Li founded the Association for Frugal Study in France (*Liufa jianxue hui*) whose aim was 'to cut down on expenditures in order to expand overseas study, and by labour and a simple life to cultivate habits of diligence and hard work'.[42] The association hailed France not only as the repository of republican ideals but also as the most economical country in which to study.[43] Wang Jingwei (1883-1944), an associate of Sun Yatsen who helped found the association and who was to join Li Shizeng in Paris after 1912, becoming as fervent a Francophile as Li himself, even suggested in 1912 that the new Chinese Republic look to France rather than the United States for its inspiration since the revolution in the former had been more thorough.[44]

A preparatory school, entirely financed by the association's founders, was opened in Beijing under the direction of Qi Rushan. No restrictions of age were imposed on potential students as long as they had a suitable grasp of Chinese. As preparation for their sojourn in France students were to be taught French and general knowledge of western culture by volunteer teachers, including André d'Hormont, a French adviser to the Chinese Foreign Ministry. The school also aimed to train students in 'hard work and frugality' (*qinlian*) by insisting they perform all menial tasks around the school. In this way expenditures were also kept to a minimum, allowing for lower tuition fees.⁴⁵ Cai Yuanpei, as Minister of Education, officially endorsed the enterprise and allowed the school to be located in the former Imperial College (*Guozijian*).⁴⁶

After their training in China the association planned to send groups of at least twenty to France where Li Shizeng, through contacts he had made before 1912, arranged for the students' reception at schools and colleges in Paris, Montargis, and Fontainebleau. It was hoped the year's expenses would not exceed 600 Chinese dollars.⁴⁷ Wu Zhihui predicted that within the following five years the association would be able to send 3 000 frugal study students to France; if the children of the rich could be attracted to the scheme so much the better, he continued, since it would cure them of their idleness and extravagance.⁴⁸ By the time the First World War broke out the association had been able to send nearly one hundred frugal study students to France, seventy of whom went to Montargis College since Li Shizeng personally knew its principal.⁴⁹ Montargis, significantly, was noted for its anti-clericalism and was home to many anarchist-inspired frugal study societies. The town authorities, in an open letter to the inhabitants, thanked Li Shizeng for sending Chinese students to Montargis, who would bring benefit to its businessmen and 'add to the charm of our town an unexpected and picturesque element'.⁵⁰ Some of the first group of students who arrived in France were brothers, thus setting a pattern that was frequently to occur in the later work-study movement after 1918 whereby members of the same family (brothers, parents and children, husbands and wives) would embark on the trip together.⁵¹ As in the case of the Chinese workers, Li laid down strict rules concerning the students' behaviour, which now included proscriptions against 'being improperly familiar with prostitutes' (*xiaji*).

The frugal study scheme was not only designed to allow the less well-off to study abroad, in contrast to the government-sponsored scheme during the late Qing of sending a restricted and privileged few to study armaments technology and industry in the United States and Europe.⁵² As Wang Jingwei remarked, such a scheme would help raise the educational level of the population as a whole.⁵³ The scheme also, however, was very much linked to the idea that the people, and students in particular, needed to be 'reformed'. Li Shizeng and Wu Zhihui shared the views of many educators who condemned the new-style modern schools during the late Qing and early years of the Republic. Instead of benefiting the country, they bewailed, the modern schools had simply produced a new elite of pleasure-seeking and idle graduates who disdained any kind of manual work. For Li and the others, frugal study was not intended as the means to acquire specialised knowledge but rather to cultivate habits of humility, 'clean living', and hard work. As Wang Jingwei dramatically declared, it would only be when the intellectual elite could lead simple and unostentatious lives that they would be able to join ranks with the 'great majority of the suffering ordinary people'.⁵⁴ The association further pointed out there was no bigger danger in society than when 'a minority of people who have some knowledge regard themselves as different from the ordinary people'.[55] Wu Zhihui may have been overstating his case when he insisted that even if frugal study students did not study anything, 'providing they at least learn how to clean toilets it will be worth it',[56] but all the promoters of frugal study hoped that such students, their behaviour and attitudes suitably reformed and their outlook shaped by the ideals of republican France, would lead the way in a widescale reform of Chinese society on their return.

Frugal study, in fact, was part of a wider movement for social reform that occupied the attention of Chinese educators during the early Republic. It is no coincidence, therefore, that the founders of the Frugal Study Association – Li Shizeng, Wu Zhihui, Cai Yuanpei, Wang Jingwei and Zhang Jingjiang – also created in 1912 the Association for the Advancement of Virtue *(Jinde hui)* to promote the abolition of gambling, opium-smoking and concubinage, as well as the Social Reform Association *(shehui gailiang hui)* which, among other things, advocated widespread birth control in China.[57]

The ambitious hopes Li Shizeng and the others had of the frugal study scheme were not fulfilled. Already the association had lost official support when Cai Yuanpei resigned as Education Minister in the summer of 1912. The following year Yuan Shikai, identifying the scheme with subversive anarchism, closed down the preparatory school. In any event, the outbreak of war in Europe brought to a temporary halt the sending of students to France.[58] Paradoxically, however, the war was to enable Li to restart the scheme on a new footing.

CHINESE LABOUR IN FRANCE AND WORK-STUDY

In 1915 severe labour shortages in France prompted the French government to consider recruiting Chinese workers on a large scale. Even before the First World War a decline in the French birth rate had resulted in growing numbers of immigrant labourers being employed in France. By 1911, for example, there were already 1 159 835 foreigners in the country, comprising principally Italians, Belgians, Spaniards and Portuguese.[59] Whereas immigration before the war had been largely unregulated and involved the free movement of peoples from countries adjacent to France, during the war the French government became more actively involved in the recruitment and organisation of immigrant labour, which was now utilised in major cities and smaller centres of war production (such as Bourges, Brest and Le Havre). For the first time, also, large numbers of non-European labourers were recruited, especially from the French colonies in North Africa and Indo-China. During the course of the war France was to recruit in total 662 000 foreign workers, of whom 132 321 came from North Africa (Algeria, Morocco, Tunisia) and 48 955 from Indo-China.[60]

In late 1915 a recruiting mission from the French Ministry of War under Lieutenant-Colonel Truptil visited China. Since China was still officially neutral, Truptil described himself as an 'agricultural engineer' in order to avoid German suspicions and dealt with the ostensibly private Huimin Company. In fact the company was controlled by Liang Shiyi, acting Minister of Finance and a close confidant of Yuan Shikai.[61] Liang was enthusiastic about the project. By supplying labourers for the French government China could claim that she had made a positive contribution to the allied cause and hence gain participation in the future peace conference.[62] In May 1916 Truptil signed a contract with the Huimin Company (which came under the control of the Bureau for Overseas Chinese Workers when China officially declared war on Germany in 1917); recruiting centres were variously established at Tianjin, Hong Kong, Pukou, and Qingdao and the first group of Chinese workers arrived in France in August 1916.[63] The British government, which had previously been involved in the recruitment of Chinese contract labour when nearly 64 000 workers were employed to work in the Transvaal gold mines between 1904 and 1907,[64] soon followed suit and recruited Chinese labour from its leasehold territory of Weihaiwei in northern Shandong for war-service work in France.[65]

Eventually there were to be 135 000 Chinese workers in France, 100 000 under British control and 35 000 under French control.[66] Most of them came from poor rural areas in the north (particularly Zhili and Shandong); Fu Baozhen, a member of the Chinese YMCA who participated in educational activities in France, later noted that amongst those who signed up were students, unemployed minor officials, soldiers and poverty-stricken lower degree-holders (*xiucai*).[67] Those under British control worked in dockyards and ordnance workshops, while those under French control went to work in arms manufacturing, metallurgical and chemical plants, and construction enterprises.[68] By 1918 some were also to be involved in digging trenches, burying war-dead, repairing roads and building aerodromes. While Chinese workers under British control had three-year contracts (most of them were repatriated by 1920), those under French control had five-year contracts and their repatriation was not completed until 1922.[69] As will be noted later, the continued presence of Chinese workers in France provided an important rationale for sending work-study students there.

Li Shizeng, already anticipating the arrival of large numbers of Chinese workers in France as the negotiations between Truptil and the Huimin Company were in progress, announced the creation in 1915 of the Diligent Work And Frugal Study Association (*qingong jianxue hui*) to promote 'diligence and perseverance in work, and frugality (in order to save money) for study, thereby advancing the labourers' knowledge'.[70] Chinese sources indicate that Li also became involved in labour recruitment when he received permission from the French Ministry of Labour to recruit workers in Yunnan on behalf of the Association.[71] He insisted that Chinese workers receive similar rates of pay as their French counterparts and that they be given the opportunity to study in their spare time.[72]

Shortly afterwards, in 1916, Li opened a Chinese Workers' School in Paris to teach French, Chinese and science.[73] The first batch of twenty-four students were those workers already in France before 1914[74] and it was hoped that some of them could be trained as interpreters and teachers in the factories for the newly-arrived Chinese workers. Significantly, whereas Chinese officials in the 1870s had insisted that students going abroad to the United States retain their cultural identity and not allow themselves to be seduced by western customs and values, the Chinese Workers' School in Paris urged its students to abandon their old habits and adapt to western ways of dress, food, and public hygiene. Cai Yuanpei, for example, who gave lectures at the school, drew attention to the bad habits of the Chinese people, such as extravagance, uncleanliness, cursing in public, and adherence to superstitious beliefs. Chinese workers, Cai declared, needed to adopt western customs such as politeness and a sense of decorum (which included standing up for women on public transport), a love of animals, and a concern for the public welfare.[75] Another topic of instruction was the history and organisation of trade unions, an indication of the educational importance work-study promoters attributed to them, seeing in trade unions an ideal environment in which the individual worker would learn to subordinate his own interests to those of the group.

Li Shizeng confidently predicted in 1916 that enormous benefits would accrue to China as a result of France's recruitment of Chinese labour.[76] Not only would the unemployment problem in China be solved, but also Chinese workers in France would form the nucleus of an educated workforce, contributing to the diffusion of industrial skills on their return to China. Such workers, Li continued, would also be civilised. In contrast to backward Chinese culture, he maintained, French culture had freedom of thought and no superstitious religious influences.[77] Furthermore, Li argued, the French were diligent and proficient at 'accumulating money' (*zhuji*), which would provide a positive example to the irresponsible and spendthrift Chinese worker. Lastly, an underlying motive for the importance Li Shizeng placed on the education of Chinese workers in France was the desire to avoid the mishaps of previous overseas Chinese, especially those in the United States, who had often been the targets of vicious racial abuse. In Li's view this was an inevitable result of their 'corrupt habits and low level of education'. Like Chinese educators and reformers from the end of the Qing onwards Li was especially sensitive to the negative image westerners had of the Chinese people and of Chinese popular culture. Only a thoroughgoing reform of the people could alter this situation.[78]

In the same year Li founded the Chinese Workers' School, he organised the Sino-French Education Association (*Huafa jiaoyu hui*) with the aim of 'developing relations between China and France and, especially, with the aid of French scientific and spiritual education to plan for the development of China's moral, intellectual and economic well-being'.[79] Anticipating the slogans of the New Culture Movement after 1917, the founders of the association expressed their determination to introduce the spirit of European (i.e. French) civilisation to China, a spirit that encompassed 'scientific truth' and 'humanism'.[80] Wu Yuzhang in 1917 also noted that the association's encouragement of Chinese overseas study in France would allow China to obtain direct knowledge of western developments in the sciences and arts without being dependent on Japanese translations.[81]

Presided over by Cai Yuanpei and the French academic Alphonse Aulard, the association not only aimed to promote Sino-French cultural relations but also described itself as the umbrella organisation overseeing the interests of all Chinese students and workers in France. In this way both the Frugal Study Association (founded in 1912) and the Diligent Work and Frugal Study Association (founded in 1915) came under its auspices. Branch associations were to be set up in a number of Chinese cities, including Shanghai, Guangzhou and Chengdu.[82] By 1919 the provinces of Hunan, Shandong, and Fujian had also created branch organisations. At the inaugural meeting of the association in 1916 Cai Yuanpei and Aulard, speaking of each other's culture, indulged in a show of mutual admiration. Cai praised the freedom of thought that underpinned French education (claiming also that China had always enjoyed this because Confucianism had never been a rigid state orthodoxy), while Aulard praised Confucius as the forerunner of the French Revolution because of his humanist ideals.[83] Lofty and grandiose hopes were expressed about the future of Sino-French relations, one aspect of which was to be the work-study movement.

THE STUDENT WORK-STUDY MOVEMENT 1917-21

The new opportunities for work in France that the war had brought about prompted Li Shizeng to turn his attention once again to Chinese students. In 1917 the Beijing preparatory school, closed since 1913, was reopened with the aim of preparing students for work-study in France.[84] It is therefore from this time on that work-study became associated with a *student* movement. Other preparatory schools were opened in Baoding and Chengdu where students were trained in such skills as metalwork, in addition to being taught French.[85] Regulations for the schools specifically stipulated that students going to France were to help educate Chinese workers in their spare time.[86] Another interesting feature of the regulations was the proposal that products made by the students during their practical training be sold to help with the upkeep of the schools, an idea that was already being implemented by other vocational schools in this period. Fees were minimal, ranging from one to three *yuan* a month, and training was to last up to two years. Students were expected to pay their own passage to France (although provision was made for loans) and, once there, were to be placed in factories or secondary schools by the Sino-French Education Association.[87]

The association embarked on a vigorous public relations campaign to promote the benefits of work-study in France. Hua Lin, a member of the association who returned to China in 1917, urged the provinces to send as

Table 26. Number and Provincial Origin of Work-Study Students

Province	August 1920[a]	October 1920[b]	1921[c]
Hunan	326	331	346
Guangdong	214	238	254
Sichuan	188	279	378
Zhili (Hebei)	110	111	147
Zhejiang	84	84	86
Fujian	65	87	89
Jiangsu	63	70	69
Anhui	41	38	40
Hubei	29	35	40
Shanxi	28	28	28
Jiangxi	25	27	29
Henan	21	22	25
Shandong	14	14	15
Guizhou	9	9	9
Fengtian	5	5	5
Jilin	5	20	0
Yunnan	4	4	6
Guangxi	3	7	7
Shaanxi	3	5	7
Total	1237	1414	1580

Sources: a. FFSL, 1: 85-6. b. NA 47 AS, A/2-1. c. MAE, E-27-4 S/d.

many students as possible to France, claiming that such students would be able to 'revitalise education and expand industry' on their return.[88] The association, in fact, succeeded in obtaining recognition as a public organisation by the Beijing government and hence gained official patronage. Some branches within China were headed by officials, such as the one in Shaanxi,[89] while others had the support of officially-recognised organisations. In Shanghai, for example, the branch association was patronised by the Chinese Vocational Education Association, headed by prominent educators like Huang Yanpei and Fan Yuanlian.[90] Official supporters and patrons were initially enthusiastic about the scheme because they viewed it as a convenient way to give students practical industrial training and experience which they could put to good use on their return to China.[91]

Students, too, viewed the scheme in practical economic terms. Jia Peizhi wrote in his diary while at the Baoding preparatory school in 1918 that he wanted to go to France to study aircraft design; the money he earned while working there, he hoped, would be used to create an enterprise on his return to China that would manufacture aeroplanes and motor cars.[92] The scheme's promoters also indulged in whimsical, if imaginative, hopes for the movement. Wu Zhihui, for example, suggested that women work-study students set up their own embroidery businesses while in France. The natural skill of Chinese women, he predicted, would ensure that such businesses would flourish and lead to an increased demand for Chinese handicraft products in Europe.[93]

Between March 1919 and December 1920 nearly 1 600 work-study students arrived in France, a large majority of whom came from the provinces of Hunan, Guangdong and Sichuan (see Table 26).[94] Figures produced by the Sino-French Education Association in November 1920 show that 498 were working in factories, 579 were in schools, and the remaining 337 were 'unplaced'. Of those working in factories, the largest numbers were located in iron and steel plants in Firminy and Saint-Chamond, near the large industrial centre of Saint-Etienne in south-central France (115), and at the Schneider armaments plants at Harfleur, Le Creusot, and Chalon-sur-Saône (75). Others worked in automobile factories, paper works, chemical plants, and metallurgical workshops. Most of the students in educational establishments were in secondary schools at Montargis, Melun and Fontainebleau, while 71 were in *lycées* and 34 in specialised vocational schools.[95] By May 1921 the Sino-French Education Association listed over 1 700 students, of whom 1 000 were in factories, 200 were studying in school, and 530 were 'unplaced'.[96] Included in the total were 21 women students, most of whom once again came from Hunan (10), Guangdong (5) and Sichuan (4). The ages of the students ranged from under 15 to over 30. Out of the 1 230 students who had arrived up to August 1920, for example, 600 were aged between 21 and 25 years, 500 between 16 and 20 years, 20 were 15 years or under, and 10 were over 30 years old.[97] One of the youngest was Deng Xiaoping, aged 16, while one of the oldest was Xu Teli, future Commissar of Education at Yanan in 1937, who was 42 when he abandoned his teaching post at the Hunan No.1 normal school to go to France at the end of 1919.[98]

Since sources do not give the social origins of the work-study students, the only criteria available to measure the impact of the movement are provincial origin and educational background. The large number of students coming from the inland provinces of Sichuan and Hunan, areas that had not been as exposed to the tides of modernisation experienced by the southern and central coastal provinces, clearly show that the work-study movement had a wider impact than previous attempts at overseas study. Amongst those who went to Japan during the early years of the twentieth century, for example, students from Zhejiang and Jiangsu had predominated. Traditionally two of the richest provinces, Jiangsu and Zhejiang had always been noted for having the highest number of traditional degree-holders in comparison with other provinces and there was a clear link between this tradition and the high numbers of students from this region going to Japan at the turn of the century. Although students from another inland province, Hubei, also figured prominently amongst those who went to Japan, this was principally due to the official encouragement of Governor-General Zhang Zhidong, one of the first high Qing officials to promote overseas study in Japan.[99]

As for educational background, a significant feature was the high number of graduates from middle-school level or below amongst work-study students, suggesting again that the movement gave the opportunity for overseas study to a wider range of people. In 1916 the Education Ministry had insisted that students going abroad on *official* scholarships had to be graduates of universities or higher specialist schools.[100] Yet the Beijing preparatory school only required of its entrants that they have the equivalent of a middle-school education, while the schools at Baoding and Changxingdian stipulated that entrants were simply to have a basic knowledge of Chinese and that they were not to possess 'bad habits' such as smoking and gambling.[101] Of the 1 237 students who went to France between May 1919 and August 1920, 500 were middle or primary school graduates, 300 were from the various preparatory schools, 90 were university students, and 100 were normal school graduates.[102] The low tuition fees charged by the preparatory schools, the specially reduced boat fares that Li Shizeng negotiated with French authorities,[103] and the opportunities provided by the scheme for students to work in order to finance their studies allowed a greater range of people, in terms of educational background, provincial origin, and age to avail themselves of the opportunity to study abroad.

The original anarchist promoters of the scheme like Li Shizeng and Wu Zhihui hoped that work-study would bring about the interaction of Chinese students and workers in France, which would help reduce the gap between mental and manual labour they claimed had been such an integral part of Confucian culture. In this way, they argued, genuine social equality would be achieved.[104] Both students and workers would become 'reformed' in the process: students would divest themselves of their elitist attitudes and disdain for hard physical work by working with, and helping to educate, workers, while the latter would become more knowledgeable and less susceptible to backward and immoral customs. It is no coincidence that the work-study movement took place at a time when Chinese educators were already calling for a new kind of vocationally-oriented education that would accord more prestige to manual work (see Chapter Five), Cai Yuanpei insisting in 1915 for example, that work was everyone's 'sacred task'.[105] The work-study promoters drew attention to the value of manual labour not only to highlight the vital role workers played in society (and hence dispel the contempt they felt Chinese intellectuals had traditionally shown towards them), but also to justify their right to be educated.

Writing in 1915 Wu Zhihui warned that the continuing division between mental and manual work would 'indirectly preserve the vestiges of imperial and official power and directly serve the power of the rich capitalists, who are succeeding them [i.e. the Emperor and his officials]'.[106] There was no need, Wu insisted, for a separate ruling class based on the monopoly of knowledge, a situation that was often described as a 'dictatorship of scholarship' (*xueshu zhi zhuanzhi*).[107] Li Shizeng also expressed confidence that work-study students would contribute to the dismantling of this monopoly by sharing their knowledge with Chinese workers. Once educated, Li assumed, workers would not only achieve economic betterment but would be less vulnerable to exploitation and deception by a privileged few.[108] This extraordinary faith in education, and the underlying assumption that all social and economic inequalities were primarily due to inequality in educational opportunities, had underpinned the educational debate in China since the turn of the century.

For Li Shizeng, the work-study movement also heralded the beginnings of a new era, one in which everyone was a worker (*gongren*), thus making the traditional social hierarchy redundant.[109] Praising Benjamin Franklin and Jean-Jacques Rousseau as typical examples of how great scientists and thinkers could emerge from the ranks of the lower classes, Li insisted that there were millions of 'potential' Franklins and Rousseaus among artisans and labourers.[110] He also wrote laudatory articles on the nineteenth-century French utopian thinker Charles Fourier and, in particular, what Li referred to as Fourier's 'ideology of mutual assistance' (*xieshe zhuyi*), which envisaged a society where no one group of people would have a monopoly of skills and knowledge and where competition would be replaced by harmony.[111] As one contributor to a journal published by the work-study- promoters put it: 'If everyone has an equal education then classes based on knowledge and ability will be abolished. Then all other various classes will soon disappear.'[112] Other journals predicted that Chinese workers eventually returning from France would have the necessary education, capital and patriotic commitment to contribute to peace and economic development, while the student-workers would lead the way in transforming Chinese society into one based on co-operation and social equality.[113]

The students who embarked for France in 1919-20 at the height of the May Fourth Movement were fired by similar ideals. This was not surprising given the fact that the enthusiasm work-study promoters displayed for popular education, their stress on the importance of labour and the significance of the worker in society, and their ideal of a future society in which intellectuals and workers would interact, anticipated the social issues of the May Fourth Movement and had a considerable influence on the activities of intellectuals and students at this time. University students formed public lecture groups,[114] organised work-study mutual-assistance groups (*gongdu huzhutuan*) and spare-time schools for workers,[115] and along with prominent intellectuals such as Li Dazhao proclaimed the importance of the labouring masses.[116]

Work-study students who wrote of their reasons for going to France often echoed the ideas of Li Shizeng and Wu Zhihui. Xu Teli noted that he went on the scheme to gain practical working experience because, in his view, the most important members of society were those who worked with their hands.[117] Wang Ruofei, future CCP representative to the Comintern, maintained that work-study was the ideal way to cultivate the habit of labour and gain knowledge of the labouring world.[118] Another student, explaining his reasons for going to France in 1920, noted that:

> We intended to do at least three things. Firstly, that poor students with no money could go abroad, thus breaking the monopoly held by wealthy official students; secondly, to allow middle school and even primary school students go to the West ... thirdly, and especially important, it was to enable students who came from a society in which the masses were considered inferior and only the intellectual was considered worthy to take off their long gowns and get down off their high horses and personally enter factories to work.[119]

Of course, other students had more immediate aims in mind. Chen Yi, future foreign minister of the Chinese People's Republic, wrote that he went to France not because he was responding to the slogan, 'the sanctity of labour' (*laogong shensheng*) but because he needed quick work in order to obtain the means for study.[120]

Support for the students came from a number of official organisations and wealthy patrons. One group of students that responded eagerly to the movement, for example, was the New Peoples Study Society (*xinmin xuehui*), which had been formed in Hunan by Cai Hesen and Mao Zedong in April 1918.[121] Cai met Li Shizeng in Beijing and Li was able to arrange for the Hunanese students to receive funds from the Overseas Chinese Workers' Bureau to study at the Beijing preparatory school.[122] In 1920 another group of Hunanese students received funds from two prominent Hunanese officials, Fan Yuanlian and Xiong Xiling.[123] Chou Enlai was financed by Yan Xiu, the founder of Nankai University and educational official in the last years of the Qing and early years of the Republic, while Cai Chang, later to be an important member of the CCP's Women's Department, received money from a wealthy relative, a factory manager in Shanghai.[124] Deng Xiaoping and Nie Rongzhen, future marshal of the People's Liberation Army, were apparently provided with travelling expenses by the head of the Chongqing Chamber of Commerce.[125] Another student, Jiang Zimin, who came from a poor peasant family in Sichuan, was sponsored by the patron of the charitable school he attended. The patron, a bank manager by the name of Yang Xizhong, provided funds for Jiang to attend the preparatory school in Chongqing (which Deng Xiaoping also attended).[126] Jiang noted in his memoirs that he continued to receive money from Yang Xizhong while in France.[127] Finally, the director of the Guangdong branch of the Sino-French Education Association, Huang Qing, was able to obtain funds from the Guangdong Governor by appealing to provincial pride. If Guangdong students went to France on the work-study scheme, Huang claimed, the province would be better equipped to participate in the future national revival.[128]

As far as the French were concerned, the work-study movement, by increasing the number of Chinese students familiar with French industry and educational institutions, would enhance French prestige and influence in China. French publications continually bewailed the increasing dominance of Anglo-Saxon cultural influence in China,[129] especially since 1908 when the United States had decided to remit its share of the Boxer indemnity in order to subsidise the sending of Chinese students to American colleges. Significantly, the arrival of Chinese workers in France in 1916 had been welcomed by French politicians such as Marius Moutet (1876-1968) because, in his view, they would 'become the best agents for French propaganda in their own country'.[130] Not surprisingly, the large number of Chinese work-study students arriving in France in 1919-20 were also welcomed by French commentators. An article in *Le Temps* in 1919 noted that 'it was obvious that these newly-arrived students, educated in France, knowing our country, and imbued with our ideas, will have an influence in China beneficial to us'.[131] It was also frequently observed that China would naturally look to France to exert her cultural independence in the face of Anglo-Saxon dominance because French culture was the most liberal and humanistic, as well as being the least ambitious in its desire to dominate others. As the French Minister to China pompously declared in 1919, France's role was 'to allow the development of, and to assist, all national cultures ... French culture does not therefore denationalise the foreign culture with which it comes into contact, it enriches such a culture'.[132] This grandiose role charted for French culture was, of course, an important component of the *mission civilisatrice* to which French colonial administrators often referred.

The high-sounding rhetoric, however, could not disguise the fact that for many French observers the work-study movement presented a unique opportunity to achieve French cultural hegemony in China.[133] An article in the newspaper *L'Information* in 1921 drew attention to the influence of Japan and the United States because of the educational opportunities extended to Chinese overseas students. The article continued: 'The Chinese is a person who is extremely and curiously pliable ... thus he takes on the cultural attributes of the country in which he is educated. He becomes American, Japanese or English if he is educated in America, Japan or England. He becomes French if educated in France.'[134]

The high hopes held by the work-study promoters in France, Chinese supporters back home, and the students themselves soon had to confront harsh reality. The post-World War One economic depression had become particularly acute in France by 1920. Many factories were to lay off workers or close down completely. At the end of that year several hundred Chinese students in the Paris region were unable to attend school (because of a lack of money) or find a job.[135] Some, like He Changgong, were able to do a variety of odd jobs,[136] but many had to rely on the temporary subsidies and facilities provided by the Sino-French Education Association at their headquarters at Colombes, just outside Paris. Students were either accommodated twenty to a room three-and-a-half metres square or else 'camped' outside in tents furnished by the association.[137] Some became sick and the association had to pay out over 1 000 francs in medical expenses.[138] By 1921 sixty-one students had died (mainly of tuberculosis) while another eighty were in hospital.[139]

For those who did find work the schedule was punishing. In his diary Wang Ruofei outlined his working day at the Saint Chamond steelworks. He studied in the morning before reporting for work at 6.45 a.m. and then after work at 5 p.m. he studied again until 9 p.m.[140] Another student, Luo Xuezan, noted that he and his compatriots in the Montargis area worked eight hours a day and then studied for up to six hours in the evening.[141] Students working at Le Creusot and La Rochelle had to work in the open and suffered because they could not afford outdoor clothing. While some saw this as a salutary experience, claiming that 'having gone through this ordeal our former bad habits of leading extravagant and idle lives have imperceptibly been shed,'[142] others became disillusioned. Chen Yi complained that factory life had nothing to do with the ideals of equality, freedom and fraternity supposedly characteristic of French society. Rather, it had shown him the 'evil nature' of European capitalism at first hand.[143]

Interestingly, students also retained elitist (and racist) attitudes despite the rhetoric of the movement that had championed the sanctity of labour. Wang Ruofei, for example, insisted on moving when he was initially lodged in an immigrant dormitory that housed blacks and Arabs. He also expressed disappointment that the French treated Chinese students and workers with equal contempt.[144] Chen Yi, writing from Château-Thierry in 1921 made it clear that he resented illiterate French workers treating him the same as blacks.[145] Li Fuchun, future chairman of the State Planning Commission after 1949, referred disparagingly to the 'uncleanliness' of Chinese workers at the Schneiders plant in Le Havre.[146] Neither Wang Ruofei nor Chen Yi thought much of French workers either, dismissing them as idle and pleasure-seeking. A revealing letter from the principal of Montargis College in 1921 to the Chinese Legation noted that of the 110 students at Montargis some had decided to continue with their studies, while those unable to pay fees would 'accept suitable work that could be found for them, that is to say *not* manual work' (emphasis mine).[147]

Nevertheless, the work-study movement was a bold experiment, providing the opportunity for student-worker interaction as well as the stimulus for worker education and organisational activities amongst workers themselves. In a factory near Toulouse Chinese students organised spare-time classes for the seven hundred Chinese workers there.[148] In Montargis a student lecture group regularly visited workers in neighbouring factories and gave talks on hygiene and science.[149] A night school for one hundred workers was opened near Lyon by Gao Yihan, later to be a noted contributor to New Youth (*Xin qingnian*), while other night schools were organised at Toulon and Rouen, where there were nine hundred Chinese workers.[150] One source gives information on the progress of workers' education organised by work-study students at a match factory in Vonges between May

1917 and March 1919. By the later date, amongst the 930 Chinese workers employed at the factory, 20 per cent were attending lectures, 50 per cent were studying in their spare time, and 30 per cent were reading *The Chinese Worker* (*Huagong zazhi*), a journal published by the Sino-French Education Association.[151] Sometimes Chinese workers took the initiative themselves in setting up their own spare-time schools and then inviting the students to help with the teaching, such as the four hundred or so who worked at a factory in Fargniers.[152] The instruction was not always one way, however. Work-study students in factories often had to rely on Chinese workers for instruction and advice since they mostly worked side by side.[153]

There were, of course, practical motives involved in organising literacy classes in Chinese and French. If Chinese workers were literate in their own language they would be able to read letters sent from home and not have to be dependent on the official Chinese interpreters who had accompanied the workers to France, one of whom was severely assaulted by a Shandong worker in Caen when he apparently got the gist of a letter wrong.[154] Likewise, Chinese workers acquainted with French would not be involved in unfortunate misunderstandings such as the worker at Le Creusot who did not take his bread ration ticket when he went to a local bakery (not understanding its significance) and then smashing a window in frustrated anger when he was refused bread.[155]

Yet there is also evidence to show that work-study students stimulated a sense of patriotism and concern for the home country amongst Chinese workers. When news of Zhang Xun's abortive attempt in 1917 to restore the last Qing emperor reached France, protesting telegrams were sent in the name of 'Chinese workers, merchants, and students residing in France'.[156] Workers at a factory in Capdenac in southern France were encouraged to make a national flag in October 1919 to celebrate national day.[157] More significantly, hundreds of Chinese workers responded to the floods that engulfed the metropolitan province of Zhili (Hebei) in 1918 by contributing money towards famine relief. Thus 500 workers at Le Creusot donated 557 francs, 550 at Suresnes donated 1 643 francs, while the 1 000 workers at Vonges contributed 2 070 francs.[158]

Work-study promoters also devised a set of rules for Chinese workers that reflected the general concern amongst Chinese educators since the turn of the century to 'reform' the people's behaviour and customs. As such, the rules laid down were similar to the exhortations issued by the Beijing popular education research association during the early years of the republic (see Chapter Five). It was felt especially urgent that Chinese workers in France adopt suitable behaviour lest they become a target of ridicule and abuse. As usual, the rules pertained to the minutiae of daily living. Thus Chinese workers were advised to wipe their shoes before entering premises, not to open the window in the morning if still dressed in nightclothes, always to knock and wait for a reply before entering a room, not to spit in public, not to splash water while washing, not to throw rubbish out of the window, not to gesticulate and shout in public, not to pick a fight if they were pushed or shoved in a crowd, and, lastly, to read assiduously the newspapers on Sunday![159]

Workers themselves organised 'self-governing associations' (*zizhihui*) of their own, whose purpose was to oversee behaviour and encourage the elimination of undesirable habits such as gambling (one worker in Le Creusot committed suicide after losing 1 000 francs in a gambling spree),[160] drinking, fighting, and frequenting prostitutes.[161] Members could be fined for breaking the rules.[162] These associations also insisted that it was the workers's patriotic duty to save money and study.[163] At the end of 1919 a General Association of Chinese Workers in France (*Liufa Huagong gonghui*) was founded under the auspices of the work-study promoters and, according to a 1920 report by the Prefect of Police in Paris, had nearly 1 500 members in the Paris region alone. Although the association was to serve as the intermediary between workers and their French employers, the principal aim was one of self-improvement and mutual aid. Members, who had to pay 24 francs a year in subscriptions, had to sign a pledge promising not to be involved in politics, not to frequent prostitutes or to gamble, nor to waste money and time.[164]

The work-study movement itself ended in 1921 when the Sino-French Education Association, drained of resources, decided to cut subsidies for the students and advise the Ministry of Education in Beijing that no more work-study students be permitted to leave for France.[165] For those students in France increasing resentment with their economic plight led to angry demonstrations in front of the Chinese Legation in Paris in February 1921.[166] French authorities became concerned at the growing radicalisation amongst Chinese students, some of whom later dated their opposition to capitalism and interest in communism from this time.[167] Students also vented their growing hostility to western involvement in China when they denounced loan negotiations being carried out between China and France in August 1921. When news in the French press indicated that the Chinese government was prepared to accept a French loan to be secured on domestic tobacco, alcohol and stamp duties, Chinese students forced the Chinese Legation in Paris to denounce publicly the loan. The French and Chinese governments, embarrassed by the publicity and fearing potential opposition from the other powers (especially as they had just resurrected the banking consortium in 1920 to facilitate joint loans to China) quietly dropped the scheme.[168]

If French authorities were becoming increasingly disenchanted with the Chinese work-study students,[169] it is apparent that Li Shizeng, Wu Zhihui and Cai Yuanpei had lost interest in the scheme by 1921 as they now concentrated their efforts on developing formal cultural and educational links with France. In particular, Li sought to negotiate the creation of a Sino-French Institute at Lyon,[170] whose Chinese students would be recruited in China on the basis of competitive examinations. (It was also expected that potential students were to have a certain level of income and knowledge of French before being accepted.)[171] Work-study students already in France demanded that the proposed Institute be open to them without prior conditions, only to be met by Wu Zhihui's insistence that the Institute was designed to train an advanced specialised elite.[172] Over one hundred work-study students thereupon converged on Lyon and 'occupied' the Institute soon after it was formally opened in September 1921.[173] They were arrested by French police and one month later 104 of the students were deported from Marseille.[174] The 'Lyon Incident' was a dramatic finale to a movement that had begun with so much enthusiasm and idealism and ended in mutual recrimination as Chinese students accused the work-study promoters of betrayal and Li Shizeng expressed his disenchantment with 'unruly' work-study students.

EPILOGUE

Although French politicians and businessmen, along with representatives of the Chinese Legation and the Sino-French Education Association, had created the Sino-French Committee of Support (*Comité Franco-Chinoise de patronnage*) the previous May to provide emergency funds for work-study students throughout the summer[175] and help place some of them in factories and schools,[176] the emphasis was very much on training a selected elite. At a meeting of the committee in March 1922 the co-chairman, E. Bradier (representing the French Foreign Ministry) noted that only a minority amongst the work-study students were intelligent or capable enough to benefit from a higher education in France. The rest, he concluded, should be repatriated as soon as possible and in future only highly qualified students recommended by French or Chinese authorities should be received.[177] In 1923 the committee was amalgamated with the *Association Amicale Franco-Chinoise* to form the Sino-French Association of Friendship and Support, which was far more concerned with placing qualified students in prestigious institutions of higher learning in France and with promoting top-level cultural contacts between France and China.

The radical work-study students who remained in France after the Lyon incident created the Chinese Communist Youth Party in Europe (*Lü-ou Zhongguo shaonian gongchandang*) in June 1922 and by February of the following year it had become formally linked with the CCP. At the beginning of 1925 there may have been as many as 300 members, although this represented the high point as increasing numbers of work-study students, including the more radical leaders, left France between the spring of 1923 and the beginning of 1926.[178]

The last major incident involving the Chinese in France occurred on 21 June 1925, and served to confirm the fears of French authorities that Chinese students and workers had become 'infected' by Bolshevik propaganda. Following the May 30 Incident in Shanghai, when Chinese workers protesting against the brutality of a Japanese factory owner were fired on by the International Settlement police force (under British command), Chinese students and workers in France organised mass protest meetings. On 14 June 1925 over 800 took part in a protest march in Paris. Pamphlets were issued not only denouncing British and French 'barbarity' in China but also appealing to the French people to put pressure on their government to pull its troops out of the concession areas in China. Significantly a report from the Prefect of Seine-et-Oise noted that copies of the pamphlets were distributed by Chinese *workers* among their French colleagues at the Renault factory in Billancourt.[179]

The climax of the protest, on 21 June 1925, saw one hundred students forcing their way into the Chinese Legation and compelling the luckless Chinese Minister, Chen Lu, to issue a telegram of support to the workers, students and merchants of Shanghai and to request the French government to withdraw its troops from China.[180] Forty-seven students were arrested and police raids on student residences in Paris and Billancourt resulted in twenty further arrests. Seventeen were deported, while fifty left the country voluntarily.[181]

As for the Chinese workers who remained in France after 1922, they too fell on hard times. Reports from French authorities in 1925-6 indicate that unemployment was rife amongst the 3 000 workers and apprentices; particularly hard hit were those who had previously worked at Renault, Citroen and Schneiders.[182] Another report in 1927 noted that two hundred of the nearly three hundred Chinese workers in the Billancourt region had had to look for work in the provinces.[183] The General Association of Chinese Workers in France, hitherto an organisation that primarily encouraged self-improvement and mutual assistance, began to adopt a more assertive stance.[184] In April 1925, for example, the association wrote to the French Foreign Ministry requesting that Boxer indemnity funds be used to offer free repatriation and that the contribution of Chinese workers to the allied war effort be recognised by the building of a commemorative monument, the establishment of a national cemetery for those Chinese workers who had died in France, and the offer of financial compensation to the families of the dead and the wounded.[185] As late as 1934 fifty unemployed Chinese workers from Billancourt took part in a demonstration calling for free repatriation, a demonstration organised by the Association of Chinese Volunteers in the First World War (*Association Amicale des Engagés Volontaires Chinois de la Grande Guerre*) which had been formed in 1931.[186]

Li Shizeng's ambitious hope that the work-study movement would be the blueprint for the realisation of unity and harmony in Chinese society was not fulfilled; many work-study students returned to participate in the Communist-led class struggle, while Chinese workers returning from France joined the ranks of the expanding proletariat.[187] Nevertheless, the movement had done much to draw attention to the importance of workers and manual labour and to break down the traditional attitude of according social prestige solely to the scholar. In many ways the work-study promoters were similar to the Russian populists of the 1870s. Both groups comprised alienated intellectuals who sought to forge a new relationship between elites and people against a background of economic and social backwardness. Yet while the ideal society of the Russian populists was to be built upon peasant traditions, Li Shizeng's ideal was to create a modernised working class by rejecting 'backward' customs.

Furthermore, with its aim of combining mental and manual work, the work-study movement occupies an important place in China's educational history. In its distrust of a purely academic education in formal schools it echoed the dissatisfaction voiced by so many Chinese educators with the modern schools since the last years of the Qing. It is also important to note that although the aims of the movement reflected the anarchist beliefs of its promoters, the optimism and faith in the power of education was just as much a feature of the thought of Chinese officials, reformers and revolutionaries in the early years of the century as it was of Li Shizeng. Finally, the movement pointed very much to the future since many of the ideas it raised, such as the necessity for students and intellectuals to gain first-hand experience of the labouring world, and the importance of raising workers' educational and cultural levels, anticipated the social radicalism of the May Fourth Movement in 1919[188] and were to form an integral part of Maoist educational philosophy.

NOTES

1. For information in English on the work-study movement, see J. Kong-cheong Leung, 'The Chinese Work-Study Movement' (Ph.D., Brown University, 1982); C. Brandt, 'The French-Returned Elite in the Chinese Communist Party', in E. F. Szczepanik (ed.), *Symposium on Economic and Social Problems of the Far East* (Hong Kong, 1962), pp. 229-39; Chow Tse-tsung, *The May Fourth Movement* (Cambridge, Mass., 1960), pp. 35-40; R. Scalapino, G. Yu, *Modern China and its Revolutionary Process*, pp. 513-7, 618-25; M. Levine, 'The Diligent-Work Frugal-Study Movement and the New Culture Movement', *Republican China*, 12: 1 (1986); Y. C. Wang, *Chinese Intellectuals and the West* (Chapel Hill, 1966), pp. 105-11; P. Bailey, 'The Chinese Work-Study Movement in France', *China Quarterly*, no. 115 (September, 1988), pp. 441-61. For information in French, see J. Van der Stegen, 'Les Chinois en France 1915-1925' (Mémoire de Maitrîse, Univ. de Paris-Nanterre, 1974); A. Kriegel, *Communismes au Miroir Français* (Paris, 1974), pp. 57-93; N. Wang, 'Paris-Shanghai: Débats d'Idées et Pratique Sociale, les Intellectuels Progressistes Chinois 1920-1925' (Doctorat d'Etat, Univ. de Paris, 1986). Some of these work-study students included Zhou Enlai, Deng Xiaoping, Li Lisan, Chen Yi, Li Fuchun, and Nie Rongzhen.
2. *Lü'ou zhoukan*, no. 67 (19 February 1921).
3. A number of documentary collections on the movement have

recently been published in China. See FFSL (Beijing, 1979-81), 3 vols; QGYD (Shanghai, 1980, 1986), 2 vols. See also Chen Sanjing (comp.) *Qingong jianxue yundong* (Taibei 1981).
4. For information on Li Shizeng see H. Boorman, R. Howard (eds.), *Republican China*, 2: 319-21 After his father's death, Li was awarded official rank, qualifying him to hold a post of department head. In 1924 he became a member of the Guomindang Supervisory Committee. After leaving the mainland in 1949 Li eventually settled in Taiwan, where he became a policy adviser to Chiang Kai-shek.
5. For information on Li Hongcao, see A. Hummel (ed), *Eminent Chinese of the Ch'ing Period* (Washington, 1943), 1: 471-2.
6. Sun Baoqi's family had been neighbours of the Li household in Beijing. *Li Shizeng xiansheng wenji* (Taibei, 1980), 2: 19. Li also remembers that high officials such as Weng Tenghe and Zhang Zhidong were frequent visitors to his home. *Ibid.*, 2: 20. For Li's reminiscences on his early education see *Shizeng biji* (Taibei, 1961), pp. 77, 148. One work-study participant, He Changgong, even claims that Li was the 'adopted son' *(gan erzi)* of the Empress-Dowager and that he received a yearly stipend from her of 8 000 *liang*, which was gratefully made use of by Li's future revolutionary colleagues Cai Yuanpei, Wu Zhihui, and Sun Yatsen. He Changgong, *Qingong jianxue huiyi* (Beijing, 1958), p. 6.
7. For information on Zhang Jingjiang, see H. Boorman, R. Howard (eds.), *Republican China*, 1: 73-7.
8. S. Leibo, *Transferring Technology to China: Prosper Giquel and the Self-Strengthening Movement* (Berkeley, 1985), pp. 126-8; Y. C. Wang, *Chinese Intellectuals and the West*, pp. 46-9. In 1876 Li Hongzhang sent seven students from the Tianjin Military School to Germany to study military technology. One of the students who went to France in 1877 was Ma Jianzhong, who became the first Chinese to receive the *baccalauréat*. M. Banno, 'Furansu ryūgaku jidai no Ba Kenchu', *Kokka Gakkai Zasshi*, no. 5 (August 1971), p. 271. See also P. Bailey, 'The Sino-French Connection 1902-1928', in D. Goodman (ed.) *China and the West: Ideas and Activists* (Forthcoming).
9. Qu Lihe, *Qingmo liuxue jiaoyu* (Taibei, 1973), p. 116; Shu Xincheng, *Jindai Zhongguo liuxue shi* (Shanghai, 1927), p. 21.
10. Y. C. Wang, *Chinese Intellectuals and the West*, pp. 54-5.
11. *Ibid.*, pp. 42-5, 73, 147. The students who went to the United States in the 1870s were to be recalled in 1881, only two of them having completed their college education.
12. The number of Chinese students in Japan declined after 1906 with increasing government restrictions. By 1912 the total had fallen to 1 400. Lui Wangling, '1896–1906 nianjian Zhongguo liuri xuesheng renshu buzheng' (Supplement on the Numbers of Chinese Students in Japan between 1896 and 1906) in *Xinhai geming lunwenji*, pp. 333-44; H. Abe, 'Borrowing from Japan: China's First Modern Educational System', pp. 75-7. For general accounts of Chinese students in Japan, see Huang Fuqing, *Qingmo liuri xuesheng* (Taibei, 1975); Saneto Keishū, *Chūgokujin Nihon Ryūgaku shi* (Tokyo, 1960).

13. Li Shizeng, 'Zhongfa jiaoyu wenti' (The Question of Sino-French Education), *Zhongfa daxue banyuekan*, no. 1 (1925), pp. 5-6.
14. *Zhongfa jiaoyujie*, no. 2 (November 1926), p. 49.
15. See, for example, Li's articles in *Lü'ou zazhi*, no. 2 (1 September 1916), *Iunshuo*, pp. 3-9; *Lü'ou zhoukan*, no. 2 (22 November 1919); no. 3 (29 November 1919).
16. In 1925 Li was to be awarded the Legion of Honour for his contributions to Sino-French cultural and educational relations.
17. On Li's friendship with Paul Reclus, see the account by his son Jacques in *Zhuanji wenxue*, 45: 3 (1984), pp. 87-8. See also *Li Shizeng xiansheng jinianji* (Taibei, 1973), p. 236.
18. On Elisée Reclus, see M. Fleming, *The Anarchist Way to Socialism* (London, 1979).
19. *Minguo bairen zhuan* (Taibei, 1971), 1:424. Zhang's father reportedly contributed 300 000 Chinese dollars to launch the venture. Zhang later opened branches of his trading company in London and New York. *Li Shizeng xiansheng jinianji*, p. 206.
20. *Lü'ou jiaoyu yundong* (Tours, 1916), p. 3. The editor of the pictorial magazine was a woman by the name of Yao Hui. Unfortunately, I have been unable to find any further references to this person.
21. H. Boorman, R. Howard (eds.), *Republican China*, 3: 416-9. See also P. Clifford, 'The Intellectual Development of Wu Zhihui' (Ph.D., University of London, 1978), p. 27.
22. On Zhang Ji, see H. Boorman, R. Howard (eds.), *Republican China*,1:15-20. For his stay at the Aiglemont communal village, see *Zhang Puchuan xiansheng quanji* (Taibei, 1951), p. 236; Li Shuhua, 'Xinhai geming qianhou de Li Shizeng xiansheng' (Li Shizeng at the time of the 1911 Revolution), *Zhuanji wenxue*, 24: 2 (February,1974), p. 44. The village, a self-sufficient community cultivating 100 *mu* of land, comprised several nationalities. Wu Zhihui also apparently stayed there for a time. See *Xin shiji*, no .57 (1908).
23. On Chu Minyi, see H. Boorman, R. Howard (eds.), *Republican China* 1:467-9.
24. *Les Temps Nouveaux* had begun publication in 1895. The name was changed to *Nouveau Siècle* in 1909.
25. For a discussion of the Chinese anarchists in Paris, see A. Dirlik, 'Vision and Revolution', *Modern China*, 12: 2 (April, 1986), pp. 123-62. For a general account of Chinese anarchism, see R. Scalapino, G. Yu, *The Chinese Anarchist Movement* (Berkeley, 1961). For a concise discussion of Sun Yatsen's views, see R. Scalapino, G. Yu, *Modern China and its Revolutionary Process*, pp. 148-67,176-7,186-92. The journal's anti-Manchu stance was sufficiently prominent to attract the attention of the Chinese authorities. In 1907 the Foreign Affairs Ministry ordered the Chinese Legation in Paris to stop its publication. Li Shuhua, p. 43. A French language publication in Shanghai in 1907 also stressed that most of the Chinese in Paris had 'subversive ideas'. *Echo de Chine* (18 July 1907).
26. Li Shizeng's translation of *Mutual Aid is* reprinted in *Li Shizeng xiansheng wenji* (Taibei, 1980),1:102-73. On Kropotkin, see M.

Miller, *Kropotkin* (Chicago, 1976).
27. 'Huijia tan' (A Discussion Concerning the Abolition of the Family), *Xin shiji*, no. 82 (1909).
28. On the Chinese anarchist group in Tokyo, see M. Bernal, *Chinese Socialism to 1907*, pp. 201-26. See also R. Scalapino, G. Yu, *Modern China and its Revolutionary Process*, pp 231-59, 506-13; Peng Yingming, 'Lun xinhai geming qian de wuzhengfu zhuyi sichao' (On Anarchism before the 1911 Revolution) in *Xinhai geming lunwenji* (Guangzhou, 1980), pp 143-65; Kui Yingtao, *Xinhai geming shi* (Beijing, 1980), pp 190-222.
29. Cited in D. Kwok, *Scientism in Chinese Thought* (New Haven, 1965), p 37.
30. Li's articles, 'Wuzhengfu shuo' (The Theory of Anarchism), are reprinted in Zhang Nan, Wang Renzhi (comp), *Xinhai geming qian shinianjian shilun xuanji* (Beijing, 1977), 3: 133-79
31. *Ibid.*, 3:225-6.
32. 'Lun cike de jiaoyu' (On the Education of Assassination), *Zhongguo baihua bao*, no. 17 (1904), *lunshuo*, pp. 1-6.
33. *Xin shiji*, no .65 (1908) .
34. *Xin shiji*, no. 82 (1909). Chu also urged Chinese revolutionaries to utilise the traditional secret societies as the bases for modern trade unions. *Xin shiji*, no. 42 (1908).
35. Some of these workers may have had some schooling, since one source refers to three graduates of a rural half-day school being included in the group. *Lü' ou jiaoyu yundong*, p. 81. One of them, Li Guang'an, was later to assist Li Shizeng in the negotiations with the French Ministry of Industry concerning the recruitment of Chinese workers.
36. See Li's discussion of the beancurd in *Asie Française*, no. 158 (May 1914), pp. 196-8.
37. *Bulletin de l'Association Amicale Franco-Chinoise*, 2: 1 (January 1910), p. 62. Another exhibition devoted to the beancurd was opened in the Salon d'Alimentation at the Grand Palais in Paris during the same year. *Ibid.*, 2: 4 (October 1910), pp. 336-46.
38. Both Qi Rushan and Qi Zhushan had studied French at the School of Languages *(Tongwenguan)* in Beijing. Qi Rushan was later to become one of the first Chinese scholars to do extensive research on traditional Chinese drama. H. Boorman, R. Howard (eds.), *Republican China*, 1: 299-301.
39. *Shizeng biji* (Taibei, 1961) p. 78; Li Shuhua, 'Xinhai geming qianhou Li Shizeng xiansheng', p. 44.
40. A report on the beancurd factory in 1919 noted that it had expanded during the war, and that the number of workers employed there had increased to nearly seventy. Whereas before the war the factory had been unable to sell large quantities of soya-bean milk because of the competition from cheap milk, the rising price of milk after 1918 prompted more interest in soya-bean milk as a viable alternative. FFSL, 1: 221-2 .
41. *Lü' ou jiaoyu yundong*, p. 50.

42. QGYD 1: 15. The regulations for the association are in *Lü'ou jiaoyu yundong*, pp. 50-5; QGYD, 1: 14-8; FFSL, 1: 169-74; DFZZ, 14: 6 (1912) *neiwa shibao*, pp. 193-5.
43. The association placed a notice in a Beijing newspaper claiming that 'frugal study' in France would be cheaper than studying in Japan. QGYD, 1: 25.
44. DFZZ, 14: 9 (1912), *neiwai shibao*, pp. 178-9. Wang admitted that France's imperialist record in Indo-China was bad but still insisted that the French Revolution had completely renewed politics, culture and society.
45. For a class of twenty students, the monthly fees were 6 *yuan* a month, plus 5 *yuan* board and lodging. Shu Xincheng (ed.), *Shiliao*, 1: 317-20.
46. A similar school was opened in Chengdu, Sichuan, under the direction of Wu Yuzhang (1878-1966), who had joined the *Tongmenghui* while studying in Japan. In 1914-16 he studied political science and economics in Paris.
47. It was calculated that an ordinary overseas student in Europe or the United States would need at least 2 000 Chinese dollars FFSL, 1: 174; QGYD, 1: 19.
48. QGYD, 1: 25-6
49. QGYD, 1:31. The students travelled to France via the Trans-Siberian railway, the trip taking fifteen days to complete in contrast to the thirty days needed if they had gone by sea. Most of the students came from Jiangsu and Hubei. *Lü'ou jiaoyu yundong*, p. 49.
50. A. Kriegel, *Communismes au Miroir Français*, p. 78.
51. Among the first group who went to France in 1912-13 were the brothers Zhu, Li, Zhang, Nie, and Wei. *Lü'ou jiaoyu yundong*, p. 55. Some of them were also quite young; in the second group that went, for example, there were two fourteen year-olds from a poor people's home in Beijing. One of them was reported to have said on the eve of his departure that he intended to engage in serious study so as to contribute to the country's economy. QGYD, 1: 30. See also JYZZ, 5: 4 (1913), *jishi*, pp. 31-2.
52. On this, see K. Biggerstaff, *The Earliest Modern Government Schools in China* (Ithaca, 1961).
53. *Liufa jianxue baogaoshu* (Guangzhou, 1918), pp. 66-71. Some of the frugal study students who went to France before 1914 achieved considerable academic success. One graduated top of his class in chemistry at Toulouse University, while another came first in the graduating class at a Montargis secondary school. Lin Zixun, *Zhongguo liuxue jiaoyushi* (Taibei, 1976), p. 350; QGYD, 1: 75.
54. *Lü'ou jiaoyu yundong*, p .35 .
55. *Ibid.*, p. 9.
56. Cited in Tao Yinghui, 'Ji Minguo silao' (On the Four Elder Statesmen of the Republic), *Zhuanji wenxue*, 23: 5 (November 1973), p. 23. The 'four elder statesmen' referred to Li Shizeng, Cai Yuanpei, Wu Zhihui, and Zhang Jingjiang, all of whom were to occupy

important posts in the Guomindang. See also QGYD, 1: 26; *Li Shizeng xiansheng wenji*, 2: 61; P. Clifford, 'The Intellectual Development of Wu Zhihui', pp. 274-9.
57. Tao Yinghui, 'Ji Minguo Silao', pp. 20-3; *Li Shizeng xiansheng wenji*, 1: 178-82.
58. Those already in France either transferred to schools and colleges in the southwest or worked full-time alongside Chinese workers in Li's beancurd factory or Zhang Jingjiang's publishing enterprise. QGYD,1: 31.
59. G. Cross, *Immigrant Workers in Industrial France* (Philadelphia, 1983), pp. 21-2.
60. J. Horne, 'Immigrant Workers in France during World War One' *French Historical Studies*, 14: 1 (Spring, 1985), pp. 57-88; G. Cross, 'The Politics of Immigration during the Era of the First World War', *French Historical Studies*, 11: 4 (Autumn, 1980), pp. 610-32. By the 1920s France was second only to the United States as an industrialised immigrant society.
61. Liang Shiyi (1869-1933) was a metropolitan degree holder (*jinshi*) under the ancien régime. He worked for Yuan Shikai when the latter was Governor-General of Zhili and in 1907 was put in charge of railways by the newly-established Ministry of Posts and Communications. In 1912 he became Yuan's chief secretary and Director of the Bank of Communications. H. Boorman, R. Howard (eds.), *Republican China*, 2: 354-7; *Minguo renwu zhuan* (Beijing, 1977), 1: 221-6. See also S. Mackinnon, 'Liang Shiyi and the Communications Clique', *Journal of Asian Studies*, 29: 3 (May, 1970). For the negotiations, see the report by the French Minister in Beijing in February 1916, *Archives du Ministère des Affaires Etrangères* (hereafter cited as MAE), E-110-2, E-22-15. See also *La Politique de Pékin*, no. 34 (25 August 1918).
62. FFSL, 1: 227-8; Bai Jiao, 'Shijie dazhanzhong zhi huagong' (Chinese Workers during the First World War), *Renwen yuekan*, 8:1 (1937), p. 2. In fact, Yuan Shikai twice proposed Chinese military participation in the war; in 1914 he suggested that Chinese troops help expel the Germans from Shandong and in 1915 he proposed sending Chinese troops to the Dardanelles. M. Chi, *China Diplomacy, 1914-1918* (Cambridge, Mass., 1970), pp. 20,72; Lo Hui-min (ed.), *The Correspondence of G. E. Morrison* (Cambridge, 1978), 2: 559-61. At the end of 1917 Beijing's new strongman, Duan Qirui, actually proposed sending Chinese troops to France. The offer was not taken seriously (despite French interest), principally because of the lack of transportation and the lukewarm response shown by Britain and the United States. MAE, E-22-14. See also P. Wou, *Les Travailleurs Chinois et la Grande Guerre* (Paris, 1939), which notes (p. ll) that Marshal Foch in 1917 also proposed the despatch of Chinese military units to the western front.
63. *Lü'ou zazhi*, no. 3 (September,1916), p. 3. For the contract, see FFSL, 1: 229-33. Nearly 19,000 out of the 31,000 workers recruited from these centres were recruited from Pukou.

64. On this, see P. Richardson, *Chinese Mine Labour in the Transvaal* (London, 1982).
65. For information on the recruitment of Chinese workers by the British, see M. Summerskill, *China on the Western Front* (London, 1985); A. P. Jones, 'Britain's Search For Co-operation in the First World War' (Ph.D., London School of Economics, 1977); P. Atwell, *British Mandarins and Chinese Reformers* (Oxford, 1985), pp. 106-7. Britain's initial motive for recruiting Chinese workers was to use them to replace British workers who were already working in French dockyards. Trade union opposition discouraged the Lloyd George government from utilising Chinese labour within Britain.
66. On the history of Chinese labour in France during the First World War, see Chen Sanjing, *Huagong yu Ouzhan* (Taibei, 1986). See also Chen Ta, *Chinese Migrations with Special Reference to Labor Conditions* (US Dept. of Labor, Bureau of Labor Statistics, Washington, 1923). pp. 142-58; H. McNair, *The Chinese Abroad* (Shanghai, 1924), pp. 235-8; J. Blick, 'The Chinese Labor Corps in WWI', *Harvard Papers on China* (August, 1955), pp. 111-45; J. Chesneaux, *The Chinese Labor Movement* (Stanford, 1968), pp. 138-40. It is interesting to note that in 1915-16 58 000 Chinese workers were also recruited to work in Russia, most of them in factories east of the Volga.
67. *Jiaoyu yu minzhong*, 2: 7 (March, 1931), p. 3
68. Chen Ta, *Chinese Migrations*, pp. 147-8. For a first-hand account of the labour battalions (from Africa and the Middle East as well as Asia) recruited by Britain and France during the First World War, see *The Times* (26, 27, 28 December 1917).
69. A report by the French Interior Ministry in 1925 noted the presence of 3 000 Chinese workers and apprentices in France. *Archives du Ministère de l'Intérieur* (hereafter cited as AMI), F7 1348. Chinese workers under French control also had the option of staying on in France after 1922, in which case their return home would not be paid.
70. QGYD. 1: 52-3; *Lü'ou jiaoyu yundong*, pp .71, 80-1.
71. *Lü'ou zazhi*, no. 1 (August, 1916), p. 9; QGYD, 1: 56. 2 500 workers from Yunnan were apparently recruited, although reports from the French Minister in Beijing in August 1916 indicate that the mission failed because of protests from German consular representatives. MAE, E-110-2, E-22-15. The French also recruited directly in China without going through the Huimin Company, mostly in Guangdong and Shanghai. *Lü'ou zazhi*, no. 10 (January,1917), p. 10.
72. *Lü'ou zazhi*, no. 1 (August, 1916). p. 9; *Lü'ou jiaoyu yundong*, p. 96; QGYD, 1: 56. Chinese workers recruited by France in any event were to be paid more than their counterparts under British control, mainly because of the insistence by French trade unions that Chinese workers not be used as a source of cheap labour to compete with French workers.
73. Curiously, although Chinese sources (QGYD,1: 56) note that the

school received funds from the French government (up to 10 000 francs), a circular from the French Foreign Ministry, dated 29 April 1916, warned that it was 'to be feared that the school would make socialists out of the students, and that Chinese workers about to come to France would be encouraged to demand equal pay with French workers'. MAE, E-110-2, E-22-15.
74. QGYD, 1: 54. In addition to the workers in Li's beancurd factory and Zhang Jingjiang's printing works, another forty-nine had been recruited in 1913 to work at an artificial silk factory in Argues-la-Bataille in Normandy. For a 1914 report on these Chinese workers by the Commissioner of Police in Dieppe, see AMI, F7 1348.
75. QGYD, 1: 55; *Cai Yuanpei xiansheng quanji* (Taibei, 1969), pp. 197, 202-5, 210-20.
76. *Lü'ou jiaoyu yundong*, pp. 82-3. See also a 1917 article by Li Shizeng, which further underlined the role of Chinese workers in France to help with the reform of Chinese society on their return. *Li Shizeng xiansheng wenji*, 1: 220-5. For the views of Cai Yuanpei and Wu Zhihui on the role Chinese workers could play in developing China's economy, see QGYD, 1:81, 84.
77. Li and his colleagues also claimed that the French were less racist than the British or Americans. This did not prevent the Interior Ministry prohibiting French women from marrying Chinese workers. FFSL, 1: 243.
78. The sensitivity to China's potential image abroad can also be seen in a 1917 report by the Chinese Minister in Paris in which he warned that Chinese workers in France would have to be seen to be frugal and industrious if China's reputation was not to be impaired. He referred to a group of Hubei workers who were forced by straitened financial circumstances to sell paper flowers in a Paris street. Their shabby and unkempt appearance, he bewailed, had aroused ridicule and laughter among passers-by. DFZZ, 14: 7 (1917), *neiwai shibao*, p. 172.
79. For the regulations of the Sino-French Education Association, see FFSL, 1: 206-9; QGYD, 1: 75-9; *Lü'ou jiaoyu yundong*, p. 115; Shu Xincheng (ed.), *Shiliao*, 1: 321
80. QGYD, 1: 102 .
81. QGYD, 1: 83; FFSL, 1: 180-3.
82. The chairman of the Shanghai branch was Li's anarchist colleague, Zhang Ji, while the vice-chairman was the French consul, Veroudart. Wang Jingwei was an executive member of the Guangdong branch; its regulations specifically referred to the aim of promoting economic ties between south China and France. QGYD, 1: 180-3.
83. *Lü'ou jiaoyu yundong*, pp. 63-41, 112 .
84. In a speech to the first class Cai Yuanpei again praised France as a haven for republican education. His previous admiration for Germany did not deter him from insisting that France had as glorious a scientific tradition as did Germany and, moreover, possessed the creativity that Germany lacked. QGYD, 1: 40-2.
85. QGYD, 1: 63-8, 100, 164-6.

86. QGYD, 1: 66. In 1918 a preparatory class was opened in Changxingdian on the Beijing-Hankou railway. It was financed by the Overseas Chinese Workers Bureau on the understanding that students would contribute to the education of Chinese workers in France. QGYD, 1: 164.
87. Applicants had also to be between 18 and 22 years of age, although this condition must have been waived later on since there were to be work-study students younger than 18 and older than 22.
88. Shu Xincheng (ed.) *Shiliao*, 2: 328-9; QGYD, 1: 46-8. Hua calculated that at least 10 000 students might eventually be sent to France if every district sponsored two to three students.
89. The chairman of the Shaanxi branch was Chen Tao, who worked in the Beijing Finance Ministry.
90. QGYD, 1: 94; FFSL, I: 95.
91. Thus the provincial Governor of Sichuan, through the efforts of the French consul in Chengdu, obtained an assurance from the Ministry of Industry in France that job openings would be created for Sichuanese students. Shu Xincheng, *Jindai Zhongguo liuxueshi*, pp. 90-1.
92. FFSL, 2.1: 28.
93. QGYD, 1: 301-2. See also *Liufa jianxue baogaoshu*, p. 90.
94. FFSL, 2.1: 65-158; QGYD, 1: 506-7, 518-9, 522-5, 528-9, 615-23, 679-83, 711-13 ,775-7, 790-1.
95. These figures are from the documents of the Sino-French Education Association and the Sino-French Committee of Support (*Comité Franco-Chinois de Patronnage*), now kept in the National Archives, Paris (hereafter cited as NA 47 AS). The lists of students were part of a report in November 1920. See NA 47 AS, A/2-1. For a guide to these documents, see G. Barman, N. Dulioust, *Etudiants-Ouvriers Chinois en France 1920-1940* (Paris, 1981) .
96. MAE, E-27-4. A distinction is often made in the documents between 'frugal study students' and 'work-study students' but in practice, as Zhou Enlai noted (FFSL, 1: 19), there was no difference between them since most of the former had little money and sought work as soon as they arrived in France. It might also be noted that the *precise* number of work-study students at any one time is difficult to arrive at since some of them (including Zhou Enlai) did not register with the Sino-French Education Association.
97. FFSL, 1: 86-7.
98. During the last years of the Qing the government ordered that no-one over the age of 20 was to study abroad. This was not only because it would be more difficult for them to learn foreign languages, the government maintained, but also because older students would 'corrupt' the younger ones with their 'undisciplined and pleasure-seeking natures'. Shu Xincheng, *Jindai Zhongguo liuxueshi*, p. 40.
99. Note also that the group of students who accompanied Sun Baoqi to France in 1902 mostly came from Jiangsu, Zhejiang, and Fujian. *Li Shizeng wenji*, 1: 69.
100. Shu Xincheng, *Jindai Zhongguo liuxueshi*, p. 134.

101. QGYD, 1: 65.
102. FFSL, 1: 85-7. 150 were from higher specialist schools, 10 from mining schools, 7 from medical schools, 10 from army colleges, 30 from schools in Japan, and 20 from overseas Chinese communities in south-east Asia. Details are also given for the previous occupations of 155 of these students. 60 had been teachers, 50 had been engineers, 10 journalists, 10 in politics, 9 military officials, 5 in banks, 4 in the book trade, 3 tradesmen, 2 hospital workers, and 2 in agriculture.
103. Boat fares were reduced from 200 *yuan* to 100 *yuan*. QGYD, 1: 208.
104. *Lü'ou jiaoyu yundong*, pp .75, 76-80 .
105. FFSL, 1: 184. For Cai Yuanpei's speech on the 'sanctity of labour' (*laodong shensheng*) see Gao Pingshu (ed.), *Cai Yuanpei jiaoyu wenxuan* (Beijing, 1980), p. 57; *Cai Yuanpei xiansheng quanji*, p. 523.
106. *Lü'ou jiaoyu yundong*, pp. 78-9.
107. *Lü'ou zazhi*, no. 4 (1 October 1916), *lunshuo*, pp. 1-7.
108. *Lü'ou zazhi*, no. 7 (15 November 1916); *Lü'ou zhoukan*, no. 4 (6 December 1919). See also Wang Jingwei's preface to Cai Yuanpei, *Huagong xuexiao jiangyi* (Tours, 1919), in which he argued that education would protect the Chinese workers' inherent virtue (*guyi zhi meide*) that is, their natural diligence and proclivity for cooperation .
109. *Huagong zazhi*, no. 39 (25 October 1919). Li referred approvingly to France where, he noted, even teachers and state functionaries were considered as 'workers' because they all belonged to trade unions.
110. *Lü'ou zazhi*, no. 1 (15 August 1916); no. 4 (1 October 1916); no. 5 (5 October 1916). A frontispiece picture of Benjamin Franklin in the opening issue of *Lü'ou zazhi* described him as a 'magnificent diligent worker and frugal study student'. Another educator described by Li Shizeng as a pioneer of work-study, and whom he claimed he met in Paris was the Spanish educator, Francisco Ferrer (1859-1909). Ferrer founded a school in Barcelona which propagated anarchist ideals and instructed its pupils in manual work. Ferrer later participated in the creation of the International League for a Rational Education of Children. See E. Chanel, *Pédagogie et Educateurs Socialistes* (Paris, 1975), pp. 38-42. For Li's article on Ferrer, see *Lü'ou zazhi*, no. 7 (15 November 1916).
111. *Lü'ou zazhi*, no. 8 (1 December 1916); no. 9 (15 December 1916); no. 10 (1 January 1917); no. 11 (15 January 1917); no. 12 (1 February 1917). On Charles Fourier (1772–1837), see D. Zeldin, *The Educational Ideas of Charles Fourier* (New York,1969), especially pp. 21-6, 32-3, 34,108-9.
112. *Lü'ou zhoukan*, no. 23 (17 April 1920).
113. *Huagong zazhi*, no. 18 (25 January 1918); no. 23 (25 June 1918); no. 39 (25 October 1919); no. 40 (25 November ,1919); *Huagong xunkan* , no. 3 (3 November 1920).
114. On the Beijing University public lecturing group, see *Wusi shiqidi shetuan* (Beijing, 1979), 2: 134-265. See also 'Beijing Daxue

pingmin jiaoyu jiangyan tuan' (The Beijing University Popular Education Lecturing Group), in *Jindaishi ziliao*, no. 2 (1955), pp. 124-60.

115. A. Dirlik, *The Origins of Chinese Communism* (Oxford, 1989) translates *gongdu huzhutuan* as 'labor-learning mutual aid groups' (p. 91). The Beijing group ran eating halls, washed clothes, and produced handicrafts while also attending university lectures. On these groups, see *Wusi shiqidi shetuan*, 2: 367-496; FFSL, 1: 277-343.
116. Numerous publications devoted to labour appeared during this period. They included *Laodong yin* (The Voice of Labour), *Laodongjie* (The Labouring World), and *Laodongzhe* (The Labourer). See *Wusi shiqi qikan jiesao* (Beijing, 1979), 2 .1: 61-85, 92-9, 167-9 .
117. FFSL, 2.1:246. Xu argued that work-study had been practised in China during ancient times and that those who laboured as well as studied were always looked up to and respected. *Xu Teli jiaoyu wenji* (Beijing, 1979), p. 256.
118. FFSL, 2.1: 212-38.
119. QGYD,1: 8; FFSL, 1: 84.
120. FFSL, 3: :47-53.
121. FFSL, 2 .1: 3, 6-7.
122. FFSL, 2.1: 51-2; He Changgong, *Qingong jianxue shenghuo huiyi*, pp. 8-11. See also Cai Hesen's letter to Luo Xuezan, in *Cai Hesen wenji* (Changsha, 1978), 2: 242 (reprinted in QGYD, 1: 142-3). Cai noted that the Overseas Chinese Workers Bureau gave up to 6 000 *yuan* to twenty-five of his comrades. Eighteen members of the society were to go to France and Mao Zedong saw off the first group in March 1919 before returning to Hunan. QGYD, 1: 141.
123. QGYD, 1: 136, 139, 716-7; He Changgong, *Qingong jianxue shenghuo huiyi*, p. 24.
124. FFSL, 3: 400, 402.
125. Li Huang, 'Liufa qingong jianxue yu Zhongguo gongchandang' (The Work-Study Movement in France and the Chinese Communist Party), *Mingbao yuekan*, no. 48 (December 1969), pp 27-8.
126. FFSL, 3: 448. It is interesting to note that Jiang was allowed to attend the preparatory school even though he had not graduated from middle school.
127. FFSL, 3: 449, 453.
128. QGYD, 1: 491.
129. See, for example, *Asie Française*, no. 159 (June 1914); *La Politique de Pékin*, no. 16 (21 April 1918).
130. *Archives Nationales: Section Outre Mer*, NF 269 (1).
131. 'La Réforme de l'Enseignement', *Le Temps* (September 1919), pp. 4-5.
132. *La Politique de Pékin*, no. 1 (4 January 1920). Note also a 1922 speech in the Chamber of Deputies by the socialist, Marius Moutet, in which he claimed that France had none of the imperialist 'vices' and therefore Chinese students chose to come to France . *La Politique de Pékin*, no. 5 (4 February 1923).
133. It is no coincidence that the work-study movement occurred at a

time when increased efforts were being made to popularise the study of the French language in China and to create French higher educational institutions there. For a more detailed discussion of this, see P. Bailey, 'The Sino-French Connection 1902-1928', in D. Goodman (ed.), *China and the West* (Forthcoming).
134. *L'Information* (4 January 1921). Chinese students themselves were not averse to exploiting this conviction. Thus an application by two work-study students in 1922 for a French government scholarship to study chemistry at Lyon University noted: 'Later, we shall always remember the kind hospitality and supreme generosity you have extended us. We shall thus carry with us to China the memory of your wonderful education and glorious culture and we shall enthusiastically work for the common interest of our two great countries.' MAE, E-541-3.
135. See Zhou Enlai's report in FFSL, 1: 6-11, 55 .
136. He Changgong, *Qingong jianxue shenghuo huiyi*, pp. 36, 48. He noted that he carried milk to market, emptied garbage, polished shoes, peeled potatoes, and worked on building sites.
137. See the personal account of one student in FFSL, 2.1: 302-3 .
138. FFSL, 1: 97.
139. Li Huang, 'Liufa qingong jianxue yu Zhongguo gongchandang', *Mingbao yuekan*, no. 46 (October 1969), p. 16.
140. FFSL, 2.1: 212-38. Wang arrived in France in December 1919 with 800 francs. After studying in Fontainebleau for four months he went to work at Saint Chamond.
141. FFSL, 2.1: 291-2.
142. *Jindaishi ziliao*, no. 2 (April 1955), pp. 182-3; FFSL, 1: 101.
143. FFSL, 3: 47-57. See also the comments of another student at Schneiders in Le Havre in FFSL, 2.1: 249-51.
144. FFSL, 2.1: 218, 220. Wang also recounts that he and his two friends met five Chinese workers from a nearby silk factory in a park, and that his two friends wanted to 'avoid' them.
145. FFSL, 3: 56. Note also He Changgong's surprise at French girls going out with blacks. *Qingong jianxue shenghuo huiyi*, p. 35 .
146. FFSL, 3: 107-16.
147. NA 47 AS B/6-2 (2).
148. *Lü'ou zazhi*, no. 24 (1 October 1917).
149. *Lü'ou zhoukan*, no. 1 (15 November 1919); no. 5 (13 December 1919).
150. *Lü'ou zhoukan*, no. 5 (13 December 1919); *Huagong zazhi*, no. 27 (25 October 1918).
151. *Jiaoyu gongbao*, no. 4 (April 1919), *jizai*, pp. 22-5 .
152. *Lü'ou zhoukan*, no. 8 (3 January 1920). See also a 1920 report on the 290 Chinese workers in the Dunkirk area which notes that workers sometimes chose teachers from amongst their own ranks. FFSL, 1: 258-60.
153. *Lü'ou zhoukan*, no. 10 (17 January 1920); no. 12 (31 January 1920).
154. *Huagong zazhi* no. 29 (25 December 1918).
155. *Huagong zazhi*, no. 17 (10 January 1918).

156. *Lü'ou zazhi*, no. 20 (15 July 1917).
157. DFZZ, 15: 6 (1919), pp. 54-60.
158. *Huagong zazhi*, no. 18 (25 January 1918); no. 20 (25 March 1918); no. 21 (25 April 1918); no. 22 (25 May 1918); no. 24 (25 July 1918). Other contributions included 881 francs from 35 workers in Boulogne and 688 francs from 190 workers at Alençon.
159. *Huagong zazhi*, no. 2 (25 January 1917); no. 3 (10 February 1917). Work-study promoters were confident that Chinese workers in France would prove superior to their compatriots in the United States or South-East Asia, who remained backward in their behaviour and were treated with contempt by their host country. *Huagong zazhi*, no. 39 (25 October 1919).
160. *Huagong zazhi*, no. 5 (10 April 1917).
161. 'Self-governing associations' were set up amongst Chinese workers at Montargis, Caen, Captieux, and Clermont Ferrand. *Lü'ou zhoukan*, no. 1 (15 November 1919); *Huagong zazhi*, no. 28 (25 November 1918); no. 35 (25 June 1919). Chinese workers in England set up similar organisations, such as the four hundred or so in Birmingham. *Huagong zazhi*, no. 21 (25 April 1918).
162. One such association punished two of its members for getting drunk by fining them one franc each. *Huagong zazhi*, no. 19 (25 February 1918)
163. See the article 'Xucai yu aiguo' (Saving Money and Patriotism), *Huagong xunkan* (15 February 1921). The article noted that workers could use their saved earnings to set up small businesses when they returned to China. A 1920 report on Chinese workers in Dunkirk noted, in fact, that some had been able to save up to 5 000 francs. FFSL, 1: 258-60.
164. AMI, F7 12900. The Prefect noted that the Association was no 'trouble' and that it was concerned mainly to procure work for those workers whose contracts had expired. For a Chinese account of the Association, see FFSL, 1: 266-71. This account claims that the membership was 4 000 and that the membership fee was 3 francs a month. It had over 50 branches, which all urged their members not to 'mix with prostitutes, gamble or drink'.
165. FFSL, 1: 13-4; 2.1: 399-400, 402-3. Chen Lu, the Chinese Minister to France, also warned Beijing that the growing numbers of impoverished Chinese students in the Paris region might harm China's reputation. FFSL, 2.1: 378.
166. For a report on the incident by the Paris Prefect of Police to the Ministry of the Interior on 4 March 1921, see AMI, F7 12900. For the recollections of Zhou Enlai and Li Lisan, see FFSL, 1: 27-30, 3: 435-9.
167. See, for example, Sheng Cheng, *Haiwai gongdu shinian jishi* (Shanghai, 1932), p. 54; Jiang Zimin's recollections in FFSL, 3: 454-8; He Changgong, *Qingong jianxue shenghuo huiyi*, pp. 38-41.
168. FFSL, 2 2: 459-66, 483-92, 493-504.
169. By 1920, for example, the French Minister in Beijing was advising the Foreign Ministry in Paris that all correspondence addressed to

Chinese residents in France be carefully scrutinised. Letter dated 21 June 1920 in AMI, F7 12900.
170. As early as 1919 Li Shizeng and Cai Yuanpei had met the Rector of Lyon University to discuss funding for such a project.
171. The Institute was to 'train a university and technical elite capable of directing China's development'.*La Politique de Pékin*, no. 3 (21 January 1923); 'L'Association Universitaire Franco-Chinoise', *Annales Franco-Chinoises*, no. 1 (March 1927), pp. 1-3.
172. FFSL, 2 .2 : 528-32, 537 .
173. Chinese accounts indicate that the Chinese Minister, Chen Lu, gave the students travelling expenses in the hope that their demonstration in Lyon would prompt the French authorities to take the initiative and deport them. FFSL, 1: 74; QGYD, 1: 24.
174. AMI, F7 12900. Amongst those deported were Cai Hesen, Li Lisan, Chen Yi, and Xiang Jingyu, all of whom were to become influential members of the CCP. FFSL, 2.2: 620-3, gives the names of 76 students who arrived in Shanghai at the end of 1921 after being deported from Marseille. Of these, 27 were from Hunan and 28 from Sichuan .
175. The Committee guaranteed the payment of tuition fees up to 15 May 1921. During the rest of the summer further subsidies were paid of up to 5 francs a day.
176. For the correspondence between the Committee and the various enterprises and schools, see NA 47 AS, A/1-2 (5); B/l-1 (2); B/6-10 (5); B/16-4 (5); C/4-3 (12); C/10-1 (1).
177. NA 47 AS, A/l-1 (3). The other co-chairman was Chen Lu.
178. QGYD, 1: 55-6. Zhou Enlai left in August 1924, while Deng Xiaoping left in January 1926.
179. AMI, F7 1348.
180. AMI, F7 12900. See also MAE, E-544-1sd.
181. *Le Matin* (25 June 1925). For a discussion of the 21 June incident, see N. Wang, 'Da Chen Lu: le Mouvement du 30 mai à Paris', *Appröches Asie* (Université de Nice, 1983).
182. See the reports by the President of the Commission at the Ministry of War (26 June1925) in AMI, F7 1348 and by the Ministry of Foreign Affairs (27 December 1926) in AMI, F7 13522 .
183. Report by the Ministry of the Interior (24 May 1927) in AMI, F7 1348.
184. It should be pointed out, however, that Chinese workers were not deterred from protesting about their working conditions if they felt suitably aggrieved. For one example, see *Lü'ou zhoukan*, no. 6 (20 December 1919), which refers to Chinese workers at a Montargis factory who wrote to the Ministry of War complaining of their treatment by the French foreman and demanding that he be replaced.
185. MAE, E-544-1. The authorities turned down all the Association's requests.
186. AMI, F7 13518.
187. The activities of the returned Chinese workers from France await

research. For a brief reference, see J. Chesneaux, *The Chinese Labor Movement 1917-1927* (Stanford, 1968), pp .138-40,160.
188. On social radicalism during the May Fourth Movement, see A. Dirlik, *The Origins of Chinese Communism* (Oxford, 1989). Even Li Dazhao, however, retained the assumption that the people needed to be 'reformed', arguing in 1918 that intellectuals had to enter the villages to 'enlighten' the peasants and help eliminate their superstitious beliefs. See his article 'Qingnian yu nongcun' (Youth and the Villages) in *Li Dazhao xuanji* (Beijing, 1978), pp. 146-50.

Conclusion

It is now generally recognised that political, social, economic, and cultural trends during the last years of the Qing represented the first important steps in China's route to modernisation. As a result many of the themes and developments hitherto identified solely with the May Fourth Movement in the late 1910s can be traced back to this period. The beginnings of a mass nationalism, new patterns of political thought and practice, the emergence of new social elites and an autonomous intelligentsia, the growing public role of an urbanised gentry, the appearance of an urban proletariat, and the critique of the Confucian tradition all have their origins in the late Qing.[1] Changes in attitudes towards popular education that began with the Qing promotion of general education after the turn of the century and culminated in the work-study movement in the early years of the republic are a crucial element in this process. Education, after all, had formed the very core of traditional Chinese culture. Changing perceptions of its role and content are therefore in the forefront of China's transition from Confucian empire to modern nation-state.

I have chosen to focus on both the last years of the Qing and early years of the Republic since there was much continuity in educational thought and personnel that spanned the political change of 1911. By also looking at how some of the ideas raised in the educational debate worked out in actual practice during the early Republic, when the Chinese polity was entering a period of disintegration, I hope to have shown an essential continuity in this aspect of China's modernisation process.[2] A number of significant points emerge from this study of educational thought in the early years of the twentieth century.

First, interest in popular education clearly predated the May Fourth Movement, which specifically referred to student demonstrations on 4 May 1919 against government corruption and the treatment of China by the allied powers at the Versailles Peace Conference, but which in a wider sense referred to the campaign by Chinese intellectuals to regenerate Chinese society and culture. The promotion of popular education by Qing officials and educators after 1900 began with the aim of consolidating the position of the monarchy and ensuring social stability. Later, influenced by the concept of 'social education' imported from Japan and convinced that western strength now lay in the quality of its peoples, Chinese educators focused on the active 'reform' of the lower classes. Decadent and immoral customs had to be eliminated and the people trained to become hard-working, self-sufficient, frugal, and public-minded citizens before China could hope to survive in the international arena. The urgency with which some Chinese educators and reformers (from Kang Youwei to Li Shizeng) called for the reform of the people was heightened by their acute sense of the contempt they assumed westerners had for the 'backwardness' of China's popular culture.

Second, since one of the aims of popular education was now to make the people economically productive, an increasing emphasis was placed on the importance of vocational training. This, in turn, led to changes in attitudes towards manual labour, a process that began with the introduction of handicrafts in the primary school curriculum in 1904 to acquaint students with 'productive work' and the 'habits of labour' and which reached full fruition during the work-study movement when labour was bestowed with moral qualities. The championing of labour by radical Chinese intellectuals during the May Fourth Movement, symbolised by the frequently cited slogan 'the sacredness of labour' (*laodong shensheng*), was not simply due to the influence of the Bolshevik Revolution,[3] but was rather the culmination of trends set in motion at the end of the Qing.

Third, it has often been assumed that Japan provided the educational model for Chinese educators during the last years of the Qing, while after 1912 the Anglo-American model became more significant. It is, in fact, difficult to speak of any one educational model exerting influence at any one time. An analysis of the Chinese educational press and educational thought in this period reveals that while Japan remained a frequently cited model, other countries provided inspiration. The work-study promoters, for example, looked to France as the embodiment of republican education. Perhaps the most interesting example is that of Germany, whose education system was enthusiastically described by Chinese educators in the late Qing[4] and throughout the early years of the republic. This was principally because education in Germany was seen to have contributed to national wealth and strength, but it was also a reflection of the fact that many of Germany's educational strategies and concerns seemed relevant to China's situation.

Much interest, for example, was shown by late Qing educators in both Prussia's promotion of 'citizen education' after 1806 to stimulate nationalism and purge the country of its 'national shame' in the wake of Napoleon's invasion[5] and in Germany's attempts in the late nineteenth and early twentieth centuries to implement compulsory vocational education for primary-school leavers. There was also considerable sympathy for German educators' criticisms of the excessive teaching of Greek and Latin in secondary schools because of their fear that students might become 'denationalised' (comparable to Chinese educators' concern over the excessive teaching of English in modern schools). During the early Republic, Chinese educators also followed with interest the debate in Germany over the potential threat to national identity and prosperity that would come with the 'invasion' of Anglo-American ideas of freedom and libertarianism. Articles in the Chinese educational press noted the concern by German educators that such ideas would undermine the sense of discipline and public duty so carefully inculcated in the schools.[6]

Even during the First World War, when allied propaganda in China painted an unflattering picture of German culture, positive accounts of German education continued to appear in the educational press. Articles described German education as the most developed in the world and Germany as the 'centre of world culture'.[7] In 1915 Germany's system of general education was contrasted favourably with that of England where, it was claimed, the school system accentuated class differences instead of producing a united citizenry.[8] The educational philosophy of Georg Kerschensteiner was discussed and praised by Chinese educators throughout this period; in their view Kerschensteiner had successfully wedded a more vocationally-oriented education with one that emphasised concern for the collectivity and state.[9] After 1918, when the ideas of John Dewey and the American model were being promoted by some Chinese educators, interest in Germany's situation and progress persisted. Articles described Germany's transition from a monarchy to a republic and how this affected education.[10] The fact that Chinese educators often looked to France and Germany for their inspiration provides a much-needed corrective to the undue emphasis on the importance of the Anglo-American model in accounts of Chinese education after 1912.

Fourth, an analysis of Chinese educational thought in the early years of the twentieth century shows that western influence is much more ambiguous than has hitherto been supposed. Previous works have described the western impact on Chinese education in terms of its 'democratic' influence, associated usually with the theories of John Dewey.[11] Yet Chinese educators during this period looked to quite different aspects of western educational practice. Centralisation, uniformity, strict supervision of textbooks, the inculcation of patriotic ideals, and the efficient surveillance of popular culture were all hailed by Chinese educators as crucial factors contributing to western strength. All Chinese educators, whether progressive or conservative, admired what they saw as the paternalistic aspect of popular education in the West, ensuring that the people were law-abiding, hard-working, patriotic, and well-behaved citizens. It is precisely these aspects of western educational practice that are emphasised in the recent 'revisionist' approach to educational history in the West, which sees the development of formal school systems more in terms of elite attempts to discipline and control the populace rather than in terms of democratic ideals.[12]

Fifth, a common assumption underpinned all educational discussion during this period. Whether the aim was to instil loyalty to the dynasty, create a united and patriotic citizenry, train an economically productive workforce, or raise the social and cultural level of the lower classes, everyone shared a boundless, almost naïve, faith in the power of education to bring about the desired aim. The ultimate expression of this faith was the assumption by many that widespread education would eliminate classes in society by, as Chinese educators often put it, breaking down the divisions between 'rich and poor' and 'the knowledgeable and the foolish'. Such faith owed as much to Confucian notions of education as it did to perceived causes of western superiority.[13]

After 1920, as anarchists and communists finally split over the relative merits of cultural versus social revolution, and those who championed Bolshevik ideology and organisation won out over their other socialist rivals (symbolised by the creation of the Chinese Communist Party in 1921),[14] a less idealistic approach to education increasingly took hold. This culminated in the first systematic analysis of education by a Chinese Marxist in 1929-30. Yang Xianzhang (1895-1931), a school teacher and administrator, joined the CCP in 1923 and helped edit its journal *Zhongguo qingnian* (Chinese Youth)[15]. Fiercely critical of all forms of education divorced from radical political and social movements, Yang published *Jiaoyushi ABC* (An ABC of Educational History) in 1929 and *Xin jiaoyu dagang* (An Outline of the New Education) in 1930,[16] in which he poured scorn on the idea of education as a panacea, summed up in the frequently cited slogan 'education can do everything' (*jiaoyu wanneng lun*).[17] Without political or social change, he argued, formal and popular education were merely ploys to maintain the status quo and train a submissive working class.[18]

Although Yang Xianzhang, as China's first Marxist educational thinker, deserves further study, the long-term significance of the educational issues and dilemmas discussed in the late Qing and early Republic cannot be underestimated. Previous studies of Chinese education after 1949 have tended to provide a brief description of traditional Confucian education before proceeding directly to Marxist educational thought in general which serves, in turn, as the background for post-1949 developments in China. Yet it was precisely in the early years of the twentieth century that Chinese educators first confronted issues that were to have continuing relevance in the People's Republic after 1949.

The disagreement that emerged in the 1950s between Mao, who favoured a wide network of spare-time schools (particularly in the rural areas) and his colleagues Liu Shaoqi and Deng Xiaoping, who preferred to see a concentration of resources on a more restricted and formal school system echoed, for example, the debate in the early twentieth century when the advocates of literacy, half-day and supplementary schools criticised the excessive preoccupation with creating a well-endowed and over-formalised school system.[19] It is also significant that one of the most serious 'crimes' Liu Shaoqi was charged with during the Cultural Revolution was that he favoured a double-track system in which the children of cadres and officials would attend full-time, academically superior schools, while the children of workers and peasants would remain in inferior spare-time schools.[20] There is a striking parallel here with Chinese educators' rejection of Yuan Shikai's dual-track scheme in 1915. The debate continues to this day as some educators have voiced concern over Deng Xiaoping's educational strategy, which seeks to create a small elite sector comprising 'keypoint' secondary schools and universities (to train scientists and engineers) while consigning the majority of the school-age population to a mass sector which offers basic literacy and vocational skills.[21] The problem of how to balance the demands for 'popularisation' (*puji*) with the 'raising of standards' (*tigao*), first confronted at the turn of the century when officials and educators argued the merits of either 'education for talent' (*rencai jiaoyu*) or 'general education' (*putong jiaoyu*), is still very much on the educational agenda in contemporary China.

Another prevalent contemporary concern is the fear of party propagandists that Deng Xiaoping's economic reforms, which have encouraged entrepreneurship and profitmaking, have had an adverse affect on the morals of cadres and people alike. In the countryside reforms have led to the virtual dismantling of the commune and to individual peasant households leasing land from the collective. A greater proportion of their crops can now be sold on a free market and official campaigns have encouraged peasants to get rich.[22] In the cities greater autonomy has been given to economic enterprises and the stress put on greater profitability. Some have argued that in the process socialist ideals and concern for the collective good have been sacrificed in the name of greater competition and individual prosperity.[23] Once again this fear echoes the debate in the early Republic when some Chinese educators argued that excessive promotion of vocational training as a means to improve individual livelihood would lead to selfishness, competition, and neglect of collective welfare.

Thirdly, when Mao during the Cultural Revolution belittled formal school education and academic instruction, condemned examinations, and stressed practical learning,[24] how much was he echoing the views of Chinese educators during the late Qing and early republic, who had criticised the modern schools for fostering elitism and disdain for manual labour? Mao's hostility towards 'bookish' intellectuals, in fact, rather than being a 'leftist' aberration as some have thought, owes much to the approach adopted by work-study promoters like Li Shizeng and Wu Zhihui, who had condemned intellectuals for their bookish learning and inability to understand the labouring world.

Finally, the campaign begun by Chinese educators at the turn of the century to reform the people by eliminating decadent customs and improving behaviour heralded an obsession that has continued to occupy the minds of Chinese political and intellectual elites throughout the twentieth century. Chiang Kai-shek, for example, launched the New Life Movement in 1934 to 'reform' the Chinese people. Arguing (as had Chinese officials and educators after 1900) that Japan and Germany derived their strength from the quality of their peoples, Chiang insisted that inculcation of Confucian ethics and Prussian-style militarism would make the people more disciplined, hardworking, frugal and hygienic.[25] Echoing the approach taken by work-study promoters in the 1910s, Chiang issued a host of rules and regulations to govern every aspect of behaviour. These included exhortations not to make noises while eating, not to crowd and shove in public places, and not to spit or urinate in public, as well as reminders that people had to respect public property, cut down on wasteful expenditures, and be punctual at all times.

The various campaigns to promote 'socialist spiritual civilisation' which have accompanied Deng Xiaoping's economic reforms since 1978,[26] while aimed primarily at warding off what party propagandists see as the potentially harmful effects of 'bourgeois liberalism' and 'spiritual pollution' (both identified with western political and cultural values) have also attempted to 'reform' the people's customs and behaviour, in terms that would have been familiar to early-twentieth-century educators and officials. People have been harangued for their lack of hygiene (e.g. spitting in public), lack of politeness and decorum (e.g. pushing and shoving in queues) and their failure to respect public property.[27] All this, it was argued in the 1980s, made the Chinese appear 'uncivilised' to the outside world at a time when increasing numbers of foreigners were visiting China. At the same time, the increased standard of living in some of the rural areas has led to a revival of traditional practices such as extravagant weddings and funerals. Echoing Chinese educators in the early twentieth century, the official press has repeatedly condemned such practices as backward and unseemly for a nation embarked on modernisation. *Plus ça change*. Clearly, it is only when full account is taken of the educational debate in the early twentieth century that China's path to modernisation can begin to be seen in a wider perspective.

NOTES

1. The first to stress the long-term significance of political, social and economic developments in the late Qing was M. Wright, 'Introduction: The Rising Tide of Change' in M. Wright (ed.), *China in Revolution: The First Phase 1900-1913* (New Haven, 1968), pp. 1-63. See also M. Bastid, *L'Evolution de la Société Chinoise à la Fin de la Dynastie des Qing 1873-1911* (Paris, 1979) for an analysis of social trends in this period, particularly changes in the composition of the elite and the emergence of an urban proletariat. M. Rankin, *Elite Activism and Political Transformation in China* (Standford, 1986) and R. K. Schoppa, *Chinese Elites and Political Change* (Cambridge, Mass., 1982) chart the growing public role of an urbanised gentry in the province of Zhejiang. E. Fung, *The Military Dimension of the Chinese Revolution* (Vancouver, 1980) analyses the development of a new military class and changing attitudes towards the military. J. Fincher, *Chinese Democracy* (New York, 1981) looks at constitutionalism in the late Qing, while Hao Chang, *Liang Ch'i-ch'ao and Intellectual Transition in China 1890-1907* (Cambridge, Mass., 1971) traces the long-term significance of Liang Qichao's political thought. Finally,

the late Qing origins of literary reform are discussed in M. Dolezelova-Velingerova, 'The Origins of Modern Chinese Literature' in M. Goldman (ed.), *Modern Chinese Literature in the May Fourth Era* (Cambridge, Mass., 1977).
2. For a stimulating discussion of the need for intellectual and social historians to see their work as complementary rather than separate, see L. Kramer, 'Intellectual History and Reality: The Search For Connections', *Historical Reflections/Réflexions Historiques* 13: 2/3 (1986), pp. 517-45. By attempting to show how ideas on education were worked out in practice, my approach tends towards a methodology that stresses the social history of ideas. Clearly, however, given the paucity of reliable data on a nationwide scale, much more extensive and painstaking research will have to be done in local gazetteers before one can begin to draw a more detailed picture of educational developments at the local level (funding, availability and distribution of schools) which characterise the sophisticated studies being done in, for example, France. See W. Frijhoff, *Ecole et Société dans l'Ancien Régime* (Paris, 1975); F. Furet, J. Ozouf, *Lire et Ecrire: l'Alphabétisation des Français de Calvin à Jules Ferry* (Paris, 1977).
3. For an example of this view, see Ding Shouhe, *Shiye geming dui Zhongguo de yingxiang* (Beijing, 1957), pp. 134-5.
4. The first issue of *Dongfang zazhi* in 1904 published an advertisement by the Commercial Press of a book recently translated from the Japanese on the German school system. The Commercial Press observed that since German scholarship was the most developed it followed that the country's education system was superior and should, therefore, be a suitable model for China. Articles on the German school system appeared in *Xuebu guanbao*, no. 13 (1907), *xiguo xiaoxue jiyao*, pp. 19-22; no. 18 (1907), *deyizhi jiaoyu*, pp. 1-10; no. 19 (1907), *deyizhi jiaoyu*, pp. 11-18.
5. A Hunanese student later recalled how he and his classmates in the early years of the Republic hoped to make Hunan another Prussia and lead the way in building a united and strong China. Lai Jinghu, 'Minchu shidai de Hunan qingnian' (Hunan Youth in the Early Republic), *Zhuanji wenxue*, 16: 3 (March 1970), p. 39.
6. JYZZ 7: 5 (1915), *yilun*, pp. 53-4.
7. *Jingshi jiaoyubao*, no. 22 (1915), *zhuanshu*, pp. 19-30; no. 40 (1917), *yishu*, pp. 1-8.
8. JYZZ, 7: 15 (1915), *yilun*, pp. 50-2. The stress on the unified German system is common in most articles at this time, despite the fact that Germany had a dual-track system. Yuan Shikai, of course, referred to the dual-track system in Germany when he proposed to create elite preparatory schools.
9. German universities also attracted much attention. More articles were written or translated in this period on the German university system than that of any other country. For example, the journal published by the Education Ministry, *Jiaoyubu bianzuanchu yuekan* (Monthly Journal of the Ministry's Compilation Bureau) featured

articles on the organisation, administration, courses, and research at German universities in nine out of the first ten issues in 1913.
10. *Jiaoyu*, no. 6 (1920), *cizong*, pp. 20-3; JYZZ, 10: 8 (1918), *diaocha*, pp. 33-7; 10: 9 (1918), *diaocha*, pp. 39-41; 11: 5 (1919), *diaocha*, pp. 27-30. See also the article on the reform of Prussia's education system by Tao Zhixing, in *Xin jiaoyu*, 1: 2 (1919), pp. 125-9. For a recent study of economic and cultural relations between China and Germany during the 1920s and 1930s, see W. Kirby, *Germany and Republican China* (Stanford, 1984).
11. See, for example, B. Keenan, *The Dewey Experiment in China* (Cambridge, Mass., 1977). In a wider sense, other scholars have argued that Chinese reformers advocated change 'in terms of western democratic and scientific ideas and values'. Lin Yu-sheng, *The Crisis of Chinese Consciousness* (Madison, 1982), p. 11.
12. Mary Jo Maynes, *Schooling in Western Europe* (Albany, 1985). Nowhere has this revisionist approach been more in evidence than in the United States where, as one scholar remarks, 'public schooling is seen, not as the product of democracy, humanitarianism, and nationalism, but of class interest and the fear of disruption'. C. Kaestle, 'Between the Scylla of Brutal Ignorance and the Charybdis of a Literary Education: Elite Attitudes Toward Mass Schooling in Early Industrial England and America', p. 177.
13. A study of reformist thought in general from the 1890s to the May Fourth Movement makes a parallel point in stressing the indigenous sources of inspiration in the intellectual content of reform. See C. Furth, 'Intellectual Change: From The Reform Movement to the May Fourth Movement 1895-1920' in J. Fairbank (ed.), *The Cambridge History of China*, vol. 12 (Cambridge, 1983), pp. 322-405. Furth argues that reformers like Kang Youwei, Tan Sitong, and Liang Qichao were able to draw on traditional utopian thought to produce a new 'evolutionary cosmology' that underpinned a faith in world historical progress. The West served not only as a model but also as a repository for ideal images projected out of the historical imagination of the Chinese themselves.
14. For a brilliant new study of the origins of Chinese communism, which seeks to highlight the importance of anarchism and other non-Marxist socialisms during the May Fourth Movement, see A. Dirlik, *The Origins of Chinese Communism* (Oxford, 1989).
15. For information on Yang Xianzhang, see Luo Bingzhi, *Zhongguo jindai jiaoyujia* (Wuhan, 1958), pp. 169-88; Saitō Akio, *Chūgoku Gendai Kyōiku Shi* (Tokyo, 1962), pp. 148-9; Pan Maoyuan, 'Yang Xianzhang jiaoyu sixiang' (Yang Xianzhang's Educational Thought), *Xiamen Daxue xuebao*, no. 1 (1954), pp. 127-39. Yang died of TB in Tokyo, in 1931.
16. *Jiaoyushi ABC* went through four reprints by 1931, while *Xin jiaoyu dagang* had gone through three reprints by 1937. Some schools apparently used them as texts. Pan Maoyuan, 'Yang Xianzhang jiaoyu sixiang jianjie' (A Brief Introduction to Yang Xianzhang's Educational Thought) in Yang Xianzhang, *Xin jiaoyu dagang* (repr.

Beijing, 1961), p. 167.
17. For an example of the kind of view Yang was criticising, see Jia Dianzhi, 'Jiaoyu wanneng shuo' (Education Can Achieve Anything), JYZZ, 6: 1 (1914), *yanlun*, pp. 18-25.
18. Excerpts from *Xin jiaoyu dagang* appear in JYZZ under Yang's penname Li Yi. The fact that Yang's writings could appear in this moderate journal devoted to education and that Shu Xincheng could cite Yang approvingly in one of his works indicates a widespread disillusionment with education. Shu Xincheng, *Zhongguo jindai jiaoyushi gaoxuan cun* (Shanghai, 1936), p. 179.
19. For general accounts of education after 1949, see T. Chen, *The Maoist Educational Revolution* (New York, 1974); J. Hawkins, *Mao Tse-tung and Education* (Hamden, Conn., 1974); T. Chen, *Chinese Education Since 1949* (New York, 1981). A wide variety of part-time schools and educational programmes were created during the Great Leap as part of Mao's attempt to reduce the need for specialized universities and schools in the cities. Significantly, most of them were closed down when Liu Shaoqi and Deng Xiaoping assumed greater control of party and government affairs after 1960. By 1964 state-run primary and secondary schools comprised the majority of remaining rural schools and these were generally located in the commune market towns and county capitals. M. Meisner, *Mao's China* (New York, 1977), pp. 238-84; J. Unger, *Education Under Mao* (New York, 1982), pp. 50-2.
20. See 'Chronology of the Two-Road Struggle on the Educational Front in the Past Seventeen Years' in P. Seybolt (ed.), *Revolutionary Education in China: Documents and Commentary* (New York, 1973), pp. 53-4. In 1964 Liu Shaoqi favoured the revival of agricultural half-work half-study secondary schools but complaints were later made that they were substandard and that it was virtually impossible for the students to pass the entrance examinations for senior high schools or universities. In the urban areas a network of schools with a shortened ten-year curriculum coexisted in the early 1960s with a system of more well-endowed regular schools. J. Unger, *Education Under Mao*, pp. 55-9.
21. On recent educational reforms, see S. Pepper, 'Chinese Education After Mao: Two Steps Forward, Two Steps Back and Begin Again?', *China Quarterly*, no. 81 (March 1980), pp. 1-65; M. Bastid, 'Chinese Educational Policies in the 1980s and Economic Development', *China Quarterly*, no. 98 (June 1984), pp. 189-219; S. Rosen, 'Recentralization, Decentralization, and Rationalization: Deng Xiaoping's Bifurcated Educational Policy', *Modern China*, 11: 3 (July, 1985), pp. 301-46.
22. For a general account of Deng Xiaoping's reforms, see H. Harding, *China's Second Revolution: Reform After Mao* (Washington, 1987). On the changing peasant economy, see E. Croll, 'The New Peasant Economy in China' in S. Feuchtwang, A. Hussain, T. Pairault (eds.) *Transforming China's Economy in the Eighties*, vol. 1 (London, 1988), pp. 77-100.

23. Disquiet over campaigns to encourage peasants to get rich compelled the *People's Daily* to insist in December 1983 that it was wrong to equate the rich peasant campaign with bourgeois egoistic ideology, which had 'nothing in common with the peasant's mentality of becoming well-off through hard work'. See J. Burns, S. Rosen (eds.), *Policy Conflicts in Post-Mao China* (New York, 1986), p. 261. See also *ibid.*, pp. 57-8, 68-70, for examples of the contemporary debate over the danger posed by selfish individualism to the continuing adherence to collective values. A recent study has also argued that the fundamental contradiction between the encouraging of individual competition and the fostering of socialist ideals of co-operation was built into the school system itself during the 1950s and early 1960s. S. Shirk, *Competitive Comrades* (Berkeley, 1982).
24. T. Chen, *Chinese Education Since 1949*, p. 4.
25. On the New Life Movement, see A. Dirlik, 'The Ideological Foundations of the New Life Movement', *Journal of Asian Studies*, 34: 4 (August 1975), pp. 945-80; S. Chu, 'The New Life Movement Before the Sino-Japanese Conflict: A Reflection of KMT Limitations in Thought and Action' in G. Chan (ed.), *China At The Crossroads: Nationalists and Communists 1927-1949* (Boulder, 1980), pp. 37-68; W. Kirby, *Germany and Republican China*, pp. 176-85.
26. See H. Harding, *China's Second Revolution*, pp. 187-200.
27. On one such campaign, see A. Dirlik, 'Spiritual Solutions to Material Problems: The Socialist Ethics and Courtesy Month in China', *The South Atlantic Quarterly*, 81: 4 (1982), pp. 359-75.

Bibliography

Archival Sources (French)
ARCHIVES NATIONALES:
Ministère du l'Intérieur, F7 12900, F7 1348, F7 13518, F7 13522.
Section Outre-Mer, NF269.
47As (Étudiants-Ouvriers en France).
ARCHIVES DU MINISTÈRE DES AFFAIRES ÉTRANGÈRES:
Série E: Asie 1918-1929 (Chine).

Works in Chinese and Japanese.
Abe Hiroshi, 'Shinmatsu no kindai gakkō, kōsei-shō o chūshin ni' (Modern schools at the end of the Qing, based on Jiangxi province), *Rekishi Hyōron* (Historical Criticism), no. 1 (January 1965), no. 3 (March 1965).
Abe Yō, 'Ryō kei-chō no kyōiku shisō to sono katsudo' (Liang Qichao's educational thought and activities), *Kyūshu Daigaku Kyōiku Kiyō* (Educational Bulletin of Kyūshu University), no. 6 (1959).
Anhui jiaoyu yuekan (Anhui Education Monthly), 1918-19.
Anhui suhua bao (Anhui Vernacular Journal), 1904.
Bai Jiao, 'Shijie dazhanzhong zhi Huagong' (Chinese workers during the First World War), *Renwen yuekan* (Humanities Monthly), 8: 1 (1937).
Banno Masataka, 'Furansu ryūgaku jidai no Ba Kenkyu' (Ma Jianzhong in France), *Kokka Gakkai Zasshi* (National Society Journal), no. 5 (Aug. 1971).
Beijing Daxue Lishixi, *Beijing daxue xuesheng yundong shi* (A history of the Beijing University students' movement). Beijing, 1979.
Cai Hesen, *Cai Hesen wenji* (Collected writings of Cai Hesen). 2 vols. Changsha, 1978.
Cai Yuanpei, *Cai Yuanpei xiansheng quanji* (Complete works of Cai Yuanpei). Taibei, 1969.
Cai Yuanpei, *Cai Yuanpei xuanji* (Selected works of Cai Yuanpei). Hong Kong, n.d.
Cai Yuanpei, *Cai Yuanpei zishu* (Autobiography of Cai Yuanpei). Taibei, 1967.
Cai Yuanpei, *Huagong xuexiao jiangyi* (Teaching materials for the Chinese workers school). Tours, 1919.
Cai Yuanpei et. al., *Wanqing sanshiwunian lai zhi Zhongguo jiaoyu* (Chinese education in the thirty-five years since the end of the Qing). Hong Kong 1969.
Chen Baoquan, *Tuisi zhai wencun* (Writings from the withdrawn thinker's studio). 2 vols. Taibei, 1971.
Chen Baoquan, *Zhongguo jindai xuezhi bianqian shi* (A history of changes in China's recent education system). Beijing, 1927.
Chen Guofu, *Zhongguo jiaoyu gaige zhi tujing* (The route of China's educational change). Shanghai, 1947.
Chen Jingpan, *Zhongguo jindai jiaoyushi* (A history of China's modern education). Beijing, 1979.
Chen Qingzhi, *Zhongguo jiaoyushi* (A history of Chinese education). Shanghai, 1936.

Chen Qitian, *Zuijin sanshinian Zhongguo jiaoyushi* (A history of Chinese education in the last thirty years). Shanghai, 1930.
Chen Rong'gun, *Chen Zibao xiansheng jiaoyu yiyi* (Bequeathed educational views of Chen Zibao). Guangzhou, 1952.
Chen Sanjing, *Huagong yu Ouzhan* (Chinese workers and the First World War). Taibei, 1986.
Chen Sanjing (comp.), *Qingong jianxue yundong* (The work-study movement). Taibei, 1981.
Chen Xinxian et. al. (ed.), *Hu Zhimo ziliao* (Historical materials on Hu Zhimo). Changsha, 1981.
Chen Yuanhui, *Zhongguo xiandai jiaoyushi* (A history of China's modern education). Beijing, 1979.
Cheng Benhai, *Xiangcun shifan jingyantan* (Experiences at a rural normal school). Shanghai, 1939.
Cheng Jihua, *Zhongguo dianying fazhan shi* (A history of the development of Chinese cinema). 2 vols. Beijing, 1963.
Cihai: jiaoyu xinli fen'ce (Dictionary of education and psychology). Shanghai, 1980.
Da Qing Dezong jing huangdi shilu (Veritable records of the Qing dynasty, Guangxu reign). Taibei, 1964.
Datong baihua bao (The Great Commonwealth Vernacular Journal). Shanghai, 1908-9.
Dongfang zazhi (The Eastern Miscellany). Shanghai, 1904-19.
Donghua lu (Donghua records). Guangxu reign. 10 vols. Taibei, 1963.
Ding Shouhe et. al. *Cong wusi qimeng yundong dao makesi zhuyi de chuanbo* (From the enlightenment movement of May Fourth to the propagation of Marxism). Beijing, 1979.
Ding Shouhe et al. *Shiye geming dui Zhongguo geming de yingxiang* (The influence of the October Revolution on the Chinese revolution). Beijing, 1957.
Ding Zhipin, *Zhongguo jin qishinian lai jiaoyu jishi* (A record of education in the last seventy years). Taibei, 1961.
Diyici Zhongguo jiaoyu nianjian (The first China education yearbook). 5 vols. Taibei, 1971.
Du Zuozhou, *Jinbainian lai zhi Zhongguo jiaoyu* (China's education in the last one hundred years). Taibei, 1969.
Fang Hao, 'Ma Xiangbo xiansheng choushe hanxiakao wenfan shimo' (The history of Ma Xiangbo's proposal to establish a research academy), in *Fang Hao liushi ziding gao* (Fang Hao's collected works), vol. 1. Taibei, 1970.
Feng Ziyou, *Geming yishi* (An unofficial history of the revolution). 5 vols. Taibei, 1970.
Fu Baozhen, *Minzhong jiaoyu yanjiu yu pinglun* (Studies and evaluation of mass education). Beijing, 1932.
Fufa qingong jianxue yundong shiliao (Historical materials on the Work-Study Movement in France). 3 vols. Beijing, 1979-81.
Gaimushō (comp.), *Chūka minkoku kyōiku sono ta no shiretsu gaiyō* (Summary of educational measures in the Chinese Republic). Tokyo, 1931.
Gan Cao, *Xiangcun jiaoyu* (Rural education). Shanghai, 1939.
Gao Pingshu (comp.), *Cai Yuanpei jiaoyu wenxuan* (Selected essays of Cai Yuanpei on education). Beijing, 1980.
Ge Gongzhen, *Zhongguo baoxue shi* (A history of Chinese journalism). Hong Kong, 1964.

Geming wenxian (Documents on the revolution). 61 vols. Taibei, 1953-.
Gongde jianghua (Lectures on civic morality). Beijing, n.d.
Gu Mingyuan et. al., Lu Xun de jiaoyu sixiang he shijian (Lu Xun's educational thought and practice). Beijing, 1981.
Gu Xuhou, Pingmin jiaoyu shishi fa (Ways to carry out popular education). Shanghai, 1925.
Guangdong jiaoyu tongji tubiao (Statistical charts on education in Guangdong). Guangzhou, 1918.
Guizhou jiaoyu guanbao (Guizhou Educational Bulletin). 1907.
Guo Moruo, Moruo Zizhuan (Autobiography of Guo Moruo). 2 vols. Hong Kong, 1978.
Hangzhou baihua bao (Hangzhou Vernacular Journal). 1901-4.
Hashikawa Tokio, Chūgoku bunkakai jimbutsu sōkan (Biographical dictionary of Chinese cultural figures). Beijing, 1940.
He Changgong, Qingong jianxue shenghuo huiyi (Memories of work-study life). Beijing, 1958.
Hu Shengwu, Jin Chongji, 'Sun Zhongshan zai linshi zhengfu shiqi de douzheng' (Sun Yatsen's struggles at the time of the provisional government), in Xinhai geming lunwenji (Collection of essays on the 1911 Revolution). Guangzhou, 1980.
Huagong xunkan (Chinese Worker Fortnightly). Paris, 1920.
Huagong zazhi (Chinese Worker Magazine). Paris, 1917-20.
Huang Fuqing, Qingmo liuri xuesheng (Chinese students in Japan at the end of the Qing). Taibei, 1975.
Huang Yanpei, Huang Yanpei kaocha jiaoyu riji (Huang Yanpei's diary concerning an investigation of education). 2 vols. Shanghai, 1914-15.
Huang Yanpei, 'Qingji gesheng xingxue shi' (An account of the promotion of education in each province at the end of the Qing), Renwen yuekan (Humanities Monthly), 1: 7 (Sept. 1930).
Huang Yanpei, 'Zhongguo ershiwu nianjian quanguo jiaoyu tongji de zong jiancha' (General overview of China's educational statistics in the last twenty-five years), Renwen yuekan (Humanities Monthly), 4: 5 (June 1933).
Huang Yanpei, Zhongguo jiaoyu shiyao (A concise history of Chinese education). Shanghai, 1930.
Huang Zunxian, 'Riben guozhi wenxue shi' (A record of Japan and its literature), Jindaishi ziliao (Historical Materials on Modern History), no. 2 (1963).
Hubei xueshengjie (Hubei Students' World), Tokyo, 1903.
Huo Yiping, 'Lun Cai Yuanpei zai Zhongguo jindaihua jiaoyushang de diwei' (A discussion of Cai Yuanpei's position in the modernization of Chinese education), Renmin jiaoyu (People's Education), no. 2 (1980).
Igarashi Shōichi, Chūgoku kinsei kyōikushi no kenkyū (Studies in recent Chinese educational history). Tokyo, 1979.
Jia Dianzhi, Shicha jiaoyu shijie yizhou ji (A record of a week's education in the world). Shanghai, 1921.
Jia Shiyi, Minguo caizheng shi (A financial history of the Republic). 2 vols. Shanghai, 1917.
Jian Bocan (comp.), Wuxu bianfa (The 1898 reforms). 4 vols. Shanghai, 1953.
Jiang Jianbai, Zhongguo shehui jiaoyu xingzheng (The administration of social education in China). Shanghai, 1937.

Jiang Menglin, *Guodu shidai zhi sixiang yu jiaoyu* (Thought and education in a period of transition). Taibei, 1963.
Jiang Menglin, *Xichao* (Tides from the West). Taibei, 1974.
Jiang Shuge, *Zhongguo jindai jiaoyu zhidu* (China's modern education system). Shanghai, 1934.
Jiang Weiqiao, *Jiangsu jiaoyu xingzheng gaikuang* (General situation of Jiangsu's educational administration). Shanghai, 1924.
Jiang Weiqiao, 'Minguo jiaoyubu chushe shi zhi zhuangkuang' (The situation of the Republican Education Ministry at the time of its initial organization), *Zhuanji wenxue* (Biographical Literature), 32: 1 (January 1978).
Jiang Zhuocheng, *Daode jiaoyulun* (A discussion of moral education). Shanghai, 1925.
Jiangning xuewu zazhi (Journal of Jiangning Education). Nanjing, 1907.
Jiangsu (Jiangsu Journal). Shanghai, 1903-4.
Jiangsu jiaoyu gailan (A survey of education in Jiangsu). 2 vols. Taibei, 1971.
Jiangsu sheng jiaoyutuan gongyoulin baogaoshu (Report of the Jiangsu Education Corps on public forests). Shanghai, 1916.
Jiaoyu (Education). Beijing, 1919-20.
Jiaoyu chao (Educational Tide). Hangzhou, 1919.
Jiaoyu fagui huibian (Compilation of educational laws and regulations). Beijing, 1919.
Jiaoyu gongbao (Bulletin of Education). Beijing, 1914-19.
Jiaoyu jie (Educational World). Tianjin, 1915-16.
Jiaoyu shijie (The Educational World). Shanghai, 1901-4.
Jiaoyu yanjiu (Educational Research). Shanghai, 1913-14.
Jiaoyu yu minzhong (Education and the Masses). Shanghai, 1929-30.
Jiaoyu yu shiye (Education and Industry). Beijing, 1917-20.
Jiaoyu zazhi (Educational Review). Shanghai, 1909-20.
Jiaoyu zhoubao (Education Weekly). Hangzhou, 1915-19.
Jiaoyubu (comp.), *Zhonghua Minguo diyici jiaoyu tongji tu* (The first set of educational statistics of the Chinese Republic). Beijing, 1913.
Jiaoyubu (comp.), *Zhonghua Minguo diwuci jiaoyu tongji tu* (The fifth set of educational statistics of the Chinese Republic). Beijing, 1917.
Jiaoyubu bianzuanchu yuekan (Monthly Journal of the Education Ministry's Compilation Bureau). Beijing, 1913.
Jiaoyubu xingzheng jiyao (Summary of the administration of the Education Ministry). Beijing, 1916.
Jinghua xinbao (Beijing Speech Journal). Beijing, 1906.
Jingshi jiaoyu bao (Beijing Educational Review). Beijing, 1914-19.
Jingshi Yixue Guan (comp.). *Jiaoyu cihui* (Record of educational vocabulary). Beijing, 1904.
Jingzhong ribao (Alarm Bell Daily). Shanghai, 1904.
Kui Yingtao et. al. *Xinhai geming shi* (A history of the 1911 Revolution). vol. 2. Beijing, 1980.
Lai Jinghu, 'Minchu shidai de Hunan qingnian' (Hunanese youth at the beginning of the Republic), *Zhuanji wenxue*, 16:3 (March 1970).
Lei Guodian, *Zhongguo jiaoyu xingzheng zhidu shi* (A history of China's educational administration). Taibei, 1983.
Li Dazhao, *Li Dazhao xuanji* (Selected writings of Li Dazhao). Beijing, 1978.

Li Huang, 'Liufa qingong jianxue yu Zhongguo gongchandang' (Work-study in France and the Chinese Communist Party), *Mingbao yuekan* (Clear-sighted Journal Monthly), no. 45 (Sept. 1969), no. 46 (Oct. 1969) no. 47 (Nov. 1969), no. 48 (Dec. 1969).
Li Shizeng, *Li Shizeng xiansheng wenji* (Collected writings of Li Shizeng). 2 vols. Taibei, 1980.
Li Shizeng, *Shizeng biji* (Personal notes of Li Shizeng). Taibei, 1961.
Li Shizeng, 'Zhongfa jiaoyu wenti' (The question of Sino-French education), *Zhongfa daxue banyuekan* (Fortnightly Journal of the Sino-French University), no. 1 (1925).
Li Shizeng xiansheng jinian ji (Commemorative volume to Li Shizeng). Taibei, 1973.
Li Shuhua, 'Xinhai geming qianhou de Li Shizeng xiansheng' (Li Shizeng at the time of the 1911 Revolution), *Zhuanji wenxue*, 24:2 (Feb. 1974).
Li Yanhan, *Jiaoyu conggao* (Collected essays on education). Shanghai, 1921.
Li Yanhan, *Pinmin jiaoyu tan* (A discussion of poor people's education). Shanghai, 1912.
Li Youning et. al. (comp.), *Jindai Zhongguo nüquan yundong shiliao* (Historical materials on the women's movement in modern China). 2 vols. Taibei, 1975.
Li Zongtong, 'Lüfa zayi' (Memories of study in France), *Zhuanji wenxue*, 1:3 (March 1962)
Liang Rongruo, 'Ji Fan Jingsheng xiansheng' (A recollection of Fan Yuanlian), *Zhuanji wenxue*, 1:6 (June 1962).
Liangguang guanbao (Official Gazette of Guangdong and Guangxi). Guangzhou, 1911.
Lin Zixun, *Zhongguo liuxue jiaoyu shi* (A history of Chinese students abroad). Taibei, 1976.
Linqing xianzhi (Gazeteer of Linqing county, Shandong). vol. 1. Taibei, 1978.
Linshi gongbao (Temporary Official Gazette). Beijing, 1912. Reprint, Taibei, 1968.
Linshi zhengfu gongbao (Temporary Government Gazette). Nanjing, 1912. Reprint, Taibei 1968. 3 vols.
Liu Shaotang (ed.), *Minguo renwu xiaozhuan* (Biographies of republican figures). Taibei, 1975.
Liu Wangling, '1896-1906 nianjian Zhongguo liuri xuesheng renshu buzheng' (Additional information on the number of Chinese students in Japan between 1896 and 1906), in *Xinhai geming lunwenji*.
Liufa jianxue baogaoshu (A report on frugal study in France). Guangzhou, 1918.
Lu Feigui, *Jiaoyu wencun* (Collection of writings on education). Shanghai, 1922.
Lü'ou jiaoyu yundong (The educational movement in Europe). Tours, 1916.
Lü'ou zazhi (Journal for Chinese Students in Europe). Tours, 1916-18.
Lü'ou zhoukan (Weekly Journal for Chinese Students in Europe). Paris, 1919-21.
Luo Bingzhi, *Zhongguo jindai jiaoyujia* (Modern Chinese educators). Wuhan, 1958.
Luo Dunhe, 'Jingshi daxuetang chengli ji' (An account of the establishment of Beijing University), *Yongyan* (Justice), 1:6 (June 1913).
Ma Jianzhong, *Shike zhai jiyan* (Recorded words from the Shike studio). Beijing, 1970.
Ma Zongrong, *Bijiao shehui jiaoyu* (Comparative social education). Shanghai, 1933.
Ma Zongrong, *Shehui jiaoyu de sheshi ji lilun* (Theory and practice of social education). Shanghai, 1935.
Mai Zhonghua (comp.), *Huangchao jingshi wen xinbian* (New essays on statecraft).

vol. 1. Taibei, 1972.
Meng Er'chang (comp.), *Beizhuan jibu* (Supplementary biographies to the Guochao Beizhuan). Beijing, 1932.
Minguo bairen zhuan (Biographies of one hundred republican figures). Taibei, 1971.
Minguo jingshi wenbian (Essays on statecraft in the Republic). 5 vols. Taibei, 1970.
Minguo renwu zhuan (Biographies of republican figures). 3 vols. Beijing, 1978-80.
Minli bao (The People's Stand). Shanghai, 1911-12.
Nakamura Tadashi, 'Chūgoku ni okeru kakumeiteki minshū shugi ka no to' (The career of a Chinese revolutionary democrat), in *Higashi Ajia Kindaishi no Kenkyū* (Studies in modern East Asian history). Tokyo, 1967.
Nakamura Tsune, 'Shinmatsu gakudō setsuritsu o meguru kōsetsu nōson shakai no ichi danmen' (A look at rural society in Jiangsu and Zhejiang when schools were established at the end of the Qing), *Rekishi Kyōiku* (Historical Education), 10:11 (1962).
Ogawa Yoshiko, 'Shindai ni okeru gigaku setsuritsu no kiban' (The foundations for the establishment of charitable schools in the Qing), in Hayashi Tomohara (ed.), *Kindai Chūgoku Kyōikushi Kenkyū* (Studies in modern Chinese educational history). Tokyo, 1958.
Onogawa Hidemi, *Shinmatsu Seiji Shisō Kenkyū* (Studies in late Qing political thought). Tokyo, 1969.
Pan Maoyuan, 'Yang Xianzhang jiaoyu sixiang' (Yang Xianzhang's educational thought), *Xiamen daxue xuebao* (Study Journal of Xiamen University), no. 1 (1954).
Peng Yingming, 'Lun xinhai geming qian de wuzhengfu zhuyi sixiang' (Chinese anarchist thought before the 1911 Revolution), in *Xinhai geming lunwenji*.
Peng Zeyi (comp.), *Zhongguo jindai shougongye shi ziliao* (Materials on modern China's handicraft industry). 2 vols. Beijing, 1957.
Pingmin jiaoyu (Education for the Common People). Beijing, 1919-20.
Pingmin jiaoyu chubu chengji baogao (A report on the initial results of mass education). Shanghai, 1922.
Qian Xingcun (pseud. A Ying) comp. *Wanqing wenxue congchao: xiaoshuo xiqu yanjiu juan* (Collection of writings on late Qing literature: fiction and drama). Beijing, 1960.
Qingmo choubei lixian dang'an shiliao (Archival materials on the preparation for a constitution at the end of the Qing). 2 vols. Beijing, 1979.
Qingyi bao (Pure Discussion Journal). Yokohama, 1899-1901.
Qiu Renliang, 'Lun baihua wei weixin zhi ben' (The vernacular is the basis of reform), *Jindaishi ziliao*, no. 2 (1963).
Qu Lihe, *Qingmo liuxue jiaoyu* (Overseas study at the end of the Qing). Taibei, 1973.
Qu Lihe, *Zhang Jian de jiaoyu sixiang* (Zhang Jian's educational thought). N.p., n.d.
Quanguo jiaoyu huiyi baogao (Report on the All-China Education Conference). 2 vols. Shanghai, 1928.
Ren Shixian, *Zhongguo jiaoyu sixiang shi* (A history of Chinese educational thought). Taibei, 1974.
Renmin jiaoyu (People's Education). Beijing, 1950-.
Renmin tiyu chubanshe, *Jianshen yu xing* (Health and sex). Beijing, 1980.
Saitō Akio, 'Chūgoku gakusei kaikaku no shisō to genjitsu' (Theory and practice in the reform of China's education system), *Senshū Jimbun Ronshū* (Symposium on the Humanities), no. 4 (Dec. 1969).

Saitō Akiō, *Chūgoku Gendai Kyōiku Shi* (A history of modern Chinese education). Tokyo, 1962.
Sanetō Keishū, *Chūgokujin Nihon Ryūgaku Shi* (A history of Chinese students in Japan). Tokyo, 1960.
Sha Guzhong, 'Huang Yanpei de zhiye jiaoyu sixiang' (Huang Yanpei's ideas on vocational education), *Jiaoyu yanjiu* (Educational Research), no. 6 (June 1980).
Shang Zhizhong, *Minzhong jiaoyu* (Mass education). Shanghai, n.d.
Shao Kelü (Jacques Reclus), 'Wo suo renshi de Li Yuying xiansheng' (The Li Shizeng I knew), *Zhuanji wenxue*, 45: 3 (1984).
Shehui jiaoyu jiangyan dagang (Outline of lectures on social education). Zhengzhou, 1929.
Sheng Cheng, *Haiwai gongdu shinian jishi* (A record of ten years work-study abroad). Shanghai, 1932.
Shiwu bao (The Chinese Progress). Shanghai, 1896-8.
Shu Xincheng, *Jiaoyu tonglun* (A general discussion of education). Shanghai, 1927.
Shu Xincheng (ed.), *Jindai Zhongguo jiaoyu shiliao* (Historical materials on modern Chinese education). 4 vols. Shanghai, 1928.
Shu Xincheng, *Jindai Zhongguo jiaoyu sixiang shi* (A history of modern Chinese educational thought). Shanghai, 1929.
Shu Xincheng, *Jindai Zhongguo jiaoyushi gaoxuancun* (Miscellaneous writings on modern Chinese educational history). Shanghai, 1936.
Shu Xincheng (ed.), *Jindai Zhongguo jiaoyushi ziliao* (Materials on modern Chinese educational history). 3 vols. Beijing, 1961.
Shu Xincheng, *Jindai Zhongguo liuxue shi* (A history of overseas study in modern China). Shanghai, 1927.
Shu Xincheng, *Wo he jiaoyu* (Myself and education). Shanghai, 1945.
Shu Xincheng, *Zhongguo jiaoyu jianshe fangzhen* (Directions in China's educational construction). Shanghai, 1932.
Su Yunfeng, *Zhang Zhidong yu Hubei jiaoyu gaige* (Zhang Zhidong and educational reform in Hubei). Taibei, 1976.
Sun Bangzheng, *Liushinian lai de Zhongguo jiaoyu* (Chinese education in the last sixty years). Taibei, 1971.
Sun Zhifen, 'Chen Tianhua de aiguo geming sixiang' (Chen Tianhua's patriotic and revolutionary thought), in *Xinhai geming wushi zhounian jinian lunwenji*, vol. 2.
Taga Akigorō (ed.), *Kindai Chūgoku Kyōiku Shi Shiryō* (Materials on the history of education in modern China). 5 vols. Tokyo, 1972.
Taga Akigorō (ed.), 'Kindai Chūgoku ni okeru zokujuku no seikaku' (The nature of clan schools in modern China), *Kindai Chūgoku Kenkyū* (Modern China Research), no. 4 (1960).
Takeuchi Minoru (ed.), *Mō Taku-to Shū* (The collected works of Mao Zedong). vol. 1. Tokyo, 1971.
Tan Bi'an, *Wanqing de baihuawen yundong* (The vernacular movement at the end of the Qing). Wuhan, 1956.
Tanaka Issei (comp.), *Shindai Chihōgeki Shiryō Shū* (Collection of materials on local drama during the Qing). 2 vols. Tokyo, 1968.
Tanaka Kenji, 'Kyū Shina ni okeru jidō no gakujuku sei katsu' (Student life in the private schools of traditional China), *Tōhō Gakuhō* (Eastern Journal), 15: 2 (January 1945).
Tao Menghe, *Shehui yu jiaoyu* (Society and education). Shanghai, 1922.

Tao Yinghui, 'Ji Minguo silao' (A recollection of the four elder statesmen of the Republic), *Zhuanji wenxue*, 23:5 (Nov. 1973).
Terahiro Teruo, 'Ryūfa kinkō-kengaku undo ni tsuite' (On the diligent work and frugal study movement in France), *Rekishi Kenkyū* (Historical Research), no. 11 (1974).
Tongsu jiaoyu yanjiu hui diyici baogaoshu (The first report of the Popular Education Research Association). Beijing, 1916.
Tongsu jiaoyu yanjiu hui dierci baogaoshu (The second report of the Popular Education Research Association). Beijing, 1917.
Tongsu jiaoyu yanjiu hui disanci baogaoshu (The third report of the Popular Lducation Research Association). Beijing, 1918.
Tongsu jiaoyu yanjiu hui disici baogaoshu (The fourth report of the Popular Education Research Association). Beijing, 1919.
Tongsu jiaoyu congkan (Collection on popular education). Beijing, 1922.
Wang Ermin, 'Qingji xuehui huibiao' (A chart on late Qing study societies), *Dalu zazhi* (Continental Review), 24:2 (Jan. 1962), 24:3 (Feb. 1962).
Wang Ermin, *Wanqing zhengzhi sixiang shilun* (Essays on the history of political thought in the late Qing). Taibei, 1969.
Wang Fengjie, *Zhongguo jiaoyushi* (A history of Chinese education). Shanghai, 1945.
Wang Guangsong, *Shexue gangyao* (An outline for school inspectors). Shanghai, 1919.
Wang Jingyu (comp.), *Zhongguo jindai gongye shi ziliao* (Materials on the history of modern industry in China). 2 vols. Beijing, 1957.
Wang Lanyin, 'Zhang Zhidong zhi fuqiang zhengce' (Zhang Zhidong's policies for wealth and strength), *Shida yuekan* (Monthly Journal of Beijing Normal School), Dec. 17, 1934.
Wang Qingbin (ed.), *Diyici Zhongguo laodong nianjian* (The first China labour yearbook). Beijing, 1928.
Wang Wenbin et. al. *Xing de zhishi* (Knowledge about sex). Beijing, 1980.
Wang Xiaochuan (comp.), *Yuanmingqing sandai jinhui xiaoshuo xiqu shiliao* (Historical materials on the censorship of plays and novels in the Yuan, Ming and Qing dynasties). Beijing, 1958.
Wang Yunwu, *Gexin shidai jiaoxue sixiang* (Pedagogical thought in the reform period). Taibei, 1971.
Wei Shaochang (comp.), *Yuanyang hudiepai yanjiu ziliao* (Research materials on the mandarin duck and butterfly school). Shanghai, 1962.
Wu Qiping, *Gailiang sishu* (The reform of traditional schools). Shanghai, 1939.
Wu Xiangxiang (comp.), *Dingxian nongmin jiaoyu* (Rural education in Ding district). 2 vols. Taibei, 1971.
Wu Xiangxiang (comp.), *Minguo bairen zhuan* (Biographies of one hundred Republican figures). Taibei, 1971.
Wu Xiangxiang, 'Pingmin jiaoyu yundong de chuqi shishi' (The early stages of the popular education movement), *Shi bao* (The Times), Feb. 17, 24, March 2, 1980.
Wu Zhihui, *Wu Zhihui xiansheng wencui* (Writings of Wu Zhihui). 2 vols. Shanghai, 1929.
Wu Ziqiang, *Riben xiandai jiaoyu gailun* (An introduction to Japan's modern education). Shanghai, 1935.
Wusi shiqi de shetuan (Societies of the May Fourth period). 4 vols. Beijing, 1979.

Wusi shiqi qikan jieshao (An introduction to publications in the May Fourth period). 3 vols. Beijing, 1979.
Xia Chengfeng, *Xiandai jiaoyu xingzheng* (Modern educational administration). Shanghai, 1932.
Xiang Zhutan, *Shehui jiaoyu* (Social education). Taibei, 1958.
Xiangxue xinbao (New Journal of Hunan Learning). Changsha, 1897.
Xin jiaoyu (New Education). Beijing, 1919-20.
Xin qingnian (New Youth). Shanghai, 1915-20.
Xin shiji (New Century). Paris, 1907-9.
Xin xiaoshuo (New Fiction). Shanghai, 1902.
Xinhai geming huiyi lu (Memories of the 1911 Revolution). 6 vols. Beijing, 1961.
Xinhai geming lunwenji (Collection of essays on the 1911 Revolution). Guangzhou, 1980.
Xinhai geming shiqi qikan jieshao (An introduction to periodicals at the time of the 1911 Revolution). 2 vols. Beijing, 1982.
Xinhai geming wushi zhounian jinian lunwenji (Collection of essays commemorating the fiftieth anniversary of the 1911 Revolution). 2 vols. Wuchang, 1961.
Xinmin congbao (New People's Miscellany). Yokohama, 1902-7.
Xiu Lingzhong, *Shehui jiaoyu xingzheng* (The administration of social education). Taibei, 1974.
Xu Teli, *Xu Teli jiaoyu wenji* (Xu Teli's writings on education). Beijing, 1979.
Xuebu (comp.), *Diyici jiaoyu tongji tubiao* (The first set of educational statistics). Beijing, 1909.
Xuebu (comp.) *Disanci jiaoyu tongji tubiao* (The third set of educational statistics). Beijing, 1911.
Xuebu guanbao (Official Journal of the Board of Education). Beijing, 1907-10.
Yang Shouyuan zouyi jiyao (Selected memorials of Yuan Shikai). Beijing, 1937.
Yang Tianshi et. al. (comp.), *Ju'E yundong* (The movement to resist Russia). Beijing, 1979.
Yang Xianzhang, *Jiaoyushi ABC* (An ABC of educational history). Shanghai, 1929.
Yang Xianzhang, *Xin jiaoyu dagang* (An outline of new education). Shanghai, 1930.
Yinbing shi quanji (Collected works from the ice-drinker's studio). Tainan, 1986.
Youxue yibian (Translations from students abroad). Tokyo, 1902-3.
Yu Gang, 'Chen Jiageng xiansheng de banxue jingshen' (Chen Jiageng's vigour in establishing schools), *Renmin Jiaoyu*, no. 10 (1979).
Yuan Shikai zouzhe zhuanji (The memorials of Yuan Shikai). 8 vols. Taibei, 1971.
Yunnan zazhi (Yunnan Journal). Tokyo, 1906.
Zeng Chubai, *Zhongguo xinwen shi* (A history of Chinese newspapers). 2 vols. Taibei, 1966.
Zhang Ji, *Zhang Puchuan xiansheng quanji* (The Collected works of Zhang Ji). Taibei, 1951.
Zhang Jinglu (comp.), *Zhongguo jindai chuban shiliao* (Historical materials on modern Chinese publishing). 4 vols. Beijing, 1954-1959.
Zhang Jinglu (comp.), *Zhongguo chuban shiliao, bubian* (Supplement to historical materials on Chinese publishing). Beijing, 1957.
Zhang Nan et. al. (comp.), *Xinhai geming qian shinianjian shibian xuanji* (A selection of articles from the ten years before the 1911 Revolution). 3 vols. Beijing, 1962, 1977.
Zhang Yunhou et. al. (comp.), *Liufa qingong jianxue yundong* (The work-study

movement in France). 2 vols. Shanghai, 1980, 1986.
Zhang Zhidong, *Zhang Wenxiang gong quanji* (Complete works of Zhang Zhidong). 6 vols. Taibei, 1963.
Zhao Qin, 'Xinhai geming qianhou de Zhongguo gongren yundong' (The workers' movement at the time of the 1911 Revolution), *Lishi yanjiu* (Historical Research), no. 2 (1959).
Zhejiang chao (Tides of Zhejiang). Tokyo, 1903.
Zheng Guanying ji (The works of Zheng Guanying). Shanghai, 1982.
Zheng Hailin, *Huang Zunxian yu jindai Zhongguo* (Huang Zunxian and modern China). Beijing, 1988.
Zheng Shixing, *Zhongguo xiandai jiaoyu shi* (A history of modern Chinese education). Taibei, 1981.
Zhengfu gongbao (Government Gazette). 92 vols. Beijing, 1912-19.
Zhengzhi guanbao (Official Government Gazette). 42 vols. Beijing, 1907-11.
Zhong Lingxiu, *Shehui jiaoyu xingzheng* (The administration of social education). Taibei, 1968.
Zhongfa jiaoyujie (The World of Sino-French Education). Beijing, 1926.
Zhongguo baihua bao (China Vernacular Journal). Shanghai, 1903-4.
Zhongguo jiaoyu cidian (A dictionary of Chinese education). Shanghai, 1930.
Zhongguo jiaoyu tongji gailan (Overview of China's educational statistics). Shanghai, 1923.
Zhongguo Jiaoyu Xuehui (ed.), *Shehui jiaoyu yanjiu* (Researches into social education). Taibei, 1968.
Zhongguo Shi Xuehui (comp.), *Xinhai geming* (The 1911 Revolution). 8 vols. Shanghai, 1957.
Zhongguo Shi Xuehui (comp.), *Yangwu yundong* (The foreign affairs movement). 8 vols. Shanghai, 1961.
Zhongguo xuebao (China Study Journal). Beijing, 1913.
Zhonghua jiaoyujie (Chinese Educational World). Shanghai, 1913-20.
Zhonghua Minguo kaiguo wushinian wenxian (Documents on the fifty years since the founding of the Republic). vol. 1. Taibei, 1964.
Zhu Youxian (ed.), *Zhongguo jindai xuezhi shiliao* (Historical materials on modern China's educational system). Shanghai, 1983.
Zhu Yuanshan, *Zhiye jiaoyu zhenyi* (The true significance of vocational education). Shanghai, 1917.
Zhuang Yu (ed.), *Zuijin sanshiwu nian zhi Zhongguo jiaoyu* (Chinese education in the last thirty-five years). Shanghai, 1931.
Zhuanji wenxue (Biographical Literature). Taibei, 1962-.
Zouding xuetang zhangcheng (Regulations on the schools). Taibei, 1972.

Works in English and French
Abe, Hiroshi. 'Borrowing from Japan: China's First Educational System', in R. Hayhoe, M. Bastid (eds.), *China's Education and the Industrial World.* New York, 1987.
Abe, M. 'Spare-time Education in Communist China: A General Survey', in S. Fraser (ed.), *Education and Communism in China.* London, 1971.
Alitto, G. *The Last Confucian: Liang Shu-ming and the Chinese Dilemma of Modernity.* Berkeley, 1979.
Anderson, R. *Education in France 1848-1870.* Oxford, 1975.

Asie Française. Paris, 1910-17.
Ayers, W. *Chang Chih-tung and Educational Reform in China*. Cambridge, Mass., 1971.
Bailey, P. 'The Chinese Work-Study Movement in France', *China Quarterly*, no. 115 (Sept. 1988).
Bailey, P. 'The Sino-French Connection 1902-1928', in D. Goodman (ed), *China and the West: Ideas and Activists* (Manchester, forthcoming).
Baker, K. *Condorcet: From Natural Philosophy to Social Mathematics*. Chicago, 1975.
Banno, M. *China and the West 1858-1861: The Origins of the Tsungli Yamen*. Cambridge, Mass., 1964.
Barendson, R. 'Half-work, Half-study Schools in Communist China', *U.S. Office of Education Bulletin*, no. 24 (1965).
Barman, G. and Dulioust, N. *Etudiants-ouvriers Chinois en France 1920-1945*. Paris, 1981.
Barnard, H. *Education and the French Revolution*. Cambridge, 1969.
Bastid, M. *Aspects de la réforme de l'enseignement en Chine au début du XXème siècle: D'après des écrits de Zhang Jian*. Paris, 1971. (Trans. by P. Bailey under the title: *Educational Reform in Early Twentieth-Century China*. Ann Arbor, 1988).
Bastid, M. 'Chinese Educational Policies in the 1980s and Economic Development', *China Quarterly*, no. 98 (June 1984).
Bastid, M. *L'Evolution de la société Chinoise à la fin de la dynastie des Qing*. Paris, 1979.
Bauer, W. and Hwang, Shen-chan. *German Impact on Modern Chinese Intellectual History*. Wiesbaden, 1982.
Bays, D. *China Enters the Twentieth Century: Chang Chih-tung and the Issues of a New Age*. Ann Arbor, 1978.
Beahan, C. 'Feminism and Nationalism in the Chinese Women's Press 1902-1911', *Modern China*, 1: 4 (Oct. 1975).
Beahan, C. 'The Women's Movement in late Ch'ing China'. Ph.D. diss., Columbia University, New York, 1976.
Bennett, A. *Missionary Journalist in China*. Athens, Georgia, 1983.
Bergère. M. C. *La bourgeosie chinoise et la révolution de 1911*. Paris, 1968.
Bergeron, R. *Le cinéma chinois 1905-1949*. Lausanne, 1977.
Bernal, M. *Chinese Socialism to 1907*. Ithaca, 1976.
Bernstein, T. *Up to the Mountains and Down to the Villages*. New Haven, 1977.
Biggerstaff, K. *The Earliest Modern Government Schools in China*. Ithaca, 1961.
Black, J. *Citizens for the Fatherland*. New York, 1979.
Blick, J. 'The Chinese Labor Corps in World War One', *Harvard Papers on China* (Aug. 1955).
Bonner, J. *Wang Kuo-wei: An Intellectual Biography*. Cambridge, Mass., 1986.
Boorman, H. and Howard, R. *Biographical Dictionary of Republican China*. 4 vols. New York, 1967.
Borthwick, S. *Education and Social Change in China*. Stanford, 1983.
Bowen, J. *Soviet Education: Anton Makarenko and the Years of Experiment*. Madison, 1962.
Bouchot, J. 'Les écoles françaises en Chine', *La Chine*, no. 27 (Oct. 1922).
Bradier, G. 'La réforme de l'enseignement en Chine', *Bulletin de l'Association Amicale Franco-Chinoise*, no. 3 (July 1911).
Brandt, C. 'The French-Returned Elite in the Chinese Communist Party', in E. Szczepanik (ed.), *Symposium on Economic and Social Problems in the Far East*.

Hong Kong, 1962.
Brickman, W. (ed.) *John Dewey's Impressions of Soviet Russia and the Revolutionary World: Mexico, China, Turkey.* New York, 1964.
Britton, R. *The Chinese Periodical Press 1800-1912.* Taibei, 1968.
Brou, A. 'Les réformes scolaires en Chine', *Etudes*, vol. 127 (April-June 1911), vol. 128 (July-Sept. 1911).
Brunnert, H. and Hagelstrom, V. *Present-Day Political Organization of China.* Shanghai, 1912.
Buck, D. 'Educational Modernization in Tsinan 1899-1937', in M. Elvin and W. Skinner (eds.), *The Chinese City Between Two Worlds.* Stanford, 1974.
Buck, D. *Urban Change in Modern China: Politics and Development in Tsinan, Shantung 1890-1949.* Madison, 1978.
Buck, P. *Tell the People: Talks with James Yen about the Mass Education Movement.* New York, 1945.
Bulletin de l'Association Amicale Franco-Chinoise. Paris, 1910-15.
Burke, P. *Popular Culture in Early Modern Europe.* London, 1978.
Burns, J. and Rosen, S. (eds.), *Policy Conflicts in Post-Mao China.* New York, 1986.
Burton, M. *The Education of Women in China.* New York, 1911.
Cameron, M. *The Reform Movement in China 1898-1912.* Stanford, 1931.
Canovan, M. *Populism.* London, 1981.
Chan, Sin-wai. *Buddhism in Late Ch'ing Political Thought.* Hong Kong, 1985.
Chan, W. *Merchants, Mandarins and Modern Enterprise in Late Ch'ing China.* Cambridge, Mass., 1977.
Chanel, E. *Pédagogie et éducateurs socialistes.* Paris, 1975.
Chang, Chung-li. *The Chinese Gentry.* Seattle, 1970.
Chang, Hao. *Liang Ch'i-ch'ao and Intellectual Transition in China 1890-1907.* Cambridge, Mass., 1971.
Chang, Tai-hung. *Going to the People: Intellectuals and Folk Literature 1918-1937.* Cambridge, Mass., 1985.
Chateau, J. (ed.). *Les grands pédagogues.* Paris, 1980.
Ch'en, J. *China and the West.* London, 1979.
Ch'en, J. *Yuan Shih-k'ai.* Stanford, 1972.
Chen, Ta. *Chinese Migrations, with Special References to Labor Conditions.* Washington, 1923.
Chen, T. *Chinese Education since 1949.* New York, 1981.
Chen, T. *The Maoist Educational Revolution.* New York, 1974.
Chen, Xiqi. 'Sun Yat-sen and the Founding of the Provisional Nanjing Government', in Eto Shinkichi, H. Schiffrin (eds.), *The 1911 Revolution in China.* Tokyo, 1984.
Cheng, R. Yu Soong. *The Financing of Public Education in China.* Shanghai, 1935.
Chesneaux, J. *The Chinese Labor Movement 1919-1927*, Stanford, 1968.
Chi, M. *China Diplomacy 1914-1918.* Cambridge, Mass., 1970.
Chisick, H. *The Limits of Reform in the Enlightenment.* Princeton, 1981.
Chow, Tse-tsung. *The May Fourth Movement.* Cambridge, Mass., 1960.
Christian Education in China. Shanghai, 1922.
Chu, S. *Chang Chien: Reformer in Modern China.* New York, 1965.
Chu, S. 'The New Life Movement before the Sino-Japanese Conflict: A Reflection of KMT Limitations in Thought and Action', in G. Chan (ed.), *China at the Crossroads: Nationalists and Communists 1927-1949.* Boulder, 1980.

Chu, You-kuang. *Some Problems of a National System of Education in China.* Shanghai, 1933.
Chuang, Chai-hsuan. *Tendencies toward a Democratic System of Education in China.* Shanghai, 1922.
Clark, P. *Chinese Cinema: Culture and Politics since 1949.* Cambridge, 1987.
Clifford, P. 'The Intellectual Development of Wu Zhihui'. Ph.D. diss. London University, London, 1978.
Clopham, R. and Ou, Tsuin-chen. *John Dewey: Lectures in China 1919-1920.* Honolulu, 1973.
Croll, E. 'The New Peasant Economy', in S. Feuchtwang, A. Hussain, T. Pairault (eds.), *Transforming China's Economy in the Eighties: vol. 1.* London, 1988.
Cross, G. *Immigrant Workers in Industrial France.* Philadelphia, 1983.
Cross, G. 'The Politics of Immigration during the Era of the First World War', *French Historical Studies*, 11: 4 (Autumn, 1980).
Crump, J. *The Origins of Socialist Thought in Japan.* London, 1983.
Day, M. *Mao Zedong 1917-1927: Documents.* Stockholm, 1975.
de Bary, Wm. 'Individualism and Humanitarianism in late Ming Thought', in Wm. de Bary (ed.), *Self and Society in Ming Thought.* New York, 1970.
de Francis, J. *Nationalism and Language Reform in China.* Princeton, 1950.
Dietrich, T. *La pédagogie socialiste.* Paris, 1973.
Dirlik, A. 'Spiritual Solutions to Material Problems: The Socialist Ethics and Courtesy Month in China', *The South Atlantic Quarterly*, 8: 4 (1982).
Dirlik, A. 'The Ideological Foundations of the New Life Movement', *Journal of Asian Studies*, 34: 4 (Aug. 1975).
Dirlik, A. *The Origins of Chinese Communism.* Oxford, 1989.
Dirlik, A. 'Vision and Revolution', *Modern China*, 12:2 (April 1986).
Dirlik, A. and Krebs, E. 'Socialism and Anarchism in Early Republican China', *Modern China*, 7:2 (April 1981).
Djung, Lu-dzai. *A History of Democratic Education in Modern China.* Shanghai, 1934.
Doar, B. 'The Boxers and Chinese Drama: Questions of Interaction', *Papers on Far Eastern History*, no. 29 (March 1984).
Dolezelova-Velingerova, M. (ed.) *The Chinese Novel at the Turn of the Century.* Toronto, 1980.
Dolezelova-Velingerova, M. 'The Origins of Modern Chinese Literature', in M. Goldman (ed.), *Modern Chinese Literature in the May Fourth Era.* Cambridge, Mass., 1977.
Dore, R. 'The Legacy of Tokugawa Education', in M. Jansen (ed.), *Changing Japanese Attitudes Towards Modernization.* Princeton, 1965.
Drège, J. P. *La Commercial Press de Shanghai 1897-1949.* Paris, 1978.
Duiker, W. *Ts'ai Yuan-p'ei: Educator of Modern China.* University Park, Pa., 1977.
Edmunds, C. *Modern Education in China.* Washington, 1919.
Elman, B. 'The Hsueh-hai T'ang and the Rise of New Text Scholarship', *Ch'ing-shih Wen-t'i*, 4: 2 (Dec. 1979).
Elvin, M. 'The Administration of Shanghai 1905-1914', in M. Elvin, W. Skinner (eds.), *The Chinese City Between Two Worlds.* Stanford, 1974.
Elvin, M. 'The Gentry Democracy in Chinese Shanghai 1905-1914', in J. Gray (ed.), *Modern China's Search For a Political Form.* London, 1969.
Esherick, J. *Reform and Revolution: The 1911 Revolution in Hunan and Hubei.* Berkeley, 1976.

Esherick, J. *The Origins of the Boxer Uprising*. Berkeley, 1987.
Feigon, L. *Chen Duxiu*. Princeton, 1983.
Feuchtwang, S. 'School Temple and City God', in W. Skinner (ed.), *The City in Late Imperial China*. Stanford, 1977.
Feuerwerker, A. *China's Early Industrialization: Sheng Hsuan-huai (1844-1916) and Mandarin Enterprise*. Cambridge, Mass., 1958.
Fincher, J. *Chinese Democracy*. New York, 1981.
Fitzpatrick, S. *Education and Social Mobility in the Soviet Union 1921-1934*. Cambridge, 1979.
Fitzpatrick, S. *The Commissariat of Enlightenment*. Cambridge, 1970.
Fleming, M. *The Anarchist Way to Socialism*. London, 1979.
Franke, W. *The Reform and Abolition of the Chinese Examination System*. Cambridge, Mass., 1960.
Fraser, S. (ed.) *Education and Communism in China*. London, 1971.
Fraser, W. 'Education and Society in Modern France', in R. Havighurst (ed.), *Comparative Perspectives on Education*. Boston, 1969.
Fridell, W. 'Government Ethics Textbooks in Late Meiji Japan', *Journal of Asian Studies*, 29: 4 (Aug. 1970).
Fung, E. *The Military Dimension of the Chinese Revolution*. Vancouver, 1980.
Furth, C. 'Intellectual Change: From the Reform Movement to the May Fourth Movement 1895-1920', in J. Fairbank (ed.), *The Cambridge History of China: vol. 12*. Cambridge, 1983.
Galt, H. *Oriental and Occidental Elements in China's Modern Educational System*. Beijing, 1929.
Gamble, S. *Peking: A Social Survey*. New York, 1921.
Gardner, J. 'Educated Youth and Urban-Rural Inequalities 1958-1966', in J. Lewis (ed.), *The City in Communist China*. Stanford, 1971.
Garrett, S. *Social Reformers in Urban China: The Chinese YMCA 1895-1926*. Cambridge, Mass., 1970.
Gasster, M. *Chinese Intellectuals and the 1911 Revolution*. Seattle, 1969.
Gewurtz, M. 'Social Reality and Educational Reform: The Case of the Chinese Vocational Association', *Modern China*, 4: 2 (April 1978).
Gipoulon, C. *Qiu Jin: Pierres de l'oiseau Jingwei*. Paris, 1976.
Gluck, C. *Japan's Modern Myths*. Princeton, 1985.
Goldstrom, J. 'The Content of Education and the Socialization of the Working Class Child 1830-1860', in P. McCann (ed.), *Popular Education and Socialization in the Nineteenth Century*. London, 1977.
Grieder, J. *Intellectuals and the State in Modern China*. New York, 1981.
Hall, I. *Mori Arinori*. Cambridge, Mass., 1973.
Halliday, J. *A Political History of Japanese Capitalism*. New York, 1975.
Handlin, J. *Action in Late Ming Thought*. Berkeley, 1983.
Hao, Yen-p'ing. *The Comprador in Nineteenth Century China*. Cambridge, Mass., 1970.
Harding, H. *China's Second Revolution: Reform After Mao*. Washington, 1987.
Harper, P. 'Problems of Industrial Spare-time Schools', in S. Fraser (ed.), *Education and Communism in China*. London, 1971.
Havighurst, R. (ed.) *Comparative Perspectives on Education*. Boston, 1968.
Hawkins, J. *Mao Tse-tung and Education*. Hamden, 1974.
Ho, Ping-ti. *The Ladder of Success in Imperial China*. New York, 1962.

Horne, J. 'Immigrant Workers in France during World War One', *French Historical Studies*, 14:1 (Spring 1985)
Hsia, C.T. 'Yen Fu and Liang Ch'i-ch'ao as Advocates of New Fiction', in A. Rickett (ed.), *Chinese Approaches to Literature from Confucius to Liang Ch'i-ch'ao*. Princeton, 1978.
Hsiao, Kung-ch'üan. *A Modern China and a New World: Kang You-wei, Reformer and Utopian 1858-1927*. Seattle, 1975.
Hsiao, Kung-ch'üan. *Rural China: Imperial Control in the Nineteenth Century*. Seattle, 1960.
Hsiao, T. *The History of Modern Education in China*. Shanghai, 1935.
Hsueh, Chun-tu. *Huang Hsing and the Chinese Revolution*. Stanford, 1961.
Huang, P. *Liang Ch'i-ch'ao and Modern Chinese Liberalism*. Seattle, 1972.
Hummel, A. *Eminent Chinese of the Ch'ing Period*. 2 vols. Washington, 1943.
Hurt, J. 'Drill, Discipline and the Elementary School Ethos', in P. McCann (ed.), *Popular Education and Socialization in the Nineteenth Century*. London, 1977.
Iriye, A. 'Public Opinion and Foreign Policy', in A. Feuerwerker et. al. (eds.), *Approaches to Modern Chinese History*. Berkeley, 1967.
Jansen, M. 'The Japanese and the Chinese Revolution of 1911', in J. Fairbank, Kwang-ching Liu (eds.), *The Cambridge History of China: vol. 11*. Cambridge, Mass., 1980.
Jansen, M. and Stone, L. 'Education and Modernization in Japan and England', *Comparative Studies in Society and History*, no. 9 (1967).
Johnson, D., Nathan, A., Rawski, E. (eds.), *Popular Culture in Late Imperial China*. Berkeley, 1985.
Johnson, D. 'Communication, Class and Consciousness in Late Imperial China', in D. Johnson, A. Nathan, E. Rawski (eds.), *Popular Culture in Late Imperial China*.
Kaestle, C. 'Between the Scylla of Brutal Ignorance and the Charybdis of a Literary Education: Elite Attitudes Towards Mass Schooling in Early Industrial England and America', in L. Stone (ed.), *Schooling and Society*. Baltimore, 1976.
Kaigo, Tokiomi. *Japanese Education: Its Past and Present*. Tokyo, 1965.
Kamachi, N. *Reform in China: Huang Tsun-hsien and the Japanese Model*. Cambridge, Mass., 1981.
Keenan, B. *The Dewey Experiment in China: Educational Reform and Political Power in the Early Republic*. Cambridge, Mass., 1977.
King, H. *The Educational System of China as Recently Reconstructed*. Washington, 1911.
Kinmonth, E. *The Self-Made Man in Meiji Japanese Thought*. Berkeley, 1981.
Kirby, W. *Germany and Republican China*. Stanford, 1984.
Kramer, L. 'Intellectual History and Reality: The Search For Connections', *Historical Reflections/Réflexions Historiques*, 13: 2/3 (1986).
Kriegel, A. 'Aux origines françaises du communisme chinois', in A. Kriegel, *Communismes au miroir français*. Paris, 1974.
Kuhn, P. 'Local Self-Government under the Republic', in F. Wakeman, C. Grant (eds.), *Conflict and Control in Late Imperial China*. Berkeley, 1975.
Kuo, Ping-wen. *The Chinese System of Public Education*. New York, 1914.
Kuo, Ting-yee. 'Self-Strengthening: The Pursuit of Western Technology', in J. Fairbank (ed.), *The Cambridge History of China: vol 10*. Cambridge, 1978.
Kwok, D. *Scientism in Chinese Thought*. New Haven, 1965.
Kwong, L. *A Mosaic of the Hundred Days*. Cambridge, Mass., 1984.

La Chine. Beijing, 1921-4.
La Politique de Pékin. Beijing, 1918-26.
League of Nations Commission (comp.) *The Re-Organization of Education in China*. Paris, 1932.
Lee, Leo Ou-fan. *Voices From the Iron House*. Bloomington, 1987.
Lee, Leo Ou-fan and Nathan, A. 'The Beginnings of Mass Culture: Journalism and Fiction in the late Ch'ing and Beyond', in D. Johnson, A. Nathan, E. Rawski (eds.), *Popular Culture in Late Imperial China*.
Lee, T. Hong-chi. 'Education in Northern Sung China'. Ph.D. diss. Yale University, 1974.
Leibo, S. *Transferring Technology to China: Prosper Giquel and the Self-Strengthening Movement*. Berkeley, 1985.
Leung, J. Kong-cheong. 'The Chinese Work-Study Movement'. Ph.D. diss., Brown University, 1982.
Levine, M. 'The Diligent-Work Frugal-Study Movement and the New Culture Movement', *Republican China*, 12 :1 (1986).
Lewis, C. *Prologue to Revolution: The Transformation of Ideas and Institutions in Hunan Province 1891-1907*. Cambridge, Mass., 1976.
Lewis, I. *The Education of Girls in China*. New York, 1919.
Leyda, J. *Dianying: An Account of Films and the Film Audience in China*. Cambridge, Mass., 1972.
Li, Jui. *The Early Revolutionary Activities of Comrade Mao Tse-tung*. New York, 1977.
Li, Yu-ning, *The Introduction of Socialism into China*. New York, 1971.
Li, Zongyi. 'The Bourgeois Revolutionaries in the Movement to Regain Economic Rights Towards the End of the Qing Dynasty', in Eto Shinkichi, H. Schiffrin (eds.), *The 1911 Revolution in China*. Tokyo, 1984.
Liao, T'ai-ch'u. 'Rural Education in Transition', *Yenching Journal of Social Studies*, 4: 2 (Feb. 1949).
Liao, T'ai-ch'u. 'School Land: A Problem of Educational Finance', *Yenching Journal of Social Studies*, 2: 2 (Feb. 1940).
Lin, Paotchin. *L'instruction féminine en Chine*. Paris, 1926.
Lin, Yu-sheng. *The Crisis of Chinese Consciousness*. Madison, 1982.
Linden, A. 'Politics and Education in Nationalist China: The Case of the University Council 1927-1928', *Journal of Asian Studies*, 27:4 (Aug. 1968).
Link, P. *Mandarin Ducks and Butterflies*. Berkeley, 1981.
Liu, Hui-chen Wang. *The Traditional Chinese Clan Rules*. New York, 1959.
Lund, R. 'The Imperial University of Peking'. Ph.D. diss. University of Washington, Seattle, 1956.
Lutz, J. *China and the Christian Colleges*. Ithaca, 1971.
Lyell, W. *Lu Hsun's Vision of Reality*. Berkeley, 1976.
Mackinnon, S. 'Liang Shiyi and the Communications Clique', *Journal of Asian Studies*, 29,: 3 (May 1970).
Mackinnon S. *Power and Politics in Late Imperial China*. Berkeley, 1980.
Mandeville, B. *The Fable of the Bees or Private Vices and Public Benefits*. Oxford, 1957.
Mann, S. *Local Merchants and the Chinese Bureaucracy 1750-1950*. Stanford, 1987.
Marshall, B. 'The Late Meiji Debate over Social Policy', in H. Wray, H. Conroy (eds.), *Japan Examined: Perspectives on Modern Japanese History*. Honolulu, 1983.
Maybon, A. *La république chinoise*. Paris, n d.
Maynes, M. J. *Schooling in Western Europe*. New York, 1985.

Bibliography

McCann, P. (ed.), *Popular Education and Socialization in the Nineteenth Century*. London, 1977.
McClelland, J. *Autocrats and Academies*. Chicago, 1979.
McNair, H. *The Chinese Abroad*. Shanghai, 1924.
Meskill, J. *Academies in Ming China: A Historical Essay*. Arizona, 1982.
Montague, H. and Woodhead, H. (comp.), *The China Year Book: 1912*. London, 1912.
Muller, D., Ringer, F., Simon, B. (eds.). *The Rise of the Modern Education System*. Cambridge, 1987.
Munro, D. *The Concept of Man in Early China*. Stanford, 1969.
Munro, D. *The Concept of Man in Contemporary China*. Ann Arbor, 1977.
Nagai, Michio. 'Westernization and Japanization: The Early Meiji Transformation of Education', in D. Shively (ed.), *Tradition and Modernization in Japanese Culture*. Princeton, 1971.
Naquin, S. and Rawski, E. *Chinese Society in the Eighteenth Century*. New Haven, 1987.
Nasaw, D. *Schooled to Order*. New York, 1979.
Neuberg, V. *Popular Education in Eighteenth Century England*. London, 1971.
Orb, R. 'Chihli Academies and Other Schools in the Late Ch'ing: An Institutional Survey', in P. Cohen, J. Schrecker (eds.), *Reform in Nineteenth Century China*. Cambridge, Mass., 1976.
Palmer, R. *The Improvement of Humanity*. Princeton, 1985.
Passin, H. *Society and Education in Japan*. New York, 1965.
Peake, C. *Nationalism and Education in Modern China*. New York, 1932.
Pelissier, R. *Les bibliothèques en Chine pendant la première moitié du vingtième siècle*. Paris, 1969.
Pepper, S. 'Chinese Education After Mao: Two Steps Forward, Two Steps Back and Begin Again?", *China Quarterly*, no. 81 (March 1980).
Péri, N. 'L'éducation nouvelle en Chine', *La Revue de Paris* (May-June 1907).
Péri, N. 'Note sur l'enseignement en Chine et au Japon', *Revue Indo-Chinoises* (November 1910).
Peterson, A. *A Hundred Years of Education*. London, 1971.
Pollard, H. *Pioneers of Popular Education 1760-1850*. London, 1956.
Price, R. *Education in Communist China*. New York, 1970.
Price, R. *Marx and Education in Russia and China*. London, 1977.
Purcell, V. *Problems of Chinese Education*. London, 1936.
Pusey, J. *China and Charles Darwin*. Cambridge, Mass., 1983.
Rankin, M. *Early Chinese Revolutionaries: Radical Intellectuals in Shanghai and Chekiang 1902-1911*. Cambridge, Mass., 1971.
Rankin, M. *Elite Activism and Political Transformation in China*. Stanford, 1986.
Rankin, M. 'The Emergence of Women at the End of the Ch'ing: The Case of Ch'iu Chin', in M. Wolf, R. Witke (eds.), *Women in Chinese Society*. Stanford, 1975.
Rawski, E. 'Economic and Social Foundations of Late Imperial Culture', in D. Johnson, A. Nathan, E. Rawski (eds.), *Popular Culture in Late Imperial China*.
Rawski, E. *Education and Popular Literacy in Ch'ing China*. Ann Arbor, 1979.
Rhoads, E. *China's Republican Revolution: The Case of Kwangtung 1895-1913*. Cambridge, Mass., 1975.
Rodes, J. *La Chine nouvelle*. Paris, 1910.
Rodes, J. *Scènes de la vie révolutionnaire en Chine*. Paris, 1917.

Rosen, S. 'Recentralization, Decentralization and Rationalization: Deng Xiaoping's Bifurcated Educational Policy', *Modern China*, 11:3 (July 1985).
Rottbach, E. *La Chine en révolution*. Paris, 1914.
Rozman, G. (ed.). *The Modernization of China*. New York, 1981.
Russell, B. *The Problem of China*. London, 1922.
Sakai, Tadao. 'Confucianism and Popular Educational Works', in Wm. de Bary (ed.), *Self and Society in Ming Thought*.
Samuel, R. and Thomas, R. *Education and Society in Modern Germany*. London, 1949.
Savioz, R. 'Georg Kerschensteiner', in J. Chateau (ed.), *Les Grands Pédagogues*. Paris, 1980.
Scalapino, R., 'Prelude to Marxism: The Chinese Student Movement in Japan 1900-1910', in A. Feuerwerker et. al. (eds.), *Approaches to Modern Chinese History*.
Scalapino, R and Yu, G. *The Chinese Anarchist Movement*. Berkeley, 1961.
Scalapino, R. and Yu, G. *Modern China and its Revolutionary Process*. Berkeley, 1985.
Schiffrin, H. 'The Enigma of Sun Yatsen', in M. Wright (ed.), *China in Revolution: The First Phase 1900-1913*. New Haven 1969.
Schoppa, R.K. *Chinese Elites and Political Change: Zhejiang Province in the Early Twentieth Century*. Cambridge, Mass., 1982.
Schram, S. *Une étude de l'éducation physique*. Paris, 1962.
Seybolt, P. (ed.) *Revolutionary Education in China*. New York, 1973.
Sheridan, J. *China in Disintegration*. New York, 1977.
Shirk, S. *Competititve Comrades*. Berkeley, 1982.
Silver, H. *English Education and the Radicals*. London, 1975.
Silver, H. *The Concept of Popular Education*. London, 1965.
Simon, D. *Georg Kerschensteiner*. London, 1966.
Smith, R. *China's Cultural Heritage*. Boulder, 1983.
Spence, J. *The Gate of Heavenly Peace*. New York, 1981.
Stone, L. (ed.), *Schooling and Society*. Baltimore, 1976
Stone, N. *Europe Transformed 1878-1919*. London, 1983.
Summerskill, M. *China on the Western Front*. London, 1982.
Talbott, J. *The Politics of Educational Reform in France 1918-1940*. Princeton, 1969.
Teng, T.Y. *Education in China*. Beijing, 1922.
Tobar, J. 'La réforme des études en Chine', *Etudes*, vol. 97 (1903).
Troen, S. 'The Discovery of the Adolescent by American Educational Reformers 1900-1920: An Economic Perspective', in L. Stone (ed.), *Schooling and Society*.
Tsang, Chiu-sam. *Nationalism in School Education in China since the Opening of the Twentieth Century*. Shanghai, 1933.
Tsau, Shu-ying. 'The Rise of New Fiction', in M. Dolozelova-Velingerova (ed.), *The Chinese Novel at the Turn of the Century*.
Tsurumi, E.P. 'Meiji Primary School Language and Ethics Textbooks: Old Values for a New Society?", *Modern Asian Studies*, 8:2 (1974).
Unger, J. *Education Under Mao*. New York, 1982.
Van der Stegen, J. 'Les chinois en France 1915-1925'. Mémoire de maîtrise, Université de Paris-Nanterre, 1974.
Wakeman, F. *The Fall of Imperial China*. New York, 1975.
Walton-Vargo, L. 'Education, Social Change and Neo-Confucianism in Sung-Yuan China'. Ph.D. diss., University of Pennsylvania, Phil., 1978.

Wang, Feng-gang. *Japanese Influence on Educational Reform in China from 1895 to 1911*. Beijing, 1931.
Wang, N. 'Da Chen Lu: le mouvement du 30 mai à Paris', *Approches-Asie*, Nice, 1983.
Wang, N. 'Paris-Shanghai: Débats d'idées et pratique sociale, les intellectuels progressistes chinois 1920-1925' . Doctorat d'état, Université de Paris,1986.
Wang, Y. *Chinese Intellectuals and the West 1872-1949*. Chapel Hill, 1966.
Weber, M. *The Religion of China*. New York, 1951.
Wieger, L. *Chine Moderne*. 9 vols. Beijing, 1920-23.
Wilbur, M. *Sun Yat-sen: Frustrated Patriot*. New York, 1976.
Woodside. A. 'Some Mid-Qing Theorists of Popular Schools', *Modern China*, 9:1 (Jan. 1983).
Woon, Yuen-fong. *Social Organization in South China 1911-1949*. Ann Arbor, 1984.
Wou, P. *Les travailleurs chinois et la grande guerre*. Paris, 1939.
Wright, M. (ed.) *China in Revolution: The First Phase 1900-1913*. New Haven, 1968.
Wright, M. *The Last Stand of Chinese Conservatism*. New York, 1967.
Yen, Sun Ho. *Chinese Education from the Western Viewpoint*. New York, 1913.
Yin, Chiling. *Reconstruction of Modern Educational Organizations in China*. Shanghai, 1926.
Yip, Ka-che. 'Warlordism and Educational Finances 1916-1927', in J. Fogel, W. Rowe (eds.), *Perspectives on a Changing China*. New York, 1981.
Young, E. *The Presidency of Yuan Shih-k'ai*. Ann Arbor, 1977.
Young, E. 'Politics in the Aftermath of Revolution: The Era of Yuan Shih-k'ai 1912-1916', in J. Fairbank (ed.), *The Cambridge History of China: vol. 12*. Cambridge, Mass., 1983.
Young, E. 'Yuan Shih-k'ai's Rise to the Presidency', in M. Wright (ed.), *China in Revolution: The First Phase 1900-1913*.
Yu, G. *Party Politics in Republican China*. Berkeley, 1966.
Zeldin, D. *The Educational Ideas of Charles Fourier*. New York, 1969.
Zito, A. 'City Gods, Filiality and Hegemony in Late Imperial China', *Modern China*, 13: 3 (July 1987).

Index

aesthetics, 117n145, 148, 149, 152
anarchism, 227, 228-30, 239, 266
Aulard, Alphonse, 236

behaviour, 72, 142, 200, 231, 232, 233, 235, 239, 243, 244-5, 268
Beijing popular education research association, 186, 189, 191, 244
Bolshevik Revolution, 135, 154, 264
Boxer rebellion, 1, 26, 29, 74, 110; settlement and indemnity, 26, 228, 242, 247
Boxers, 64, 73, 188
Britain, 191-2, 210-11; as educational example, 2, 39-40, 77; Chinese students in, 228, 229; education in, 2, 30, 41-2, 150, 211
Buddhism, 25-6, 107-8, 143n44
buildings, 100, 107-8, 113, 204; *see also under* schools

Cai Chang, 241
Cai Hesen, 241, 246n174
Cai Yuanpei, 72, 135, 139-42, 143, 144, 145n59, 146, 148-9, 152, 191, 192, 208, 227n6, 231, 232, 233, 235, 236, 239, 245
Cen Chunxuan, 36-7, 42-3
censorship, 65, 142, 185, 187-94
ceremonies, 72, 152, 164, 209
Chambers of Commerce, 112-13, 115, 155n131
Chen Baoquan, 138, 151, 188n13, 196, 208
Chen Duxiu, 72, 73
Chen Lu, 227, 247
Chen Tianhua, 71, 80
Chen Xiefan, 75
Chen Yi, 241, 243, 246n174
Chen Zibao, 5, 73-4, 78, 117
Chiang Kai-Shek, 267-8
China: constitutions, 45, 65-6, 185; political history, 1, 17, 25, 36, 45-6, 65-6, 134-5, 139, 143-4, 185-6
China Popular Education Association, 144, 186
Chinese Educational World, The, 6, 191, 198, 199
Chinese people, views of, and sensitivity to foreign opinion, 21, 26, 64, 72, 76n79, 78, 79-81, 200, 209, 235, 242, 243, 244-5, 268
Chinese Vocational Education Association, 110, 208, 237
Chou Enlai, 241
Chu Minyi, 229, 230
Cixi, Empress-Dowager, 1, 26-7, 115n134, 135n2
class division, 3, 69, 70-1, 79, 84, 163, 164, 230, 239-40
classics, European, 150, 151, 264
coeducation, 137, 154, 201, 202
Commercial Press, 64-5, 117, 136, 189
Communist Party, Chinese, 20, 186, 227, 246, 266
Confucian classics, 22, 43, 116, 117; in curricula, 2, 4, 20+n24, 25, 26, 31, 32, 74, 116, 117, 137, 139-42, 150, 151, 157, 164
Confucianism/Confucian thought, 17, 29, 69, 110, 116-17, 149, 192-3, 209, 236; and education, 21, 29, 43
Confucius, 2, 26, 43, 152, 164
crime, 30, 42, 77, 110, 114, 198
curricula, 18, 19, 21, 23-4+n48, 25, 27-8, 148, 150, 154, 155, 157, 207-8; apprentice school, 111, 112; half-day school, 200-1; normal school, 142, 157; open-air school, 202; primary school, 4, 32-4, 39-40, 116-17, 136-7, 139-42, 154; supplementary school, 202; vocational school, 35

Index

degrees, 28, 29, 36, 137, 139
Deng Xiaoping, 5n33, 26n68, 238, 241, 266, 267, 268
Denmark, 204
Dewey, John, 7, 137n21, 265
Dongfang zazhi, see *Eastern Miscellany*
drama, 73, 186, 188-9, 190, 193
Duan Fang, 30, 36-9, 43

Eastern Miscellany, 65, 66, 67, 72, 77-8, 79, 80
education: aims, 2, 3, 6, 29, 34, 36, 40, 43, 68-9, 83, 111, 117, 119, 145, 147, 148-9, 152, 155, 163, 167, 208-9, 227, 230, (as producing/cultivating talent), 17, 18, 20, 21, 22-3, 26-7, 28-9; belief in power of, 2, 81-2, 240, 265-6 (*see also* reform); compulsion and/compulsory, 29-30, 31-2, 34, 41-2, 99, 149-50; control of, 27, 98-102, 117-18, 119-20; debates/discussions on, 6, 64-6, 68-84, 135-9, 145-51; foreign influences on *see under* West *and under* individual countries; mass/popular, 3-4, 20, 102, 146, 196, 198; pre-primary, 43; *see also* schools *and* vocational education
Education, Board of, 37, 39, 40, 47-8, 66, 98-100, 102-3, 104-6, 109-10, 112, 117, 118, 136-8, 139
Education Ministry, 5, 67, 142-5, 151-3, 157, 163, 165, 186, 187-9, 191, 194, 198-9, 200, 205
Education Promotion Bureaux, 99, 100, 103, 118
Educational Review, The (Jiaoyu zazhi), 5, 6n41, 64, 66, 67, 74, 78, 81, 102, 109, 116-17, 138, 146, 147, 151, 200, 202, 211n203
Educational World (Jiaoyu shijie), 5, 64, 66, 69-70, 71, 76n86, 78, 83
elitism, 4, 6-7, 149, 163, 198, 243, 246
examinations, 17n7, 18n8, 24, 28, 31, 106, 139, 165, 198, 246; civil service, 2, 7, 21, 22, 36, 37, 118

factories, 69, 70, 115; in France, 230, 231, 233n58, 235n74, 238, 243-4; in schools, 210
Fan Yuanlian, 5, 138, 144, 146, 152, 198, 237, 241
Feng Guifen, 17
fiction, 73, 100, 117, 188-90
film, 142, 154n125, 186n6, 191-2
finance, 46-7, 103-4, 108, 113, 119, 138, 157-8, 163, 202-3
France: and China, 18, 228, 233-4, 242; as cultural example, 235-6, 242; as educational example, 2, 19, 27n71, 147, 152-3, 264; as political example, 147n72, 240; censorship in, 191; education in, 42, 143n49, 145, 149-50, 151; work-study movement and, 227-48
French Revolution, 70n31, 135, 150n93, 152, 153, 154, 231

Gao Fengqian, 67, 146, 147
Gao Yihan, 243
Germany: as educational example, 2, 7, 21, 25, 37, 38, 110, 146, 164, 200, 202, 204, 211, 264-5; censorship in, 191, 192; Chinese students in, 228; education in, 106, 145, 146, 150
Guangxu Emperor, 1, 25, 26, 67, 134, 135n2
Guo Moruo, 37, 165
Guomindang (Nationalist Party), 143, 164, 185, 186

handicrafts, 34, 111, 136-7, 142, 154, 155, 210
He Changgong, 227n6, 242
higher education, 137, 146, 157, 203
Hou Hongjian, 151, 198, 199, 204
Huang Yanpei, 5, 72n45, 101, 110, 138, 151, 155, 186, 192, 202, 207-8, 209+n177, 237
Huang Zunxian, 25, 27, 65n8, 73
individual and common good, 78-9, 81, 99-100, 110, 148, 152, 198, 209-11, 267

industry, 69, 111, 199, 211; aesthetics and, 117n145, 149; in schools, 210; supporting Chinese, 152, 199; *see also* vocational education/training
Italy, 38, 150

Japan, 66, 73n57, 76n82; as educational example, 2, 3, 7, 8, 18, 25, 27, 32, 36n120, 37, 39, 66, 69-71, 76, 117-18, 142, 145-6, 191, 264; as source of Western thought, 6; Chinese relations with, 18, 22; Chinese students in, 47n171, 68, 70n33, 144, 145, 196, 228; education in, 106n48, 109, 145-6, 147
Jia Dianzhi, 138, 149, 151, 166
Jiang Kanghu, 147-8
Jiang Weiqiao, 5, 67, 72, 75, 76, 77, 102, 142, 208
Jiaoyu shijie, see *Educational World*
Jiaoyu zazhi, see *Educational Review*
journals, 5-6, 20, 64-5, 68, 71, 72, 75, 76-7, 80-1, 151, 189, 191, 198, 205, 229, 240, 244, 266

Kang Youwei, 1, 21-2, 24, 25, 26, 64, 65n8, 67, 73, 77, 101, 108, 192-3, 266n13
Kerschensteiner, Georg, 211, 265

labour: and status, 20, 79, 137, 209, 211, 212, 239-41, 243, 248, 264, 267; disputes, 69-70, 84; in schools, 138, 208, 231-2; 'sacredness' of, 209, 239, 264
language, 31, 73, 75, 117, 137; *see also* terminology *and* vernacular
languages: foreign, 7n49, 21, 23n48, 27, 116, 150, 155, 228; minority, 143, 144
lectures, 31, 71, 78, 99-100, 113, 142, 144, 194-200, 202, 240
Li Dazhao, 240, 248n188
Li Duanfen, 20, 21, 22-4, 204n148
Li Hongcao, 227, 230
Li Hongzhang, 7, 17, 228n8
Li Shizeng, 5, 227-31, 232, 233, 234-6, 239-40, 241, 245-6, 247-8, 267
Li Yanhan, 81-3, 199
Liang Qichao, 1, 22, 64, 67-8, 70-1+n39, 72-3, 74, 75-6, 78, 80n111, 81n122, 83, 84, 108n67, 165, 190, 197n89, 266n13
Liang Shiyi, 234
libraries, 24, 37, 99, 144, 187, 196, 203, 204-7
literacy, 2n12, 3-4, 98, 104, 150n98, 190, 244
literacy schools, 84, 104-7, 109-10, 196n85, 202
literature, 73, 100, 117, 188-90, 199
Liu Shaoqi, 20n25, 147, 266
Lu Feigui, 5, 66-7+n17, 74, 84, 138+n29, 147, 151-2, 154n118, 158, 189, 190, 200, 208
Luo Zhenyu, 5, 66, 69-70, 74, 76, 80, 83, 138, 204n148

Ma Jianzhong, 24n57, 207n164, 228n8
Mao Zedong, 20n25, 27n72, 77, 80, 82, 146-7, 149n88, 166, 209, 241, 248, 266, 267
May Fourth Movement, 7, 78, 81, 84, 137n21, 190, 209n179, 212, 240, 248, 263, 264, 266n14
Meng Zhaochang, 78, 138
militarism, 17, 39-40, 76, 77, 119, 138-9
military training/education, 27, 40, 102, 136, 138, 154
missionaries, 9n60, 20-1, 196-7
morality, 200; in education, 27, 32, 39, 148, 154, 189
museums, 144+n57, 187, 205
music, 116, 142, 187n9, 190n38, 192, 193, 202

national anthem, 152
nationalism, 7, 68, 152
New Culture Movement, 74, 212, 235-6
New People's Miscellany (*Xinmin conbao*), 68, 70, 71, 73, 76, 165
newspapers, 24, 64, 73

Index

night classes, 107, 113, 115, 243
normal schools, 19, 36, 47, 137, 142, 155-7, 210

parents, 73-4, 99, 143, 165, 198
patriotism, 34, 38, 39-40, 73, 76, 77, 100, 116, 152, 192, 244
physical education, 32, 76-7, 102, 136, 139, 154
political action, 34, 65, 69-70, 84, 143, 246-7
popular culture/customs, 26, 72, 73, 76, 80-1, 144, 145, 186, 187-94
populists, Russian, 4, 248
poverty, 77, 81-3, 102, 109
publishing, 64-5, 117, 189-90, 229, 231

Qi brothers, 230-1
Qing monarchy/government, 24, 25, 27, 28, 30, 40, 45, 64, 65, 68, 98, 100-1, 108, 111-13, 117, 118, 119, 134-5, 137, 147, 151
Qiu Jin, 75

racism, 65, 81n122, 235, 243
reform, education and, 2, 3, 21, 22, 26-7, 29, 30, 42, 72, 74-84, 111, 145, 163, 192-4, 200, 229-30, 240
religion, 26, 41, 44-5, 72, 84, 107-8
Rousseau, Jean-Jacques, 76n86, 166, 240
rural areas, 9, 80, 103, 143n49, 146-7, 204, 266
Russia, 38, 43-5, 228
Russian Revolution, 135, 154, 264

salaries, 108-9, 196, 202, 209n177
school systems, 4, 20, 21, 22-31, 145-9; 1904: 27, 28, 29-36, 102-20, 154; 1912: 135, 145-67; dual-track, 106, 109, 145-6, 158-63, 266-7
schools: age of attendance at, 109-10, 119, 154, 200, 202; apprentice, 35, 111, 112, 115; attacks on, 119, 142, 165, 198; attitudes to, 31, 37; buildings, 23, 25-6, 104, 108, 118-19, 138; clan, 118-19; control over, 27, 31, 36, 37, 157; family, 31; fees, 19, 23, 38, 78n103, 102, 103, 112, 138, 147, 154, 157; finance, 23, 46-7, 148, 157-8, 163, 201, 203, 210; half-day, 102-4, 106, 107, 109, 196n85, 200-2, 210; hours/weeks, 32, 116, 165; labour, 211; labour in, 138, 208, 231-2; missionary, 119, 163n158; numbers of, 46, 158; numbers of pupils, 163, 203-4; open-air, 202; preparatory for work-study students, 231-2, 236, 241; primary, 28, 29, 34, 103, 109, 116-17, 136-7, 138, (preparation for), 106, 109-10, 112; private, 31, 118, 143, 147, 155; selection for/in, 18-19, 23, 27n73, 83-4; selling products, 201, 210; spare-time, 240; specialist training, 17, 19, 20, 21; supplementary, 35, 202; traditional, 2, 18-20, 23, 31, 118, 143, 166, 198n92; *see also* vocational schools
self-criticism, 82, 167n192
self-strengthening movement, 17, 18, 19, 101, 110
sexual behaviour, 189-90, 200
Shen Liangqi, 118, 138
Shu Xincheng, 31, 37, 166
Smiles, Samuel, 78, 199
social education, 3, 4, 20, 24, 69-71, 142, 143, 144, 148, 186, 191, 193, 209
socialism, 67, 84, 147, 229, 248, 266, 267, 268
Spencer, Herbert, 73, 78
state and education, 4, 17, 38, 47-8, 98-102, 139, 148-9; *see also* school systems
strikes, 69, 70, 165, 210-11
students, 68, 71, 74-5, 76-7, 80-1, 83, 84, 165, 196n85, 208; finances, 38, 68, 103, 111, 138, 232; political activism, 34, 72n45, 164-6, 246-7
Sun Baoqi, 106, 227, 228, 239n99
Sun Yatsen, 67, 72+n44, 134, 135,

139nn32-3, 142, 143, 227n6, 229, 231
superstition, 26, 64, 235

teacher training, 19, 34, 35-6, 39, 47, 102, 106, 112, 143
teachers, 108-9, 137, 165, 201; control of, 118; criticisms of, 165, 166, 198, 207; foreign, 109, 112; relationships with students, 165, 166-7; salaries, 108-9, 202; shortage of, 112; volunteer, 108, 202, 231
temples, 100, 107-8, 118-19, 194, 196, 204
terminology, 3-4, 24, 69, 100n10, 102n30, 111, 144n56, 157n142, 211
textbooks, 27, 32, 67, 104-6, 117-18, 136, 266n16
Tongmenghui (Alliance League), 135, 143, 152n107, 229
trade unions, 69-70, 230, 235, 240n109
translations, 1, 6, 66, 67, 69, 73, 74, 78, 84, 100, 211, 229

uniform, 27, 30, 102, 152, 163
universities, 24, 26, 28, 146, 149n88, 157n141, 192n62
USA, 65, 166, 191-2; as educational example, 2, 7, 76; Chinese people in, 68, 228, 232, 235, 242; education in, 38, 42

vernacular, 5, 73-4, 117
vocational education/training, 4, 40-1, 78, 98, 102, 110-16, 150-1, 154, 201, 208-11, 239, 264
vocational schools, 47, 155, 210; selling products, 113
volunteer teachers, 108, 202, 213

Wang Guowei, 83-4
Wang Jingwei, 231, 232, 233, 236n82
Wang Ruofei, 240-1, 243
West, 6-7, 70, 148, 149-51, 191-2, 242; as educational example, 2, 6, 19, 21, 24, 27, 31, 32, 38, 77, 117n149, 145n62, 146n69, 165-6, 192-4, 264-5
women/girls, 69n28, 75, 76, 143n47, 193; education of, and attitudes to, 5, 6, 7n48, 9, 20+n24, 30, 31, 34-5, 73n58, 75-6, 83, 99, 102, 115-16, 137, 147, 154, 155, 157, 163n158, 201, 202, 207; work-study students, 237-8
work-study movement, 4, 5, 154n122, 227-48
Wu Da, 5, 144, 151, 186, 196, 210
Wu Zhihui, 227n6, 229-30, 231, 232-3, 237-8, 239, 240, 245, 246, 267

Yan Fu, 1, 73
Yan Xiu, 138, 241
Yang Xianzhang, 198, 266
Yuan Shikai, 24n56, 27, 28-9, 31, 36-7, 109, 111, 134-5, 143+n43, 144, 157, 158-64, 185, 233, 234, 266-7

Zhang Baixi, 29-30, 32, 34n109
Zhang Binglin, 79n108, 83n126, 108n67, 139n33, 152n111
Zhang Ji, 229, 236n82
Zhang Jian, 8, 36, 66, 69n26, 115, 136, 137n23, 148, 165-6, 209n186
Zhang Jingjiang, 227, 228, 229, 231, 233
Zhang Yuanji, 67, 79-80
Zhang Zhidong, 7, 18, 19-20, 21, 23, 24n56, 25-6, 27-30, 31, 34-5, 36-7, 46, 66, 68, 83, 100, 102n27, 108, 112, 117n149, 205, 238-9
Zheng Guanying, 21, 22, 24, 26, 75
Zhonghua jiaoyujie, see *Chinese Educational World*
Zhou dynasty, education under, 24, 29, 148
Zhou Enlai, 5n33, 138, 238n96
Zhu Yuanshan, 164, 210-11
Zhuang Yu, 67, 109, 117, 148-9, 151, 208, 209, 211
Zuo Zongtang, 20